WAR AND PUNISHMENT

THE CAUSES OF WAR TERMINATION
AND THE FIRST WORLD WAR

H. E. Goemans

PRINCETON UNIVERSITY PRESS

PRINCETON AND OXFORD

LIBRARY OF CONGRESS CATALOGING-IN-PUBLICATION DATA

GOEMANS, HEIN, 1957–

WAR AND PUNISHMENT : THE CAUSES OF WAR TERMINATION AND
THE FIRST WORLD WAR / HEIN GOEMANS.

P. CM. — (PRINCETON STUDIES IN INTERNATIONAL HISTORY AND POLITICS)

INCLUDES BIBLIOGRAPHICAL REFERENCES AND INDEX.

ISBN 0-691-04943-2 (alk. paper) — ISBN 0-691-04944-0 (pbk. : alk. paper)

1. PEACE. 2. WORLD WAR, 1914–1918—ARMISTICES. 3. PEACE TREATIES.
4. CAPITULATIONS, MILITARY. I. TITLE. II. SERIES.

D613 .G62 2000

940.4'39—dc21   00-036693

THIS BOOK HAS BEEN COMPOSED IN BERKELEY BOOK MODIFIED TYPEFACE

THE PAPER USED IN THIS PUBLICATION MEETS THE MINIMUM REQUIREMENTS
OF ANSI/NISO Z39.48-1992 (R1997) *PERMANENCE OF PAPER*
HTTP://PUP.PRINCETON.EDU

PRINTED IN THE UNITED STATES OF AMERICA

1   3   5   7   9   10   8   6   4   2

1   3   5   7   9   10   8   6   4   2

CONTENTS

052301−2635×6

LIST OF TABLES AND FIGURES

Tables

Figures

ACKNOWLEDGMENTS

ON THE LONG ROAD from my days as a disc jockey, working to pay for my studies at the University of Amsterdam, to the final completion of this book, I have incurred many debts of gratitude. From my days at the University of Amsterdam, I would like to single out Henk Leurdijk, who from very early on stimulated my interest in International Relations and gave me the confidence to continue my studies. I also would like to thank the van der Reijden family, especially Jurriaan and Mrs. and Mr. van der Reijden, who welcomed me into their family when I was facing a difficult time. Without their support I surely would not be where I am today.

For my study at the School of Advanced International Studies, the Johns Hopkins University, Bologna Center, I want to express my deep gratitude to Mevrouw van der Does-Rissik and the Hendrik Muller Vaderlandsch Fonds, the Fundatie van de VrijVrouwe van Renswoude, the Mr. Peletier Stichting, and the Knottebelt Fonds. Very special thanks are due to Isabella Aniorte-Tjepkema, who gave me the confidence to try in the first place, and Jane Zuidema, who gave me that essential little extra push. In Bologna Professors Frank Weiss and Douglas Stuart were fundamental to my intellectual development and ambitions. I also would like to thank my fellow students at the Bologna Center, who opened a new world for me by their interest and willingness and enthusiasm to discuss international relations in the broadest sense.

I would like to thank the members of my dissertation committee at the University of Chicago, Steve Walt, John Mearsheimer, Jim Fearon, and Duncan Snidal, who patiently supported me, withstood my recurring flights of fancy, and showed me by their example the importance of thinking and reasoning clearly. John Mearsheimer deserves an extra mention for giving much more than intellectual support; his hospitality and patience made all the difference.

I was extremely fortunate to find myself with a cohort without peer. Jason Cawley, Dale Copeland, Angie Doll, Atsushi Ishida, Marcus Fisher, Andy Kydd, Alicia Levine, Walter Mattli, Ashley Tellis, and Barbara Walter were all extremely influential in my studies and my life outside the university and helped me in immeasurable ways.

I could not have wished for a more supportive and friendly environment than I found when I came to Duke University. John Aldrich, John Brehm, Chris Gelpi, Joe Grieco, Paul Gronke, Ruth Grant, Peter Feaver,

Peter Lange, Scott Morgenstern, Mike Munger, Emerson Niou, and above all Bob Keohane all contributed significantly not just to this book and but also to my happiness here.

Many other people offered valuable comments on all or part of the manuscript: Scott Bennett, Ronald Bobroff, Bruce Bueno de Mesquita, Colin Elman, Page Fortna, Richard Froom, George Gavrilis, Colin Hall, Robert Jervis, Jeffrey Legro, Jane Plotke, Amy Poteete, Dani Reiter, Ken Schultz, Alastair Smith, Jack Snyder, Glenn Snyder, Allan Stam III, David Stevenson, Marc Trachtenberg, Suzanne Werner, R. Harrison Wagner, Chris Way, Dean Wilkening, and Christopher Winland. In the final stages of the book detailed comments from Bob Keohane, John Mearsheimer, Jack Snyder, Allan Stam III, Marc Trachtenberg, and Steve Walt made this a much better book than it would have been without their criticism, insights, and suggestions. I am extremely grateful to all of them. Peter Volpe did a great job proofreading and preparing the index.

For their institutional support I would like to thank the Josiah Trent Foundation, the Olin Institute at the Center for International Affairs at Harvard, and the RAND Corporation for providing time and money to work on the manuscript as it developed.

My last word of thanks is to Craig Koerner, a friend whose help has simply been invaluable and incalculable. If this book has any merits, Craig deserves a substantial part of the credit. He withstood innumerable discussions on the topic, read countless drafts, and always remained ready to help. He saved me from many errors of logic and fact and more than anybody else taught me to think. In deep and abiding gratitude, this book is dedicated to him and the standards of scholarship he represents.

WAR AND PUNISHMENT

1

INTRODUCTION

Of war men will ask its outcome, not its causes
(Seneca)

The Central Question

NOW, AS ALWAYS, states fight wars. As one of the most destructive forms of human behavior, war and its study lie at the heart of the discipline of international relations. It is not surprising, therefore, that much theoretical work has been done to explain the causes of war initiation. What is surprising, however, is the paucity of effort to understand and explain the causes of war *termination*. While it is interesting and important to know why wars break out in the first place, it is no less interesting or important to know why it often takes so much time and such enormous costs before wars end. Why, for example, did the First World War not end after the Schlieffen Plan failed? This book therefore seeks to answer the question, asked more than twenty years ago by William Fox: "What keeps wars going and what finally makes them stop?"[1]

The Central Argument

The answer to this question, the central argument of the book, is laid out in chapter 2. Wars can end only when the minimum terms of settlement of both sides become compatible, when both are asking no more than the other side is willing to give up. Therefore, the fundamental cause of war termination is a change in the minimal demands, that is, the minimum terms of settlement of the combatants. Starting with the rational unitary actor approach, the theory developed in chapter 2 first argues that changes in a nation's minimum terms of settlement are a function of new information about the outcome and the costs of war. But not all states change their war aims according to this logic because domestic politics can fundamentally affect how different regimes change their war aims. The second half of chapter 2 therefore builds

---

[1] Fox, "The Causes of Peace and Conditions of War," p. 1.

on the rational unitary actor theory and offers a theory that explains why some regimes refuse to lower their war aims—indeed, sometimes *increase* their war aims—*even when they learn they will probably lose*. Specifically, semirepressive, moderately exclusionary regimes will refuse to lower their war aims and keep fighting where nonrepressive, nonexclusionary and repressive, exclusionary regimes would prefer to lower their aims and settle because leaders of semirepressive, moderately exclusionary regimes anticipate severe domestic punishment for even a moderate defeat. Thus, the main contribution of this book is the theoretical argument and empirical evidence that the decision to continue fighting or settle depends on the nature of the domestic political regime.

Competing Explanations

An exhaustive search through the existing literature on war termination[2] yielded no well-articulated and testable competing theories. However, individual, disconnected, and sometimes contradictory propositions and generalizations abound. The existing propositions in the literature on war termination can be divided into two main strands. The first strand argues that war ends when the "loser" recognizes his position and accedes to the "winner's" demands. In other words, war ends when one side, the "loser," cries uncle. The crucial assumption in this strand of the literature is that war has only two outcomes: victory or defeat. War ends when the loser gives up his demands and accepts the demands of the winner.

The second strand argues that war ends when the combatants agree to a settlement that *both* prefer over continued fighting. In other words, war is seen as a form of bargaining in which states make rational cost/benefit calculations about war and its termination and maximize their expected value. This strand of the literature maintains that demands or war aims of both sides fluctuate during war, and that the final terms of settlement may be totally different from the combatants' original aims. In other words, the terms of settlement are endogenous. Thus, this strand of the literature maintains that there exist an infinite number of possible outcomes of war because there exist infinite combinations of potential terms of settlement.

---

[2] "War termination" provides a convenient shorthand term, but I should stipulate that I do not intend to explain specific forms of *formal* war termination such as peace treaties. Rather, I will define war termination to occur when the belligerents agree, formally or tacitly, to stop fighting.

One-Sided Termination: "The Vanquished Makes Peace"

At first glance the argument that war ends when the loser cries uncle seems plausible. Its plausibility stems from the commonly held conviction that it takes only one side to start a war. It is assumed, therefore, that it also takes only one side to end it. This view is still widely held in and outside of academia.[3]

If one aggressor can start a war by a sudden attack, this argument goes, war will simply stop when the aggressor recants or the loser submits. Calahan, for example, wrote in 1944 that "war is pressed by the victor, but peace is made by the vanquished. Therefore, to determine the causes of peace, it is always necessary to take the vanquished's point of view. Until the vanquished quits, the war goes on."[4]

In a similar vein Francis A. Beer and Thomas F. Mayer argued in 1986 that "[t]he major proposition of rational choice theory on how wars end is . . . : Wars terminate because *one or more* combatants decide they have more to gain, or less to lose, by making peace than by continuing to fight."[5] Beer and Mayer's proposition implies that if one side decides it has more to gain by making peace than by continuing to fight—in other words, when the vanquished quits—war will end. Many other students of war termination, such as Robert Randle, Paul Kecskemeti, Lewis Coser, Nicholas S. Timasheff,[6] and Hobbs,[7] all either implicitly or explicitly argue that war ends when the vanquished quits.

---

[3] Carroll noted in 1980: "It is still generally held that wars do for the most part end in victory for one side, defeat for the other; stalemates and settlements with no discernible victor or defeated are regarded as relatively rare. This is not often stated as a general principle, and has sometimes been subjected to challenge. Nevertheless it appears repeatedly, sometimes as an underlying assumption in the theoretical analysis of war endings" ("Victory and Defeat,'" p. 50).

[4] Calahan, pp. 18–19.

[5] Beer and Mayer, p. 98, emphasis added. Max Manwaring makes a very similar argument: "War is terminated and peace resumes when one or both of the adversaries rationally agree that the costs of armed struggle exceed the benefits expected" (Manwaring, p. 60).

[6] Carroll argues convincingly that these authors start from a similar assumption ("Victory and Defeat," pp. 50–52). Coser argues that "no matter how the activities of the potential winner have facilitated an early termination of the conflict, the final decision to end the war remains with the potential loser" (Coser, p. 349). See also Randle, *The Origins of Peace*; Kecskemeti, *Strategic Surrender*. Timasheff argues that "it is for the weaker party to ask for the termination of hostilities and thus to induce negotiations" (Timasheff, pp. 217–18).

[7] Hobbs argues, for example: "To sum up the limited warfare of this period then, the objective of nineteenth-century warfare was the creation of risks which made continued resistance appear more costly than the peace terms offered. As the peace terms were more moderate, the margin of superiority required was smaller. *These wars ended when a*

More recently Allan Stam has offered a theory of war termination that argues that "war ends when one or both sides see costs as exceeding benefits."[8] Stam argues that war has three possible outcomes: one side quits, the other side quits, or both quit—as he puts it in the title of his book, *Win, Lose, or Draw*.[9] Among the scholars who have tried to operationalize their version of the "vanquished makes peace" argument, such as Frank Klingberg and Lewis Richardson, Stam's work stands out. While Klingberg and Richardson have tried to predict when the loser will quit by focusing on battle deaths, Stam and his co-author Bennett offer a far richer model.[10] In their article Bennett and Stam do not try to offer a model or a test of the causes of war termination but focus on the closely related topic of war duration.[11] Overcoming difficult data problems and incorporating tremendous amounts of research, Bennett and Stam present a rich model that includes variables such as strategy, terrain, capabilities, and government type and that generates strong and surprising statistical support.

A crucial assumption in their model is that

> wars occur over some issue, with some fundamental benefit at stake, such as a piece of territory, economic influence over an area, or some government policy. *We also assume these issues to be fixed and exogenous*, despite the possible manipulation of the apparent stakes by political leaders. Unlike benefits, the costs of continuing a war rise over time.[12]

This assumption that the stakes of the war are *fixed* also defines the arguments of the scholars who propose variants of the vanquished makes peace argument.[13] Richardson even went so far as to argue that

---

sovereign government agreed to the victor's terms thereby assuming responsibility for their execution" (Hobbs, p. 20, emphasis added).

[8] Stam, p. 28; see pp. 28–47. On p. 32 he repeats the claim: "Actor A quits fighting when the costs imposed upon it by Actor B cross A's benefit threshold."

[9] Stam, p. 36.

[10] Klingberg, pp. 167–68; Richardson, "War Moods." As Arthur Stein and Bruce Russett note, "there has been no scholarly consensus on the narrower issue of predicting duration or point of termination on the basis of battle deaths, regardless of whether those deaths are suffered by the winner and/or loser and without attempting to predict victor or vanquished. . . . These works, which attempt to predict war's outcome by reference to battle deaths, focus on the loser and the point at which costs lead a nation to give up; in other words, they assume the loser's role to be decisive in terminating war" (Stein and Russett, p. 403). The argument developed below offers additional suggestions why no relationship could be found.

[11] See Bennett and Stam.

[12] Ibid., p. 240, emphasis added. I am grateful to Suzanne Werner for pointing out this quotation to me.

[13] Randle, "The Domestic Origins of Peace," pp. 77–78; Kecskemeti, *Strategic Surrender*, pp. 18–19. However, Kecskemeti seems to have changed his mind subsequently. In 1970

the "possible terms of peace" do not significantly affect the course of the war and the prospects of its termination.[14] The assumption that war aims are fixed poses a fundamental puzzle.

Why the Argument Is Flawed

The above argument claims that war ends when the "loser" decides to submit to the "winner's" demands. This argument is fundamentally flawed because it simply assumes that the winner does not raise his demands once he realizes his advantage. This model of war termination describes only the extreme and relatively rare case of unconditional surrender[15] or "absolute war," where the winner cannot possibly ask for more. In most cases, however, a winner can raise his demands if he discovers an unexpected advantage.

During the First World War the negotiations at Brest-Litovsk provide a classic example of the flaw in this argument. On February 10, 1918, some among the new Bolshevik leaders, in particular Trotsky, thought Russia could end the war on the Eastern Front simply by refusing to fight; *literally* the vanquished quit. The Germans, however, thought otherwise and on the 16th announced they would continue the war. Facing little opposition, they quickly and easily advanced. After the Bolsheviks formally announced on February 21 that they would accept Germany's terms, the Germans issued new and harsher terms on the 23d. On the 24th the Bolsheviks signaled their acceptance of the new terms.[16]

---

he wrote: "The criterion of balancing the war effort with the political stake, which is fundamental to the Clausewitzian strategic theory, raises considerable difficulties. To begin with, the belligerent's political stakes are by no means fixed once and for all in each war" ("Political Rationality in Ending War," p. 109). See also Staudenmaier, p. 27; Craig and George, pp. 229–30.

[14] Richardson, "War Moods," part 1, pp. 154–55.

[15] Pillar records only eleven capitulations out of sixty-nine inter-state wars but twenty capitulations out of fifty-two extra-systemic wars. However, he warns that "Capitulations may include "unconditional" surrenders as well as agreements that are much less one-sided; all that matters is how the agreement was reached" (i.e., imposition by one side). Pillar, p. 15; see also pp. 22, 25. The theory developed in the next chapter explains why some wars do continue until the unconditional surrender of one side.

[16] Wheeler-Bennett, pp. 227, 245–61. Wheeler-Bennett also records that the German legal expert Ministerial-Director Kriege, "after exhaustive researches, reported that a similar case of a unilateral declaration of peace had occurred several thousand years before, after a war between the Greeks and the Scythians" (p. 228). See also Ludendorff, *My War Memories*, pp. 551–66, and especially the map on p. 565, which shows the advance of the German army after it resumed the offense. See also the map in Wheeler-Bennett, opposite p. 274. Compare these events with William Fox's statement that "*Unless one side chooses simply to abandon the field* or unconditionally surrenders, it takes two to end a war" ("The Causes of Peace and Conditions of War," p. 5, emphasis added).

The argument that the vanquished makes peace, thus, leaves unanswered this theoretical puzzle: When a "winner" realizes his advantage, why would he not raise his demands?[17] While empirical examples where states do not raise their war aims exist, for example, the coalition war against Iraq in 1990, they beg the question. Why did the United States not raise its demands after its brilliantly successful and relatively costless military victory in the war against Iraq? Note that this is also a clear case where it was the winner who decided to end the war. Iraq would have been happy for the fighting to have stopped earlier.

Aside from its conceptual shortcomings, the argument that it takes only one side to end a war also suffers from poor implementation and testing. The proposition is theoretically underspecified because it provides no mechanism that causes a "loser" to cry uncle. This makes it very difficult to empirically test the claim. Klingberg and Richardson have both tried to provide mechanisms, mainly by focusing on the number of battle deaths, but no general relationship between fatalities and war termination has been found.[18] Moreover, the argument is also difficult to test since it is problematic to identify the loser ex ante, that is, independent of the outcome.

Two-Sided Termination: Both Must Prefer Peace over War

The second current explanation of war termination is that it takes both sides to end a war.[19] Intuitively, and with the example of Brest-Litovsk in mind, this argument seems to be much more compelling. However, as the argument currently stands in the literature, it is incomplete at best. The best statement and elaboration of this argument can be found in an excellent article by Donald Wittman. He argues that "An agreement (either explicit or implicit) to end a war cannot be reached unless the agreement makes both sides better off; for each country the expected utility of continuing the war must be less than the expected utility of the settlement."[20]

---

[17] The argument has other flaws. See Carroll, "How Wars End," pp. 303–5; and Carroll, "Victory and Defeat." For example, it seems to assume that the "winner" and "loser" of any war are somehow predetermined. In reality, war seems much more probabilistic.

[18] Klingberg, pp. 167–68; Richardson, "War Moods."

[19] Halperin, p. 87; Kecskemeti, "Political Rationality in Ending War," p. 107; Blainey, pp. 122, 293; Ikle, p. 13; Pillar; Seabury and Codevilla, p. 243; Schelling, ch. 1; Wagner, "The Causes of Peace"; Wagner, "Peace, War, and the Balance of Power"; Wittman.

[20] Wittman, p. 744.

Some authors, such as Geoffrey Blainey, Paul Pillar, and R. Harrison Wagner, most likely endorse this statement in toto.[21] Even some wary of the rational unitary actor approach, such as Janice Gross Stein and Charles Fred Ikle,[22] would probably largely agree with Wittman's statement.

Why the Argument Is Flawed

This second argument claims that states end a war because they reach an agreement that makes both sides better off than continued fighting. The argument is incomplete for two reasons. First, it provides no mechanism that brings such an agreement in reach for both sides and fails to explain why a bargaining space opens up. Second, it completely ignores the enforcement problems of any agreement to end war. Thus, the argument overlooks the fundamental anarchic nature of international relations. How can agreements that change the relative power of the antagonists be enforced? The argument truncates the problem by omitting considerations of the possibility of future war and other potentially dangerous consequences of changes in relative power.

Focusing on the first problem, most authors assume (implicitly or explicitly) that when the belligerents agree more about the outcome on the battlefield, an agreement to end war becomes more likely.[23] In other words, it is assumed that when belligerents agree more on their estimates of their probability of winning it becomes more likely that a bargaining space opens up. However, Wittman's analysis suggests that even when both sides agree more on the outcome of the war, settlement need not become more likely.[24] The combatants adjust their estimates of their probability of winning as a result of new information and unexpected events on the battlefield. When one side raises its estimate of its probability of winning, its reservation value increases, and it will therefore raise its demands. When the other side lowers his estimate of his probability of winning, he will lower his demands. Both sides now

[21] See Blainey; Pillar; Wagner, "The Causes of Peace"; Wagner, "Peace, War, and the Balance of Power."

[22] See Janice Gross Stein, "War Termination and Conflict Reduction or How Wars Should End"; Janice Gross Stein, "War Termination and Conflict Resolution." Ikle argues that "To bring the fighting to an end, one nation or the other almost always has to revise its war aims. This revision is stimulated by a reevaluation of the military prospects, but *not in so direct a linkage nor in so logical a fashion as a rational approach to national policy would dictate*" (p. 96, emphasis added).

[23] See, for example, Halperin; Kecskemeti, "Political Rationality in Ending War"; Blainey; Staudenmaier; Mandel.

[24] Wittman, pp. 749–51. See also Ikle, p. 42; Janice Gross Stein, "The Termination of the October War," pp. 233–34; and Pillar, p. 49.

agree more on their probability of winning; however, it is not necessarily true that the difference in their demands diminishes. Agreement becomes more likely and a bargaining space is more likely to open if and only if one side lowers his demands more than the other side increases his demands. Thus, more agreement about the outcome does not automatically make an agreement to terminate the war more likely.

The second theoretical problem is a familiar one from the literature on international cooperation: How can two states reach an agreement in an anarchic realm with no central authority to enforce its terms? This problem should be particularly severe in agreements to end a war because the settlement of a war almost always entails some shift in relative power between the belligerents. Simply put, the "winner" has more power (which is the reason he is winning), and will get still more power in the settlement. Therefore, the winner is in a better position to demand further concessions from the loser later on, whereas the loser will be in an even worse position to resist. This argument implies that no state will accept any agreement that diminishes its relative power, without some sort of insurance that the enemy will make no further claims. In other words, the stronger side must credibly commit itself not to exploit its bargaining advantage in the future. Where can such insurance come from?[25]

A historical example serves to illustrate the problem. When Hitler demanded the Sudetenland from Czechoslovakia in the 1938 Munich crisis, he promised this would be his last demand. When the Czechoslovakians conceded, they ceded territory to Germany that contained the major defensive works along the German-Czechoslovakian border. The ensuing shift in relative power not only made it easier for the Germans to invade the "rump" of Czechoslovakia in March 1939 when Hitler's promise could not be enforced but also made it easier to fight the Battle of France in 1940.[26]

Although the argument that war termination requires an agreement that leaves both sides better off than continued war has much appeal,[27] it fails to specify a mechanism that creates the necessary preconditions

[25] Wagner points to this problem in his "Peace, War, and the Balance of Power," p. 598.

[26] In 1938 it was estimated that the Czechs would call up 1.8 million men. As Shirer points out "[t]hat was as many trained men as Germany had for two fronts. Together the Czechs and the French outnumbered the Germans by more than two to one" (Shirer, p. 401).

[27] In an off-the-record briefing two days after the Yom Kippur War started, Minister of Defense Moshe Dayan was asked by senior editors about the likely termination of hostilities. He answered: "I don't think we can pinpoint a moment at which we will stop fighting. For one thing, we're not the only ones doing the fighting" (quoted in Janice Gross Stein, "The Termination of the October War," p. 230).

for any such agreement. These necessary preconditions are, first, the creation of a bargaining space (which produces the possibility for an agreement that leaves both better off) and, second, a credible commitment from the stronger side that it will not raise further demands in the future. In the next chapter I show how these puzzles can be solved.

Why the Question Is Important

The theory in chapter 2 offers a necessary condition for war termination and provides solutions to several previously unanswered theoretical puzzles about war termination. This theory, moreover, also provides new insights into the causes of war initiation in two ways. First, any competent theory of the causes of war initiation must be able to also explain the absence of war. In other words, a theory of war must explain the variation between war and peace. This is a notoriously difficult problem for the study of the causes of war initiation because in peacetime it is difficult to evaluate the costs of war and the outcome of that war. Any competent theory of the causes of war termination must similarly explain the variation between continued war and war termination, or peace. Thus, a theory of war termination must be able to explain not only why a war ends but also why a war continues. It is easier to explain the variation between war and peace by a focus on the causes of war termination than by a focus on the causes of war initiation. The reason is simple: It is much easier to compare how decision makers evaluate the consequences of a decision to settle (peace) and a decision to continue fighting (war) during war. After even a few days of fighting decision makers are better able to anticipate the consequences of continued war. Moreover, it is easy to evaluate the choice for peace because peace can always be had on the opponent's terms. Thus, in an attempt to explain the variation between war and peace a theory of war termination has a practical advantage over a theory of the causes of war initiation because it is easier to measure the expected values of peace and war during war.

This practical advantage should not be underestimated. Much of the empirical literature on the causes of war initiation suffers from some form of selection bias. Many works on the causes of war initiation sample on the dependent variable and, for example, try to explain why Germany went to war in 1914 but fail to explain why Germany did *not* go to war in 1913, 1912, 1911, or 1906. Another, less obvious, form of selection bias was exposed recently by Fearon.[28] Many scholars have

---

[28] See Fearon, "Threats to Use Force."

tried to explain war as a deterrence failure and have focused on crises. Fearon has shown, however, that the mere existence of a crisis, a failure of general deterrence, makes war, a failure of immediate deterrence, more likely. A proper focus on the causes of war termination avoids both these pitfalls. While the study of the causes of war termination therefore provides a better handle on the variation between war and peace, it can even be argued that an understanding of the causes of war termination is analytically prior to an understanding of the causes of war initiation.

A focus on the causes of war termination can, secondly, throw light on the causes of war initiation because the anticipated ex post consequences of the potential outcomes of war should influence the decision makers' ex ante calculus of war. Moreover, as R. Harrison Wagner has recently argued, the decision to go to war is not a decision to forego bargaining in favor of something else, but rather a decision to pursue bargaining over the terms of a negotiated settlement "with the admixture of other means." A rational explanation of war must therefore show how leaders evaluate this option of bargaining during war against the available prewar options, such as outright surrender for the defender or the status quo for the attacker. As R. Harrison Wagner puts it, "we must not only explain why the participants could not reach agreement without fighting, but also why they fought as long as they did before agreeing to stop."[29] It is exactly this question that is at the core of the present study.

To test my theory I address the empirical puzzle why the First World War did not end before the eleventh hour of the eleventh day of the eleventh month of 1918. The First World War remains one of the most studied wars in the fields of History and International Relations, used as a case study and example in countless theories and arguments. Its prominence probably stems from its status as a watershed in the history of the twentieth century. The First World War brought changes that reverberate still today. It changed a largely European system into a truly global international system, introduced modern forms of warfare on a continent-wide scale, caused horrible numbers of casualties, heralded vast cultural change, brought forth new nations, and spelled the demise of others.

While dozens of books and articles have been written on the causes of the First World War, no work explains why it kept going and why it finally ended in November 1918. This lacuna is all the more remarkable for two reasons. First, German, French, Austro-Hungarian, Russian, and the great majority of British troops who rushed off to war in

---

[29] Wagner, "Bargaining and War," p. 3.

the summer of 1914 all thought they would be "home by Christmas." How could all of them have been so wrong? Second, neither the terrible havoc wrought by the First World War nor its place as a turning point in history is adequately explained by the events of July 1914. Consider the counterfactual: If the war had ended in November 1914, would this war have been considered as important? Would it even be referred to as the "First World War"? To understand why so many people died, and why the war brought such important changes, we need to try to understand why the war lasted so long or, more precisely, why it continued.

Method

I employ three methods: rational choice for theory construction and statistical analysis and case studies for theory testing. The theory in chapter 2 explicitly adopts a rational choice perspective and relies heavily on insights from the recent literature on bargaining and agency problems. I develop a classic argument of backwards induction through which I offer one overarching framework to address the consequences, cessation, conduct, and causes of war. As will be readily apparent, this theory aims to provide a *rationalist baseline explanation* for the causes of war termination. Let me hasten to admit that emotions and social norms may also sometimes play significant roles in decisions to end war. However, a rational choice theory of war termination provides a baseline against which the effects of such emotions and social norms can be more effectively weighed.

I argue in chapter 2 that states cannot find an outcome that both prefer over continued war because each side expects to gain more by continued fighting than by accepting the opponent's terms of settlement. This bland expected utility argument raises the fundamental question of how both sides can prefer the continuation of costly war to a negotiated settlement. My theory offers two answers, the first an adaptation of an argument first proposed by Fearon, the second, to the best of my knowledge, new in international relations.[30]

I argue first that states have *private information* about their strength, resolve, and the expected costs of war and *incentives to misrepresent* their estimates. States have incentives to misrepresent these estimates for two reasons. First, they may want to overstate their true strength and resolve to get a more favorable outcome at the bargaining table.

---

[30] See Fearon, "Rationalist Explanations for War." For an argument similar to mine on the settlement or continuation of litigation, see Mnookin and Wilson.

Second, they may want to understate their strength and resolve or exaggerate the expected costs of war to limit their military vulnerability both to their current enemy and to potentially hostile third states. A revelation of its true strength, moreover, may encourage hostile balancing. The combination of private information and incentives to misrepresent can cause leaders on both sides to expect a more favorable result from continued war than from settlement on the opponent's terms. Extending this argument suggests that war termination becomes possible when sufficient information is revealed on the battlefield to produce consistent expectations on both sides about their relative strength, resolve, and the costs of war.

However, not all regimes necessarily react in the same fashion to the same new information. In the second half of chapter 2 I argue that rational leaders can sometimes prefer to continue war even if for the state as a rational unitary actor the expected utility of continued war is less than the expected utility of the terms of settlement. This second answer to the question of how both sides can prefer continued war over a negotiated settlement focuses on the consequences of the terms of a negotiated settlement. If the consequences of the terms of settlement appear particularly nasty for political leaders—if they can personally expect severe punishment as a result of these terms—leaders can rationally prefer to continue fighting as long as there is a chance they can get terms that prevent their punishment. Specifically, such leaders can rationally prefer to continue war as long as the variance of the potential outcomes of the war, and therefore of the terms of settlement, is high enough to include terms that would forestall their punishment. The variation of potential outcomes, crucially, can be manipulated for exactly these reasons because *leaders can deliberately and rationally adopt a high-variance war-fighting strategy.* While such a high-variance war fighting strategy would lower the overall expected utility for the state, it can, if successful, generate the required terms of settlement and save domestic political *leaders* from severe punishment. This is, of course, the logic of an agency problem where the interests of the leadership of a state, the agent, clash with the interests of the population of the state as a whole, the principal. Readers familiar with the formal literature on principal-agent problems will recognize the mechanism of *gambling for resurrection.*[31] Although this specific mechanism may not be new to

---

[31] The closest parallel to my argument can be found in the law and economics approach in legal studies. See the Mnookin and Wilson study on *Pennzoil v. Texaco*, where they argue that in the legal dispute between Texaco and Pennzoil over the acquisition of Getty Oil, the managers of Texaco chose to continue costly litigation to avoid being held personally liable. Downs and Rocke offer a formal model that shows how leaders sometimes go to war or prolong it in a gamble for resurrection.

international relations, in its application here it is new. Not only is it applied to a new substantive question, war termination, but I also propose a new argument and present evidence why certain kinds of regimes, specifically semirepressive, moderately exclusionary regimes, are particularly likely to exhibit such gambling for resurrection.

To explain war termination this rational choice theory proposes several specific causal mechanisms.[32] These causal mechanisms explain in detail why and how changes in the belligerents' minimum terms of settlement must eventually make settlement preferable to continued war for both sides; why and how states change their minimum terms of settlement; how, why, and when fear of severe punishment influences the minimum terms of settlement of one particular regime type; and finally why, when, and which leaders must fear severe punishment as a consequence of settlement.

The theory yields several observable implications and predictions. Some of the predictions are tested quantitatively, while the others are tested in detailed case studies. Chapter 3 offers statistical tests on opposite ends of the micro-macro spectrum. I test the predictions of the final mechanism, when and which leaders must fear severe punishment, by means of the statistical analysis of a new cross-national data set with 216 cases.[33] In addition, I test the implications for the duration of wars by the statistical analysis of a data set initially developed and analyzed by Scott Bennet and Allan Stam.[34] These tests show that the proposed mechanisms on the fate of leaders and the duration of wars hold generally across time and space.

In chapters 4 through 7 I test the proposed mechanisms and hypotheses on how and when states change their minimum terms of settlement in detailed case studies of the changing war aims of Germany during 1916, Russia between 1914 and 1916, and France and Britain in 1917 during the First World War. Wherever possible these case studies rely on original sources, and I have read memoirs, cabinet memoranda, diplomatic correspondence, and relevant secondary literature in the original languages.

In chapters 8 and 9 I test the proposed causal mechanism and its predictions on how and when changes in the belligerents' minimum terms of settlement eventually provide the necessary condition to make settlement preferable to continued war for both sides. Thus, for

---

[32] See Elster, ch. 1, for the epistemological status of causal mechanisms.

[33] Most of the work of gathering the necessary additional data was done during a research internship at the RAND Corporation in Santa Monica in the summer of 1994. I would like to express my gratitude for the generous help and support I received, especially from Ashley Tellis and Dean Wilkening.

[34] See Bennett and Stam.

each year of the war I then examine whether the interaction of the war aims of main belligerents created or failed to create a bargaining space. In essence, these chapters summarize an additional eighteen case studies on the "new information" and war aims of Germany, France, Britain, Russia, and the United States for each year of their participation in the war. This allows me to explain in chapter 8 why no general peace agreement could be reached in 1914, 1915, 1916, or 1917 and why a separate peace between Russia and Germany could be reached in 1917. Chapter 9 explains why a general peace agreement finally came into reach during the latter half of 1918.

The book uses both detailed case studies and statistics to test my theoretical arguments. Each method helps to compensate for some of the weaknesses in the other. As Alastair Smith and Curt Signorino have recently argued, the statistical methods commonly used in International Relations are suspect because they are poorly suited to deal with strategic interaction.[35] Because the actors anticipate the decisions of other actors when they make their choices, the decisions between actors are *inter*dependent and not independent, as most statistical estimators require. Moreover, as Smith argues,

> strategic choice models also suggest selection effects. When actors anticipate an unfavorable response by another actor they attempt to avoid the contingent circumstances under which the response will occur. Thus, their choice depends as much upon unrealized eventualities as it does upon observed events. Standard econometric techniques do not adequately deal with this censoring; as such, these methods fail.[36]

The case study method is particularly well suited to avoid these pitfalls. To illustrate, a crucial part of my argument is that leaders of semirepressive, moderately exclusionary regimes anticipate drastic punishment whether they lose a war moderately or disastrously. It is this anticipation that makes such leaders formulate their war aims by a different logic and leads them to prefer to continue a losing war where

---

[35] See Alastair Smith; Signorino. Both argue that large N work in International Relations, which uses international outcomes (e.g., war) as the dependent variable, is generally invalid when conventional techniques such as logit and probit are used. Not only the magnitudes but also the signs of the statistical coefficients are often wrong. This is not a minor result or just a qualification: It is a fundamental critique of the work that has been done in this field. Unless the critique is shown to be wrong, it becomes problematic to analyze International Relations with a large statistical database unless statistical techniques are used that make assumptions about the distribution of values of the dependent variable that are consistent with the distributions that emerge from game-theoretic analysis.

[36] Alastair Smith, p. 3.

leaders of other regimes would tend to prefer settlement on moderately losing terms. My case study of Germany during 1916 gives me an opportunity to examine the ample evidence that decision makers did indeed worry about the "off-the-equilibrium path" outcome of severe punishment if they settled the war on moderately losing terms. Historical research thus allows us to test if the actors did actually consider such "off-the-equilibrium path" outcomes and took steps to avoid them.[37] In cabinet memoranda and confidential notes we can often hear an actor arguing in favor of one course of action over another, because the latter could lead to an undesirable outcome.[38] Large N approaches based on observed behavior are particularly prone to ignore this type of critical information.

To be sure, it is not always possible to trace such considerations in the historical record, and the issue of falsifiability remains. Historians and political scientists doing historical research can easily fall prey to the subtle problem of selecting the depth of their historical research to fit their expectations. For example, if you cannot find evidence for something you strongly believe, you are easily tempted to argue you cannot find it because its is hidden, and you will keep digging until you find it. In contrast, if you were to immediately find evidence supporting your beliefs, you would be tempted to forsake deeper historical probing that could contradict your beliefs. Aware of this problem, a consistent absence of any indications that leaders of semirepressive, moderately exclusionary regimes considered the "off-the-equilibrium path" outcome of severe punishment if they settled on moderately losing terms would have led me to drastically lower my confidence in my arguments.

When it is impossible or extremely costly to develop reliable indicators for the variables of interest for a large number of cases, the best and most efficient way to proceed can often be to perform a limited number of case studies. Two crucial variables in this book, new information about the outcome of the war and the minimum terms of settlement, fall in this category. In some of the recent rational choice litera-

---

[37] These arguments mirror closely the recent call for "analytic narratives." See Bates et al.

[38] One unrecognized weakness of the case study method: The researcher should always try to keep in mind the particular audience any source is addressing. A politician who tries to persuade his domestic opposition may well use very different arguments in the back chambers of his own party, which might differ, in turn, from the arguments he would make to his wife. In other words, researchers should keep in mind the strategic nature of public speech. Throughout my case studies I have tried to be aware of such potentially distorting factors. Occasionally, where important, I warn the reader about a particular audience and its effects on the argument of the source in the footnotes.

ture in international relations, information is an important explanatory variable. It has been difficult, however, to empirically operationalize and test such theories. In this book I show how new information affects estimates of the outcome of the war and, subsequently, war aims. To show how *new* information affects estimates, it is necessary to first establish initial expectations. It would be extremely time consuming to develop reliable indicators and code expectations of the outcome of the war at subsequent stages for all participants in all wars. Such coding would also seem prohibitively costly for another variable of interest: the minimum terms of settlement. The case studies in this book therefore combine maximum empirical leverage with feasibility.

Conclusion

This book aims to provide a theoretical framework that shows how the *politics* of war termination affect the variation between war and peace, the duration of wars, and the choice of military strategy (especially when states are willing to adopt risky strategies). In addition, this framework will show how the fate of political leaders and elites, issues of electoral reform, revolution, wartime censorship, and manipulation of the media all are intricately connected with war termination. The empirical contribution in the case studies amounts to a brief but new and integrated history of the First World War that puts both battlefield and homefront developments in their proper diplomatic and strategic perspective.

2

A THEORY OF WAR TERMINATION

> We can thus only say that the aims a belligerent adopts, and
> the resources he employs, must be governed by the particular
> characteristics of his own position; but they will also conform
> to the spirit of the age and to its general character. Finally,
> they must always be governed by the general conclusions
> to be drawn from the nature of war itself.
> *(Clausewitz, Book 8, Chapter 4)*[1]

THIS CHAPTER FIRST presents a unitary rational actor baseline theory of war termination and then adds the dimension of domestic politics. In the previous chapter I reviewed the existing arguments on the causes of war termination and laid out their shortcomings. Here I reconstruct a rationalist framework of the causes of war termination that can address these shortcomings. The addition of domestic politics in the second half of this chapter leads to the surprising and counterintuitive result that one particular regime type sometimes increases its war aims even as its leaders get more pessimistic about the outcome of the war. I explain why such regimes prefer to continue a losing war in a "gamble for resurrection." Such regimes gamble that through some new strategy or luck they can still win and thereby avoid domestic political punishment. In addition I briefly address how domestic politics can affect the utility for fighting and the commitment problem.

Main Themes

The main task of this chapter is to identify causal mechanisms that explain how states at war choose between two broad options: continued fighting and settlement. When decision makers choose between these options, they weigh the potential consequences of each course of action. It is therefore essential to explicitly model the potential consequences of continued fighting and the potential consequences of settlement. On the one hand, the consequences of continued fighting include

[1] Clausewitz, p. 594.

additional costs of war and potentially better or worse terms of settlement. The terms of a settlement, on the other hand, may leave a state almost defenseless in a next round of fighting and can have important domestic political repercussions for a regime and its leaders.

My approach links the causes of war termination to the causes of war. War breaks out because one side demands more than the other is willing to concede, that is, because states have incompatible terms of settlement, and each side hopes to procure its demands through war. In other words, each side expects to do better by going to war than by conceding the opponent his demands. Such demands can vary from maintenance of the status quo to unconditional surrender and need not be explicit. In terms of bargaining theory, wars start because both sides have reservation values that preclude a bargaining space.

This basic framework of the causes of war initiation points directly to the causes of war termination. Before the war both sides have a higher expected utility for fighting than for settlement. For a war to end, however, both sides must have a higher expected utility for the available settlement than for continued fighting. Therefore, for a war to end, for at least one side either the expected utility of fighting or the expected utility of settlement must change. In other words, for at least one side continued war must become less attractive or a settlement more attractive. In bargaining terms a necessary condition for war termination is that a bargaining space opens up.

For a bargaining space to open up it is necessary that for both sides the expected utility for settlement increases relative to their expected utility for continued fighting. The expected utility for fighting changes when a state changes its estimate of its probability of victory and the expected costs of the war. The proposed mechanism is learning; during war information that was private before the war becomes public.[2] This mechanism, the revelation of new information produced by fighting wars, can explain why wars end at some time yet could have started in the first place. Before war states have incentives to exaggerate (or understate) their strength and resolve and the expected costs of war. Events on the battlefield, however, provide belligerents with the best and most direct information to estimate their relative strength and resolve and the costs of war. Thus, when states update their estimates of

---

[2] This mechanism may seem similar to Blainey's contention that "[w]ars usually end when the fighting nations *agree* on their relative strength, and wars usually begin when fighting nations *disagree* on their relative strength" (Blainey, p. 122). The main difference in my approach lies in my very different dependent variables. Whereas Blainey's dependent variable is war/peace, my dependent variable is upward/downward change in the minimum terms of settlement or war aims. The differences between Blainey's and my approach will become clearer in the section below. By "learning" I refer to the evolution of information sets over time.

their relative strength and resolve, their utility for continued fighting changes. States would change their minimum terms of settlement, or war aims, as the utility for continued fighting changes if the expected utility of settlement did not often play an important role.

The expected utility for settlement depends on the available terms of settlement and the domestic and international consequences of those terms. The domestic consequences of the terms of settlement differ in different regime types. The mechanism that affects the expected utility for settlement is that some regimes and leaders anticipate severe domestic punishment—exile, imprisonment, or even death—whether they lose moderately or disastrously and therefore gamble for resurrection.[3] I differentiate regimes by two variables: the degree of repression employed to stay in power and the proportion of the (productive) population excluded from access to power. Regimes that do not employ repression and exclude no significant proportion of the population from power (the typical "Democracy") are likely to lose power even if they lose the war moderately. Such regimes and leaders are likely to suffer severe additional punishment, such as exile, imprisonment, or even death, only if they lose the war disastrously, and then mostly at the hand of the foreign enemy. Regimes that use extreme repression and exclude the rest of the population from access to power (the typical "Dictatorship") are unlikely to lose power if they lose the war on moderate terms because they can use their repressive apparatus to suppress attempts to remove them from power. If they lose disastrously, however, they can expect not only to lose power, but to suffer severe additional punishment. Regimes that use moderate repression and exclude a large proportion of the population from access to power (the typical "Mixed Regime" or "Anocracy") can expect to lose power and face a similar likelihood of severe punishment *whenever* they lose, be it moderately or disastrously. As a result, when they learn they will probably lose the war, such regimes and leaders have incentives to gamble for resurrection. If the gamble is successful and they win the war, they are unlikely to be punished. But if the gamble fails and they lose the war disastrously, the regime and leaders are not significantly worse off than before.

Because they fear punishment, such semirepressive and moderately exclusionary regimes have a very low utility for settlement on losing terms and settle only on terms that allow them to buy off the domestic opposition. Therefore, such regimes formulate terms of settlement, that is, war aims, that will allow them to show a profit on the war. With a profit they can buy off their opposition and stay in power. Thus, if they learn they are winning the war, such regimes do not worry about their

---

[3] See Downs and Rocke; see also Mnookin and Wilson.

domestic political audience and change their war aims with their estimates of the probability of victory. However, if they learn they will probably lose the war, they *increase* their war aims as the absolute costs of the war increase. Other regimes (the typical "Dictatorships" and "Democracies") always change their war aims in the same direction as they change their estimates of the probability of victory.

The international consequences of the terms of settlement revolve around the consequences of shifts in relative power, as they affect not just the (former) belligerents but also third parties. If the terms of settlement increase one state's relative power, that state will be in a better position to demand even more concessions later on. The central puzzle is: How can the "winner" credibly commit himself not to exploit his bargaining advantage in the future? If the "winner" cannot credibly commit himself to abstain from further and higher demands in the future, the "loser" must include the value of such further demands and the probability they will be made in his expected utility calculation. The commitment problem can be overcome, in an anarchic system, when the terms of settlement are self-enforcing

The terms of settlement are self-enforcing when the marginal benefits of additional demands are less than the marginal costs of fighting to achieve those demands on the battlefield. In other words, the "defender" can be sure the "attacker" will not raise further demands after the settlement, if both sides know that in a war over such new demands the additional costs of war are higher than the value of those demands for the attacker but not for the defender. I propose three mechanisms that increase the marginal costs of fighting. The first mechanism is outside intervention; the second focuses on geography; a potential third relies on a straightforward extension of the principal-agent model developed earlier.

The Theoretical Framework, Part I: Unitary Rational Actors

Like Schelling, Pillar, and Wagner, I view warfare as a bargaining process.[4] In this process both sides try to find out each other's reservation value. The "reservation value" is an important concept from the bar-

---

[4] Schelling; Pillar; Wagner, "The Causes of Peace"; Wagner "Peace, War, and the Balance of Power." Wagner aptly summarizes the bargaining context of war: "While adversaries can certainly choose to negotiate without fighting, if they fight it is because each sees fighting as a way to influence the outcome of negotiations" ("Peace, War, and the Balance of Power," p. 595).

gaining literature. The reservation price of a negotiator is the minimum price he prefers to pay or receive for the good over no agreement at all. In other words, a "negotiator's reservation price or 'bottom line' depends directly on the value of no agreement alternative to a proposed agreement."[5] This "bottom line" must change for the combatants to make an agreement possible where no such agreement was possible before. The reservation prices of both sides combine to create a bargaining space or a bargaining gap. As long as one side asks for more than the other side is willing to give up, a bargaining space does not exist.

Hence, a necessary condition for war termination is that a bargaining space opens up. If there exists no bargaining space before the war starts, such a bargaining space can be created only if the reservation value of the belligerents changes. In simpler terms, the minimum demands of both sides must become compatible. The reservation value of the belligerents depends on how they value no agreement compared with the value of the proposed agreement. To examine how the reservation values of the belligerents change, we must first identify the causes of changes in their value for no agreement (the expected utility of continued fighting) and their value for agreement (the expected utility of settlement). Then we must show how changes in the expected utility for fighting affect the expected utility for settlement. To avoid jargon as much as possible, I prefer to use "minimum terms of settlement" and "war aims" rather than "reservation price," but all three formulations refer to essentially the same concept: the minimum agreement a belligerent would prefer over continued fighting.

Below I flesh out and complete the argument that war ends when for both sides the expected utility of continued fighting is less than the expected utility of settlement. I present the mechanisms missing in the competing explanation that create the necessary preconditions for an agreement that leaves both sides better off than continued fighting. These mechanisms focus on both sides of the equation. The first mechanism reveals how the expected utility for continued war changes, and the second reveals how the expected utility for settlement changes.

For purposes of exposition I overemphasize the distinction between the expected utility from war and the expected utility from settlement. However, the two are of course related. In each period, states compare

---

[5] Lax, "Optimal Search in Negotiation Analysis," p. 456. As Morrow remarks, "No bargainer should ever accept an agreement that it believes to be worse than no agreement at all" ("Social Choice and System Structure in World Politics," p. 81). Rational decision makers weigh the value of any proposed agreement against the value of the absence of agreement. They choose to accept an agreement if it gives them a higher utility than they expect to get by rejecting that agreement.

the terms of settlement that currently are on offer versus the settlements that might be on offer in the next period (once more information is revealed) minus the costs of fighting for that period. Thus, the expected utility of continued fighting includes expectations about future settlement offers.

The Expected Utility for Fighting

For the purposes of exposition I assume in this section that the terms of settlement have no domestic or international consequences. (Subsequently these assumptions will be relaxed.) Looking at the problem in a slightly different way, I assume that the system is made up of only two actors, both unitary. In addition, I assume no one values fighting in itself.

One of the fundamental features of war is that it is costly. If they could, opponents would want to avoid the costs of war. In President Truman's words, "Warfare, no matter what weapons it employs, is a means to an end, and if that end can be achieved by negotiated settlement of conditional surrender, there is no need for war. I believe this to be true even in the case of ruthless and terroristic powers ambitious for world conquest."[6]

In a system of two actors, as Truman noted, if both sides knew the outcome on the battlefield, war would be unnecessary and wasteful. War is costly; it destroys lives and property. Because of the costs of war, the overall pie to be divided between belligerents after war is smaller than it was before the war. In other words, war is a *negative* sum game. If both sides knew how the pie would be divided after the war, both would be better off if they divided the pie accordingly before the war. Although their share of the pie would be the same, they would be dividing a larger pie and would therefore gain in absolute terms. In other words, because fighting is inefficient ex post there should exist ex ante bargains that rational states would both prefer to war.[7]

Why can states not avoid the costs of war? The best-known answer in international relations comes from Blainey, who suggested: "Wars usually end when the fighting nations agree on their relative strength, and wars usually begin when fighting nations disagree on their relative strength."[8] Earlier in this century Simmel had already argued that "The most effective prerequisite for preventing struggle, the exact knowledge of comparative strength of the two parties, is very often

---

[6] Truman, *Memoirs of Harry S. Truman*, vol. 1, p. 210.

[7] Fearon, "Rationalist Explanations for War," pp. 380, 383, 387–88.

[8] Blainey, p. 122.

obtainable only by the actual fighting out of the conflict."[9] The argument implies that events on the battlefield tell the belligerents something they did not and could not know before the war. It is this new information that makes it possible to reach an agreement to end war. To predict how disagreement about relative strength changes into agreement, we need to know the fundamental cause of such disagreement. If we cannot explain how rational states can disagree on their relative strength and/or resolve before the war, we cannot explain how they can later come to agree. In other words, if wars end when the causes of war initiation are removed, we need to know the causes of war initiation in order to explain war termination.

If disagreement must be explained by "misperception" or some other irrational behavior, a rational choice model could only partially predict war termination. At a minimum, it would be necessary to control for irrational behavior. Most often that would require additional insights from political psychology. I do not deny the potential of such an approach, but as shown below a rational choice model can explain why states sometimes cannot agree on their relative strength and resolve and the expected costs before war. Such a model also starts to explain how war produces agreement on relative strength, resolve, and the costs of war.

Some recent work in international relations, by scholars such as James Fearon, James Morrow, and R. Harrison Wagner, has followed up on Blainey's insight.[10] Fearon, Morrow, and Wagner have filled many of the theoretical holes in what essentially was a one-liner in Blainey. I call this new approach *rationalist learning theory*. Rationalist learning theory provides a mechanism to account for the lack of agreement on relative strength and resolve between rational leaders. Below I sketch the main theoretical underpinnings of rationalist learning theory and apply it to the question of war aims.

Rationalist learning theory postulates that states are expected utility maximizers. In straightforward expected utility terms: "Each state considering war will calculate its expected utility for war by weighting its utility for each possible outcome by the probability of that outcome occurring and subtracting the expected costs of war."[11]

---

[9] Quoted in Rosen, p. 183.

[10] Fearon, "Rationalist Explanations for War"; Fearon, "War, Relative Power and Private Information"; Fearon, "Threats to Use Force"; Morrow, "A Continuous-Outcome Expected Utility Theory of War"; Morrow, "Social Choice and System Structure in World Politics"; Morrow, "Capabilities, Uncertainty, and Resolve"; Wagner, "The Causes of Peace"; Wagner, "Peace, War, and the Balance of Power"; Wagner, "Bargaining and War." See also Bueno de Mesquita and Lalman, *War and Reason*.

[11] Morrow, "Social Choice and System Structure in World Politics," p. 88.

In simple terms, a fundamental cause of war is that the most each side is willing to cede (rather than fight) may be less than what the other side thinks it can get by fighting minus the costs of war. What one side is willing to cede and what the other side demands depends on each side's estimate of its relative strength, resolve, and the expected costs of war.[12] The relative strength of the belligerents depends on a host of factors, including the quality of the leadership, troops, their equipment, training and morale, technology, strategy, tactics, and logistics.[13] A state's resolve is determined by how much that state values the issues at stake; it reflects the importance a state attaches to these issues.[14] The expected costs of war depend on beliefs about relative strength, relative resolve, and structural factors such as the offense-defense balance and random factors such as the weather.

Rationalist learning theory argues that leaders are strategic calculators who go to war because they have competing wants and imperfect information about the real balance of military power between their states. Leaders also have less than perfect knowledge about how much the other side values the issues at stake, that is, its resolve. Finally, leaders can only estimate the costs of war.

If the leaders of one side have such private information,

> they should understand that their own estimates based on this information are suspect because they do not know the other side's private information. In principle both sides could gain by sharing information, which would yield a consensus military estimate (absent bounded rationality). And . . . doing so could not help but reveal bargains that both would prefer to a fight.[15]

Because the costs and risks of war surely supply leaders and states with incentives not to miscalculate and thus to find out what other leaders and states will or will not agree to, a rationalist explanation for war must explain what prevents leaders and states from sharing their private information. The answer, Fearon argues, must be that

> rational leaders may be unable to locate a mutually preferable negotiated settlement due to *private information* about relative capabilities or resolve

---

[12] Ibid., pp. 82, 84. See also Morrow, "A Continuous-Outcome Expected Utility Theory of War."

[13] See Stam, chs. 2 and 3. Michael Howard's four dimensions of strategy, logistical, operational, social, and technological, offer an attractive and relatively simple framework. Howard, *The Causes of Wars and Other Essays*, p. 105.

[14] Since the issues at stake vary endogenously during war, I assume that a state's utility function for all potential issues at stake is given before the war and does not change during war.

[15] Fearon, "Rationalist Explanations for War," p. 393.

and *incentives to misrepresent* such information. Leaders know things about their military capabilities and willingness to fight that other states do not know and in bargaining situations they can have incentives to misrepresent such private information in order to gain a better deal. . . . Given these incentives, communication may not allow rational leaders to clarify relative power or resolve without generating a real risk of war.[16]

On the basis of the insights of Fearon, Morrow, and Wagner, I construct a theoretical framework to explain war termination: *strategic learning theory.* As the reader will note below, the word "strategic" does double duty. First, the strategic interaction of the war aims of the belligerents creates or fails to create a bargaining space. (Fearon argues, of course, that technically a bargaining space always exists; the players are just unable to identify it because of their private information and incentives to misrepresent.) Second, and in contrast to the usual game-theoretic approach, the strategic interaction does not just lie in attempts to discover or signal each player's preferences—as in attempts to discover each side's cost tolerance—but also in attempts to signal or discover each other's relative strength and the costs of war. This signaling, moreover, does not take place in a series of offers and counteroffers, but occurs on the battlefield, in the interaction of the belligerents' military strategies. Specifically, each side designs its military strategy to present the other with new information about relative strength and resolve and the costs of war. Thus, I believe that most of the strategic interaction of war termination is to be found in military strategy and tactics, which provide credible signals of relative strength, resolve, and the expected costs of war. (Note that, if this is correct, a much deeper understanding of the "art of war" itself, of strategy, tactics, and their interactions, is needed than is usually assumed to fully understand the bargaining that is war.)

War makes agreement possible because *war provides information.*[17] On the battlefield each side can measure its relative strength and resolve directly on the basis of their actions and performance. Once a war starts, and the belligerents spend some time fighting each other, they acquire new information about their own as well as their adversaries' capabilities and the costs of war.[18] They also begin to learn more about

---

[16] Ibid., p. 381. Statesmen seem to be well aware of their adversaries' incentives and attempts to misrepresent information to them. See Hankey, vol. 2, p. 479.

[17] "An agreement reached after a costly conflict would prompt regret that a similar agreement was not reached initially—unless the information of one or both parties has changed during the conflict" (Kennan and Wilson, p. 101).

[18] "[S]ince incentives to misrepresent military strength can undermine diplomatic signaling, states may be forced to use war as a credible means to reveal private information

both sides' resolve. Specifically, continuous combat will tell both sides all sorts of things about the final outcome on the battlefield that they can never know before the war.[19]

Events that confirm previous expectations do not influence estimates; belligerents adjust their estimates only when they get *new* information. Assume, for example, that before the war both sides agreed on their relative resolve, but each expected to be twice as strong as their opponent (because they developed a new weapon or some innovative strategy). As the war progresses, at least one side must discover that its estimate was wrong. As *unexpected* defeats and failures on the battlefield mount, the relatively weaker side learns it overestimated its strength. A rational actor then lowers his estimate of his relative strength. In this manner combatants continuously adjust their estimates until they agree on their relative strength.[20] In more technical terms, states adjust their probability density functions of the outcome on the battlefield until they are consistent. In a similar manner combatants learn each other's resolve and the costs of war. Combatants still have incentives to exaggerate their resolve to their opponent, but each can now directly observe the other's resolve on the battlefield and the homefront.

As the warring states get new information about their "true" relative strength, resolve, and the costs of war, their expectations about the outcome of the war change, and therefore the expected utility for continued fighting changes. Because we assumed that there are no domestic consequences to the terms of peace, what each side is willing to cede rather than fight should change as a result of the changing expected utility for fighting. Changes in estimates of these three factors, relative

---

about their military capabilities" (Fearon, "Rationalist Explanations for War," p. 400). Timasheff argued well before Blainey that in the course of the war "estimates and expectations of the parties as to their relative strength, including the eventual intervention of neutrals, are gradually replaced by facts. Through fighting it is established beyond reasonable doubt that one party is stronger than the other.... Then, one of the conditions of warfare, uncertainty as to relative strength, is eliminated" (Timasheff, pp. 204–5).

[19] This, of course, raises the question of where each side's priors come from, how they construct their initial expectations. It seems reasonable to posit that in the era of the General Staff system countries formulate their priors through extensive war games. In the pre–General Staff system era, I would assume that military leaders form priors based on past engagements and readings of military history.

[20] An empirical problem could be that states come up with new private information as they invent new weapons, tactics, and strategies. Such new private information will only temporarily derail this process of adjustment of expectations and estimates of relative strength.

strength, resolve, and the costs of war, therefore lead to changes in war aims during the fighting.[21]

First, when one side learns that he is stronger than he previously thought and upwardly revises his subjective estimate of his relative strength, what he thinks he can get by continued fighting minus the costs of war should increase. Therefore, his minimum demands or war aims will go up.[22] In other words, changes in the estimated battlefield outcome and in war aims should move in the same direction. Thus, the following hypothesis:

> *Hypothesis 1*: As unitary rational belligerents get new information about their relative strength, they change their war aims. If they learn they are stronger than they previously estimated, they increase their war aims; if they learn they are weaker, they lower their war aims.

Second, when a belligerent learns his opponent is more resolved (i.e., the opponent values issues at stake higher than previously estimated) he will lower his war aims. I should note that I have a slightly unconventional view of a belligerent's resolve and its relationship to his strength. This unconventional view may have important implications for the enforceability of agreements. The fundamental point in my view is that a state's resolve at least partly determines the force he mobilizes on the battlefield. Nobody would dispute that the United States could have defeated the North Vietnamese if the United States had mobilized as it did during the Second World War. Why, then, did the United States deploy only relatively limited forces? The answer must be that the United States did not care enough about the issue at stake.[23] How much your side can hurt the other obviously depends at least partly on your own willingness to suffer. In other words, the costs you can inflict depend partly on your own cost tolerance, whether you are willing to pay the costs it takes to hurt the enemy.

The bargaining strength of states is therefore determined by a combination of strength and resolve, not by the simple addition of their individual values. In my view *resolve is the total amount of resources one side is willing to expend for the issue and relative strength is the numbers of troops and casualty ratio*. Thus, the higher your resolve, that is, your willingness to suffer, the higher your expected utility for fighting.

---

[21] See Morrow, "A Continuous-Outcome Expected Utility Theory of War": "Among the new conclusions [of Morrow's article] is the finding that nations shifting their level of acceptable outcomes to a conflict upward or downward after fighting starts is perfectly consistent with a rational model" (p. 473).

[22] See Wittman; Morrow, "A Continuous-Outcome Expected Utility Theory of War."

[23] Morrow, "Social Choice and System Structure in World Politics," p. 83.

Hypothesis 2: As unitary rational belligerents get new information about their opponent's resolve, they change their war aims. If they learn their opponent has a lower resolve than estimated previously, they increase their war aims; if they learn he has a higher resolve, they lower their war aims.

Relative power and relative resolve interact to determine each state's relative bargaining strength. Relative power functions as an "exchange rate" that translates resolve in overall relative bargaining strength.

Third, when one side learns the costs of war will be lower than he previously estimated, his utility for continued fighting will go up. If he expects the same probability of victory, but now for a lower price, what he thinks he can get by continued fighting minus the costs of war should increase. Changes in estimates of the costs of war therefore lead to changes in war aims in the opposite direction.

Hypothesis 3: As unitary rational belligerents get new information about the expected costs of war, they change their war aims. If they lower their estimate of the costs of war, they increase their war aims. If they increase their estimate of the costs of the war, they lower their war aims.

In summary, a rational unitary state will lower its war aims when it lowers its estimate of its relative strength, raises its estimate of the opponent's resolve, and raises its estimate of the costs of war.

Over time, combatants must come to agree on their relative strength and resolve because the mechanisms that prevent such agreement before war cannot survive prolonged fighting. Indeed, war may be the only way to credibly reveal private information about each side's relative strength and resolve. Private information becomes public once relative strength, resolve, and the costs of war can be directly observed on the battlefield. Although states may still have incentives to misrepresent this private information, it becomes much harder to plausibly claim greater resolve and strength than you are willing to show on the battlefield.

A change in war aims depends on the revelation of private information and random factors, such as the weather, which help determine the battlefield outcome. It is the very essence of private information and random factors that they are not known in advance. Therefore, most of the time we can also not predict exactly when private information will become public and when random factors will play a less important role. However, we can sometimes predict whether some events will decisively alter estimates of strength, resolve, and the costs of war. An example would be the credible and determined intervention by a third state of overwhelming power.

I do not claim that in the real world states learn their relative strength and resolve easily and without the intrusion of complications. For example, states could come up with new weapons and secret plans during the war, creating, in effect, new private information; it can be argued that the pace of innovation tends to speed up during war. Moreover, the information processing and evaluative apparatus of a state can significantly affect how quickly a state learns.[24] In his important book *Strategic Assessment in War*, Scott Gartner has recently shown how political actors develop and apply indicators to evaluate the military's performance and prospects on the battlefield.[25] Gartner shows convincingly that the indicators different actors choose can substantially affect their estimates of the probability of victory. Nevertheless, the underlying logic still holds: Over time private information becomes public.

The Expected Utility for Settlement

So far, I have argued that states choose between continued fighting and settlement on the basis of the probable consequences of their choice. If a state expects a better payoff from continued fighting than from the terms of settlement offered, it will rationally decide to continue fighting. Above I outlined how the expected utility for fighting changes. In this section I focus on the consequences of the alternative course of action: settlement. Postponing an analysis of the potential effects of domestic politics for the moment, I argue that the international consequences of the available terms of settlement can decisively affect the expected utility of settlement.

In an anarchic international system any terms of settlement that change the relative balance of power between the two actors threaten to trigger the commitment problem. How can the "loser" be sure that the "winner" will not try to take advantage of his increased power in

---

[24] Basically, belligerents and nonbelligerents move from incomplete to more complete information. There are three factors that affect this updating: the quantity of information the war provides, the quality of information, and the evaluative apparatus of each side. If a state receives more or clearer information, its estimates are more accurate, and the state learns faster. Some states possess a better evaluative apparatus than others. In a fascinating paper entitled "Why States Believe Foolish Ideas," Stephen Van Evera shows that sometimes it can be in the narrow self-interest of an evaluative organization to suppress information about the war. The better the evaluative apparatus, the faster and the more accurate a state will learn. Scott Gartner incorporates some of these effects in "I'm OK, You're OK."

[25] Gartner, *Strategic Assessment in War*.

the future? If the "winner" cannot credibly commit himself not to exploit his bargaining advantage in the future, the "loser" must include the value of any further demands and the probability they will be made in his expected utility calculation.[26] In anarchic international systems, thus, agreements must be self-enforcing.[27]

Agreements will be self-enforcing at terms where for both sides the marginal benefits of additional demands are less than the marginal costs of fighting to achieve those demands on the battlefield. The marginal benefit of an additional demand can be less than the marginal costs of fighting for the stronger side that is actually winning if the additional demand triggers third-party intervention. Potential interveners will balance against one side if that side's war aims threaten the interests of the potential intervener.[28] As a result of intervention, the previously winning side must now lower its estimate of its relative strength and lower its war aims. The presence of potential interveners can make agreements self-enforcing because states can anticipate intervention and its consequences. If the winner raises his demands, against the interests of a third state, he should increase his estimate of the probability of hostile intervention. As he increases his estimate of the probability of intervention, his expected utility for war goes down. The winner's additional demand is "self-defeating" if it makes hostile intervention so much more likely that the winner must lower his expected utility for fighting to the point where he would prefer to settle on the *original* demands.

Two historical examples may serve to illustrate the point. The first shows the mechanism in action after war termination and the terms of settlement became known. The second is an example where the anticipation of intervention limited war aims. In the 1877 Russo-Turkish War

---

[26] This problem has not gone unnoticed by students of war termination. As William Fox noted, "Hitler could not, however, translate an unimaginably vast military success into any kind of political settlement with Britain, because he had a totally insoluble credibility problem. Too many times, in too few years, too recently, he had made lightning moves of his military forces—into the Rhineland, into Austria, and into Czechoslovakia—and won reluctant acquiescence to successive *faits accomplis* by asserting in each case that he had no further demands in Europe. Given the circumstances, the British government could see little point, no matter how bleak its military prospects, in accommodating to the self-designated victor's demand for peace. The pitcher had gone to the well one too many times, and it failed Hitler on its most crucial trip" ("The Causes of Peace and Conditions of War," p. 9). See also Quester, pp. 31–32, 34, 37–38; Pillar, pp. 205, 231; Wagner, "Peace, War, and the Balance of Power." As Wagner argues in "Bargaining and War," if the disagreement outcome in the next conflict changes, the equilibrium agreement of the current conflict will change. See also Fearon, "Bargaining over Objects that Influence Future Bargaining Power."

[27] Wittman similarly notes that we must look for self-enforcing contracts but proposes only geography as a mechanism (Wittman, p. 757, note 15).

[28] See Walt.

Russia defeated Turkey, and the Ottomans accepted the Russians' maximum demands. In the Treaty of San Stefano of March 1878, the Turks accepted the creation of a large independent Bulgarian state. However, Britain and Austria-Hungary opposed this treaty because they feared Russia would totally control this new Bulgaria. As a consequence, Russia would achieve mastery over all the Balkans and the Straits. When the other European countries became aware of the consequences of the settlement of the Russo-Turkish War, they were willing to intervene to force Russia to accept lesser terms. The British demonstrated their displeasure and signaled their concern when they heard of the Treaty of San Stefano by mobilizing reserves and sending Indian troops to the Mediterranean. The threat of war was averted when the European powers, led by Britain, forced Russia to accept much lower terms of settlement at the Congress of Berlin in June 1878.

During the Seven Weeks' War Bismarck kept Germany's demands low to prevent hostile intervention, mainly by the French.[29] Bismarck *anticipated* the French would intervene if they thought Germany's demands would threaten French interests or, more generally, change the European balance of power. To keep the French out of the war Bismarck granted the Habsburgs moderate terms by the Treaty of Prague. Neither Austria nor its most faithful ally, Saxony, was asked to cede any territory. Thus, the presence of a potential intervener allows winners to credibly commit to limit their war aims if both winners and losers know that any further demands would invite balancing behavior by a third party.[30] The anticipation or actuality of third-party invention in war provides the first mechanism that makes a self-enforcing agreement to end war possible.

Geography can also help to make some terms to end war self-enforcing. On the one hand, terms of settlement that include giving up territory will increase the relative strength of the winner in the current war. On the other hand, by withdrawal the loser may gain more defensible borders. By increasing the superiority required for a successful offensive, new borders along mountain ranges, passes, or rivers can sometimes negate any increase in relative strength and make an agreement to end war self-enforcing.[31]

---

[29] Bismarck seems to have well understood the dynamics of war aims and the conduct of war: "The definition and limitation of war aims remains a political task during a war, and the way of solving it necessarily influences the conduct of the war" (quoted in Reiners, p. 197).

[30] The role of potential interveners as guarantors might explain why states sometimes "win the war, but lose the peace." A prime example is the Sino-Japanese War of 1894, and also Turkey in the war over Crete.

[31] It might also be possible that the marginal benefit of an additional demand can be less than the marginal costs of fighting for the "winning" side if the additional demand

One additional concern of the international consequences of settle-ment deserves notice. In a coalition war allies will also be concerned how the terms of settlement affect the future relative power among the coalition members. States may put downward pressures on the overall coalition's war aims to prevent too large gains to their current allies who may after all be future rivals.

If an agreement cannot be made self-enforcing, there will exist a lower bound of war aims below which states will not be willing to settle be-cause they would be dependant on the victor. If the defender's in-creased willingness to suffer does not compensate for the attacker's increase in strength, or if there exists no credible and powerful inter-vener (as in a system of only two states, or in a war in which all the members of the system are involved on two opposing camps), the loser will not settle on terms that leave it unable to defend itself in a next war.

War Aims and War Termination

As I argued above, simply more agreement about the outcome on the battlefield does not necessarily make agreement more likely. However, when both sides agree on their relative strength and resolve, a bar-gaining space must open up because war is ex post inefficient. In other words, because war is costly, once belligerents have consistent[32] expec-tations about the outcome of the fighting and their relative resolve, there exists an agreement that leaves both sides better off than contin-

---

triggers a sufficiently increased willingness to suffer on the part of the losing side. The defender's (increased) willingness to suffer must compensate for the attacker's (in-creased) advantage in relative strength. Thus, the costs the defender must be willing to suffer to make an agreement self-enforcing depend on two factors: how much the at-tacker values the (next) issue at stake and the relative strength of the combatants. For a formal model on very similar lines, deriving very similar conclusions, see Fearon, "Bar-gaining over Objects that Influence Future Bargaining Power." Note that because the disagreement outcome in the next war has not changed there is no commitment problem in this example.

The commitment problem is triggered, even if the marginal utility of territory in-creases for the conceding state, if the current settlement changes the disagreement out-come of the next war. Fearon argues that this commitment problem may also be over-come if (1) there is always a delay in the effect of territorial transfers on relative power, (2) the function relating probability of winning to territory is continuous, and (3) the alternative to an agreement now is an all-out war to the finish (Fearon, "Bargaining over Objects that Influence Future Bargaining Power"). I thank R. Harrison Wagner for clari-fying my thinking on this issue.

[32] See Wagner, "Peace, War, and the Balance of Power," for the important distinction between uncertainty and consistency.

TABLE 2.1
New Information and War Termination

	Favorable New Information for A	Unfavorable New Information for A
Favorable New Information for B	War Termination *less* likely	Indeterminate
Unfavorable New Information for B	Indeterminate	War Termination *more* likely

ued fighting. This does not imply that an agreement will be immediate. Even when a bargaining space exists, both sides may continue fighting for a while to get the best possible terms.[33] In other words, the theory outlined here offers only a *necessary* condition for war termination.

The presence or absence of a bargaining space depends on the interaction of the belligerents' reservation values, that is, their war aims. War started because the war aims of both sides precluded a bargaining space. Therefore, the creation of a bargaining space that makes war termination possible depends on how the war aims of the belligerents change, and therefore on how new information affects their prior estimates and war aims. It would seem obvious that war termination becomes more likely if both sides become more pessimistic about the outcome: Both will lower their war aims. Similarly, war termination becomes less likely when both sides become more optimistic about the outcome. When one side receives good new information and the other side receives bad new information the situation is more complicated. (It requires an estimate not only of the direction, but also of the magnitude of the change in war aims to predict whether war termination becomes more or less likely.) The effect of new information, which leads to changes in war aims, on war termination is summarized in table 2.1.

In general terms a bargaining space becomes more likely if one side lowers his minimum terms *more* than the other side raises his terms. To predict the creation of a bargaining space, therefore, we often need to know whether the change in one side's war aims is larger or smaller than the change in the opponent's war aims. The theory offers some predictions about the magnitude of such changes in each side's war aims. The worse (better) the new information about relative strength, resolve or the expected costs of war, the larger the decrease (increase) in the minimum terms of settlement. The practical value of these predictions is limited; at most they can tell us something about the order

---

[33] For more on such bargaining, see Pillar.

of magnitude of changes in minimum terms. In other words, at most we can predict whether a state's minimum terms should change little or a lot. Thus, if one state learns its relative strength is much lower than it previously estimated, it should substantially lower its minimum terms. If the enemy learns little new, because its estimates were basically correct, it should hardly change its minimum demands at all. In this case a bargaining space, and therefore war termination, will become more likely.

The Theoretical Framework, Part II:
Domestic Politics and War Termination

Many scholars have argued that the internal politics of states can affect their foreign policy.[34] They have proposed multiple mechanisms to account for the observed different behavior of different regimes. In the literature on war termination several authors similarly suggest that domestic politics can have an important impact on a state's decision whether to terminate war or continue fighting.[35] Fred Ikle, among others, suggests that a change of regime makes war termination more likely.[36] However, these authors have failed to develop a general theoretical framework to link domestic political structure and war termination.

I link domestic politics and war termination through the logic of the well-known principal-agent model. In all regimes the outcome of the war serves as a signal for the people (the principal), on the basis of which they decide to reward or punish the leadership (the agent) for their choice to go to war and their wartime performance.[37] However, the same outcome and terms of settlement can have very different consequences for leaders in different regimes.

[34] See, for example, Allison; Putnam; Tsebelis; Levy, "Domestic Politics and War"; Snyder, *Myths of Empire*; Jervis, "Cooperation under the Security Dilemma," p. 177; Jervis, "War and Misperception," p. 103; Stam, ch. 6. The democratic peace literature has spawned a whole host of potential mechanisms for how regime type affects the likelihood of war initiation. The literature is too vast to cite, but see Schultz, "Looking in Black Boxes"; Doyle; Russett, *Grasping the Democratic Peace*.

[35] See Craig and George, p. 231; Rothstein; Randle, "The Domestic Origins of Peace"; Halperin; Blainey; Ikle, pp. 59, 69, 84. Handel, "War Termination—A Critical Survey," p. 54; Shillony, p. 101; Waltz, pp. 273–74; Holl; Sigal.

[36] See Ikle.

[37] Skocpol and Tilly have shown that defeat in an international war can often lead to revolution. I go one step beyond their analysis here and suggest that one prewar regime type should be particularly susceptible to revolution because even a moderate loss suffices to coordinate the domestic opposition. See Tilly, pp. 6, 12, 102–3, 216–21, 231; Skocpol, pp. 60–64, 73–77, 94–99.

Regime Types and the Expected Utility of Settlement

One simple and attractive way to differentiate regimes is to assume that given the same terms of settlement, different regimes have different probabilities of losing power.[38] This assumption has led some scholars to conclude that Democracies are fundamentally different from other regimes.[39] However, losing power might not be so bad if you or your party could run and win again in subsequent elections. Losing power could be very bad when it almost certainly leads to additional severe punishment, such as exile, imprisonment, or death. What matters for leaders, in other words, is not just the probability but also the *consequences* of losing power. The probability of losing power and the probable consequences of losing power thus together determine the leaders' expected value of the outcome of the war. My central point is that for semirepressive and moderately exclusionary regimes the expected value of settlement remains the same, whether they lose moderately or disastrously. Therefore, when such regimes learn they will probably lose the war, they have little to lose by continuing the war and gambling for resurrection. For other regimes (repressive and exclusionary and nonrepressive and nonexclusionary), in contrast, the expected value of a settlement on moderately losing terms is significantly higher than the expected value of a settlement on disastrous terms.

My typology to differentiate regime types in some aspects closely mirrors the logic of *political opportunity structures* developed in the Comparative Politics literature.[40] However, because the typology developed here is less ambitious in scope and only aims to predict the fate of leaders as a result of war termination, I employ only two closely related variables to differentiate the three ideal typical regime types. The first variable that determines regime type is the degree of repression employed to stay in power. The degree of repression interacts with the terms of settlement to determine when leaders in the different regime types lose power. The second, and related, variable is the proportion of

---

[38] That war affects the political survival of leaders was recently shown in Bueno de Mesquita, Siverson, and Woller. Bueno de Mesquita et al. examine only one kind of punishment: the violent overthrow of regimes. I argue that the *degree* of punishment, mere overthrow or additional punishment, makes an important difference for the incentives of regimes to keep fighting or settle on losing terms. See also Bueno de Mesquita and Lalman, "Domestic Opposition and Foreign War"; and Bueno de Mesquita and Siverson, "War and the Survival of Political Leaders."

[39] See Downs and Rocke; see also Bueno de Mesquita and Siverson, "War and the Survival of Political Leaders."

[40] See especially Kitschelt; Lipsky; Eisinger; McAdam, McCarthy, and Zald; Kriesi et al.; Linz and Stepan.

the (productive) population excluded from access to the policy-making process. These two variables are related because the ability to exclude largely relies on the ability to repress to some degree those excluded from access to the policy-making process.

Together with the terms of settlement, the ability to repress the domestic opposition determines when leaders and regimes lose power. The terms of settlement of the war serve as a signal of the regime's competence and leadership abilities. In effect, the outcome of the war helps coordinate the expectations of members of the opposition and determines whether a sufficiently large group will attempt a revolt to make it successful.[41] If the war ends in even a small defeat and the regime employs no repression at all, it is extremely easy for the opposition to coordinate and remove the leader from power. However, the more the regime represses the domestic opposition, the more difficult it becomes for the opposition to coordinate an attempt to overthrow the regime. The reason is simple: the more repressive the regime, the higher the potential costs of an attempt to overthrow a repressive regime. Therefore, individual members of the opposition have to be very confident that others will join them in their attempt to remove the leader and make it successful.[42] Thus, the more repressive the regime, the worse the outcome of the war must be to coordinate the expectations of the members of the opposition so that a sufficient number will join to make the attempt to remove the leader successful. The worse the outcome of the war, the more citizens will agree that the leader should be removed simply because the worse the outcome of the war, the more the citizens will want to deter future similar behavior. If they fail to deter such behavior, they might have to pay similarly high costs of war again. Moreover, the worse the losses in war, the more the means of repression are destroyed.

The proportion of the (productive) population excluded from access to wealth and power largely determines the consequences of losing power. When groups that were previously denied access to the policy-making process come to power they have incentives to punish the former leaders to deter future attempts at exclusion.[43] Hence, the higher the proportion of the population that is excluded, the higher the likelihood that the leaders and regime will suffer severe additional punishment above and beyond their removal from power.

---

[41] See Hardin, *Collective Action*; Hardin, *One for All*.

[42] See Kuran; Lohmann.

[43] The competition between ruling elite and other groups in society can be based on many cleavages, for instance, along class, ethnic, ideological, civil-military, or kinship lines.

To be sure, the proportion of the (productive) population excluded from access is closely related to the degree of repression employed: the higher the proportion that is excluded, the more repression will be necessary to maintain the in-group(s) in power. For analytical purposes, however, the separation of the two variables usefully highlights the distinction between losing power and suffering additional severe punishment. Because we would expect both repressive but nonexclusionary and nonrepressive but exclusionary regimes to be extremely rare empirically, we can roughly distinguish three regime types. The first type is repressive and exclusionary—roughly corresponding with "Dictatorships." These regimes consist of a relatively small in-group that maintains its position by harsh repression of the rest of the population. The second type is semirepressive and moderately exclusionary—roughly corresponding with "Mixed Regimes" or "Anocracies." These regimes exclude a large proportion of the population and consist of a larger sized in-group or several in-groups that use moderate repression to maintain control. Finally, nonrepressive and nonexclusionary regimes—which can roughly be equated with "Democracies"—include all or almost all of the (productive) population and therefore need little or no repression.

If they win the war, leaders in all regimes are unlikely to lose power. (Well-known exceptions are, of course, Winston Churchill after the Second World War and George Bush after the Gulf War; note that both were leaders of nonrepressive and nonexclusionary democracies.) If they lose the war disastrously, leaders in all regimes are likely not only to lose power but also to suffer additional punishment. The fate of leaders governing under different types of regimes only significantly differs if the outcome of the war is somewhere between a total defeat and breaking even on the war. I argue that for semirepressive and moderately exclusionary regimes *any* loss is as bad as a total defeat. In either case the leadership is likely not only to lose power but in addition to suffer severe punishment such as exile, imprisonment, or even death. Such regimes would thus almost sign their own death warrant if they settle for anything less than a profit on the war. More importantly, such regimes have little to lose by continuing a losing war and gambling for resurrection. After all, a worse loss does not increase the probability of severe punishment. To avoid punishment, these regimes will settle only on terms that allow them to show a profit on the war and buy off the domestic political opposition. Hence, when such semirepressive and moderately exclusionary regimes become more pessimistic about the outcome of the war they will sometimes increase their war aims to cover the costs of the war. Leaders in nonrepressive nonexclusionary regimes will lose power if they lose a war but will only suffer severe additional punishment if they lose very badly. Thanks to their repressive apparatus, repressive and exclusionary regimes will stay in power unless they lose the war very badly, in which case they not only lose power but can also expect severe additional punishment. Because for leaders in both nonrepressive nonexclusionary regimes and repressive exclusionary regimes a worse loss significantly increases the chance of severe punishment, they have no incentive to continue a losing war and gamble for resurrection. Therefore, these regimes change their war aims as do the rational unitary actors in the baseline model considered above. When they become more optimistic about the outcome of the war they raise their war aims; when they become more pessimistic they lower their war aims.

Repressive and Exclusionary Regimes

Repressive and exclusionary regimes basically consist of one group— their inner circle—that rules at the expense of all others. The ability to exclude the rest of the population clearly relies on the regime's ability to ruthlessly repress their opposition. (These regimes thus correspond closely to what are commonly called "Dictatorships" or sometimes "totalitarian" regimes.) A good modern example of such a regime is Iraq under Saddam Hussein. The regime's ability to harshly repress the domestic opposition makes any attempt to overthrow the regime a very dangerous affair. Because the costs of an attempt to overthrow the regime are potentially very high, individual members of the opposition have to be very confident that others will join them in their attempt to remove the leader and regime and make it successful. As long as the war ends in a moderate loss and the regime's repressive apparatus remains intact, any attempt to overthrow the regime is extremely risky and unlikely to attract enough supporters to make it succeed. Only when the war ends in a disastrous loss and the regime's repressive apparatus is severely weakened will the domestic opposition be likely to attempt a revolt.

Once the leader is removed from power, however, it is very likely that he or she will suffer severe additional punishment. The previously excluded and repressed proportion of the population has strong incentives to punish the former leader severely once he loses power. We can identify at least four basic sets of incentives to punish former leaders of repressive and exclusionary regimes. The first is simple revenge for previous repression. The second incentive is that severe punishment serves to deter leaders aspiring to such repressive and exclusionary control. The third and fourth incentives come into play when members of their own in-group overthrow the leader. By punishing the former leader, the new rulers offer a scapegoat and at the same time prevent coordination of any potential opposition to their new rule from rallying around the old leader.[44]

Repressive and exclusionary regimes and their leaders who learn they will probably lose the war on anything less than disastrous terms have no incentive to gamble and continue the war. Such regimes and leaders have much more to lose than to gain by such a gamble. By continuing a losing war the regime would needlessly suffer additional costs of war and put at risk the forces they rely on to maintain their position. Because for such regimes and leaders the terms of settlement have no important domestic political consequences, unless the war ends in a disastrous defeat, they change their war aims along with their expectations about the outcome of the war.

Semirepressive and Moderately Exclusionary Regimes

Semirepressive and moderately exclusionary regimes consist of one medium sized in-group or several competing in-groups, jockeying among each other for power and influence while extracting rents from the excluded proportion of the population.[45] Unable to ruthlessly eradicate the domestic opposition like repressive regimes, repression in these regimes takes the form of occasional incarceration, bureaucratic obstructionism, and control over information. (Although there exist no consensus in the literature, such regimes roughly correspond with what the literature has referred to as "Mixed," "Anocratic," "Authoritarian," or sometimes "Oligarchic" regimes.) With only a moderate ability to repress their domestic political opposition, these regimes and their leaders stay in power by preventing the effective coordination of their opposition and through bribes to buy off the opposition. Unlike repressive regimes, thus, semirepressive regimes depend on the acquiescence of the governed. A good example of a modern semirepressive and moderately exclusionary regime is Yugoslavia under Milosevic.

---

[44] If we model the in-group as the principal, the in-group also has incentives to punish the leader only when the outcome of the war is very bad. Because in these regimes leaders have to satisfy only their one in-group, they can easily accrue reliability credits. See Bueno de Mesquita and Lalman, *War and Reason*; Bueno de Mesquita and Siverson, "War and the Survival of Political Leaders"; Morgan and Campbell. The in-group will thus forgive moderate losses and count them against past successful performance.

[45] Snyder, *Myths of Empire*. In their endeavor to exclude the opposition these regimes sometimes experience collective action problems among their constituent groups. Because repression and bribes are costly, each of the constituent groups in such moderately exclusionary regimes tries to shift these costs onto other groups. In other words, some groups will try to free-ride on others. The effect of free-riding on the probability and consequences of losing power is unclear; arguments can be made in both directions.

Semirepressive and moderately exclusionary regimes use a combination of moderate repression and bribes to affect their opposition's calculations of the costs and benefits of an attempt to overthrow the regime. Because such regimes use *moderate* repression, it is easier for their opposition to coordinate attempts to overthrow the regime than it is for the opposition in repressive exclusionary regimes. A much smaller loss in the war therefore suffices to coordinate the expectations of the domestic opposition to prompt their attempt to remove the leadership. These regimes also use bribes to buy off potential members of the opposition. Such bribes can take many forms, such as national prestige, economic growth, or possibilities for advancement (e.g., in the colonies) to siphon off ambition. When the regime can no longer afford bribes, when the losses of the war outweigh its gains so that the regime becomes unable to buy off the opposition without giving up power, the domestic opposition will attempt to overthrow the regime. For these reasons, semirepressive and exclusionary regimes face domestic revolt even if the war yields only a moderate loss.

When the leadership in such regimes loses power, it will likely suffer additional severe punishment such as exile, imprisonment, or death. As in repressive regimes, the excluded have incentives to punish the former leadership severely: revenge for previous repression and to deter leaders who aspire to such semirepressive and moderately exclusionary control. When the ruling coalition learns that it will probably lose the war and lose power, each coalition member will therefore try to blame the other for all mistakes and excesses of the past in the hope a scapegoat will satisfy the opposition. In the scramble to avoid punishment, where former allies turn against each other, it actually becomes more likely the in-groups will lose power and some of them suffer severe punishment. However, because these regimes repress their opposition less than do fully repressive regimes, and exclude a smaller proportion of the population, semirepressive and moderately exclusionary regimes are slightly less likely to be punished if they lose power than fully repressive and exclusionary regimes.

Once they learn the war will end in a loss, these regimes and their leaders can attempt two general strategies to try to avoid a loss of power and severe additional punishment: buy off the opposition or repress it. On the first strategy, they have two options if they aim to buy off the people: redistribute the international pie or redistribute the domestic pie. In other words, the leadership can choose between domestic political concessions and the redistribution of gains at the expense of the external enemy. The leadership can try to open up the regime and include (some of) the excluded population, but such transitions are difficult to control.[46] The higher the total loss on the war, the more far-reaching the domestic political concessions must be until these concessions threaten the continued dominance of the in-group members themselves. (This distinguishes moderately exclusionary regimes again from fully exclusionary regimes, who have more room to maneuver.) A shift to full participation and democracy would, of course, entail a loss of the regime's and leadership's privileges; moreover, it would also mean that the leadership would have to give up the means to protect themselves from punishment. Members and leaders of such semirepressive and moderately exclusionary regimes have reason to argue that opening up the regime could come close to suicide from fear of death. To throw themselves completely at the mercy of the new regime is a dangerous strategy, especially because the new regime still has incentives to deter future attempts at (even moderate) exclusion and repression. (Indeed, the commitment problem lurks in any regime change; how can the new regime credibly promise not to punish the old, failing regime?) The alternative way to buy off the people is to extract redistributable resources from the enemy. For example, territorial gains can be used to reward returning soldiers for their sacrifices in the form of land grants.

On the second strategy, semirepressive and moderately exclusionary regimes can also attempt to forestall a revolution by repressing the opposition. Such regimes could try to become a full-fledged repressive and exclusionary dictatorship and repress the people, but this is a very risky strategy that may make revolution even more likely. Any attempt to turn the current semirepressive and moderately exclusionary regime into a full-fledged repressive and exclusionary dictatorship would, of course, meet with the strong opposition of the groups that are currently included but in the future would be excluded from power. Moreover, since the regime lacks a strong repressive apparatus, any attempt to eliminate the people's rights would also invite resistance from the people. When the regime and leadership find themselves unable to buy off the opposition, the competing in-groups may have incentives to form a regime based on only their own group at the expense of other groups and launch a full-scale repression to try to avoid punishment. However, because each currently included group has such incentives to defect, the overall regime becomes less able to present a common front and becomes less stable and more vulnerable to an overthrow from the opposition. Furthermore, the aspiring dictator would need to create an effective force to repress the people after the war. (However, scapegoating might help to buy off the population to some

[46] See Przeworski.

degree by redistributing the rents of former in-groups and by assuring opponents there will be no future similarly ill-advised wars.) The competing groups and opposition will, of course, similarly lobby for the support of the returning soldiers. Any attempt to change the domestic regime into a fully repressive and exclusionary regime to avoid punishment is therefore a very risky strategy that could easily backfire and make the punishment of the aspiring dictators only more likely.

Thus, when the leadership of a semirepressive and moderately exclusionary regime estimates the war will end in defeat and will not yield the required profit to buy off the people, political reform, toward either inclusion or repression, is a risky and unattractive option. But settlement on losing terms will almost surely lead to a loss of power and severe additional punishment. This leaves the leadership with only one option: continue the war in the hope that a new strategy or luck will turn the tide and enable them to avoid domestic political punishment. The leadership in such regimes can rationally choose to continue or even escalate the war because if the gamble is successful and they win the war they are unlikely to be punished. Further, if the gamble fails and they lose the war disastrously, the leadership is not much worse off than if they lost it moderately. Because for the leadership the probability and level of punishment is not significantly different whether the war ends in total defeat or any more moderately losing settlement, leaders in such semirepressive and moderately exclusionary regimes have little to lose by continuing a losing war. Although the expected value of the outcome of continued fighting may be lower than that of settlement for the people as a whole, for the individual leaders the greater variance of continued conflict holds out a better possibility of somehow gaining a profit on the war and thus avoiding punishment.[47]

The leadership in such semirepressive and moderately exclusionary regimes can rationally prefer to continue war as long as the variance of the potential outcomes of the war is high enough to include terms that would forestall their punishment. In other words, and as illustrated by the figure below, such regimes maximize the area under the war outcomes probability curve to the right of the "enough profit to buy off the people" vertical line. However, the leadership does not have to take the variance of the outcome on the battlefield as given but can manipulate the variance and rationally adopt a high-variance warfighting strategy. It can be rational for leaders to adopt a high-variance strategy as long as this strategy increases the probability they achieve a

---

[47] Downs and Rocke, p. 375. Note that Downs and Rocke only allow for continued intervention or escalation. I add the dimension of strategy.

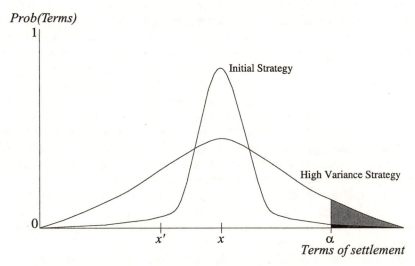

Prob(Terms)

Terms of settlement

Figure 2.1. High-Variance Strategies

settlement that will allow them to buy off the people. A high-variance strategy is rational because the likelihood of severe punishment does not increase significantly when the outcome of the war gets even worse while the likelihood of achieving terms sufficient to buy off the people increases. Hence, while both repressive and exclusionary *and* nonrepressive and nonexclusionary regimes maximize the expected value of the war, semirepressive and moderately exclusionary regimes maximize the probability of reaping a profit on the war. Figure 2.1 helps to illustrate the logic.

After each round of fighting states update their probability estimates of the outcome of the war and the terms of settlement. Assume that after the latest round of fighting the leadership of the semirepressive and moderately exclusionary regime has a probability estimate of the terms of settlement given by the high-spiked Initial Strategy probability density curve. They estimate that the terms will be at their mean, at x. Now assume that x represents a loss in the war. The leadership of the semirepressive and moderately exclusionary regime knows that if the settlement results in x they are highly likely to be severely punished. In order to forestall punishment they estimate they need to achieve terms of at least α, because α minus the costs of war leaves enough to buy off the people. (Thus, α indicates the "enough profit to buy off the people, the regime survives" line segment.) Notice that the likelihood of achieving α under the Initial Strategy is extremely low (the area under the curve is very small). The leadership of the semirepressive and moderately exclusionary regime can now rationally adopt a high-variance strategy, for example, by denuding one front to throw all troops in one offensive on another front. The high-variance strategy makes it much more likely that the threshold at α will be crossed than it was under the initial strategy (because there is a larger area under the curve to the right of the "regime survives war" line segment). However, the high-variance strategy will also make it much more likely that the outcome will be at x', a substantially worse outcome than at x. The leadership of the semirepressive and moderately exclusionary regime does not care about this increased risk of a worse outcome because it does not significantly increase the likelihood of severe punishment. Leaders of semirepressive and moderately exclusionary regime are therefore willing to trade off a much higher likelihood of a much worse outcome of the war, as long as it also gives an increased likelihood of an outcome good enough to forestall severe punishment.

The domestic opposition, in the meantime, obviously would prefer not to continue fighting for the survival of the regime and would prefer settlement on terms x. The opposition has no incentive to suffer additional costs to ensure the survival of the regime. Therefore, if the leadership learns they will probably not be able to win the war, they can continue fighting only as long as the opposition does not find out the war is probably lost. After all, the regime faces a threat to its political position when the opposition learns that the terms of settlement will not cover the costs of the war. *Whenever* the opposition learns the war is probably lost, they will be tempted to overthrow and punish the regime and its leaders. Thus, the leadership's ability to control and manipulate information is a crucial aspect of their moderate ability to repress. In all regime types leaders typically possess better information about the prospects of the war than do citizens. Semirepressive and fully repressive regimes have an added advantage over nonrepressive regimes because the leadership controls the media and thereby restricts the dissemination of bad news. Their control over the domestic flow of information allows them to manipulate their war aims for domestic political purposes. As long as they can prevent the opposition from finding out the precarious state of affairs, the leadership of semirepressive and moderately exclusionary regimes will continue a losing war in the hope they can pull a rabbit out of the hat and gain a profit.

The only terms such leaders are willing to settle on will then be those that allow them to gain the required profit on the war. Thus, even when they estimate they will probably lose, leaders of semirepressive and moderately exclusionary regimes will formulate war aims that recoup the losses of the war; as losses mount, so will the war aims to compensate the people for their sacrifices. If they are winning, these leaders need not fear punishment and change their war aims as their expected utility for war changes, similar to rational unitary actors.

> *Hypothesis 4*: Semirepressive and moderately exclusionary regimes that learn that the war probably will not bring a profit will increase their war aims with the expected costs of the war unless their aims are already high enough to cover the expected costs.

The leadership of the semirepressive and moderately exclusionary regimes will lower their war aims only when the outcome of the war is certain or when the people and potential opposition learn that the war will end in a loss. When the potential outcome of the war no longer includes an outcome sufficient to buy off the people, and there exist no further strategies to increase the variance of the outcome up to that point, for example, when the outcome of the war is determinate, leaders of semirepressive and moderately exclusionary regimes can only try to forestall punishment by domestic reforms. Similarly, when the people do find out the war is lost, the regime must shift to one of the two alternative strategies proposed above. The regime can attempt a small revolution from above to prevent a larger one from below and institute some reform to give the excluded proportion of the population greater access, in other words, attempt a transition to democracy. Alternatively, some members of the ruling elite can propose to institute a full-fledged dictatorship and harshly repress the domestic opposition. A failure to lower war aims when the people know high war aims serve merely to keep the current regime in power will only increase the chances of a revolution from below. Hence, the leadership of semirepressive and moderately exclusionary regimes will lower their war aims like unitary rational actors only when the outcome of the war is certain or when the people find out the war is lost.

Nonrepressive and Nonexclusionary Regimes

Nonrepressive and nonexclusionary regimes do not exclude a significant proportion of the (productive) population and therefore do not need to repress their opposition at all. Such regimes—but not individual governments—stay in power because they offer all groups the chance to be winners in the future.[48] At the same time leaders of such nonrepressive and nonexclusionary regimes survive because it is much easier for them to buy off their opposition without sacrificing their own access to power. Often, in such nonexclusionary regimes, issues

---

[48] See Przeworski, ch. 1.

of significant salience among the populace will be co-opted by political parties for electoral gains. Because opposition to such governments is cheap and extremely unlikely to lead to repression, it is very easy for members of the opposition to coordinate efforts to unseat the government. Leaders of such nonrepressive and nonexclusionary regimes, therefore, lose power earlier than the other two regime types. Any loss on the war suffices to lead to their removal from power.

However, because they do not systematically exclude a significant proportion of the (productive) population from access to the policy-making process, the penalty for unsatisfactory performance in such regimes is the simple loss of power. Once out of power, losers in one election can retire, go into private practice, or run again in the next election. In contrast to moderately and fully exclusionary regimes, these nonexclusionary governments do not need to fear additional punishment. Severe punishment is likely only if the regimes suffer catastrophic defeats. Even then, severe punishment most often comes from the external enemy; prominent examples are France, the Netherlands, and Belgium in the Second World War. Like leaders of repressive and exclusionary regimes, leaders of such nonrepressive and nonexclusionary regimes have strong incentives to avoid such total defeats and therefore have more to lose than to gain by a gamble on continued war and high-variance strategies to stay in power. Moreover, the free press in nonrepressive and nonexclusionary regimes makes it very difficult to keep the people in the dark about the war and the prospects for victory. Therefore, nonrepressive and nonexclusionary regimes formulate their war aims as unitary rational actors and change their war aims along with their expectations about the outcome of the war.

In summary, repressive and exclusionary regimes and leaders are least likely to lose power but most likely to be severely punished if they do. Nonrepressive and nonexclusionary regimes are most likely to lose power, but least likely to suffer additional punishment. Semirepressive and moderately exclusionary regimes live in the worst of both worlds. If they lose a war, they are almost as likely to lose power as nonrepressive regimes, and when they lose power, they are almost as likely as fully exclusionary regimes to suffer severe additional punishment. Figure 2.2 shows in graphic form the hypothesized relation between regime types, the outcome of war, and each type's probability of severe punishment.

The essential point is that for semirepressive and moderately exclusionary regimes the probability of severe punishment jumps up like a step function close to the break-even point. For both repressive and exclusionary *and* nonrepressive and nonexclusionary regimes, how-

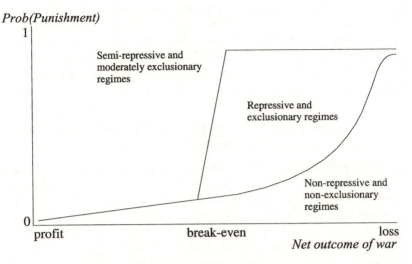

Prob(Punishment)

Semi-repressive and
moderately exclusionary
regimes

Repressive and
exclusionary regimes

Non-repressive and
non-exclusionary
regimes

profit   break-even   loss

Net outcome of war

Figure 2.2. Prob(Punishment) Depending on the
Outcome of War and Regime Type

ever, the outcome of the war has to be much worse before the probability of punishment increases to a similar level. Hence, Hypothesis 5:

Hypothesis 5: Semirepressive and moderately exclusionary leaders and regimes are likely to lose power and suffer additional severe punishment whether they lose moderately or disastrously. Repressive and exclusionary and nonrepressive and nonexclusionary regimes and leaders are only likely to suffer severe punishment when they lose disastrously.

As I argued above, to avoid such severe punishment semirepressive and moderately exclusionary leaders and regimes will continue losing wars and gamble for resurrection. As long as pessimistic semirepressive and moderately exclusionary leaders and regimes see any chance to reap a profit on the war and buy off their domestic opposition, their minimum demands will be for such a profitable settlement. However, because their winning opponent expects to settle on winning terms, both sides will ask for more than the other is willing to concede and no bargaining space exists. Thus, the following proposition:

Hypothesis 6: Wars with losers that are semirepressive and moderately exclusionary regimes will last longer than wars with other losers.

In summary, because the expected utility of settlement can have dramatic consequences for semirepressive and moderately exclusionary leaders and regimes, they formulate their war aims by a fundamentally different logic. When they get more pessimistic about the outcome of the war they sometimes even raise their war aims to cover the costs of the war. As a result, wars with losers that are semirepressive and moderately exclusionary regimes do not end until the outcome is certain or the people find out the war will be lost.

Domestic Politics, the Expected Utility for War, and the Commitment Problem

Domestic politics could also influence the expected utility for war, independent of the effect continued fighting has on the terms of settlement on offer, but, I expect, in only very rare and highly unusual circumstances. It is, however, possible that war itself confers some domestic political advantages that would disappear if a settlement is reached. Gordon Tullock provides an excellent example that shows the mechanism as well as the unusual circumstances required:

> When Mao Tse-Tung seized control of China, he actually was the head of an organization in which there were in essence 5 armies all of which had been built up by one leader from practically nothing and which were to a considerable extent loyal to that leader. Mao may have been able to deal with this by ordinary methods, but the Korean war gave him a wonderful opportunity. He in essence drafted from each of these armies specific units to send to the Korean war. These units were then rotated back to China on a regular basis, but were not returned to their original army. As a result at the end of the Korean war the 5 major armies had melded into one. Mao was then able to remove the four most important generals from their positions of personal power.[49]

Domestic politics can also help overcome the commitment problem. First, it may be possible for domestic politics to allow some regimes to credibly tie their hands. For example, a regime that won a war and promised not to raise its demands in the future could potentially face domestic political punishment if it reneged on its promise. Such audience costs might then make it possible for a winner to credibly commit himself not to raise his demands in the future.[50] This could fit well with recent developments in the Democratic Peace literature.

[49] Tullock, p. 29. Note that this incentive to continue war held only until Mao effectively integrated all five armies into one. For an example of how Milosevic similarly used the war between Serbia and Croatia to deal with his potential domestic opposition see Gagnon.

[50] See Fearon, "Domestic Political Audiences and the Escalation of International Disputes."

Second, and perhaps more interesting, the same mechanism that induced repressive and exclusionary and nonrepressive and nonexclusionary regimes *not* to gamble for resurrection may also induce them to settle on terms that change the relative balance of power in the opponent's favor. A rational unitary actor might continue fighting out of fear that the enemy would absorb and integrate any concessions such as territory into his economy and then subsequently raise new demands. However, continued fighting ensures additional costs of war and most likely worse terms of settlement. Since for repressive and exclusionary and nonrepressive and nonexclusionary regimes continued fighting would only increase their chance of severe punishment, they may prefer to settle now on more moderate terms. For this to be rational, however, these regimes and leaders must be sufficiently myopic and hope they can avoid punishment in case the opponent raises his demands in a next round of fighting. Such regimes would, in effect, gamble on a lack of recognition by the domestic opposition that today's moderate terms may lead to additional and worse terms in the future. Alternatively, they might gamble that before the people find out their military situation will improve, perhaps by a military reorganization or because other belligerents will defeat their opponent. In such cases the principal-agent logic might trump the commitment problem.

Conclusion

I have argued in this chapter that the choice between war and settlement depends on the expected utility attached to each option. I proposed a mechanism that explains how the expected utility for war changes with new information about the outcome on the battlefield. As would seem intuitively obvious, when states get more pessimistic (optimistic) about the outcome of the war on the battlefield, they lower (raise) their war aims. I proposed a second mechanism that explains when war aims are determined by the expected utility for war and when they are determined by the anticipated international consequences of the terms of settlement. States will not accept terms of settlement that threaten their own long-term survival; the losing state will have a lower bound of war aims below which it will not settle if the winning state cannot credibly commit not to exploit its advantage in the future.

A third mechanism explains when war aims change under the influence of the anticipated domestic political consequences of the terms of settlement. Although for very different reasons, repressive and exclusionary regimes and nonrepressive and nonexclusionary regimes formulate their war aims by a very similar logic. Behaving like the rational strategic unitary actors in the first half of this chapter, these regimes change their war aims in the same direction as their estimates of the outcome of the war on the battlefield. Semirepressive and moderately exclusionary regimes, in sharp contrast, formulate their war aims by a very different logic because their likelihood of punishment remains the same whether they lose moderately or disastrously. When winning, these regimes change their war aims in the same way as the other regimes. However, when losing, they formulate war aims to cover the costs of the war. Thus, when they get more pessimistic about the outcome of the war, they do not decrease but instead often increase their war aims.

The theoretical framework outlined in this chapter presents some straightforward conclusions about war termination. First, it is impossible for the combatants to predict during a war when and on what terms the war will end. Neither side knows his opponent's private information; therefore, neither side knows which events would constitute new information for his opponent, nor how he would react to it; each only knows that fighting reduces the asymmetry of information. But neither side can predict when the asymmetry in information is removed. Second, if the winner cannot credibly commit not to exploit his (increased) bargaining advantage in the future, war continues until the loser surrenders unconditionally. Third, wars with losing semirepressive and moderately exclusionary regimes will continue until either they are completely defeated on the battlefield or there is a regime change. The hypotheses of the theory must, of course, be tested empirically. To this task we now turn.

3

LARGE N: THE FATE OF LEADERS

AND THE DURATION OF WAR

THIS CHAPTER TESTS several of the hypotheses offered in the previous chapter. Using a new cross-national data set specifically constructed for this purpose, I analyze how the outcome of the war has affected the fate of leaders. I rely on a second data set constructed and analyzed previously by Scott Bennett and Allan Stam to examine the duration of wars.[1] I first describe the new data and then analyze each data set and discuss potential problems or sources of bias.

The Data

The data on the fate of leaders come from four sources.[2] The war data are taken from the *Correlates of War* data set as reported in Small and Singer's *Resort to Arms*.[3] This data set reports all wars between 1816 and 1975 with at least one thousand battle-related fatalities and identifies the initiators, winners, and losers. The data set also contains the number of battle deaths per ten thousand population. Two sets of corrections were made. First, where possible, the data on battle deaths were checked against the 4th edition of Dupuy and Dupuy's *Encyclopedia of Military History*.[4] Where there was substantial disagreement and Dupuy and Dupuy offered precise numbers, I used the latter's figures. This resulted in only a handful of corrections.

Second, a careful look quickly reveals that the *Correlates of War* project was not constructed with questions about war termination in mind. For example, that project codes the war between Japan and China as starting in 1937 and ending 7 December 1941, and a new war, the Pacific War, starting 7 December and ending in 1945. I recoded this as a single war, beginning, for China and Japan, in 1937 and ending in 1945. Also, the *Correlates of War* project codes both the date a war ended and

---

[1] Bennett and Stam.

[2] The full data set is available at www.duke.edu/~hgoemans.

[3] Small and Singer, *Resort to Arms*; Small and Singer, *Wages of War, 1816–1980*.

[4] Dupuy and Dupuy, *The Harper Encyclopedia of Military History* (New York: HarperCollins, 1993).

the outcome of the war. Sometimes, however, this leads to internal contradictions. For example, Yugoslavia and Greece are coded as winners in the Second World War although for both of them the war is coded as ending in 1941. I chose, for obvious reasons, to focus on the end date and to recode Greece and Yugoslavia as losers.

The regime-type data were taken from the May 1996 version of Ted Robert Gurr's *POLITY III*.[5] This data set "consists of annual codings of regimes' structural characteristics, institutional changes, and the directionality of changes on underlying dimensions of democracy, autocracy, and power concentration." The *POLITY III* data set offers one coding per year for each country. If there was a change in the regime type at the end of the year, the coding for this country for that whole year reflects the new regime type. Therefore, to accurately capture the regime type at the start of the war I also recorded the regime type one year before the war started. Next, I examined whether there was a regime change in the year the war started and whether that change occurred before or after the war started. If a regime change occurred in the same year but *after* the war started, I classified the regime type at the start of the war by using the *POLITY III* coding for the previous year. (Cyprus's regime score before the 1974 Turko-Cypriot conflict is coded as missing because the leadership came to power five days before the war by a coup.) There are twelve observations in the set for which the data on regime type were missing, including France in the Franco-Mexican War; Mecklenburg-Schwerin, Hesse Grand Ducal, Hesse Electoral, and Hanover in the Seven Weeks' War; Germany in the Franco-Prussian War; Greece in the war of 1919 with Turkey; Ethiopia, Italy, and Bulgaria after they switched sides in the Second World War; Israel in 1948; and Cyprus in 1974.

Third, I did a substantial amount of original research. I hypothesized that leaders in different regime types can face different degrees of punishment. Therefore, I needed information on the effective leadership, their entry and exit from power, and their fate when they lost power. For each participant in a war I coded who the effective leader was when the war started, when the war ended, and one year before the war ended. For each country I consulted the historical secondary literature to locate the person who held ultimate authority and was held accountable. In some cases effective authority was held by more than one person.[6] If a prime minister largely made policy but could be dis-

---

[5] Gurr, Jaggers, and Moore, *POLITY II: Political Structures and Regime Change, 1800–1986*; Jaggers and Gurr, *POLITY III*; Jaggers and Gurr, "Transitions to Democracy"; Gurr, Jaggers, and Moore, "The Transformation of the Western State."

[6] In only one case did I encounter significant difficulties coding the effective leader: Japan between 1931 and 1945. I did not code the emperor as the effective leader because

missed by a king or queen at his or her will, I coded the monarch as the effective ruler. If the monarch had the nominal right to remove the prime minister, but in effect the prime minister ruled and the monarch was unable to remove him or her, the prime minster was coded as the effective ruler. In addition, I coded each leader's date of entry and exit from power. Finally, I coded whether the leader was punished, that is, killed, exiled, or imprisoned, within the period one year before the war ended to one year after the war ended.[7]

I added one final variable to capture the potential for punishment of domestic political leaders by outside foreign forces. This dummy variable records the leaders who were removed from power by foreign intervention. The codings for regime change imposed by foreign intervention come from a data set constructed and analyzed by Bruce Bueno de Mesquita and Randolph M. Siverson.[8] I made some minor adjustments for countries that had been excluded from their data set. I also ran the regressions with the cases of Foreign Imposed Regime Change as operationalized by Suzanne Werner; the results remained substantively unaltered.[9] From this data set I eliminated the cases in

---

he did not set policy, nor did he appoint or dismiss prime ministers. But neither could I code the prime ministers as the effective leader because they were assassinated, almost at their whim, by radical army officers. Moreover, the assent of the army council was required to form a cabinet in the first place. Without an army minister, no cabinet could form. Although less than satisfactory, I coded the effective leadership of Japan between 1931 and 1945 as the army council, consisting of six members. After the Pacific War all leaders, except the emperor, of course, were punished. To test for its effects, I also coded the prime minister as the effective leader of Japan between 1931 and 1945. The results are not substantively different.

[7] This information was collected from a variety of sources, including Spuler; *Webster's New Biographical Dictionary* (1983); Bienen and van de Walle; *The New Encyclopedia Britannica*, 15th ed.; *Encyclopedia Britannica* (1966); *The Encyclopedia Americana*, International Edition (1987); *Worldmark Encyclopedia of the Nations*, 5th edition (1976); the *Country Studies/Area Handbooks*; Seton-Watson; Legg. As always, there will be some cases that are difficult to interpret. For example, during the Franco-Mexican War of April 1862 to February 1867 the French put Maximilian on the Mexican throne in 1864. He was executed in June 1867. He was the representative of the French government, but the French government back home suffered no punishment. Hence, the French leader at the time (Napoleon III) is coded as not removed from power or punished. Yayha Khan, effective leader of Pakistan before and during the 1971 war between India and Pakistan/Bangladesh, was kicked out of the presidency and the army and placed under house arrest. He was coded as punished. For some of the longer wars it would be essentially incorrect to focus just on the leader at the start of the war. For example, Emperor Franz Joseph of Austria-Hungary died in 1916. His grandnephew Emperor Charles took over and after the defeat fled in 1918. It would be incorrect to classify this case as merely a natural death, and the leader of Austria-Hungary was coded as punished in the First World War.

[8] Bueno de Mesquita and Siverson have analyzed this data set in Bueno de Mesquita, Siverson, and Woller, p. 641.

[9] Werner, p. 84.

which there was no clear-cut winner, for example, the participants in the Korean War. This left me with 215 observations. For the analysis of the fate of political leaders I dropped the six cases where leaders died a natural death.

To construct variables for the three regime types, I first created a composite indicator of regime type by subtracting the *POLITY III* Autocracy index from the Democracy index to produce a variable that ranges from 1 to 21. This composite index thus captures the four components used in both the democracy and autocracy index, openness of executive recruitment, competitiveness of executive recruitment, competitiveness of participation, legislative constraints on the executive, and a fifth component from the autocracy index, the regulation of participation. The composite index for Autocracy and Democracy seems a good first approximation of the number of groups that have access to the policy-making process. The higher a country scores on the Autocracy index, the higher the proportion of people it is likely to exclude from access to power. Likewise, the higher a country scores on the Democracy index, the higher the proportion of people that will have access to power. Because repression and the number of groups excluded from power are probably highly collinear, this scale is a good indicator for the variables that determine regime type. It also has the advantage of being well known and widely used.

Next, I constructed three dummy variables for each of the three regime types, nonrepressive and nonexclusionary, semirepressive and moderately exclusionary, and repressive and exclusionary regimes. (Using dummies makes it much easier to test whether leaders of different regime types faced a significantly different fate when they lost small than when they lost big.) Because I cannot directly measure the two variables that together determine regime type (repression and exclusion) and to avoid clumsy prose, in this chapter I refer to the three regime types as "Democracies" (roughly corresponding with nonrepressive, nonexclusionary regimes), "Mixed Regimes" (roughly corresponding with semirepressive, moderately exclusionary regimes), and "Dictatorships" (roughly corresponding with repressive, exclusionary regimes).

Countries that score 17 or higher on the composite indicator are coded as Democracies, countries that score from 7 to 16 are coded as Mixed Regimes, and countries from 1 to 6 are coded as Dictatorships. (I discuss the robustness of this specification below.) Although France's regime type in 1862 was coded as missing in *POLITY III*, additional research allowed me to code France in 1862 as a Dictatorship.[10]

[10] The Autocracy and Democracy scores for France are coded as −88 between 1860 and 1862; in 1860 France scored −8 on the Autocracy index and 0 on the Democracy index,

To test how different outcomes of wars affect the fate of domestic political leaders, we need data about the overall outcome of the war for each country. I know of no data that readily provide the overall outcome of the war, weighing benefits and costs in similar units. Thus, as an approximation, I focus on the *size* of a loss for losers. (Below I will discuss some of the regrettably unavoidable shortcomings of this choice.) The coding for losers comes from the adjusted data from the *Correlates of War* project. The problem lies in distinguishing moderate losses from big losses. A good approximation is available in the corrected war lethality data. The *Correlates of War* project lists for each nation its battle deaths per ten thousand population. This measure is particularly attractive because it is consistent across time and insensitive to the size of a nation's population. Because these data are highly skewed, I used a logarithmic transformation.[11] This variable was used to distinguish small losers from big losers. If a country lost a war and suffered more than one standard deviation above the mean of the natural log of battle deaths per ten thousand population, it was coded as a big loser. By definition, this qualifies about 25 percent of all losers as big losers. If a country lost a war but suffered less battle deaths, it was coded as a small loser. (I tried other codings to distinguish small losers from big losers; again, the results were not significantly different.)

The Fate of Leaders

In this section I test Hypothesis 5 presented in the previous chapter. To refresh the reader's memory, table 3.1 lists the hypothesized consequences of the outcome of war by regime type. For purposes of war termination, the crucial distinction is what happens to the leaders in different regime types when they lose the war moderately.

My central claim is that leaders of Mixed Regimes will be punished whether they lose moderately or disastrously. Dictators and Democrats, in contrast, are likely to be punished only if they lose disastrously. Therefore, for leaders of Mixed Regimes the difference between losing moderately or losing disastrously affects the probability of punishment much less than for Dictators and Democrats. Moreover,

---

and in 1863 France scored −6 on the Autocracy index and 0 on the Democracy index. For both of these years, thus, France would be a Dictatorship. I coded France in 1862 as a Dictatorship because the institutional structure remained largely unchanged between 1860 and 1862, with the possible exception of a marginal change in the allocation of financial responsibility to the Chamber on 31 December 1861. See Plessis, pp. xi, 151–58, and especially 15–57.

[11] See Bueno de Mesquita, Siverson, and Woller.

TABLE 3.1
The Outcome of War and the Fate of Leaders

Type/Outcome	Win	Lose Moderately	Lose Disastrously
Democracy	Stay in power	*Out of power*	Out and punished
Mixed Regime	Stay in power	*Out and punished*	Out and punished
Dictatorship	Stay in Power	*Stay in power*	Out and punished

TABLE 3.2
Regime Type, Outcome of the War, and Consequences

Type/Outcome	Out of Power		Punished		Total	
Democracy Winners	31%	(9)	3%	(1)	15%	(29)
Democracy Small Losers	86	(6)	29	(2)	4	(7)
Democracy Big Losers	100	(1)	100	(1)	1	(1)
Mixed Regime Winners	26	(8)	10	(3)	16	(31)
Mixed Regime Small Losers	46	(11)	46	(11)	12	(24)
Mixed Regime Big Losers	90	(9)	70	(7)	5	(10)
Dictatorship Winners	13	(5)	5	(2)	20	(39)
Dictatorship Small Losers	37	(18)	31	(15)	25	(49)
Dictatorship Big Losers	75	(6)	75	(6)	4	(8)
Total	37	(73)	24	(48)	N=198	

Note: Pearson Chi^2 (8) = 38.5865, Pr=0.000, 51.1609, Pr=0.000

whereas Democrats are hypothesized to be likely to lose power when they lose moderately, Dictators are likely to stay in power. Table 3.2 examines these predictions and reports on the combination of regime type, outcome of the war—that is, win, lose small, or lose big—and the consequences for the leaders within the period one year before the war ended to one year afterwards.

Thus, of all Democratic leaders that won a war, 31 percent neverthe-less lost power; therefore 69 percent remained in power. To interpret the "Punished" column, it is important to remember that all leaders that were punished, for example, exiled, imprisoned, or killed, of course first lost power. Therefore, the one Democratic leader that won the war but lost power and suffered additional punishment (Sodonio Pais from Por-tugal in the First World War) represents 3 percent of all Democratic win-ners but 11 percent of Democratic winners that lost power.

It is troubling, of course, that there are so many cells with a very small number of observations. Especially with regard to Democracies, therefore, any conclusions must be tenuous. With these caveats in mind, it is nevertheless striking that, as predicted, whether they won, lost small, or lost big, Dictators were far more likely to stay in power than were leaders of Mixed Regimes, who, in turn, were more likely to stay in power than were Democrats. Moreover, for leaders that lost power, the likelihood of severe additional punishment does not seem to differ much between Dictators and leaders of Mixed Regimes. Among those who lost power, only 11 percent of the Democratic winners suffered additional punishment as compared to 38 percent of Mixed Regime winners and 40 percent of the Dictatorship winners. Similarly, among small losers that lost power, only one-third of those Democratic leaders were punished, whereas *all* of those Mixed Regime leaders and 83 percent of those Dictators suffered additional punishment. Finally, among big losers that lost power, the one Democrat was punished severely, whereas 78 percent of those Mixed Regime leaders and *all* those Dictators suffered exile, imprisonment, or death.

More importantly, whether leaders of Mixed Regimes lose badly or moderately affects their probability of punishment *much less* than it does for Dictators and Democrats. In either case, whether they lose big or small, leaders of Mixed Regimes are uncomfortably likely to be punished. In sharp contrast both Democrats and Dictators are much more likely to be punished when they lose badly than when they lose moderately. For Democrats and Dictators alike, whether they lose big or small makes a big difference in their likelihood of punishment.

In the previous chapter I argued that Mixed Regimes are caught in the worst of both worlds. They have a similar likelihood of losing power as Democracies, but once they lose power they have a similar likelihood of suffering additional punishment as Dictatorships. To test this argument I construct the following logit models. First, I test whether Democracies and Mixed Regimes have a similar and high likelihood of losing power whereas Dictators have a significantly lower likelihood of losing power. I exclude the cases where the regime was overthrown by foreign intervention because all those leaders suffered additional punishment. Because the one Democratic big loser was removed from power by foreign intervention, I estimated the following logit regression:

$$\Pr(\text{Leader out in 1 year}) = 1/(1+e^{-X\beta}).$$

$X\beta = K + \beta_1(\text{Democratic small losers}) + \beta_2(\text{Mixed Regime small losers}) + \beta_3(\text{Mixed Regime big losers}) + \beta_4(\text{Dictator small losers}) + \beta_5(\text{Dictator big losers}) + \varepsilon.$

The results are reported in table 3.3.

Testing the difference among the small losers reveals that, as predicted, the Mixed Regimes were significantly more likely to lose power than were Dictatorships ($p < .05$), but about as likely as Democracies ($p < .26$, two-tailed tests). Thus, if they lose moderately, leaders of Mixed Regimes are as likely to lose power as Democrats. I argued in

TABLE 3.3

The Outcome of War and the Likelihood of Removal from Power in One Year

Removal from Power in One Year	*Coefficient (Standard Error)*
Democrat Small Loser	2.40 ** (1.18)
Mixed Regime Small Loser	1.04** (.40)
Mixed Regime Big Loser	3.09** (1.11)
Dictator Small Loser	-.055 (.47)
Dictator Big Loser	1.70* (.95)
Constant[a]	-1.30** (.25)

Notes: All tests are two-tailed: *= p < .1, **= p < .5, ***= p < .01. Logit estimates: Log likelihood—94.94, Chi^2 (5) = 22.01, P > Chi^2 = .0005, N = 176.[a] The constant picks up the winners, and the coefficients for the other variables must be interpreted against this baseline.

the previous chapter that, once removed from power, leaders of Mixed Regimes and Dictators should face a similar likelihood of additional punishment. Because all leaders of Mixed Regimes that lost small and all Dictators that lost big were punished, I did not distinguish between small and big losers but examined only losers. The regression showed that, among leaders that lost power, the likelihood of punishment was not significantly different for leaders of losing Mixed Regimes and losing Dictators (p < .79). However, both leaders of losing Mixed Regimes and losing Dictators were significantly more likely to face additional punishment than were losing Democrats (p .07 and p < .09, respectively; all two-tailed tests).

With these encouraging results, I proceed to Hypothesis 5: Leaders of Mixed Regimes are likely to lose power and suffer additional severe punishment whether they lose moderately or disastrously. Recall that punishment is coded as 1 if a leader lost office *and* was exiled, imprisoned, or killed in the period one year before to one year after the war ended, and 0 otherwise. I ran the logit regression with both indicators of "Overthrow by Foreigners." The first indicator of regimes overthrown by the foreign enemy perfectly predicts additional punishment beyond removal from office. In Model 1 I therefore dropped those cases. I also ran the regression with a second (Werner's) indicator for foreign-imposed regime change. Because in three of her twenty-four instances of foreign-imposed regime changes the leader was not removed from power, the variable no longer perfectly predicted the post-removal fate of leaders and could thus be included in the regression. Model 2 therefore reports the results for the regression that includes Werner's indicator for foreign-imposed regime change.

Furthermore, I postulated that the important distinction was between Mixed Regimes and the other two types. I argued that both Dictators and Democrats should expect basically the same likelihood of

TABLE 3.4
Regime Type, the Outcome of Wars and the Likelihood of Punishment

Death, Imprisonment, or Exile	Model 1	Model 2
Other Small Loser	.895 (.661)	1.58*** (.554)
Other Big Loser	3.33*** (1.02)	3.11*** (1.02)
Mixed Regime Small Loser	2.66*** (.623)	2.48*** (.622)
Mixed Regime Big Loser	3.21*** (.891)	3.03*** (.893)
Regime Overthrown by Foreigner	——	3.06*** (.702)
Constant	-2.92*** (.459)	-2.93*** (.444)

Notes: All tests are two-tailed: *= p < .1, **= p < .5, ***= p < .01. Model 1: Logit estimates: Log likelihood -59.09, Chi^2 (4)=32.67, Prob > Chi^2 = 0.0000, N = 176. Model 2: Logit estimates: Log likelihood = -71.75, Chi^2 (5) = 78.07, Prob > Chi^2 = .0000, N = 198. [a] The constant picks up the winners, and the coefficients for the other variables must be interpreted against this baseline.

severe punishment whether they lose big or small. Therefore, I reduced the classification of regime types to two variables: Mixed Regimes and Other Regimes. This coding also partially alleviates the low cell frequency problems that especially plagued Democracies. Additional tests reported below reveal this did not artificially distinguish Mixed Regimes from Dictatorships.

The logit model reveals the postulated effects of regime type, losing big or small, and regime change by foreign intervention on the likelihood of punishment. The estimated model was

Pr(Exile, Imprisonment, Death) = $1/(1+e^{-XB})$.
$X\beta = K + \beta_1$(Other small losers) + β_2(Other big losers) + β_3(Mixed Regime small losers) + β_4(Mixed Regime big losers) + ε.

Because of the nature of the independent variables, it was necessary to leave one outcome—winning, losing small, or losing big—out of the estimation of the model. The effect of the omitted variable is then contained in the constant. The results are reported in table 3.4.

The results of Model 1 show that for the Other regimes the probability of being punished by their domestic opponents when they lost small was only about 19 percent. When they lost big, however, they faced a 75 percent chance of being punished. Mixed Regimes that lost small faced a whopping 55 percent chance of being punished by their domestic opponents, and a 72 percent chance if they lost big. It will hardly be a surprise that Mixed Regime Small Losers and Other Small Losers were significantly different (p < .0027, all one-tailed tests). Crucially, Mixed Regime Small Losers and Mixed Regime Big Losers were *not* significantly different (p < .26), whereas Other Small Losers and Other Big Losers *were* significantly different (p < .009). Mixed Regime Big Losers and Other Big Losers were not significantly different (p < .46). Model

TABLE 3.5
Marginal Effects on P (Punishment), with Other Variables Held at Their Means

Regime Type and Outcome of the Year	Model 1		Model 2	
	IV at 0	IV at 1	IV at 0	IV at 1
Other Small Loser	9%	19%	12%	40%
Other Big Loser	10	75	16	81
Mixed Regime Small Loser	8	55	14	66
Mixed Regime Big Loser	9	72	16	79
Regime Overthrown by Foreigner	——	——	13	77

TABLE 3.6
Losing Mixed Regimes and the Fate of Their Leaders

Small Losers (War Entry)	Leader's Fate	Big Losers (War Entry)	Leader's Fate
Denmark (1864)	In power	Germany (1914)	Out and punished
France (1870)	Out and punished	Turkey (1914)	Out and punished
Guatemala (1885)	Out and punished	Bolivia (1932)	Out
Spain (1898)	In power	Japan (1937)	Out and punished
Honduras (1906 & 1907)	Out and punished	Japan (1939)	In power
Turkey (1911)	Out and punished	Finland (1939)	Out
Turkey (1912)	Out and punished	Finland (1941)	Out and punished
Yugoslavia (1941)	Out and punished		
Egypt (1948)	In power		
Lebanon (1948)	In power		
Syria (1948)	Out and punished		
Republic of Korea (1965)	In power		
Philippines (1966)	In power		
Pakistan (1971)	Out and punished		

2 includes the variable for Regime Overthrown by Foreigner as coded by Werner; its results were not substantively different. As before, Mixed Regime Small Losers and Other Small Losers were significantly different ($p < .05$). Mixed Regime Small Losers and Mixed Regime Big Losers were not significantly different ($p < .27$), while Other Small Losers and Other Big Losers were significantly different ($p < .06$). Mixed Regime Big Losers and Other Big Losers were not significantly different ($p < .47$; again all one-tailed tests). Table 3.5 lists the marginal effects of Models 1 and 2. In Model 1 the baseline probability of punishment with all variables held at their mean is about 11 percent, in Model 2 it is 18 percent.

While six leaders of Mixed Regimes that lost small stayed in power, two of them, Marcos of the Philippines and Park of the Republic of Korea, successfully turned their regimes into Dictatorships a year before the Vietnam War ended. We would expect them, as Dictators, to remain in power after a moderate defeat. Among the leaders of Mixed Regimes that lost big, President Salamanca of Bolivia was overthrown about six months before it ended by a military coup whose leaders were intent on continuing the war. He was detained for five days before he voluntarily retired to the countryside to write his memoirs in isolation, and he died a natural death one month after the war ended. Because he agreed to cooperate and make a statement to transfer power "peacefully" in order to prevent civil war in the face of an external war and his extremely short detention, he was not coded as punished. Less than one year after the war ended, a coup turned Bolivia into a Dictatorship. Japan's leaders stayed in power after Japan's defeat at Nomohan in 1939. Although this defeat had extremely important consequences, the leadership's ability to stay in power should not be surprising, given their apparent successes in China proper.

Specification Checks

I performed several specification checks. First, I examined how sensitive these results were to the cutoff points used to specify regime types. I multiplied the full composite indicator and its square with the variables for big loser and small losers. Regressing these four variables on punishment showed the expected curvilinear effect for both small and big losers. Because it was more complicated to test whether the likelihood of punishment differed significantly for small and big losers across regimes, I constructed a host of additional dummy variables. Analysis showed that the crucial thresholds for the three different regime types lay at composite indicator scores of 6 and 17. Different codings within that range all yielded substantively the same results as above. Once I coded Mixed Regimes outside that range, however, the results no longer held.

Second, it could be argued that collapsing Democrats and Dictators into one category, Other Regimes, unduly influenced these results because Democracies were unlikely to be punished in the first place. I dropped all Democracies and ran the regression with only Mixed Regimes and Dictatorial regimes. The results are again very similar. Among small losers, leaders of Mixed Regimes were significantly more likely to suffer punishment than Dictators ($p < .004$, all one-tailed tests). The likelihood of punishment was *not* significantly different for Mixed Regime small losers and Mixed Regime big losers ($p < .26$), whereas the likelihood was significantly different for Dictator small losers and Dictator big losers ($p < .01$). Finally, among big losers, leaders of Mixed Regimes were not significantly different from Dictators ($p < .46$).

TABLE 3.7
Regime Types and the Size of Loss

Type/Outcome	Small Loss	Big Loss	Total
Democracy	86% (51)	14% (8)	58% (59)
Mixed Regime	71 (24)	29 (10)	33 (34)
Dictatorship	89 (8)	11 (10)	9 (9)
Total	81 (83)	19 (19)	N=102

Note: Chi^2 (2) = 3.9440, Pr=.139.

Third, it might be argued that exile is not nearly as bad as imprisonment or death and that the inclusion of exiled leaders as punished unduly influenced the results. To check, I regressed the now familiar independent variables on a new variable for leaders who were just imprisoned or killed. The same results held as before, whether I used my or Werner's codings for foreign-imposed regime change. Democrats and Dictators were significantly more likely to be imprisoned or killed if they lost big than if they lost small. Leaders of Mixed Regimes were just as likely to be imprisoned or killed if they lost small as when they lost big.

Fourth, one might anticipate that "defenders" would not suffer the same fate as "attackers." I therefore also checked whether the initial stance of the regime type influenced the results. The dummy variable for "defender"—both separate and as an interaction with regime type—was not significant and did not influence the results.

Although these results look very encouraging, a serious endogeneity problem exists: The outcome of the war is endogenous. Unfortunately, the endogeneity problem is unavoidable, cannot be solved in this case with simultaneous equations, and does not depend on how I construct my indicators for the size of the loss. I argued that leaders of Mixed Regimes anticipate the same fate whether they lose moderately or disastrously and as a result prefer to continue fighting rather than settle on moderately losing terms. If my arguments are correct, we should expect to find evidence of a selection effect and significantly fewer moderately losing Mixed Regimes. Note, however, that settlement on moderately losing terms is rational if the domestic opposition has learned the war will probably be lost. Table 3.7 examines whether leaders of Mixed Regimes are indeed more likely to be big losers.

As the table shows, Mixed Regimes do seem to suffer more big losses, but the significance is doubtful. Another way to get at this is to look at overall costs of war in battle deaths. To examine whether losing Mixed Regimes lose worse than other regimes, I tested whether Mixed Regime losers suffered more casualties per ten thousand population

TABLE 3.8
Regime Type, Duration of War, and Battle Deaths

Battle Deaths per 10,000 Population	Model 1 Neg-binomial	Model 2 OLS
Losing Democracy	.207 (.572)	-.282 (.508)
Losing Mixed Regime	1.46*** (.332)	.907*** (.303)
Losing Dictatorship	1.04*** (.285)	.479* (.255)
Opponent of a Losing Mixed Regime	1.25*** (.327)	.876*** (.296)
Months at War	.055*** (.005)	.033*** (.004)
Constant	1.141*** (.216)	.962*** (.185)
In alpha	.873*** (.093)	

Notes: Regression estimates: Model 1: LR Chi^2(5) = 137.5, Prob > Chi^2= .0000, Pseudo R^2 = .084; alpha = 2.39 (.221), LR test of alpha Chi^2(1) = 29,567.5, Prob > Chi^2 = 0.0000. Model 2: F(5, 198) = 18.65, Prob > F = .0000, Adjusted R^2 = .303, N = 204.

than did other losers. It is necessary to include a control variable for the type of winner to conduct this test. I argued that Mixed Regimes do not want to settle but continue fighting when they estimate they will probably lose. Because their opponents are likely to estimate they will win, no bargaining space will exist, and both sides prefer to continue fighting rather than settle on the opponent's terms. This implies that I should also control for the battle deaths of countries that were fighting against a losing Mixed Regime and thereby forced to continue fighting and suffer higher battle deaths as well.

I use two different statistical estimators with related but different dependent variables to test whether Losing Mixed Regimes and their Opponents are forced to suffer higher costs of war. Because the data are highly overdispersed, I ran a negative binomial maximum-likelihood regression in Model 1; the dependent variable in Model 1 therefore is battle deaths per ten thousand population. For comparison, I include an Ordinary Least Squares regression in Model 2; the dependent variable there is the natural log of battle deaths per ten thousand population plus one. Because the duration of war significantly affects the number of battle deaths, I controlled for months at war.

As the alpha indicates, the data are indeed highly overdispersed, thus validating the choice for a negative binomial estimator. In both models, Losing Mixed Regimes were significantly more likely to suffer higher battle deaths than Losing Democracies ((Model 1) p < .02; (Model 2) p < .01). The difference between Losing Mixed Regimes and Losing Dictatorships is also supported ((1) p < .10; (2) p < .08). As expected, the regressions also show that Opponents of Losing Mixed Regimes suffer higher battle deaths than other winners. The difference between Democratic and Dictatorial losers was also significant ((1) p < .07; (2) p < .06, all for one-tailed tests). Hence, as expected, Losing Mixed Regimes suffer and force their Opponents to suffer higher costs of war.

The Duration of War

The finding that the duration of war significantly influenced the costs of war and the number of battle deaths should not surprise us; in the previous chapter I argued that the duration of war also is endogenous. Hypothesis 6 held that *wars with Mixed Regime losers will last longer than wars with other losers*. To test this hypothesis I rely on the data set on the duration of war developed by Scott Bennett and Allan Stam. To their data set I add one dummy variable: Was the loser a Mixed Regime?

Bennett and Stam offer a model of the duration of war that incorporates both realpolitik and domestic political variables.[12] Their main realpolitik variables focus on strategy, terrain, the balance of capabilities, total military capabilities, population size, quality of the military, surprise, and the salience of the issue. Their domestic political variables focus on both sides' ability to repress (based on their *combined* score on *Polity II's* "competitiveness of participation") and with an eye on the democratic peace, how democratic both sides at war were (based on their *combined Polity II* Democracy score). Two final control variables about the history of conflict between the belligerents and the number of actors involved complete their model.

Bennett and Stam code strategy as a set of dummy variables that distinguishes nine possible strategies, in ascending order of expected increased duration: *OMDM*: Offensive Maneuver, Defensive Maneuver; *OMDA:* Offensive Maneuver, Defensive Attrition; *OADM:* Offensive Attrition, Defensive Maneuver; *OADA:* Offensive Attrition, Defensive Attrition; *OMDP*: Offensive Maneuver, Defensive Punishment; *OPDM:* Offensive Punishment, Defensive Maneuver; *OADP:* Offensive Attrition, Defensive Punishment; *OPDA:* Offensive Punishment, Defensive Attrition; *OPDP:* Offensive Punishment, Defensive Punishment. Of these nine strategies they include only *OADM, OADA, OADP,* and *OPDA* as dummies in the final analysis. However, the full nine are incorporated in the interaction term with terrain. Table 3.9 lists Bennett and Stam's independent variables and hypotheses about their effect on the duration of war.

[12] Bennett and Stam, pp. 239–49.

Although one can take issue with Bennett and Stam's variables and hypotheses, I take them at face value for two reasons. First, their work is the most sophisticated and careful on the duration of wars to date. Second, the exclusion of some of their variables can of course alter the estimates of the hazard curve's shape. The fairest test is thus to test my (unconstrained) model against their (constrained) model; this will show whether and how much the inclusion of a variable for the regime type of the loser affects the duration of war. Note that Bennett and Stam's hypotheses about regime type are supposed to hold for the *combined score of all participants* involved in the war. We can therefore not infer that Democracies fight longer or shorter wars. We can infer only that as the Democracy score of the combination of all participants increases, wars would tend to last shorter. The substantive implications for individual regime types may well be difficult if not impossible to assess.

Bennett and Stam analyze seventy-seven wars between 1816 and 1985. They split up two of these wars, World War II and the Vietnam War, into multiple wars. For example, World War II is broken up into twelve separate wars, including a German-Polish, German-Belgian, Pacific, Western, and Eastern War. I dropped six of these twelve separate wars, the German-Belgian, German-Netherlands, German-Danish, German-Norwegian, German-Greek, and German-Yugoslav wars, because they clearly were part of the larger conflagration. For two wars there were missing data on the regime type of the loser: the Greco-Turkish war of 1919, and the Turko-Cypriot War of 1974.

Table 3.10 presents the results of two hazard analyses. Model 1 repeats the analysis of Bennett and Stam's Model 5 (non–Time Varying Covariate model), but this time on the more limited population of seventy-one wars. Model 2 adds only the dummy variable whether the loser was a Mixed Regime. The dependent variable is the duration in months.

Compared to Bennett and Stam's article, these results differ only marginally, with one exception. In these hazard analyses estimated with the smaller sample, the effect of the population ratio, terrain, surprise, and repression variables was reversed. Whereas Bennett and Stam originally found a positive coefficient for population ratio and terrain and negative coefficients for surprise and repression, in the models estimated here the signs were reversed. For the first three variables this is not surprising because the coefficients in the original article and in the regressions here are nowhere near significant. The reversal of the sign for repression is much more disturbing and interesting, because Bennett and Stam list a negative coefficient significant at the .1 level. My finding here runs directly contrary to their hypothesis.

TABLE 3.9

Bennett and Stam's Variables and Their Effect on the Duration of War

Independent Variables	Hypothesized Effect on the Duration of War
Realpolitik	
Strategy: OADM } Strategy: OADA }	Wars in which one or both sides use a maneuver strategy will be the shortest.
Strategy: OADP } Strategy: OPDA }	Wars in which one or both sides use a punishment strategy will be the longest.
Terrain	Wars on flat, open terrain will be shorter than those fought on inhospitable terrain.
Terrain * Strategy	Wars fought with a strategy appropriate to the terrain will be shorter
Balance of Forces	The greater the imbalance of the two sides, the shorter the war.
Total Military Personnel (in millions)	The greater the total military forces involved in a war, the longer the war.
Total Population (in billions)	The greater the total population forces involved in a war, the longer the war.
Population Ratio	The greater the disparity in the size of the opposing countries' populations, the shorter the war.
Quality Ratio	The greater the difference in the two sides' military quality, the shorter the war.
Surprise	If a state achieves strategic surprise, then the war will be shorter.
Salience	The more salient the issue at sake, the longer the war.
Regime	
Repression	Highly repressive states will select risky wars that are likely to end quickly.
Democracy	The more democratic the states involved, the shorter the war.
Other Approaches	
Previous Disputes	The more numerous the previous disputes between states, the longer the war.
Number of States	The more states involved in the war, the longer the war.

TABLE 3.10

Hazard Model Coefficient Estimates, Effects on the Duration of War

Length (Months)	Model 1 (Constrained)	Model 2 (Unconstrained)
Realpolitik		
Strategy: OADM	2.72*** (.761)	2.47*** (.74)
Strategy: OADA	2.74*** (.706)	2.45*** (.674)
Strategy: OADP	4.63*** (1.83)	4.05*** (1.64)
Strategy: OPDA	5.59** (3.07)	4.88* (2.97)
Terrain	-.505 (4.09)	-1.28 (3.99)
Terrain * Strategy	-.348 (1.06)	-.227 (1.03)
Balance of Forces	-2.62** (1.23)	-1.81* (1.28)
Total Military Personnel	.393*** (.119)	.419*** (.114)
Total Population	-.342 (.743)	-.08 (.736)
Population Ratio	-.0025 (.017)	-.007 (.022)
Quality Ratio	.0012 (.0017)	.0017 (.0017)
Surprise	-.186 (.592)	.216 (.61)
Salience	.435** (.261)	.408* (.259)
Regime		
Repression	.304** (.136)	.275** (.133)
Democracy	-.145*** (.059)	-.153*** (.058)
Losing Mixed Regime	——	.614** (.352)
Other Approaches		
Previous Disputes	.023 (.058)	.012 (.055)
Number of States	-.163** (.09)	-.184** (.092)
Constant	.75 (1.29)	.527 (1.3)
ρ (Duration Term)	1.0035	1.0358
Ln ρ	.003 (.096)	.035 (.354)
Log Likelihood	-112.53	-107.99
Chi^2 (x)	50.38	51.26
Prob > Chi^2	0.0000	0.0000
Number of Wars	71	69

Notes: Standard errors in parentheses. Significance tests are one-tailed: * = $p < .1$, ** = $p < .05$, *** = $p < .01$.

To examine whether the inclusion of the variable for combined repression affected the coefficient and significance of the Losing Leaders of Mixed Regimes dummy, I dropped the Repression variable and ran the hazard model again. Although this reduced the significance of many variables, it somewhat increased the significance and coefficient of the Losing Mixed Regime dummy. Other manipulations showed the results to be quite robust, and the coefficient for Losing Mixed Regime remained remarkably stable.

To examine whether the inclusion of the dummy for Losing Mixed Regime added significant explanatory power, I performed a log likelihood ratio test, which tests whether the inclusion of the dummy for the Losing Mixed Regime variable significantly improves the fit of the model to the data. Because this test has to be performed on the same data, I dropped the two observations for which data on regime type of the loser were missing. The inclusion of the Losing Mixed Regime significantly improved the fit with a probability well below the .1 level ($p < 0.0883$), not bad for an N of 69.

To calculate how much fighting against a losing Mixed Regime affected the duration of war, I used the estimated coefficients of Model 2 by setting all other variables to values of a base case consisting of typical (mean or median) values on the other variables, as suggested by Bennett and Stam.[13] Wars fought against other losers have an expected duration of 5.2 months; wars fought against Losing leaders of Mixed Regimes, in contrast, have an almost double expected duration of 9.6 months. Hence, Hypothesis 6 is supported: Wars against Losing Mixed Regimes lasted longer than other wars.

Conclusion

This chapter has shown that my intuitions about the connection between the fate of leaders and the outcome of the war are supported by the data. Leaders of Mixed Regimes can expect the same degree of punishment whether they lose moderately or disastrously. Democrats can expect to lose power when they lose a war moderately, but they will suffer severe punishment only when they lose disastrously. Dictators are unlikely to lose power unless they lose disastrously, in which case they can expect severe punishment. Only leaders of Mixed Regimes, therefore, have disincentives to settle on moderately losing terms and instead have incentives to continue war and gamble for resurrection. As a result, wars against losing leaders of Mixed Regimes can be expected to last longer than wars against other losers. These are new and major findings for the field of international relations with major implications for the study of war termination and potentially also for the study of war initiation (see the final chapter).

[13] The base case has strategy=OADA, balance of forces=0.75, terrain=0.34, terrain x strategy=0.68, number of states=3, total population=165 million, total military personnel=2.4 million, population ratio=2:1, quality ratio=2:1, salience=0, democracy=6.1, repression=−5.0, surprise=0.5, and past disputes=0, with expected duration of 12.1 months. Detailed information at Scott Bennett's Web page at http://www.personal.psu.edu/dsb10. Expected duration is then estimated as $E[t \mid xI]=\exp(\beta'xI) \times Y(1/\rho+1)$.

While these are encouraging results, our confidence should be tempered by the realization that the statistical tests, including the duration analysis, suffer from some problems of endogeneity. In other words, we cannot be completely confident about the casual direction of our findings: Do leaders of Mixed Regimes anticipate punishment and therefore refuse to settle on moderately losing terms; or does settlement on moderate terms cause them to suffer severe punishment? Does the choice of a particular strategy lead to a long war, or do states pick certain strategies because they anticipate a long war? With the available data it is unfortunately not possible to conclusively answer one way or another.

To get more data at a much finer resolution, the next few chapters offer detailed case studies of how Germany, France, and Great Britain changed their war aims in the First World War, which will allow us to examine the causal mechanisms up close.

4

Germany

THE NEXT FIVE chapters employ the case study method to test most of the remaining predictions and causal mechanisms proposed in the theory chapter. In chapter 2, I hypothesized that semi-repressive, moderately exclusionary regimes change their war aims to cover the costs of the war whereas nonrepressive, nonexclusionary and repressive, exclusionary regimes change their war aims along with their expectations of the outcome of the war. In chapters 4 through 7 I test how two semirepressive, moderately exclusionary regimes (Germany and, briefly, Russia in chapters 4 and 5) and two nonrepressive, nonexclusionary regimes (France and Britain in chapters 6 and 7) changed their war aims during the First World War. I chose the First World War for three main reasons. First, it is an extremely important and interesting case; World War I and its consequences are of central importance in the history of the twentieth century. Second, most of the necessary data are available. The archives of most of the participants have been opened, and many primary sources have been published. With the extremely unfortunate exception of Russia, historians have been able to examine the documentary evidence of the wartime policies of the major belligerents. As a result, an enormous secondary literature has blossomed as historians have researched and written on the military strategies, war aims, and domestic politics of many of the participants in the First World War. Third, World War I gives us a good range of variation among the independent and intervening variables: We can observe how participants on both sides react to favorable and unfavorable new information. Those participants, moreover, include regimes from at least two of the three regime types: nonrepressive, nonexclusionary regimes and semirepressive, moderately exclusionary regimes. In chapters 8 and 9 I examine the interaction of the war aims of the main belligerents to test whether there existed a bargaining space in 1914, 1915, 1916, 1917, or 1918. This allows me to examine my central claim that the creation of a bargaining space is a necessary condition for war termination.

Main Themes

To test the proposed hypotheses, the following chapters operationalize the main variables of the theory. Focusing first on how regimes change their war aims, each of the chapters samples on the independent variable: regime type. In the first section below I explain why Germany qualifies as a semirepressive, moderately exclusionary regime. To identify what constitutes new information, the intervening variable, we need two sets of historical evidence. First, we need to know what the initial expectations of the leadership were. Second, we need to know whether and how subsequent events belied these initial expectations. Hence, in the following chapters I first lay out the initial expectations of each belligerent at the beginning of the year and show what new information it received during the year. I focus on the leadership's expectations at the end of the calendar year because the campaign season ended in November, and during November and December leaders took stock of the situation and formulated new expectations and plans for the coming year. The dependent variable, war aims, includes all demands made by governments as preconditions for a return to peace.[1] However, whether a change in war aims constitutes an increase or decrease is not always so obvious. I measure changes in war aims not simply by the number of demands or square miles of territory demanded. Rather, changes constitute increases or decreases depending on how they would affect the country's postwar position in the international system and whether the addition or withdrawal of a demand would represent a net gain or loss for the country's international position. This issue is especially important in the case of the new French and British "demands" against Turkey in 1914 and 1915 that promised Russia free passage through the Straits and control over Constantinople. On the one hand, this represents an additional demand for more concessions from the Central Powers. On the other hand, this demand was against the interests of both the British Empire and France; it was an issue over which Great Britain and France had fought against Russia in the Crimean War (1853–1856). I conclude therefore that this additional demand actually constituted a lowering of British and French war aims.

Recall that the theory argues that semirepressive, moderately exclusionary regimes behave differently from the other regimes when they receive unfavorable new information and lower their estimates of the outcome of the war. Therefore, to test my predictions and the causal mechanism we need to focus on periods when the leadership became more pessimistic about Germany's relative strength, resolve, or the expected costs of war. In the second section below I offer a brief synopsis of the new information Germany's leaders received in each year of the war and summarize the resulting changes in Germany's war aims. I

---

[1] There is undoubtedly some slack between the theoretical construct reservation value and the indicator, governmental war aims. However, it seems highly likely that changes in the government's war aims closely track changes in its reservation value.

show that the First World War offers three intervals in which the German leadership received new information that forced them to lower their estimates about the outcome of the war: September to November-December 1914, December 1915 to November-December 1916, and March to November 1918. In this chapter I focus on the second interval, 1916, because by then German leaders had realized the war would end in a loss. I postpone an analysis of the third interval (March to November 1918) to chapter 9.

The analysis in this chapter will show that Germany's leaders formulated their war aims to cover the costs of the war because they feared that an "insufficient peace" would irrevocably change the political order of the empire and seriously threaten their political, economic, and even physical survival. Although it would appear irrational for the German elite to continue a war they knew they would probably lose, "we must remember," as Hans Gatzke concludes, "that to most of the beneficiaries of the Hohenzollern regime, the loss of [their] privileges was at least as vital a threat as the military defeat of their country."[2]

The chapter also examines in detail several competing explanations. The first argues that domestic politics does not matter. If domestic politics does not matter, states should behave as unitary rational actors. In short, as laid out in chapter 2, rational unitary states change their war aims as they get new information about the outcome on the battlefield. As states become more optimistic (pessimistic) about the outcome of the war, they raise (lower) their war aims. This competing explanation fails because the evidence clearly shows that Germany's war aims increased even though the leadership estimated that Germany's chances for victory were decreasing.

The second competing explanation comes from what remains the standard work on Germany's war aims in the First World War, Fritz Fischer's book *Griff nach der Weltmacht*, published in 1961.[3] Fischer argues that there was no fundamental change in Germany's high war aims during the war because its war aims were the expression of a German grab for hegemony. I will show that Germany's aims changed significantly and were not the expression of any particularly German aggressive intentions to become a world power. Instead, Germany's war aims rose with the costs of the war because its leaders believed that the alternative to high aims was revolution at home.

A third competing explanation that could also potentially explain the statistical findings in the data analysis chapter of all wars between

---

[2] Gatzke, p. 273.

[3] Fischer, *Griff nach der Weltmacht*. An abridged version of Fischer's book was published in English under the title *Germany's Aims in the First World War*.

1816 and 1975 might propose that semirepressive, moderately exclusionary regimes have specific institutional features that make them
"bad learners." It could be the case that such regimes draw systematically biased inferences about their performance and chances during
war, which would lead them to have systematically biased estimates of
their probability of winning and the costs of war.[4] These systematically
biased estimates would then, in turn, produce systematically inflated
war aims. This competing explanation fails because Germany's leadership explicitly recognized and acknowledged the implications of unfavorable new information. In fact, it could well be argued that of all
countries during the First World War, Germany was the best learner.
(However, as we will see in the next chapter, this might be a contribut-
ing factor to Russia's behavior in 1915.)[5]

Finally, I examine a fourth competing explanation for Germany's
higher war aims at the end of 1916: the change in the Army's High
Command. At the end of August 1916 Chief of Staff Erich von Falkenhayn[6] was replaced by General Paul von Hindenburg and his First
Quartermaster General, Erich Ludendorff, at German Army High
Command (OHL).[7] Subsequently, Ludendorff became enormously
powerful in the policy-making process, and his support of annexationist war aims significantly influenced the debate on Germany's war
aims at the end of 1916. Hence, it could be argued that it was the person of Ludendorff, rather than the institutional features of the German
Empire, that caused Germany's high war aims. However, I will show
that Hindenburg and Ludendorff were called to power explicitly to
maximize the chances of survival of the regime. Specifically, the leadership believed that with Hindenburg and Ludendorff at the Supreme
Command, the German people would accept worse terms of settlement than with Falkenhayn or any other general.

---

[4] An important recent book that makes an argument somewhat close to this is Snyder's *Myths of Empire*. For more on the potential of inefficient and sometimes contradictory learning, see Gartner, *Strategic Assessment in War*.

[5] See French, *The Strategy of the Lloyd George Coalition*, p. 29. It might be argued that
each in-group in Germany had a veto over a decision to end war and war aims and that
Germany's high war aims were the result of "logrolling." See Snyder, *Myths of Empire*.
However, if that were the case, we would expect to see rapidly cycling vetoes and war
aims. The historical record shows very little of such internal instability regarding war
aims.

[6] On Falkenhayn see his memoir *General Headquarters and Its Critical Decisions 1914–
1916*. On his interactions with Bethmann Hollweg see Janssen, *Der Kanzler und der General*; and Direnberger.

[7] OHL stands for Oberste Heeresleitung. After August 1916 this abbreviation could
have stood, with almost as much justification, for Organization Hindenburg-Ludendorff.
On Hindenburg and Ludendorff see Asprey; Stephen Bailey, "Erich Ludendorff as Quar-

To substantiate these claims this chapter is organized in five main sections. The first section codes Germany's regime type. The second section provides a brief overview of the new information and changes in war aims for each year of the war. The third section focuses on the second period when Germany's leaders became more pessimistic: December 1915 to November-December 1916. In sequence I present the leadership's initial expectations, the new information of 1916, and expectations at the end of 1916. Next I describe Germany's war aims at the end of 1915, followed by Germany's war aims at the end of 1916, and compare the changes. To explain why Germany's leaders raised their war aims even when they became more pessimistic about the outcome of the war during this period, the fourth section focuses on the proposed causal mechanism. I show that, as argued in the theory chapter, the need to reward the people for their sacrifices led Germany's leaders to formulate war aims to cover the costs of the war. The German regime knew that to stay in power they would have to buy off the domestic opposition after the war. The enormous costs of the war gave the regime only two options. They could buy off the people with real political concessions, specifically, a reform of the Prussian franchise and the introduction of parliamentary government. Alternatively, they could buy off the people with the spoils of a victorious war. The German regime could not grant political concessions to the opposition without endangering their own political survival. That left them only one possibility to buy off the opposition: gains at the expense of their external enemies, in other words, high war aims. The fifth section examines a competing explanation for the increase in Germany's war aims during 1916 and briefly analyzes the background and implications of the change in the Army High Command, the ascent to power of Hindenburg and Ludendorff.

The Independent Variable: Regime Type

In this section I examine whether Germany should be classified as a nonrepressive, nonexclusionary regime, a semirepressive, moderately exclusionary, or a repressive, exclusionary regime. I briefly sketch the political landscape in prewar Germany and identify the main decision makers and the sources of their political power. Germany qualifies as

termaster General of the German Army 1916–1918"; Ludendorff, *Meine Kriegserinnerungen 1914–1918*; Ludendorff, *Kriegführung und Politik*.

a semirepressive, moderately exclusionary regime for two reasons.[8] First, the ruling elite saw themselves locked in a life or death struggle with the domestic opposition, the Socialists, who were effectively excluded from access to wealth and power. At stake in this struggle, the leadership of the old order estimated, was nothing less than their political and economic primacy and their continued dominance. If they lost this struggle, the best the in-groups could hope for was a democratic regime that would remove their privileges. Second, prewar Germany was a semirepressive, moderately exclusionary regime because the leadership felt its hold on power slipping and lacked the means to eliminate the opposition by forceful repression. When the Socialists emerged from the elections of 1913 as victors and the largest party in the Reichstag (the parliament of the German Empire), the in-groups were seriously worried.

In this and subsequent sections I focus on the position of the whole elite, rather than just the individual leader. The reason is not that no evidence exists that Wilhelm II feared punishment if the war would be lost; that evidence exists and will be mentioned in passing in this chapter and in chapters 8 and 9. Rather, it is the power position of the elite and their control over the policy-making process that is at stake in the outcome of the war. A revolution would sweep away not merely the leader, but the superstructure that kept the in-groups in power.

The most important actors in prewar and wartime Germany were the Kaiser, the Chancellor, and the Chief of Staff. The three most important institutional pillars on which rested the political power of the old order were the politically strong army, the politically weak parliament, and Prussia's extraordinary position in the empire, all solidly anchored in the institutional arrangement of the empire, which sprang by and large from Bismarck's constitution of 1871. The opposition to the old order therefore tried to contain the influence of the army, strengthen parliament, and change the electoral laws of Prussia.

Bismarck's constitution, with some emendations, put a tremendous amount of power in the hands of the three strongest decision makers in imperial Germany: Kaiser Wilhelm II;[9] the Chancellor, until 13 July 1917 Theobald von Bethmann Hollweg,[10] from 14 July to 26 October 1917 Georg Michaelis, from 26 October to 30 September 1918 Count Georg Hertling, and from then until the end of the war Prince Max

---

[8] The classification developed for the data analysis in the previous chapter also codes Germany as a "Mixed Regime." On Gurr's *POLITY III* Democracy index, Germany scores a 5 in 1914; on the Autocracy index Germany scores a 3.

[9] For a close-up view of the Kaiser's role during the war see the memoirs of members of his close entourage, especially Müller.

[10] On Bethmann Hollweg see his memoirs, *Betrachtungen zum Weltkriege*.

von Baden; and the leadership of the army, Chief of the General Staff from late September 1914 to the end of August 1916 General Erich von Falkenhayn, General, later Field Marshall, Paul von Hindenburg, commander of the Oberost, commanding German forces in the Eastern Front, from 31 August 1916 onward Chief of the General Staff, and last, but definitely not least, General Erich von Ludendorff, Hindenburg's Chief of Staff at Oberost, from 31 August 1916 onward First Quartermaster General at German Army High Command.

By virtue of the *Kommandogewalt*, the royal power of command, a vague but tremendously important privilege, the Kaiser, in his capacity as King of Prussia, commanded the forces of all German states in war (and most of them in peace time as well). The *Kommandogewalt* gave the Kaiser the right to appoint the officers in the armed forces and gave him considerable administrative powers.[11] Everything that fell under the *Kommandogewalt* was subject neither to the Prussian Ministry nor to the directives of the Chancellor.[12] Upon the outbreak of the war the Kaiser increased his nominal control over domestic affairs through the imposition of martial law, the so-called *Belagerungsgesetz*, which gave him unrestricted powers. Martial law could be imposed only by the Kaiser; its imposition allowed him to name the military commanders and direct and control their efforts.[13] As Marc Trachtenberg convincingly showed, ultimate authority rested with the Kaiser, who could and did on at least one extremely important occasion overrule his chief of staff.[14]

The German army could wield tremendous independent political influence. The political leadership had minimal control over the military, especially after 1883, when the military became no longer subject to any parliamentary control except for budgetary matters. If the Chief of the General Staff, and later the Quartermaster General as well, disagreed with the civilian political leadership, they could always appeal to the Kaiser, more often than not successfully. Precisely because the army was such an important institution in German politics, the elite made sure the army remained a bulwark of the old order and as such

---

[11] See Deist, *Militär und Innenpolitik*, 1/I, p. xix.

[12] Ibid., p. XXIX.

[13] Ibid., p. XXXII.

[14] Trachtenberg shows that the Kaiser halted the Schlieffen Plan, halting the advance through Luxembourg, explicitly overruling a panicking Moltke when he heard of the British "proposal" (which turned out to be a mistake) that Britain would remain neutral if Germany did not attack France and would conduct the war only in the east. See Trachtenberg, "The Meaning of Mobilization in 1914," pp. 215–16. Apparently the Kaiser did not consult his Chancellor on the famous blank-check policy on the afternoon of 5 July. See Stevenson, *The First World War and International Politics*, p. 27.

helped to exclude the domestic opposition from access to power. The elite, for example, used both indoctrination and coercion to maintain the ideological purity of the army.[15] Officers were required to subordinate their political convictions to those of the Kaiser on the basis of their personal oath of loyalty to him. As a result, the army was overwhelmingly conservative in make-up and culture and fundamentally an expression of and loyal to the old order. Conservatives, in turn, relied on the army as "the only fixed point in the whirlpool, the rock in the sea of revolution that threatens us on all sides, the talisman of loyalty."[16] This intimate connection between conservatives and armed forces may not be unusual. However, as Deist notes, the particular interaction between the army and the domestic political opposition was a specific German development by which the army was given internal political goals.[17]

Germany's parliament was politically weak, and its influence more apparent than real. This weakness was the result of a deliberate design to prevent the accumulation of power in the hands of any opposition to the old order. The German parliament was made up of two houses, the Bundesrat (Federal Council) and the Reichstag. While the Reichstag was elected by universal male suffrage, delegates to the Bundesrat were appointed by the rulers and governments of the twenty-five federal states. To thwart the influence of the lower classes, moreover, Bismarck's constitution stipulated that Reichstag members would not receive salaries.

This parliament had no executive power or responsibility or any means of independent control over the executive because executive power and control rested firmly in the hands of the Kaiser. He held executive power together with his Chancellor and could appoint or dismiss the latter at his pleasure. The Reichstag could therefore not force the Chancellor to explain and defend his policies. The Chancellor, however, did have some independent political influence because the Kaiser needed the countersign of his Chancellor on all laws. The Kaiser also appointed all officials of the federal government, and he could "summon, prorogue, and close the Reichstag, . . . [and] he possessed the right to interpret the constitution."[18] The latter privilege, especially, should not be underestimated. Because the Kaiser also reserved the right to determine foreign policy, "with the right to make treaties and conclude alliances, as well as declare war and conclude peace,"[19] the

---

[15] For some lurid examples see Ritter, *The Sword and the Scepter*, vol. 2, pp. 102–3.
[16] Quoted in Craig, p. 159.
[17] Deist, *Militär und Innenpolitik*, 1/I, p. XIX.
[18] Craig, p. 39.
[19] Ibid.

Reichstag's political influence in both domestic and foreign policy was fundamentally limited. Thus, while the domestic opposition was represented in the Reichstag, the Reichstag did not have the right to initiate legislation and was shackled by an inherently conservative Bundesrat. As a result, the domestic opposition to the old order could effect little or no fundamental change. The lower classes were thus excluded from access to the policy-making process.

The cornerstone in the systematic exclusion of the domestic political opposition was Prussia and its privileged position in the empire. As a member of the Reichstag put it, "the federal system thus established was superimposed on the Prussian autocracy but was, in fact, dominated by feudal and reactionary Prussia."[20] It is not surprising, therefore, that since Bismarck's time and especially after 1878 the internal political conflict centered around Prussia's extraordinary position and the political ordering of the empire. At stake in this conflict were the introduction of parliamentary government in the Reichstag and especially universal suffrage in the Prussian parliament, the Landtag. If the domestic opposition could gain a foothold in the Prussian parliament, they could hope to eventually bring about the necessary changes to gain access to the federal policy-making process.

In the Prussian Landtag deputies were not elected democratically but by a system that favored the propertied classes. Since 1849 voters were divided into three classes according to the amount of taxes they paid. Each class had a third of the suffrage.[21] In practice the result was often that five or six voters from the first class elected as many delegates as fifty to sixty voters of the second, or five hundred to six hundred voters from the third class.[22] This system provided a strong bulwark against the forces of liberalism and democracy. Prussia's dominant position in the empire explains the tremendous weight the Socialists and the governing elite attached to reforms of the Prussian electoral laws. Indeed, in the words of Hans Peter Hanssen, a Reichstag deputy, "Since the government of the empire depended on Prussia, the German socialists naturally championed Prussian electoral reforms."[23] As we will see below, the issue of Prussian electoral reform became inextricably linked with the question of German war aims. Gordon A. Craig puts his finger on the essential characteristic of the prewar political struggle that was to have such a big impact on German war aims:

[20] Hanssen, p. xii.
[21] Craig, p. 43, note 9.
[22] Braun, p. 25.
[23] Hanssen, p. xiii.

There is no doubt that there were many who sincerely believed that no compromise with Social Democracy was possible, but there were more, in the councils of the Conservative, Centre, and National Liberal parties, and the Bund der Landwirte and the Centralverband deutscher Industrieller, who saw that the price of collaboration with the working class was social and political change of a kind that they thought they could not afford.[24]

In summary, prewar imperial Germany must be coded as a semirepressive, moderately exclusionary regime because some groups, mainly the lower classes, were systematically excluded from access to the policy-making process but were not systematically violently repressed as a matter of course. On the one hand, the domestic opposition was allowed to express itself politically in the Reichstag, and did so by voting for the Socialists. On the other hand, this political representation was barely more than mere window dressing, because the institutional design of imperial Germany systematically denied the domestic opposition any opportunity to effect any meaningful change in the domestic distribution of power. Power always remained effectively secured in the hands of representatives of the old order.

Overview of the War

For this study I traced the expectations, new information, and war aims of the main belligerents in each year of the war. However, to fully analyze each year for each of the main belligerents would unfortunately require too much space, amounting perhaps to a second book. Therefore, I summarize the evidence on the intervening and dependent variables, new information and changes in war aims, in condensed form in a series of tables. Table 4.1 first presents the new information and changes in war aims of Germany for 1914, 1915, 1916, 1917, and 1918. Then I briefly recapitulate for each year whether the unfavorable new information outweighed the favorable new information and whether war aims decreased or increased. As noted above, Germany's leaders became more pessimistic in 1914, 1916, and 1918. I focus on the latter two intervals in depth in this chapter and chapter 9 but must limit my analysis of 1914 to a few pages.

During 1914 the unfavorable new information of the failures of the Schlieffen Plan and the subsequent attempt to save the strategic goal in the so-called Race to the Sea forced Germany's leaders to lower their estimates of the outcome of the war. At the end of November Bethmann Hollweg explicitly noted the new information that the fighting

[24] Craig, p. 269.

TABLE 4.1

New Information and Changes in War Aims for Germany

Germany	New Information	Changes in War Aims
1914	*Unfavorable*: 14 Sept: Schlieffen Plan fails. 17 Nov: Race to the sea fails. Germany can't win if the Entente stays together. Sept–Dec: Russia inflicts serious defeats on Austria-Hungary. *Favorable*: 1–4 Nov: Turkey enters war.	9 Sept 1914–Nov–Dec 1914 *Decreases*: Demands against Russia limited to war indemnity and Polish border strip; no more annexation of Liège and Verviers? *Increases*: Longwy and Briey.
1915	*Unfavorable*: 23 May: Italy declares war. *Favorable*: May–Sept: Severe defeats of Russian army; 300-mile wide advance in the east. Sept–Oct: Bulgaria enters. Nov: Serbia defeated.	Nov–Dec 1914–Nov–Dec 1915 *Increases*: 10–11 Nov 1915: Greater political, economic, and military penetration of Austria-Hungary. Lithuania and Courland. Tracts of land in the Suwalki province. Additional territory from Poland. Oct: Annexation of parts of the Flemish coast, Ostende-Zeebrugge-Antwerp?
1916	*Unfavorable*: 18 Apr: American intervention more likely if unrestricted submarine warfare launched. 4 June–11 Aug: Brusilov offense. May: Jutland fails? 25 May: Conscription in Britain. May: Looming manpower shortage. 1 July–18 Nov: The Somme; high casualties; the British are willing to commit large numbers of their own troops. 11 July: Verdun: Operation Gericht fails. 27 Aug: Rumania enters war. 18 Dec: French recover the lost forts; Germans lose almost as many men as the French. Fall-winter: desertions increase. *Favorable*: Oct–Nov: Restricted submarine warfare successes. Nov–Dec: Rumania defeated.	Nov–Dec 1915–7 Nov 1916 *Decreases*: 5 Nov 1916: Parts of Upper Silesia. *Increases*: 5 Nov: Poland autonomous; increased economic influence in Poland; German control over the new Polish army. 7 Nov: Lithuania and Courland territory to be annexed. Enlargement of the Polish frontier strip. Higher monthly tribute from Belgium, the resources in the Campine, and (parts of?) the Congo.

New Information and Changes in War Aims for Germany

Germany	New Information	Changes in War Aims
1917	*Unfavorable*: 5 Apr: America enters war. Summer: Unrestricted submarine warfare fails. Summer: First mutiny in the fleet. 28 Jan 1918: Massive strike, including 600,000 munitions workers in Berlin. *Favorable*: 15–17 Mar: First Russian revolution. Spring-Summer: Entente offensives fail with high casualties. 27 Oct: Italian defeat at Caporetto. 13 Nov: Second Russian revolution. 6–7 Dec: Russian armistice.	Nov–Dec 1916–5 Mar 1918 *Decreases*: 2 Jan 1918: Smaller Polish borderstrip? *Increases*: Oct: Deeper penetration of Austria-Hungary: military convention, customs union, tighter financial and economic ties. 18 Dec: Liège and foreland. Belgian coast? No more concessions to France in Alsace-Lorraine. 3 Mar 1918: Brest-Litovsk: Russia broken up. Economic penetration of Ukraine and Finland. Estonia and Livonia get the right to ask for the Kaiser's "protection." Reparations ("reimbursement of maintenance of prisoners of war")? 5 May: Economic penetration of Rumania, including oil fields, railroads, Danube harbors.
1918	*Unfavorable*: Mar–May: Failure of the Stormtrooper offensives. 18 July–Sept: Allied counterattacks push back German army. 8 Aug: "Black day of the German army;" German morale crumbling; tanks. 15 Sept: Austrians cannot continue, launch peace appeal. 19 Sept: Salonica: Bulgarian army starts to disintegrate. 19–20 Sept: decisive Turkish defeat at Megiddo. 27 Sept: Hindenburg line is turned. 29–30 Sept: Bulgarian armistice and surrender. 29 Oct–3 Nov: Italian victory at Vittorio Veneto? 30 Oct: Turkish armistice. 1 Nov: Americans break through around Verdun. 1 Nov: Austro-Hungarian union dissolved. 3 Nov: Austria signs a separate peace. 4 Nov: News of the fleet mutiny reaches Berlin. 7–8 Nov: Revolution breaks out in Bavaria. 9 Nov: Revolution breaks out in Berlin.	5 Mar 1918–10 Nov 1918 *Decreases*: 6 Nov: Capitulation

Notes: Question marks indicate the uncertain status of new information and/or a change in war aims. For Germany's full war aims see chapters 8 and 9.

on the battlefield had brought when he admitted that Germany had underestimated all its enemies.[25] Germany had lost its best hope for a quick and cheap victory; now it had to face a lower probability of victory and higher costs of war. Moreover, while German forces had won some surprising victories in the east (e.g., at Tannenberg), by 18 November after the failure of the First Battle of Ypres Chief of the General Staff Falkenhayn had also given up his earlier hopes for a decisive victory in the east.[26] The next day, on 19 November, Bethmann Hollweg explicitly agreed with Falkenhayn's pessimistic assessment that as long as Russia, France, and England held together, it would be impossible to defeat them enough to get a decent peace. Rather, Germany would run the danger of slowly exhausting itself. Either Russia or France would have to be detached from the enemy coalition.[27] Bethmann Hollweg wrote Zimmermann that

> a complete victory over and destruction of our enemies in a decisive battle appears impossible, according to the of course reserved information from the General Staff. This situation will remain so during the winter and can *politically* be endured quite propitiously by us but also fails to open up possibilities for a decisive *military* victory in the future. As far as I can judge the situation, such a victory can, rather, be at least hoped for only when we can throw our Army engaged in the east at France. . . . If we fail to detach Russia we will not militarily wholly master any of our enemies.[28]

Bethmann Hollweg concluded that an attempt would have to be made to reach a separate peace with Russia.[29] He was cautiously optimistic by the beginning of December that Russia could be sufficiently defeated, for example, by the occupation of the larger part of Poland, to induce it to conclude a separate peace with Germany.[30] The good news of Turkey joining the Central Powers at the end of October opened up the possibility of a three-front war against Russia but could not compensate for the failures in the west and Austria-Hungary's defeats in Galicia. Overall, Germany's leaders had become more pessimistic about the outcome of the war.

[25] See Scheidemann's notes of a conversation with Bethmann Hollweg on 29 November 1914. Quoted in Zechlin, "Friedensbestrebungen und Revolutionsversuche," B 20/61, p. 280.

[26] Zechlin, "Friedensbestrebungen und Revolutionsversuche," B 20/61, p. 275. See also Sweet, "Leaders and Policies," p. 231.

[27] Fischer, *Griff nach der Weltmacht*, p. 218.

[28] Scherer and Grunewald, vol. 1, no. 13, p. 17, emphasis in original.

[29] Ibid., pp. 15–19.

[30] Sweet, "Leaders and Policies," p. 246; Farrar, *The Short-War Illusion*, p. 85; Scherer and Grunewald, vol. 1, no. 13, p. 18.

As a result of the new information, Germany's leaders formulated war aims to cover the costs of the war. They lowered their demands in the east while maintaining essentially similar, potentially somewhat higher war aims in the west. These war aims at the end of 1914 were intended to allow the old regime to conclude the war with gains that more than covered the costs of the war. I will make two main points here. First, Germany's leaders were aware that they needed such gains to buy off the people. Second, Germany's demands at the end of 1914 would indeed have more than covered the costs of the war. On the first point, it is crucial to emphasize again that Bethmann Hollweg was willing to conclude a separate peace, not a general peace to end the war between all combatants. He was against a general peace because he thought that realistic terms of a general peace would "appear to the people as absolutely insufficient rewards for such terrible sacrifices."[31] Already in the first months of the war, according to L. L. Farrar, "German leaders increasingly perceived an inversely proportional relationship between war aims and reforms. A victory and achievement of war aims would obviate demands for reform, while defeat and failure to achieve war aims would result in reform, if not revolution."[32]

On the second point, Germany's aims at the end of 1914 were at least partially designed to reward the people for their sacrifices. As Farrar has pointed out, Minister of the Interior Clemens von Delbrück hoped that after the war the increase in German power would make it possible to "satisfy all parties and thus resolve all political problems."[33] First, high war indemnities from France remained a central and unchanged part of Germany's demands, to which a war indemnity from Russia would be added. These war indemnities would forestall the need for postwar tax increases to pay for the war and could be used in a variety of ways to reward the people for their sacrifices in the war.[34] In addition, Germany demanded the annexation of a border strip from Poland. This border strip would reward the people for their sacrifices in two ways. First, it was explicitly intended for settlement by "loyal Germans," loyal, that is, to the old regime. Second, this area contained industrial and rich mineral resources, which were eagerly sought by Germany's industrial elite and would indirectly lead to more jobs and better wages for the working class. Furthermore, German leaders could

[31] Scherer and Grunewald, vol. 1, no. 13, p. 18.

[32] Farrar, *The Short-War Illusion*, p. 44.

[33] Ibid., p. 43; see also p. 50.

[34] From very early on Pan-Germans warned of the danger of a higher postwar tax bill and its potentially revolutionary consequences. See Gatzke, p. 28.

be confident that the gains of the war could be made to cover the costs because a separate peace with Russia would allow Germany to redeploy its forces in the west against France. Thus, by (temporarily?) giving up its demands in the east, Germany would be able to get substantially better terms in the west. The record is clear: If Germany lowered its war aims at all, these war aims would still cover the costs of the war. Bethmann Hollweg's aims of November could be used to buy off the people. Stronger still, his memorandum of 19 November clearly shows Germany would increase its demands against France, and ensure additional profit from the war, once its forces in the east could be brought to the Western Front.

During 1915 the favorable new information from the Eastern Front made the leadership more optimistic about the outcome of the war. The substantial increases in Germany's war aims, mostly in the east but also against Belgium, were probably the result of both the favorable new information of the year and domestic pressures to reward the people for their sacrifices. The events of 1916 once again made the leadership more pessimistic. The failure of the offensive at Verdun, the Brusilov offensive, the enormous casualties suffered on the Somme, the British adoption of conscription, and the successes of the French counteroffensives at Verdun far outweighed the favorable new information of Rumania's easy defeat. Although the German leadership recognized that the probability of victory had decreased during the year, they nonetheless increased their war aims, mainly in the east.

During 1917 the leadership received some unfavorable new information, in the form of the United States' entry into the war and the failure of unrestricted submarine warfare. However, the favorable new information of the Russian revolutions, the failures of the Entente offensive, and the armistice on the Eastern Front at the end of the year made the leadership overall more optimistic they could win the war on land in 1918. The new optimism of the German leadership led to increased war aims in the east, expressed in the Treaties of Brest-Litovsk and Buftea; German war aims against Belgium also increased. From March on, 1918 brought little but unfavorable new information. The break through the Hindenburg line and the Bulgarian defection at the end of September convinced the German people that they had been lied to and that the war was lost. In an attempt to forestall a large revolution from below, the leadership attempted a small revolution from above. Too little and too late, with the front crumbling and Germany's allies defecting, the regime had lost its credibility. To "save what could be saved" on the threatening home front, the leadership became willing to settle on any terms.

The theory predicts that all regimes will behave similarly and raise their war aims when they become more optimistic. Therefore, a detailed analysis of Germany's behavior during 1915 and 1917 would provide little empirical leverage on the theory. Only when they get more pessimistic and estimate they will probably lose the war do semi-repressive, moderately exclusionary regimes formulate their war aims differently. In the next section, therefore, I focus on 1916. Germany's behavior in 1918 will be examined in chapter 9.

Expectations, New Information, and War Aims in 1916

To establish what would constitute new information, we start with the leadership's initial expectations for 1916. Around Christmas 1915 Falkenhayn compiled a comprehensive review of Germany's strategic situation and summed up the prospects for future plans of operations, and he presented his conclusions to the Kaiser and Bethmann Hollweg.[35] Falkenhayn reasoned that England was Germany's main enemy, and, to defeat England, its allies must be defeated first:

> [F]or England the campaign on the continent of Europe with her own troops is at bottom a side-show. Her real weapons here are the French, Russian and Italian Armies. If we put these armies out of the war England is left to face us alone, and it is difficult to believe that in such circumstances her lust for our destruction would not fail her. It is true that there would be no certainty that she would give up, but there is a strong probability.[36]

The Chief of the General Staff then argued that Russia was as good as finished:

> Even if we cannot perhaps expect a revolution in the grand style, we are entitled to believe that Russia's internal troubles will compel her to give in within a relatively short period. In this connection it may be taken for granted that she will not revive her military reputation meanwhile. We need not be anxious about that.[37]

---

[35] See Janssen, *Der Kanzler und der General*, pp. 288–89. Janssen argues that in early January 1916 Bethmann Hollweg was even more optimistic than Falkenhayn (p. 185).

[36] Falkenhayn, p. 214. Note that at the time the Kaiser held that Germany's most dangerous enemy would be Russia, not England! Therefore, it is unlikely that Falkenhayn was playing on the Kaiser's hatred of England. See Müller, *Regierte der Kaiser?* p. 146, diary entry of 9 January 1916.

[37] Falkenhayn, p. 216.

Falkenhayn concluded that Germany should strike at France because France was almost at the breaking point. With France out of the war, England would find itself without a strong champion on the continent. Having learned from his enemies' mistakes, Falkenhayn proposed to attack at Verdun, not to break through by frontal assault, but to bleed France white, explicitly through a battle of attrition. He wrote:

> As I have already insisted, the strain on France has almost reached the breaking-point—though it is certainly borne with the most remarkable devotion. If we succeeded in opening the eyes of her people to the fact that in a military sense they have nothing more to hope for, that breaking-point would be reached and England's best sword knocked out of her hand. To achieve that object the uncertain method of a mass break-through, in any case beyond our means, is unnecessary. We can probably do enough for our purposes with limited resources. Within our reach behind the French sector of the Western front there are objectives for the retention of which the French General Staff would be compelled to throw in every man they have. If they do so the forces of France will bleed to death—whether we reach our goal or not. If they do not do so, and we reach our objectives, the moral effect on France will be enormous. . . . The objectives of which I am speaking now are Belfort and Verdun.[38]

Falkenhayn's argument is remarkable for its clear emphasis on the function of the planned offensive. The attack was designed not to "defeat" the French, but to influence the estimates of the French people and leadership of France's relative strength and the expected costs of the war.

In general terms Falkenhayn was very pessimistic about Germany's chances if the war would continue into 1917, and he made sure Bethmann Hollweg knew it.[39] Bethmann Hollweg himself was only slightly less pessimistic.[40] According to Müller, he "did not believe it would be impossible for Germany to endure one more Winter campaign."[41] Falkenhayn was convinced Germany would have its last chance at victory in 1916. To that end he strongly argued in favor of unrestricted submarine warfare, an important change in his previous position.

[38] Ibid., pp. 217–18.

[39] See the notes Bethmann Hollweg took on 7 January 1916 of his conversation with Falkenhayn about the prospects for the war. Janssen, *Der Kanzler und der General*, p. 289. Later that month, when asked directly by Holtzendorff upon Müller's prodding whether time worked for or against Germany, Holtzendorff reported that Falkenhayn had told him that time worked against Germany. He also said that Germany's allies, Austria-Hungary and Turkey, could not endure the war beyond the autumn of the year (Müller, p. 149; see also p. 154).

[40] See also Bethmann's hopeful account of operations at Verdun in 29 March 1916 in Hanssen, pp. 138–40.

[41] Müller, p. 161.

The New Information of 1916

Based on Falkenhayn's detailed review, we can confidently infer Germany's expectations and, therefore, which events in 1916 constituted "new information." As will be shown below, this new information forced Germany to revise and lower its estimate of the probability of winning the war. First, Operation Gericht, as Falkenhayn dubbed his offensive aimed at Verdun, started on 21 February and lasted until 11 July. The Germans made substantial gains, but when the French counterattacked on 24 October, under their new local commander, General Nivelle, they recaptured the forts lost in the spring.[42] The battle finally ended on 18 December. The Germans not only had failed to bleed the French beyond their recovery, but their own casualties were almost as bad. They suffered 434,000 against 541,000 French casualties.[43]

Second, on 1 July the British launched their offensive on the Somme.[44] This battle became the first big *Materialenschlacht* (battle of equipment).[45] The fighting lasted until 18 November 1916 and showed the German leadership that England was willing to carry its share of the burden, and that its commitment on the continent was no "side show."[46] Even more important in this respect was the British govern-

---

[42] Hindenburg and Ludendorff, on their first visit to Verdun, likened it to a hell and an open wound. Of the counterattack in October Hindenburg noted candidly: "On this occasion the enemy hoisted us with our own petard. We could only hope that in the coming year he would not repeat the experiment on a greater scale and with equal success" (Alistair Horne, pp. 302–3, quotation on p. 317). Note the striking similarity of views of both Hindenburg and Nivelle about the possibility and likelihood that the French successes at Verdun could be repeated on a grander scale elsewhere in 1917. For the attempt and results see the chapter on France during 1917.

[43] Herman, p. 211.

[44] Bethmann Hollweg notes about a conversation he had with Falkenhayn on 28 May 1916: "Whether the English intend to launch an offensive, which incidently could only be supported by the French through a small parallel action, the general is not able to judge. He *suspects* that the English will remain on the defensive and will only proceed actively in Asia Minor and at the Suez Canal" (quoted in Janssen, *Der Kanzler und der General*, p. 290, emphasis in original).

[45] As Falkenhayn notes, "the requirements during the simultaneous battles on the Meuse, on the Somme, in Galicia, and in Italy, 1916, ... That exceeding as they did all anticipations, brought about a critical period in the supply of ammunition for a time" (Falkenhayn, pp. 45–46).

[46] Janssen argues that Falkenhayn underestimated until the summer of 1916 the number of troops the British were sending to France (*Der Kanzler und der General*, p. 51; see also p. 221). The French contributed with twenty-six divisions even though Falkenhayn had told the Kaiser they had only six divisions in reserve. On the issue of financial strength, Admiral Holtzendorff estimated at the end of the year that British and French financial difficulties would not bring results "within a determinable period" (Stevenson, *The First World War in International Politics*, p. 76).

ment's acceptance of compulsory military service in May, with both houses of Parliament quickly passing a bill that received the King's authorization on 25 May. When compulsory military service won out over the so-called Derby Plan, which rested upon voluntary enlistment, this represented a radical break with a tradition going back centuries.[47] Moreover, the Germans were horrified by the unexpected high costs of the defense.[48] On more than one occasion Ludendorff warned against the recurrence of "Somme fighting."[49] One of his most important arguments in favor of unrestricted submarine warfare, for example, was as when he said on 9 January 1917, "We must spare the troops a second battle of the Somme."[50] Apparently, Falkenhayn was forced to scale down the offensive at Verdun because the battle of the Somme also consumed much more ammunition than was expected.[51] Ludendorff, who took over the Supreme Command with Hindenburg at the end of August, summarized the situation at the end of 1916 as follows:

> G.H.Q. had to bear in mind that the enemy's great superiority in men and material would be even more painfully felt in 1917 than in 1916. They had to face the danger that "Somme fighting" would soon break out at various points on our fronts, and that even our troops would not be able to withstand such attacks indefinitely, especially if the enemy gave us no time for rest and for the accumulation of materiel. Our position was uncommonly difficult, and a way out hard to find. . . . If the war lasted our defeat seemed inevitable. Economically we were in a highly unfavorable position for a war of exhaustion. At home our strength was badly shaken.[52]

Third, the Brusilov offensive from 4 June to 11 August 1916 proved that Russia still could fight hard and that it was Austria-Hungary who was incapable of defending itself.[53] Indeed, on the last day of the year,

---

[47] The first stage of compulsory service was not accepted until the first week of January 1916, well after Falkenhayn had composed his memorandum. For a thorough description of the process that eventually led to the imposition of full conscription, see Cassar, ch. 9. Like the Germans, Joffre apparently also worried about the British willingness to provide manpower. See his *The Memoirs of Marshal Joffre*, vol. 2, p. 418.

[48] See Ludendorff, *My War Memories*, pp. 242, 246, 266–67, 278, 290; see also Guinn, p. 168. In a speech to the Finance Committee of 25 April, 1917 Dr. Cohn, a deputy in the Reichstag for the SDP, bewailed the losses at the Somme as follows: "Among the most recent disasters may be cited the destruction during the retreat from the Somme" (quoted in Hanssen, p. 183).

[49] Terraine, *The Road to Passchendaele*, p. 16; see also Basler, p. 69.

[50] *Official German Documents Relating to the World War*, vol. 2, pp. 1320–21.

[51] See Bethmann Hollweg's notes of 19 July 1916 about a conversation with General Falkenhayn, in Janssen, *Der Kanzler und der General*, p. 296.

[52] Ludendorff, *My War Memories*, vol. 1, p. 307.

[53] The successes of the Brusilov offensive came all the more as a surprise because the Austro-Hungarians had built up strong defenses and told the German Kaiser that their

"German Intelligence considered that Russia was in a happier situation than in the previous winter because in the recent fighting only part of her Army had been engaged and her loss in material had been slight."[54] Neither military nor civilian leaders expected the collapse of Russia any time soon, and Bethmann Hollweg had given up his hopes for a separate peace with Russia in late October 1916.[55]

On 27 August, furthermore, Rumania attacked northward and joined the Entente. Germany's leaders, although aware of this possibility, were nonetheless unhappily surprised by the timing.[56] Arguably one of only two pieces of good new information during 1916 was the easy defeat of Rumania. The Kaiser's despondent cry upon hearing the news that Rumania had declared war upon Austria-Hungary "That means the end of the war!" was premature and too pessimistic.[57]

In the meantime, the war at sea had at best produced mixed results. Tensions with the United States had increased sharply: first by the German decision of 23 February to sink armed enemy merchant vessels without warning in the blockade against England, then by the sinking of the unarmed *SS Sussex* on 24 March by the German submarine U-92. On 18 April President Wilson sent a note to Germany threatening to sever diplomatic relations if Germany did not halt its submarine war against merchantmen. Although in principle the decision to go to unrestricted submarine warfare (i.e., to also target and sink unarmed merchantmen) had been taken on 4 March, final authorization remained with the Kaiser, who had tentatively scheduled 4 April as the date on which the final decision would be made.[58] Under pressure from

---

"formidable offensives" would "automatically hold" against the Russians in their present strength and numbers. Even any initial successes were ruled to be "impossible" (Stone, p. 242). From now on the Austro-Hungarian army had to be reinforced with German officers and NCOs (Stone, p. 262).

[54] Quoted from the German official account "Der Weltkrieg" in Falls, p. 535, note 1. Ludendorff notes in his memoirs that at the end of 1916 "Russia, in particular, produced very strong new formations." The Russian army was reorganized, and, according to Ludendorff, "[t]his reorganization meant a great increase in strength" (Ludendorff, *My War Memories*, vol. 1, p. 305). In August 1916 the French Commander-in-Chief Joffre reported that from 4 July to 31 July the Russians had taken 335,000 Germans, including 6,000 officers, prisoner; he estimated that the Central Powers had lost since 4 July to the Russians in killed, wounded, and prisoners more than a million men (Joffre, *The Memoirs of Marshall Joffre*, pp. 477–78).

[55] Ludendorff, *My War Memories*, vol. 1, pp. 307, 317, vol. 2, pp. 413–14, 410; Bethmann Hollweg, *Betrachtungen*, 2d part (1921), p. 135.

[56] Scherer and Grunewald, vol. 1, p. 463; see also Müller, p. 203; Falkenhayn, p. 284.

[57] Müller, p. 216. To put Rumania's easy defeat in perspective it may help to know that one of the first orders of the day on 27 August was that only officers above the rank of major would be allowed to wear make-up.

[58] Ibid., p. 162.

the United States, Germany was forced to halt the submarine warfare on merchantmen on 27 April 1916. While Germany's leaders had hoped to launch unrestricted submarine warfare without drawing the United States into the war, they now knew with almost certainty that unrestricted submarine warfare would mean war with that country. The war at sea did produce the second (but distinctly minor) piece of good new information of 1916: Restricted submarine warfare following the rules of cruiser submarine warfare did score some successes in October and November 1916. The Battle of Jutland in May 1916 had not affected the balance of power at sea in any meaningful way, and the blockade of Germany continued.

Finally, the German leadership also learned that its populace might not be willing to suffer the rising costs of war quietly. On 14 May 1916 three days of food riots broke out in Leipzig. Again, on 27 August 1916 crowds gathered before the town hall in Hamborn and pelted officials and police with rocks over food shortages. In June thousands of munitions workers in Berlin and Braunschweig went on strike.[59] In June and July the Military Governors reported to the Prussian Ministry of War that the mood among the populace had worsened markedly, largely as a result of their increased uncertainty about the outcome of the war and uncertainty about the postwar domestic political order.[60] The food shortage did not fail to leave its impression on the German population, and the winter of 1916–17 became know as the *Kohlrübenwinter*, the cabbage- or rutabaga-winter.

Most importantly, the quantity and quality of the troops were seriously declining. For the first time the concept of *abgekämpfte Truppen* (fought-out troops) was used.[61] Even worse, the number of desertions increased over the fall and winter of 1916.[62] At the end of 1915 Bethmann Hollweg had been convinced by the War Ministry that Germany could continue fighting a long time, and that Germany need not fear a shortage of raw materials or substitutes.[63] At the end of May 1916, however, Bethmann Hollweg learned from Falkenhayn that Germany had sufficient manpower reserves to replace troops only until October 1917, while Austria-Hungary had sufficient replacements only until the spring of 1917. Around the same time raw materials for the construction of artillery and munitions would run out.[64] In addition, Baron Burian, the Foreign Minister of the Austrian-Hungarian government,

[59] Dahlin, p. 83.
[60] Deist, *Militär und Innenpolitik*, 1/I, p. 378, no. 154, p. 392, no. 159.
[61] Basler, p. 69.
[62] Dahlin, p. 85, note 111.
[63] Janssen, *Der Kanzler und der General*, p. 172.
[64] Ibid., p. 290.

warned the German government on 18 October that an attempt had to be made to bring about an end to the war because the situation would only worsen: "If the war continues, we will be faced with even larger offensives by our enemies than in this summer. Even if we victoriously repel these, we would not thereby force any of our enemies to make peace, but be close to exhaustion ourselves, and therefore be worse off than at present."[65] Thus, Germany's leaders became more pessimistic about both their own capability to continue fighting and Austria-Hungary's capability to stay in the war.

Germany's leaders were certainly aware of the unfavorable news and its implications. In August 1916 Bethmann Hollweg noted the "unexpected powers of resistance of France [and] the surprising offensive power of Russia."[66] In a meeting of the Prussian Cabinet on 28 August, Bethmann again admitted that Germany's military situation had worsened seriously since March.[67] On 29 September Bethmann confessed to the members of the Finance Committee that "our military situation is more unfavorable than it was last spring. Austria has been seriously defeated, both by Russia and Italy. Rumania has joined our enemy, and we have not had the success at Verdun which we expected."[68] At the end of October Bethmann Hollweg once again admitted that the situation had become more difficult for Germany.[69] Colonel Bauer, Ludendorff's extremely conservative advisor on questions of domestic politics and a very influential voice in the German Army High Command, also admitted that the situation would be intolerable if the war would last another year because Germany's *Soldatenmaterial* (soldier material) was reaching its limits and because German industry could not compete with the whole world.[70] The fighting during the

---

[65] Bethmann Hollweg's note regarding a conversation with Baron Burian of 18 October 1916 in Scherer and Grunewald, vol. 1, no. 347, pp. 517–19. Apparently, through an agent working for the British Council General in Rotterdam, the British leadership learned of this pessimistic estimate. See French, *The Strategy of the Lloyd George Coalition*, pp. 33–34.

[66] Quoted in Fischer, *Griff nach der Weltmacht*, pp. 301–2.

[67] Scherer and Grunewald, vol. 1, p. 463.

[68] Hanssen, pp. 145–47.

[69] At the Austro-German conference of 18 October both German and Austrian leaders agreed that they were now at the apogee of their victories and force and that they would inevitably decline henceforth (French, *The Strategy of the Lloyd George Coalition 1916–1918*, p. 34).

[70] Janssen, *Der Kanzler und der General*, p. 256. For Bauer's influence see Deist, *Militär und Innenpolitik*, 1/I, pp. LV–LVI. Colonel Max Hoffmann, one of Germany's most gifted staff officers who worked very closely with Hindenburg and Ludendorff, had remarked in March 1915 that Germany could not defeat its opponents to the extent that "we can dictate them terms. . . . It is not possible to completely defeat the Russian army" (quoted in Janssen, *Der Kanzler und der General*, p. 90).

year had been extremely costly. The German army had lost over a million men, three-quarters of whom were lost on the Somme and at Verdun and the rest in the east. To combat the steady attrition of both their manpower and the economic staying power and under pressure by the new Supreme Command, the German leadership instituted the Hindenburg Program and the Patriotic Auxiliary Service Law.[71]

Expectations for 1917

By the end of 1916 the German leadership had become much more pessimistic about the war. Both civilian and military leaders now estimated it was no longer possible to win the war on land. In 1917, Ludendorff estimated, 154 German divisions would face 190 Entente divisions on the Western Front, and the military feared a massive offense by the Entente.[72] He was well aware that "Notwithstanding the successful close of the year 1916, the outlook for the coming year was exceedingly grave. It was certain that in 1917 the Entente would again make a supreme effort, not only to make good their losses, which they were certainly in a position to do, but to add to their strength everywhere and swell their superiority in numbers."[73]

Ludendorff therefore planned to conserve his forces and remain on the defensive in the west; he prepared the troops for defensive warfare and intended, by means of the "Alberich maneuver," to shorten his lines and withdraw to the Siegfried line (subsequently known as the Hindenburg line).[74] Underscoring the growing superiority of the Entente and the effects of the Battle of the Somme, he warned that even German troops could not withstand "Somme fighting" indefinitely.[75] Ludendorff also had little faith in any peace moves, whether instigated by the Germans or President Wilson. He had concluded that "[the En-

[71] French, *The Strategy of the Lloyd George Coalition, 1916–1918*, p. 31.

[72] This fear tied in to OHL's support for unrestricted submarine warfare. Ludendorff told the Chancellor: "The U-boat war will also bring our armies into a different and better situation. Through the lack of wood needed for mining purposes and for lack of coal, the production of ammunition is hard-pressed. It means that there will be some relief for the western front. *We must spare the troops a second battle of the Somme*" (*Official German Documents Relating to the World War*, II, pp. 1320–21, emphasis added).

[73] Ludendorff, *My War Memories*, vol. 1, p. 305. Ludendorff gives more reasons for his pessimism on pp. 305–17.

[74] Czernin, p. 116. Ludendorff, *My War Memories*, vol. 1, pp. 308, 386–88; vol. 2, p. 405. As we shall see in subsequent chapters, this retreat had serious implications for the French plans for 1917. Especially the new tactics of defense in depth, designed by Colonel Bauer and Captain Geyer, were to prove their worth.

[75] Basler, pp. 69–71; Ludendorff, *My War Memories*, vol. 1, p. 307. See also *Official German Documents Relating to the World War*, II, pp. 1320–21.

tente's] prospects for 1917 were so much more favorable than ours that, even while I hoped for it, I had grave doubts as to the success of any step by President Wilson."[76]

Although, strictly speaking, it probably falls outside of the time-frame under analysis here, we now turn to an analysis of Germany's decision on 9 January 1917 to launch unrestricted submarine warfare. This decision requires attention for two main reasons. First, it could be argued that Germany's leaders had very high estimates of the efficacy of unrestricted submarine warfare and at the end of 1916 were optimistic about their probability of victory on that basis alone. The analysis below will show that is not the case and that, rather, the decision to launch unrestricted submarine warfare shows how pessimistic Germany's leaders had become by the end of 1916. Second, I will show that unrestricted submarine warfare probably qualifies as a high-variance strategy, that is, a risky strategy that increases both the chance of better terms of settlement but also the chance of substantially worse terms.

In January 1917, after Bethmann Hollweg's peace move had failed and with no chance of victory on land, the German leadership finally decided to try to gain victory at sea. It deserves emphasis that high expectations about the efficacy of unrestricted submarine warfare did not lead Ludendorff or the Chancellor to propose and/or accept high war aims in early November. At the time of the deliberations on the peace move by the Central Powers, Chancellor Bethmann Hollweg, Secretary of State of Foreign Affairs Zimmermann, and the Secretary of State for the Interior Karl Hellferich were firmly opposed to un-restricted submarine warfare. It was only after the failure of the peace move that the military forced Bethmann Hollweg's hand. Reichstag representative Hanssen accurately analyzed why Bethmann had to concede the issue when he wrote in his diary on 20 December 1916:

> When the Junkers asked Bethmann last spring how he would conclude an acceptable peace for Germany, since he had rejected submarine warfare, he answered by referring to Verdun. But he made no reply when they con-fronted him with the same question this fall, after the failure of the Verdun offensive. His stand was untenable. In his extremity he thereafter held to the peace offering of December 16th, but on its rejection he was forced to recognize the Kaiser and the generals so completely, especially Hindenburg and Ludendorff, that a battle was bound to result. And thus his opposition to submarine warfare has been broken. Unless he yields, his days as Chancellor are numbered.[77]

[76] Ludendorff, *My War Memories*, vol. 1, p. 309.
[77] Hanssen, p. 156.

As Gatzke notes, with the options dwindling, "Germany's ruling class saw in the unrestricted use of the submarine the only means to gain a victorious peace, which in turn, they felt, was necessary to maintain the existing political and social order."[78]

Every member of the leadership now agreed that Germany could not win a long war. As we saw above, even Ludendorff admitted that "[i]f the war lasted our defeat seemed inevitable."[79] And, as Ludendorff and Hindenburg told Bethmann Hollweg in the third week of December—after the peace move of 16 December had failed—"[u]nrestricted submarine warfare [is] now the only means left to secure a victorious end to the war within a reasonable time."[80] Not only did their conclusion that without ruthless submarine warfare Germany would lose the war therefore *not* surprise the Chancellor, it was also the explicit justification for unrestricted submarine warfare invoked by the Germans in discussions with the Austro-Hungarians.[81]

It is not the case that Germany's leaders became very optimistic about submarine warfare; rather, they became so pessimistic about the current prospects of the war that unrestricted submarine warfare by comparison offered a better chance of securing the required terms of settlement. In early January 1916 Secretary of State for Foreign Affairs Zimmermann, for example, said, "Show me a way to obtain a reasonable peace and I would be the first to reject the idea of the U-boat warfare."[82] Bethmann Hollweg was also decidedly not optimistic about the prospects of submarine warfare.[83] The exchange between the naval authorities and the Chancellor reported by Hohenlohe on 12 January 1917 to the new Austro-Hungarian Foreign Minister Czernin is instructive:

[78] Gatzke, p. 166. See also Hoffman's remark, ibid., pp. 165–66.

[79] Ludendorff, *My War Memories*, p. 307. For Bethmann Hollweg's conclusion that "time was running against us," see his *Betrachtungen*, 2d part (1921), pp. 133–34.

[80] Ludendorff, *War Memories*, vol. 1, p. 312; Bethmann Hollweg, *Betrachtungen*, 2d part (1921), pp. 130, 133–34. It deserves notice that Ludendorff and Hindenburg had opposed unrestricted submarine warfare when they came to power on 30 August 1916 on the grounds that the time had "not yet come for it" and as recently as the first week of October (Ludendorff, pp. 127–28).

[81] Bethmann Hollweg, *Betrachtungen*, 2d part (1921), p. 129; see also Czernin, pp. 118–19. The same reasoning can be found in the report of the conference of 20 January in Vienna with Zimmermann and German Admiral von Holtzendorff present, on pp. 121–24.

[82] Quoted in Czernin, p. 120.

[83] *Official German Documents Relating to the World War*, vol. 2, pp. 1320–21. See also Bethmann Hollweg's discussion of 9 January 1917 with Admiral von Müller in Müller, p. 249. Moreover, already in August 1916 the Chancellor had noted that the British could take effective countermeasures against unrestricted submarine warfare: The British could use convoys. See *Official German Documents Relating to the World War*, vol. 2, pp. 1154–63.

"The leading naval authorities reassert that they may be relied on, even though they are not considered capable of crushing England, at least to be able, *before* America can come in, so to weaken the British Island Empire that only one desire will be left to English politicians, that of seating themselves with us at the Conference table."[84] When the Chancellor objected that success and failure of unrestricted submarine warfare were equally impossible to prove and asked "in what position should [Germany] find [itself] in case the admirals were mistaken," the Admiralty gave a revealing reply. Rather than argue for the prospects of success, the Admiralty pointed out the poverty of alternatives when it "promptly asked what sort of position the Chancellor expected to find when autumn arrived without having made a proper use of the U-boats and we found ourselves, through exhaustion, compelled to *beg* for peace."[85] Ludendorff, finally, also did not think that unrestricted submarine warfare would produce a decisive victory. He told General von Eisenhardt-Rothe in the beginning of 1917, "Don't think I approach the matter in some sort of jubilant mood. In spite of all promises by the Navy, I do not indulge in the hope to bring England to her knees by U-boat warfare. But I certainly hope that the lack of shipping space in England will be so large that it will be ready for a sensible peace."[86]

The decision to launch unrestricted submarine warfare in early 1917 is a good example of a high-variance strategy, as laid out in the theory chapter. The German leadership was now willing to try a very risky strategy because they estimated that was the only way to achieve the terms of settlement necessary to stave off punishment, as the quote by Zimmermann above illustrates. The leadership seems to have been well aware of the downside of unrestricted submarine warfare and the greatly increased risks it brought. Bethmann Hollweg, for example, warned: "should success not materialize, then the worst end awaits us."[87] He thought this "leap into the dark" could

---

[84] Czernin, p. 116, emphasis in original.

[85] Hohenlohe's report of the debate between Bethmann Hollweg and the military authorities, in Czernin, p. 117, emphasis in the original. Bethmann's warning that neither success nor failure could be proven is found in Bethmann Hollweg, *Betrachtungen*, 2d part (1921), p. 137.

[86] Quoted in Direnberger, p. 24; see also Müller, p. 258. In his memoirs Ludendorff defends the decision in favor of unrestricted submarine warfare by arguing, "If submarine warfare in this form could have a decisive effect—and the Navy held that it could— then in the existing situation it was our plain military duty to the German nation to embark on it" (*My War Memories*, vol. 1, p. 312).

[87] Bethmann Hollweg, *Betrachtungen*, 2d part (1921), p. 137. He had earlier compared unrestricted submarine warfare to an "all-or-nothing gamble" (Va-banquespiel) (p. 286). See also Fischer, *Griff nach der Weltmacht*, pp. 362, 367. Other German politicians had similar fears; see Czernin, p. 116.

spell the end of Germany.[88] Ludendorff calculated that "in case U-boat warfare would not work, [the United States' entrance would mean] a serious increase in the enemy's power and a significant shift in the balance of forces. It could not be doubted that America, if she entered the war, would arm herself in the same way that England had done, and that the Entente would call forth from the United States ever more armaments by virtue of its view and energy."[89] Secretary of State for the Interior Karl Helfferich not only feared the greater variance produced by unrestricted submarine warfare but apparently even believed this strategy had a lower expected value. In late August he warned, "I see nothing but catastrophe following the application of the U-boat weapon at this time. *A method which will lead us out of one serious situation into the toils of another more serious*, is not practical if we are not able to adopt counter-measures for the purpose of rendering the other disadvantageous result [probable U.S. entry] ineffectual."[90] The infamous Zimmermann telegram, proposing an alliance with Mexico, finally shows that the German leadership was far from convinced by assurances that American entry would be irrelevant. Zimmerman's telegram was an attempt at an insurance strategy in case the United States should enter the war. If Germany's leaders were confident that the United States would not effectively play a part in the war because Great Britain would be defeated before it could contribute, this risky ploy of an alliance with Mexico would make little sense.

The Change in German War Aims

To trace how the new information of 1916 affected Germany's war aims, I compare Germany's war aims of November 1915 with those of November–December 1916. The first section lays out the war aims of November 1915, the second section those of November 1916, and the

---

[88] Fischer, *Griff nach der Weltmacht*, p. 362.

[89] Ludendorff, *Meine Kriegserinnerungen 1914–1918*, p. 247. A couple of pages later he acknowledges the effect the new American armies would have when he recalls that, while he did not take the navy's estimates literally, "I believed I could count on a critical effect before the new year, thus, before America could appear on the battlefield with its new forces" (p. 249).

[90] *Official German Documents Relating to the World War*, vol. 2, p. 1158; see esp. pp. 1154–63. Admiral von Capelle's reply is revealing: "According to the course which the war has followed up to this time, I am convinced that *we are not on the road to a peace acceptable to us if we continue along the lines pursued thus far*. . . . If complete success were not to result from the U-boat war, this would not, in my opinion, lead to a catastrophe, but would, at the very worst, merely result in prolonging the war of exhaustion, just as the situation is at this time" (ibid., emphasis added).

third section compares these aims and highlights the changes. The main conclusion is that Germany's war aims increased from January to November 1916. This evidence falsifies the first two competing theories. First, on the basis of a steady flow of bad new information, the unitary actor model (e.g., domestic politics is irrelevant) would predict that Germany's war aims would go down. Second, Fischer's thesis that Germany's war aims basically remained constant throughout the war is also shown to be false.

Central to Germany's war aims at the end of 1915 were the newly occupied territories of Poland and the Baltic provinces. With regard to Poland, Bethmann Hollweg preferred the so-called Austro-Polish solution whereby Poland would be incorporated into Austria-Hungary, "perhaps like Croatia is incorporated in Hungary."[91] In return Germany would gain stronger political, military, and economic ties chaining the Austro-Hungarian monarchy to Germany, border adjustments along the Prussian-Polish border and autonomy for Courland and Lithuania.

In a conference with Austro-Hungarian Foreign Minister Baron Burian on 10 and 11 November 1915, Bethmann laid out the German conditions for the Austro-Polish solution.[92] He warned that if Germany could find no other compensations for its great sacrifices, German domestic public opinion would not tolerate Austria-Hungary gaining all rewards of victory. As usual, German conditions were broken up into military, political, and economic aspects. For allowing Austria-Hungary to annex Poland, Germany would demand deeper and broader military, economic, and political ties between the German and Austro-Hungarian empires. These ties would draw Austria-Hungary tighter into the proposed Middle-European bloc under Germany's control. The German leadership also warned that the addition of Poland could not be allowed to damage the political influence of the "German element" in the Austro-Hungarian Empire. Since the power of the Germans in the Dual Monarchy formed a guarantee for Austria-Hungary's

[91] Bethmann Hollweg to Falkenhayn, 11 September 1915; Scherer and Grunewald, vol. 1, no. 140, p. 176; see pp. 173–78.

[92] There are two slightly differing memoranda on this conference by Jagow. The first is Jagow's "Note of the conversations with Baron Burian in Berlin of 10 and 11 November," dated 14 November 1915, in Scherer and Grunewald, vol. 1, no. 167, pp. 218–21. The second Promemoria note was sent by Jagow to the Austrian Foreign Ministry. It is dated 13 November and has been cited by Fritz Fischer in his *Griff nach der Weltmacht*, p. 254. Fischer cites the Auswärtiges Amt, Österreich-Ungarn, 23, vol. 1, Promemoria Jagows, 13.11.1915. Note that this version differs from Jagow's memorandum in Scherer and Grunewald, mainly in the demand for Lithuania and Courland.

continued friendly relations with Germany, so argued Bethmann, public opinion would not allow any weakening of their position.

In return for leaving Poland to Austro-Hungarian control, Germany would require the following terms against Russia. First were strategic border adjustments: "Besides the tracts of land necessary for the improvement of Germany's borders in the province of Suwalki and in addition to Courland and Lithuania, also several for Germany very valuable tracts of . . . Poland."[93] When asked for guidance on specific military conditions by Bethmann Hollweg in mid-October, the Prussian Minister of War demanded border rectifications along the line Kowno-Grodno-Ostrolenka-Plozk-Warthe.[94] With regard to Courland and Lithuania, Bethmann was on record against annexation; both he and the Kaiser favored their independence from Russia and consolidation into an autonomous dukedom under a German prince.[95] Colonization and "Germanification" would further strengthen its political connection with the German Empire. Militarily, this dukedom would, of course, be joined with the German Empire; economically, it would be joined by means of a customs union and a common railway system. The "very valuable tracts" of Poland included territory in the Upper Silesian industrial area. Furthermore, Germany demanded many and far-reaching guarantees that would bring the fundamental economic infrastructure of the Polish economy under absolute German control. Railroads and waterways would be taken over by German private corporations and thereby give Germany control over all transportation. Finally, Germany laid claim to part of the Polish Crownlands for the purposes of re-colonization (*umsiedlung*); these were to form integral parts of the enlarged so-called Polish Frontier Strip.[96]

It seems that the Central Powers' war aims against Russia in Poland might nevertheless be modified and substantially lowered if Russia would only finally accept a separate peace. At their discussion both the German Chancellor and the Austro-Hungarian Foreign Minister agreed that if Russia would soon offer a separate peace and the general situation would make the acceptance of that offer desirable, Poland might have to be returned to Russia. However, when made aware of Bethmann's caveat, the Kaiser ruled out a return of Poland to Russia

[93] Quoted in Fischer, *Griff nach der Weltmacht*, p. 254.

[94] Scherer and Grunewald, vol. 1, no. 147, pp. 188–89.

[95] See Jagow's note of 2 September 1915, enclosed by Bethmann Hollweg in his letter of 11 September to Falkenhayn (Scherer and Grunewald, vol. 1, no. 140, p. 179). For the Kaiser's approval, see note 13. See also nos. 104 and 222.

[96] Geiss, *Der Polnischen Grenzstreifen*.

at the end of 1915.[97] Nonetheless, in a conversation with Reichstag leaders later in December Bethmann continued to insist that in case Russia offered a separate peace, at least a large part of Poland would have to be returned to Russia.[98] Since at this time much of Poland was to be brought under Austro-Hungarian control, most if not all of this potential "moderation" of the Central Powers' war aims would undoubtedly be at Austria-Hungary's expense.

There remains uncertainty about Germany's demands against Belgium at the end of 1915. On the one hand, Bethmann noted on 1 January 1916 that probably the most that could be achieved in Belgium would be a defensive alliance with political, military, and economic guarantees, while it remained undecided whether Liège would be annexed or not.[99] On the other hand, at the end of October the Kaiser expressed his complete agreement with the navy's demands for the annexation of parts of the Flemish coast, specifically, the port triangle of Ostende-Zeebrugge-Antwerp.[100] However, it is unclear whether the Kaiser's agreement would survive a Crown Council with the Chancellor and Chief of the General Staff.

One year later, in October and November 1916, Germany and Austria-Hungary drew up their war aims in detail in preparation for their peace offer of 12 December. It is striking to see how, in spite of all the bad news of 1916, Germany's war aims increased during 1916 (and increased even further if we include the additional demands of the army and the navy in December). It should be noted that the additional demands should not be simply explained as bargaining chips. Bethmann Hollweg, wary of public commitment and aware of the possible audience costs, explicitly warned representatives of the press against such a strategy in March 1916 because "[h]e did not consider it wise to bluff with far-reaching annexationist demands and then become more and more modest."[101] During November and December 1916

---

[97] Fischer, *Griff nach der Weltmacht*, p. 258.

[98] Ibid., p. 259.

[99] Scherer and Grunewald, vol. 1, no. 180, pp. 243–44. For terms offered Belgium if it would make a separate peace, see no. 183, pp. 247–51; see also Fischer, *Griff nach der Weltmacht*, pp. 264–65.

[100] Fischer, *Griff nach der Weltmacht*, p. 332.

[101] Quoted in Gatzke, pp. 72–73. Gatzke's book is an impressive effort with many valuable insights and mostly careful scholarship. However, there is at least one important mistake. On pages 139–40 he argues that on 2 September Bethmann sent a telegram to Germany's ambassador in Washington that asked "Would mediation by Wilson be possible and successful if we were to guarantee Belgium's unconditional restoration? Otherwise the unrestricted U-boat warfare will have to be carried out in dead earnest." As the source of this quote he refers to Forster, *The Failures of Peace*, p. 41. While the reference

Bethmann Hollweg reformulated Germany's war aims in consultation with Austria-Hungary and the Supreme Command. After an exchange of notes between the Supreme Command and the Chancellor in the first week of November, Bethmann Hollweg telegraphed the Kaiser on 7 November with a list of Germany's war aims as they were to be communicated to the Austro-Hungarian Foreign Minister Baron Burian:[102]

1. Recognition of the Kingdom of Poland.
2. Annexation of such Courlandian and Lithuanian territory that with the inclusion of the Kingdom of Poland a good strategic border with Russia will be won, running from the north to the south.
3. Trade agreement with Russia, respectively economic advantages.
4. Guarantees in Belgium, as much as possible to be determined in negotiations with King Albert. Would these not be obtainable to a sufficient degree, annexation of Liège with suitable environs (*Landstreifen*).
5. Evacuation of the occupied French territory with the exception of Briey and Longwy in return for evacuation of the parts of Alsace-Lorraine occupied by the French and strategic border adjustments for [Germany] in Alsace-Lorraine, as well as war indemnity, or else compensations.
6. Restitution of the colonies with exception of Kiautschou, the Caroline and Mariana islands, or else a general colonial agreement, acquisition of the Congo, or part of it.
7. Indemnity for the Germans living abroad and German property abroad, to the extent it is damaged.
8. Incorporation of Luxembourg in the German Empire. This appears necessary for the case that we acquire Briey and Longwy.[103]

On 8 November the Kaiser gave his formal consent to these demands. The only suggestion he made was to demand that English mining concessions in Russia be transferred to Germany.[104] As Bethmann Hollweg

---

is correct, Forster mistranslates the original German. The original German note can be found in Scherer and Grunewald, vol. 1, no. 319, pp. 465–66. Its correct translation is very different: "Would . . . peace mediation by Wilson be possible and successful if we guarantee Belgium's *conditional* restoration? Otherwise unrestricted U-boat warfare must be seriously considered" (emphasis added).

[102] For Bethmann Hollweg's initially suggested list of 4 November 1916, see Scherer and Grunewald, vol. 1, no. 361, pp. 542–43. Note that this telegram also contains Baron Burian's proposal for Austro-Hungarian war aims for 1916. Hindenburg replied the next day and offered some emendations; see no. 365, pp. 548–49. Bethmann Hollweg expressed his agreement with the suggestions of the Supreme Command with one minor reservation that could well have been based on a misunderstanding on 6 November. See no. 367, pp. 550–51; see also Fischer, *Griff nach der Weltmacht*, pp. 402–12.

[103] Scherer and Grunewald, vol. 1, no. 369, p. 552.

[104] On 15 December Bethmann Hollweg presented a list of the German minimum demands to Baron Burian. This list differs from the list sent for approval to the Kaiser and

explicitly intended, this list of eight main German war aims was kept as much as possible in general terms, but as we shall see, he had formally agreed to some more detailed demands left out of this list.

On 6 November Bethmann Hollweg explicitly agreed to Hindenburg and Ludendorff's elaboration of his proposed war aims.[105] The demands suggested by Supreme Command on 5 November 1916 were more specific on several points. On the first demand about recognition of the Kingdom of Poland, the Supreme Command demanded border improvements along the Prussian-Polish border, economic union of Poland with Germany, decisive influence on the railroads, and further economic advantages in Poland. On the second demand for a good strategic border with Russia, the Supreme Command demanded border adjustments in the east by means of annexations up to the line from the Gulf of Riga, west of Riga, and east to past Wilna in the direction of Brest-Litovsk. On the German demands in Belgium the Supreme Command included the demand for the exploitation of the raw materials of the Campine ('t Kempen) area, economic union with Germany, and the right of occupation. In return for this conditional restoration of Belgium, the Supreme Command wanted to ask England for a war indemnity.[106] Bethmann Hollweg explicitly rejected this demand in his reply, arguing that the conditional delivery of Belgium would be traded for the return of Germany's colonies, most of which were occupied by England. Moreover, as the Chancellor pointed out, Germany would demand the Congo from Belgium, and Belgium had already paid far more than a billion marks in contributions to the war. However, he would be willing to raise Belgium's current levy of 40 million marks a month to 50 million.[107]

How do Germany's demands of November 1916 compare to the demands at the end of the previous year? We start again in the east. With regard to Poland, German demands increased substantially. The Aus-

---

includes several additional demands, of which the two most important were freedom of the seas and freedom of navigation on the lower Donau (see Basler, p. 65).

[105] See Scherer and Grunewald, vol. 1, no. 367, pp. 550–51. For Bethmann's explicit acceptance of Ludendorff's list of war aims in a letter to the German ambassador in Vienna in which he announced his support of the war aims of the OHL, see Stephen Bailey, p. 17, note 1, referring to Bethmann's letter to Count Wedel of 23 November 1916 in Michaelis, vol. 1, p. 65.

[106] Scherer and Grunewald, vol. 1, no. 365, pp. 548–49. Compare with Fischer, *Griff nach der Weltmacht*, pp. 274–76. On 27 August 1916 Bethmann Hollweg had told Müller that Germany needed peace as soon as possible. He generally would strive for the status quo ante but indicated he was willing to give up parts of Alsace-Lorraine in return for a part of Briey! (Müller, p. 215).

[107] Bethmann to the Supreme Command, 6 November 1916, in Scherer and Grunewald, vol. 1, no. 367, pp. 550–51.

tro-Polish solution had died a quick death. Already by January 1916, Falkenhayn declared that the Austro-Polish solution could no longer be recommended "from a military point of view," and Bethmann Hollweg had similarly abandoned it by the end of February.[108] By August the allies agreed to reconstitute an "autonomous" Poland.[109] (At least for the Chancellor if not for the Kaiser, this represents an increase of war aims against Russia because it made impossible the trade of Poland for a separate peace with Russia.)[110] On 5 November 1916 Kaisers Wilhelm II and Franz Joseph declared a "Kingdom of Poland" into existence that was to consist entirely of former Russian territory. As Clarence Jay Smith notes, "The Austrians consented to the step with great bitterness."[111] Bethmann Hollweg would allow an Austrian Archduke on the Polish throne but remained firm in his desire to control the Polish economy and raw materials. The value of this Polish kingdom to Austria-Hungary becomes even more questionable since the Dual Monarchy was forced to agree to complete German control over any new Polish army.[112] All in all, Germany's demands at the end of 1916 would give Germany tremendous additional influence in Poland at the expense of its ally.[113] Although the demand for parts of Upper Silesia was now off the table, Germany gained more than enough to make up for this in Poland and elsewhere. As Fritz Fischer shows, the German Empire would make substantial additional territorial gains in the east under the guise of a "good strategic border against Russia."[114] Not only were Courland and Lithuania now to be annexed, but the so-called Polish borderstrip was also drastically enlarged. The additional territory "from the Gulf of Riga to east past Wilna in the direction of Brest-

---

[108] Fischer, *Griff nach der Weltmacht*, p. 260; Ritter, *The Sword and the Scepter*, vol. 3, p. 113.

[109] Stevenson, *The First World War and International Politics*, pp. 97–98.

[110] See, however, Janssen, *Der Kanzler und der General*, pp. 243–44, who argues that Zimmermann in August 1916 still wanted to hold out the option of giving Poland back to Russia.

[111] Smith Jr., *The Russian Struggle for Power, 1914–1917*, p. 384; see also Fischer, *Griff nach der Weltmacht*, p. 293

[112] Fischer, *Griff nach der Weltmacht*, pp. 293–99; Stevenson, *The First World War in International Politics*, p. 98; see also Scherer and Grunewald, vol. 1, nos. 221, 227, 261, 303, 304, and 305.

[113] For a discussion on Poland's future between Austria-Hungary and Germany of 6 January 1917, see Scherer and Grunewald, vol. 1, no. 461, pp. 663–67.

[114] Fischer, *Griff nach der Weltmacht*, p. 295; see also pp. 340–44, 404. See also Bethmann's aims as expressed against Baron Burian on 14 April in Ritter, vol. 3, p. 116. Note also the increase as compared with Bethmann Hollweg's earlier communication to Falkenhayn, on 4 August 1915, Scherer and Grunewald, vol. 1, no. 121, p. 149.

Litovsk" adds up to tens of thousands of square kilometers.[115] Even if we assume that the demand for Courland and Lithuania remained unchanged—unlikely because the demand was now for outright annexation—the addition of the Wilna district alone would add thousands of square kilometers to the German Empire.[116] Further south, as Fischer shows, the area demanded as the Polish Frontier Strip had substantially expanded by the end of 1916, to well over 30,000 square kilometers.[117] To add insult to injury, it would seem, Russia would be forced not just to give up all that territory but in addition to agree to a treaty of commerce with Germany. Germany's demands in the west also increased. France would have to cede additional territory (most likely involving the western slopes of the Vosges). Belgium would now have to pay a higher monthly tribute, give up the raw materials in the Campine, and also parts if not the whole of the Congo. I am uncertain whether demands against Belgium changed in other aspects.[118]

Even by the most conservative estimates, therefore, between November 1915 and November 1916 Germany substantially increased its war aims. Good arguments can be made that Germany's aims were even substantially higher at the end of December 1916. On 23 December, less than two weeks after the Chancellor launched his "peace move," the Supreme Command presented an additional list of demands that "reached far beyond the goals discussed with Bethmann Hollweg early in November."[119] The Supreme Command now de-

---

[115] See the map in Fischer, *Griff nach der Weltmacht*, between pages 340 and 341. Fischer calculates that Suwalki, Courland, Kowno, and parts of Grodno and Wilna would constitute an area of about 60,000 square kilometers (p. 293). Elsewhere he argues that Kowno and Suwalki alone comprised 53,000 square kilometers; Courland would add about 27,000 square kilometers (p. 344).

[116] Fischer, *Griff nach der Weltmacht*, p. 404.

[117] Ibid., pp. 295, 340–43.

[118] Compare also the demands proposed by Count Toerring for negotiations between Germany and Belgium of 1 December 1915 in Scherer and Grunewald, vol. 1, no. 172, p. 232, note 3. Note also that, on the one hand, the war aims of November 1916 do not refer to the previous demand for German "protection" of the Flemish coast. On the other hand, the demands of November 1916 include "guarantees" and annexation of Liège and vicinity in the case of insufficient occupation rights. Compare with Fischer, *Griff nach der Weltmacht*, pp. 259, 264ff., 269. Also note Ritter's contention that on 26 November the navy presented Bethmann Hollweg with the first of two memoranda on Germany's maritime war aims (Ritter, *Staatskunst und Kriegshandwerk*, vol. 3, pp. 290–91). By June 1916 it appears that Germany's leaders had decided to content themselves with the attachment of Luxembourg through a customs union. See for this and more on the Congo, Fischer, *Griff nach der Weltmacht*, p. 273.

[119] Ritter, *The Sword and the Scepter*, vol. 3, p. 290; see esp. pp. 290–92; Steglich, *Bündnissicherung oder Verständigungsfrieden*, p. 157.

manded additional annexations from Belgium and Russia. Upon Ludendorff's urging Hindenburg demanded increased annexations from Poland and remarked, "I cannot accept anything less than these demands."[120] Although the Chancellor held Hindenburg to their earlier exchange of telegrams of November, he carefully avoided a commitment about a peace program and an open struggle for power in the knowledge that he would have come out the loser.[121] Nevertheless, three months later he was forced to concede all these demands in the Kreuznach conference of 23 April 1917.[122]

The Causal Mechanism: The Domestic Consequences of the Terms of Settlement

This section first shows how the questions of war aims and domestic political reforms were closely linked during the war. The German regime knew that the people would have to be bought off after the war. They could either grant political concessions or use the spoils of a victorious war to satisfy the demands of the people. The first option was deemed unacceptable. Therefore, the beneficiaries of the regime continuously pressed for high war aims in the belief that substantial gains could prevent the democratization of Germany and the ensuing permanent loss of their privileges. As they became more uncertain about the outcome of the war, their efforts to keep war aims high enough to

---

[120] Hindenburg to Bethmann Hollweg, in Scherer and Grunewald, vol. 1, no. 435, pp. 630–31; see also Fischer, *Griff nach der Weltmacht*, p. 352. Field Marshall Hindenburg presented the Chancellor with a new list of demands, under the pretext that the exchange of views on war aims between Bethmann Hollweg and the Supreme Command "had not yet led to a definite agreement." See Scherer and Grunewald, vol. 1, no. 435, pp. 630–31. The navy sent the Chancellor its own list of war aims the next day. The navy's main demand was for authority over the Belgian coast with bases in the important maritime triangle of Brugge, Ostende, and Zeebrugge. In its conclusion the navy's memorandum summarized the navy's need for strategic bases. At home, the coast of Belgium and of Courland [with Vindava and Lepaya,] the islands of Oesel and Mohn, and the Faroe Islands. Abroad, in addition to an African colonial empire, as new gains the Azores, Valona, Dakar with Senegambia, Tahiti; keep the previous possessions: New Guinea with the Bismarck Archipelago and Yap. Potentially Portuguese Timor was to be gained instead, and Tsingtau as a German trading port. See Scherer and Grunewald, vol. 1, no. 437, pp. 633–37; see also Ritter, *The Sword and the Scepter*, vol. 3, p. 292.

[121] See Ritter, *The Sword and the Scepter*, vol. 3, p. 292.

[122] As Renouvin notes, this further increase in German war aims came after the Germans had reason to become less pessimistic. The French Nivelle offensive of 16 April had failed, and the unrestricted submarine warfare still seemed to hold great promise ("Les tentatives de paix en 1917 et le gouvernement français," p. 507).

cover the costs of the war mounted. The second part of this section establishes that the additional demands of 1916 were indeed intended to buy off the populace. First, the additional territorial demands could be used to reward the returning soldiers with land grants and the like. Second, high war indemnities and economic advantages would prevent the need for higher taxes after the war.

Politicians of all stripes knew that after the war, at the latest, they would have to defend their actions, their choice of (continuing) the war, to the people.[123] As I argued in the theory chapter, in effect, the people would retrospectively judge the regime on the basis of the costs and gains of the war. This conclusion is shared by the large majority of historians of Germany in the First World War. The historian Egmont Zechlin makes the point in terms that very closely mirror my theoretical arguments:

> It almost looks as if human and economic sacrifices of the German people should be made good by the acquisition of territory, and to use the resulting possible improvement of wages to head off the coming political claims of the work force. . . . [T]he war reparations in the form of land or money appear as a safety valve for a future social revolution.[124]

Fritz Fischer similarly concludes that, by 1917,

> The leading circles of Germany in property and education were apparently stronger than ever of the opinion that they could maintain their political and social system against the pressures of forces from below only then when they could terminate the World War victoriously and with profit, since already a drawn peace on the basis of the status quo would shake their internal political power position.[125]

[123] For example, the National-Liberal Ludwig Roland-Lücke warned already in December 1915: "Our decision to continue the war must be made with the thought in mind that we will have to defend ourselves before our people" (quoted in Hanssen, p. 118). Ludendorff wrote in a letter of 29 June 1916 to Zimmermann, "doesn't the Chancellor see . . . that one day an explanation will be demanded from the Monarchy." This is one of several original sources provided by Janssen, *Der Kanzler und der General*, appendix 6, no. 2, p. 292.

[124] Zechlin; "Friedensbestrebungen und Revolutionsversuche," B 20/61, pp. 271–72; see also Farrar, *The Short-War Illusion*, pp. 133–34, p. 150; Gatzke, pp. 126–31, 166, 188, 294; and Janssen, *Der Kanzler und der General*, pp. 52–53.

[125] Fischer, *Griff nach der Weltmacht*, pp. 559–60; see also Deist, *Militär und Innenpolitik*, 1/II, no. 286, p. 719, note 10, where Tirpitz argues at the end of April 1917 that an annexationist peace would distract the people from their demands for domestic democratic reforms. Ludendorff told the Austro-Hungarians on 5 February 1918 in very similar language that a peace that brought only the status quo would mean that Germany had lost the war (ibid., p. 653).

If the people could be "rewarded for their sacrifices," their judgment would surely be more favorable. While both the in-groups and their opponents recognized that the people would have to be rewarded for their sacrifices, they vehemently disagreed over the form and substance of such rewards.[126] The Socialists and more moderate elements including Bethmann Hollweg and some other Prussian Cabinet members emphasized political reforms to give the people a greater say. Their conservative opponents, in contrast, emphasized economic and territorial gains. The two issues of war aims and domestic political reform thus were basically two sides of the same coin: How the people should be rewarded or bought off after the war.

As Bethmann Hollweg and many others have noted, the domestic fight over political reforms was publicly fought out over the issue of war aims.[127] "The controversy of war aims," Prussia's Minister of the Interior wrote in February 1918, "which ... dominates the domestic scene in Germany, has been able to gain its depth and intensity only because each side recognizes in the representative of opposing peace demands also its opponent in domestic issues."[128] This link is generally accepted in the historical literature. L. L. Farrar's conclusion can stand for the general historical consensus: "German leaders increasingly perceived an inversely proportional relationship between war aims and reforms. A victory and achievement of war aims would obviate demands for reform, while defeat and failure to achieve war aims would result in reform, if not revolution."[129] However, as a report by the Bavarian War Ministry of early August 1916 acknowledged, the requirement of the *Burgfrieden* (truce) at home prohibited open attacks on Bethmann's moderately pro-reform policies (known as *Neuorientierung* (new orientation) and *Politik der Diagonale* (politics of the diagonal)). Therefore, the report concluded, the conservatives hoped that Bethmann would fall over the war aims and peace-settlement questions— as happened in the spring of 1917.[130]

Agitation in favor of high war aims started very soon after the war broke out, and the beneficiaries of the old order wasted no time in

---

[126] Farrar comes to exactly the same conclusion: "The arguments of the reformers and annexationists were consequently analogous but antithetical. Both sides expected the German people would have to be paid for their war effort, but one side advocated reforms and the other annexations as the payment" (*The Short-War Illusion*, p. 144).

[127] Gatzke, p. 192, note 244; Deist, 1/II, p. 663, letter of Colonel Mertz v. Quirnheim to the Bavarian Minister of War on the controversy between the Bavarian Prime Minister and the Army High Command, 15 February 1917.

[128] Quoted in Gatzke, p. 249.

[129] Farrar, *The Short-War Illusion*, pp. 44, 50.

[130] Deist, *Militär und Innenpolitik*, 1/I, pp. 406–13, no. 165, 5 August 1916.

warning about the dire domestic consequences of a "meager peace." Interest groups, such as intellectuals[131] and industrialists,[132] as well as members of the political establishment[133] argued that the war had to bring rewards to the people or serious domestic unrest would result. To pick just one of many examples, General Baron von Gayl, Deputy Commander in Westphalia (one of the twenty-four Army Corps districts into which Germany was divided), wrote the Chancellor at the end of June 1915 on the topic of war aims. Von Gayl told Bethmann that "national circles" believed that substantial territorial gains were needed in the west as well as in the east, to distract the people from "internal quarrels." "If in this fateful hour an insufficient peace will be made," he warned Bethmann, "then the fate, not only of the Empire, but most of all the monarchy and the Dynasty of the Hohenzollerns—

[131] The famous Petition of the Intellectuals of April 1915 warned that "A statesman who returns without Belgium—soaked with German blood—, without strong extensions of the frontier in east and west, without a substantial indemnity, and before all, without the most ruthless humiliation of England, such a statesman will have to expect not only the worst discontent from the lower and middle classes about the increased burden of taxation; he will also find much bitterness among leading circles, which will endanger internal peace and may even affect the foundations of the monarchy. The disappointed nation would believe that it sacrificed in vain the flower of its youth and manhood" (quoted in Gatzke, p. 121). The explicit purpose of such reports and memoranda was to pressure the Chancellor not to give up what had been won and to "conclude a premature peace which even excludes the compensation for the costs" of the war (Hirsch to Schifferer, 13 March 1915; quoted in Zechlin, "Friedensbestrebungen und Revolutionsversuche," B 22/63, p. 24).

[132] The most prominent example is the so-called Petition of the Six Economic Organizations of March and May 1915. See Gatzke, pp. 38, 45ff.; Deist, Militär und Innenpolitik, 1/I, p. 406, no. 165. Already in September 1914 the Bund der Industriellen and the Verband deutscher Industriellen pushed to have their own delegate in General Headquarters to prevent settlement on low terms. See Deist, 1/I, no. 83, p. 200. Hugenberg, of the Krupps concern, agitated on numerous occasions for high war aims on the grounds that the people had to be distracted from their demands for internal reforms. See Klein et al., p. 391; Thieme, pp. 65–66; Zechlin, "Friedensbestrebungen und Revolutionsversuche," B 20/61, pp. 271–72.

[133] Count Hertling, the Bavarian Prime Minister, for example, warned Bethmann Hollweg in a letter of 28 March 1915 that a disappointing peace would endanger the monarchy and especially the position of the Kaiser. See Zechlin, "Friedensbestrebungen und Revolutionsversuche," B 22/63, p. 26, note 16. Farrar also notes that the "Pan-Germans were among the first to recognize and articulate a relationship between war aims and prewar political conflicts." Apparently the Conservative leader Count Westarp also warned that the (unacceptable) alternative to achieving extensive war aims was domestic political reform (The Short-War Illusion, p. 44, see also p. 50). For the warnings of the conservatives that an insufficient peace would endanger the monarchy and the political system, see Gatzke, p. 22. Throughout his book Gatzke gives numerous examples of similar warnings of beneficiaries of the old order. See also Stevenson, The First World War and International Politics, p. 101.

together with all other dynasties—would be put into question. . . . Then the revolution [will be] only a question of time."[134] He warned that, without reparations, taxes would have to rise permanently, and the returning soldiers would be left with nothing but higher taxes for all their sacrifices. Even the Kaiser himself, at the end of November 1915, told Austro-Hungarian leaders that the returning soldiers would have to be bought off, and he claimed to be prepared to do so.[135] The Kaiser and conservative forces hoped that victory and the gains of the war would result in a political shift to the right.[136] In support of their hopes they could point to the domestic consequences of the victory in the Franco-Prussian War.[137]

The conservative forces warned that the gains from the war had to outweigh the costs to prevent domestic troubles; hence, as the costs of the war increased, so, too, would war aims have to increase.[138] Very much along these lines, the Centrist Deputy Herold declared in January 1916 in the Prussian Landtag that, although prevented from discussing war aims by the censorship laws, he nevertheless wanted to say that the longer the war lasted, the more demands would be included in the war aims.[139] The leader of the Center, Groeber, also demanded higher war aims to cover the additional costs of war when the peace offensive of December 1916 failed. In a speech in the Reichstag in late January 1917 he said, "Still a few words regarding peace aims. The world has recently heard about our offers of peace. We take the

---

[134] Deist, *Militär und Innenpolitik*, I/I, no. 105, pp. 244–46.

[135] Scherer and Grunewald, vol. 1, no. 170, pp. 227–29.

[136] See Deist, *Militär und Innenpolitik*, 1/I, p. 206, no. 87, a report, dated 27 October 1914 of Captain Hopman to the Imperial Navy Command about opinions in General Headquarters regarding reforms of the Prussian electoral system. Hopman notes: "Admiral von Müller remarked that he agreed with von Schulze-Gaevernitz's standpoint (necessity of the common franchise in Prussia). Regrettably those in the Emperor's entourage are of a different opinion and they hope that the consequences of the war in internal politics would be a swing to the right." Hopman added in a footnote "[t]he Chancellor certainly does not share this last opinion and he has said that he would not take part in such a policy." See also Bethmann Hollweg, *Betrachtungen* (1989), p. 240; and Deist, *Militär und Innenpolitik*, 1/I, p. 275, note 15: "Loebell [Prussian Minister of the Interior (Königlichen Staatsminister und Minister des Innern)] was on the other hand of the opinion that Social Democracy, since it had not been the 'Bearer of the National Ideal,' potentially would have to accept a substantial loss of votes after the war."

[137] Craig, p. 8.

[138] Zechlin, "Friedensbestrebungen und Revolutionsversuche," B 20/61, pp. 271–72; Deist, *Militär und Innenpolitik*, 1/I, no. 105, p. 245, no. 159, pp. 392–93, both reports of the Stellvertretende Generalkommandos to Bethmann Hollweg and the Prussian War Ministry; Gatzke, pp. 26–28, pp. 126–29. Scherer and Grunewald, vol. 2, 1966; no. 113, p. 191: Kaiser Wilhelm II to Kaiser Karl I, 11 May 1917.

[139] Dahlin, p. 72.

stand that our former overtures of peace can no longer be considered. The continuance of the war has required such tremendous sacrifices that we must increase our demands."[140]

On the other side of the political spectrum demands for rewards were no less loud. The Left, however, urged electoral reform in Prussia. The New Fatherland Society, for example, warned in 1915 that "the people must be rewarded for their sacrifices" but instead of territorial gains demanded political reforms.[141] Similarly, in 1914 "Eduard David, a moderate Socialist, warned Imperial Minister of the Interior [Clemens] Delbrück, that 'a chasm will be created between the people [and the government] which will not be bridged for decades' if the Socialist soldier was not rewarded with reforms for his support of the war."[142] Not just the Socialists but also Bethmann Hollweg hoped to reward the people by domestic political reforms, specifically a democratization of the political system.[143] I do not intend to argue here that Bethmann Hollweg had socialist sympathies, but merely that he hoped to follow a middle course between the two extremes (his "new orientation" and "politics of the diagonal"): some reform and moderate war aims.[144] The crucial difference between the conservative elements and Bethmann Hollweg was that Bethmann believed that reforms would be necessary, even if Germany managed to "win" the war.[145] As he noted in his memoirs,

That a defeat at minimum would threaten the old foundations of the State, endanger if not overthrow the privileged position of the classes that hitherto carried the state, was clear. But even the most complete victory

---

[140] Quoted in Hanssen, p. 165.

[141] Dahlin, pp. 53–54; see also Farrar, *The Short-War Illusion*, p. 144.

[142] Farrar, *The Short-War Illusion*, p. 40.

[143] Already at the end of August 1914 the Socialist Deputy David forewarned the Prussian Minister of the Interior that political reforms were needed after the war to reward the people for their sacrifices in the war. David hinted at the threat of domestic internal unrest if the government failed to produce such reforms. See Zechlin, "Friedensbestrebungen und Revolutionsversuche," B 20/63, p. 46, Delbrück to Bethmann Hollweg, 13 September 1914. Bethmann Hollweg and Delbrück both believed in the necessity of political reforms and hoped initially that such reforms could be postponed until after the war. See Hanssen, p. 87; Bethmann Hollweg, *Betrachtungen* (1989), p. 29, in the introduction by Jost Dülfer; pp. 235–37.

[144] See Farrar, *The Short-War Illusion*, pp. 42–43, 145–47; Birnbaum, pp. 145–46.

[145] Bethmann Hollweg, p. 169. Also see Bethmann's letter to Valentini of 9 December 1915 where he argues: "The framework in which we will have to conduct our governmental affairs after the war is already determined and cannot be fundamentally affected by a more or less fortunate design of the conclusion of the peace" (quoted in Deist, 1/I, p. 272, no. 119). Bethmann's advocacy for reforms did not constitute a sudden change of heart. Already as Vice Chancellor in 1907 Bethmann had persuaded the Kaiser that some sort of electoral reform was necessary. See Craig, p. 281.

should lead to the influence of the lower classes on the state, their cooperation and shared responsibility. Upon their return from this war, victorious
solders cannot be denied the removal of a state of affairs they perceive as
political degradation. But even those who denied this, for whom internal
reform was not a matter of political conviction, but only a question of tactics, could not fail to notice that neuorientierung was a necessity of war.[146]

Bethmann's support for reforms was thus not ideologically inspired,
as it was for the Socialists, but the acknowledgement of necessity.[147]
He never favored parliamentary government during the war and only
supported the equal franchise for Prussia under the pressure of events
shortly before the Russian Revolution. Initially, Bethmann hoped to appease the populace with much more modest reforms.[148] He argued that
after the war, the Monarchy should "voluntarily and joyfully" give the
returning soldiers and the brave people increased rights and so turn
them into new supporters of the state: "Then also the unavoidable,
heavy internal battles with the existing bearers of the parliamentary
power in Prussia and their supporters at the Court and in the Army
could be fought out without danger for the state."[149] However, by 1917
Bethmann Hollweg argued that the longer the war lasted and the
greater the sacrifice, the more internal concessions would have to be
made.[150] This, of course, stood in sharp contrast with the conservatives,
who intended to cover the rising costs of the war with higher war aims.
Thus, the failure of Bethmann Hollweg's policy of neuorientierung and
his ouster from the chancellorship in July 1917 constituted an important victory for the conservatives.[151]

---

[146] Bethmann Hollweg, Betrachtungen (1989), p. 169.

[147] In October 1914 Bethmann agreed that if peace was not concluded within five
months, doubts and bitterness would spread, and then Liebknecht, a Socialist leader,
would have an easier job winning over the populace (Janssen, Der Kanzler und der General, p. 53, footnote 18).

[148] See Bethmann Hollweg, Betrachtungen (1989), introduction by Jost Dülfer, p. 30.

[149] Bethmann Hollweg, Betrachtungen (1989), p. 235.

[150] Deist, Militär und Innenpolitik, 1/II, p. 694, no. 272, telegram Reichskanzlers an Le-
gationsrat Freiherr v. Grünau betr. die Rückwirkungen der russischen Revolution auf
die Politik der "Neuorientierung" of 28 March 1917; see also Dahlin, pp. 63–64.

[151] Bethmann Hollweg had been warned early in the war of a danger of conservative
reaction if the government granted the Socialists' demand for reform. See Farrar, The
Short-War Illusion, p. 41. For the fight over neuorientierung, see Ritter, The Sword and the
Scepter, vol. 3, pp. 188, 205–6, 209, 283, 290–93, vol. 4, pp. 96–100; Müller, pp. 183, 206,
234, 289, 304; Janssen, Der Kanzler und der General, pp. 85, 94, 173, 215, 243, 291–92; Bethmann Hollweg, Betrachtungen (1989), pp. 175–76, 226, 487; Craig, pp. 368, 374, 380, 390;
Deist, Militär und Innenpolitik, 1/I, pp. LXIV–LXVI, LII–LIII, 1/II, p. 783; Stephen Bailey,
pp. 33, 39–40, 45, 101, 122; Gatzke, pp. 191–92, 281, 287; Knesebeck, pp. 163–65; Hanssen,
pp. 152–56, 255. Bethmann Hollweg wrote in 1921: "Partisanship for large war aims and

However, while he recognized the necessity of some reforms, Beth-mann also noted in March 1915 that Germany would need a peace "which would be felt and recognized by the German people as a full compensation for the colossal sacrifices made."[152] Bethmann Hollweg thus also favored moderately high war aims, but because he hoped to buy off the people partially with domestic reform, Bethmann was willing to settle for much lower war aims than the anti-reform conservatives. In contrast to Fritz Fischer's arguments, therefore, Bethmann Hollweg's war aims, for example, were much lower than the war aims of the anti-reform Hindenburg and Ludendorff.[153]

The crux of any political reforms dealt with Prussia's extraordinary position in the empire and specifically its electoral laws.[154] As outlined above, Prussia's position in the Reich enabled the conservative Prussian forces to thwart any constitutional reforms and maintain a large measure of control over domestic society. Small wonder, then, that the arguments for political reforms centered around the Prussian electoral laws and parliamentary government. It should be noted, however, that Prussia did not stand alone in its battle against reforms: In Bavaria, Württemberg, and Saxony conservative forces opposed similar electoral reforms just as vehemently.[155] The probably frankest admission

---

opposition against the so-called Neuorientierung usually went hand in hand" (quoted in Gatzke, p. 1). Georg Bernhard of the *Vossische Zeitung* wrote: "There can be no doubt that a large number of the attacks upon the Chancellor's alleged attitude towards the question of peace are made from motives of internal policy.... Doubtless those, who view a change of the existing forces in domestic policy with alarm, often use foreign policy as a pretext to vent their anger on him." The banker Paul von Schwabach wrote to a friend in July 1916: "They speak of peace terms and they really mean the Prussian franchise." Both quotations are in Gatzke, p. 130; see also Gatzke, p. 173; Direnberger, p. 70; Deist, *Militär und Innenpolitik*, 1/I, pp. 406–13, no. 165; Dahlin, pp. 142–43.

[152] Quoted in Fischer, *Griff nach der Weltmacht*, p. 228. Farrar concludes that Bethmann concluded early on that the anticipated postwar domestic political problems could "certainly not be resolved by a return to principles" rooted in the past. According to Farrar, Bethmann thought that "Partisan politics in the sense of a process of resolving domestic differences would be unnecessary because Germany's increased power would allow it to satisfy all parties and thus resolve all political problems" (*The Short-War Illusion*, pp. 42–43).

[153] Compare Bethmann's war aims as presented to the Prussian Cabinet on 27 October and 30–31 October 1916, in Ritter, *The Sword and the Scepter*, vol. 3, pp. 277–78, with his list of war aims sent to Hindenburg on 4 November 1916, in Scherer and Grunewald, no. 361, p. 542, and with Hindenburg's reply of 5 November 1916, in Scherer and Grunewald, no. 365, pp. 548–49. The aims presented to the Prussian Cabinet most likely represent his true aims, while the later list sent to Hindenburg must have anticipated Hindenburg's and Ludendorff's reactions. See also Müller, p. 215. On the majority Socialists see Gatzke, p. 185.

[154] Bethmann Hollweg, *Betrachtungen* (1989), pp. 235–37.

[155] Dahlin, p. 92.

that the German leadership feared such domestic political reforms more than anything comes from Ludendorff, who played a leading role against reforms and, by extension, favored high war aims after he became First Quartermaster General at the end of August 1916. On the first day of the last year of the war, Ludendorff wrote a letter to Alexander Wynecken, editor of the *Königsberger Allgemeine Zeitung*, with whom Ludendorff had privately corresponded for a number of years. Ludendorff wrote, "I always hope that the [equal] franchise in Prussia falls through. If I did not have this hope, I would recommend any peace. With the [equal] franchise we cannot live. . . . Let the disturbances come. Rather an end with terror than a terror without end. . . . *It would be worse than a lost war.*"[156]

I have argued that Germany's war aims, as well as the increase in war aims during 1916, were designed to cover the costs of the war and buy off the populace.[157] In this section I therefore examine how Germany's war aims could be used to buy off the people. First, the annexed territories would be used for colonization by "reliable" Germans. In Germany's demands in the east, as Fischer notes, "settlement and resettlement [of the current population] stood in the center of all plans regarding the border strips."[158] In this regard the Polish Frontier Strip deserves special attention, because it became official policy that this "Strip was to be settled with nationally reliable German elements,"[159] as was Courland.[160] The German and Prussian Ministries of the Interior became officially involved with settlement plans in the summer of 1916.[161] Similar plans for settlement and colonization were proposed for annexations in the west. In his famous memorandum of September 1914, Bethmann Hollweg noted with approval the Kaiser's plan to reward "deserving noncommissioned officers and troops" in the form of land grants and settlement of the territories to be annexed from Belgium and France.[162]

Second, the conservative forces worried about the postwar consequences of the enormous financial costs of the war. Higher taxes to pay for these costs would almost certainly lead to domestic unrest. These

---

[156] Knesebeck, pp. 164–65, emphasis added. Similarly, Ludendorff warned the Austrian Foreign Minister Czernin on 5 February 1918: "If Germany makes peace without profit, then Germany has lost the war" (quoted in Ikle, p. 82).

[157] Ludendorff hoped to reward the returning soldiers with cheaper housing; see Knesebeck, p. 163.

[158] Fischer, *Griff nach der Weltmacht*, p. 341; see also Müller, p. 122, diary entry of 11 August 1915.

[159] Fischer, *Germany's Aims in the First World War*, p. 271.

[160] Fischer, *Griff nach der Weltmacht*, pp. 345–51.

[161] Ibid., p. 349.

[162] Basler, p. 382.

fears were echoed by Pan-Germans, National Liberals, Conservatives, Foreign Minister Jagow, and even the Kaiser himself.[163] Higher taxes could only be avoided by shifting the costs of the war onto Germany's enemies. Germany's demands therefore included war indemnities. (Recall the demand to increase Belgium's "contributions" from 40 to 50 million marks.) Third, a strengthened economy would ensure economic prosperity and higher wages for the working classes. This strengthened economy would be the result of the famous *Mitteleuropa* plan for a large economic trading bloc and preferential economic agreements. The hope of the conservative forces that the working class could be bought off by annexations and war reparations was not unfounded. Significant parts of the working class agreed with war aims that included the acquisition of land for settlement and a war indemnity. For example, one association of workers organizations demanded "a peace which will guarantee an indemnity for the sacrifices imposed by the enemy and . . . which will offer the working population the opportunity of a secure livelihood and unhindered development."[164]

In conclusion, Germany's increased territorial demands at the end of 1916, such as the additional land demanded from Poland, were intended to reward the populace in the form of land grants and settlements. Other demands, such as increased economic penetration of Poland and Austria-Hungary, the treaty of commerce with Russia, the exploitation of Belgian mineral resources, and compensations for German losses in other countries, were intended to prevent higher postwar taxes and, through a stronger economy, improved wages.

A Competing Explanation: OHL and High War Aims

In this section I briefly examine a competing explanation for Germany's high war aims at the end of 1916 and analyze the change in the Supreme Command of August 1916, the replacement of Falkenhayn by Hindenburg and Ludendorff. It could be argued that Hindenburg and particularly Ludendorff were in large part responsible for Germany's high war aims at the end of 1916, and, therefore, the increase in German war aims could be attributed to a shift to more extremist leadership rather than the nature of the regime.[165] However, this begs the

---

[163] Dahlin, pp. 101–2; Deist, *Militär und Innenpolitik*, 1/I, no. 105, pp. 244–46; Thieme, p. 54; Janssen, *Der Kanzler und der General*, p. 281; Gatzke, pp. 26–28; Scherer and Grunewald, vol. 2, no. 113, p. 191.

[164] Quoted in Gatzke, pp. 202–3; see also p. 19.

[165] It is important to note that the increase in Germany's war aims during 1916 cannot simply be explained by any alleged greater optimism on the part of Hindenburg and

question why these "extremists" were allowed to take over this position of leadership. I will argue that the change in the Supreme Command was explicitly intended to make it possible for the regime to accept lower war aims and make peace. The regime hoped that Hindenburg's prestige and popularity would convince the people if he said that a "meager peace" was the best that could be attained. With Hindenburg's signature under such a peace, they thought, the chances for a violent overthrow of the old regime would be minimized. Thus, with Hindenburg at the head of Germany's armed forces, Germany's minimum demands could be lower than under Falkenhayn. The change in command, therefore, must be understood as an insurance policy for the regime. Given any set of terms of settlement, the regime would have a higher probability of surviving in power with Hindenburg and Ludendorff than with Falkenhayn in command. The appointment of Hindenburg and Ludendorff thus shows the regime would have liked to adjust its war aims as a democracy, if they thought they could survive doing so.

The proximate cause of Falkenhayn's removal was Rumania's declaration of war on 27 August 1916. However, long before that, Ludendorff and Bethmann Hollweg had argued strongly for the replacement of Falkenhayn by Hindenburg. Bethmann was convinced that the only way to prevent a revolutionary overthrow of the old order was to have Hindenburg with his enormous prestige and popularity as the victor of Tannenberg and the Masurian Lakes at the head of Germany's armed forces. If Hindenburg told the people this was the best peace to be had, they would believe him and accept it.[166]

In June 1916, after the Brusilov offensive, Bethmann expressed his pessimism about Germany's chances to Valentini, the chief of the Kaiser's Civil Cabinet.[167] Less than two weeks later, 23 June 1916, in a letter

---

Ludendorff than had previously prevailed with Falkenhayn as Chief of Staff. Ludendorff admitted, once called to command, that the situation on the Western Front was much worse than he had previously thought. Moreover, as a product of the General Staff system, it is unlikely that Ludendorff's expectations would be so different from Falkenhayn's. See Ludendorff, *Meine Kriegserinnerungen*, pp. 187ff. Ludendorff's war aims increased during the rest of the war with the costs of the war, until they went down in the fall of 1918. Thus, in terms of the theory, his increase in war aims in 1916 is consistent with the subsequent instances of reformulations of Germany's war aims.

[166] Bethmann Hollweg argued in his memoirs: "But also only with Hindenburg as leader and with his consent would Germany have accepted a meager peace" (Bethmann Hollweg, *Betrachtungen* (1989), p. 175). See also Janssen, *Der Kanzler und der General*, pp. 243–44, and Ritter, *The Sword and the Scepter*, vol. 3, p. 205, who explicitly agree with this interpretation. Fischer disagrees. For a convincing argument against Fisher's position on this issue, see Janssen, *Der Kanzler und der General*, pp. 243–44.

[167] Janssen, *Der Kanzler und der General*, p. 210.

to the chief of the Kaiser's Army Cabinet that was, of course, to go on to the Kaiser, Bethmann explained in plain language why Hindenburg should replace Falkenhayn:

> The name Hindenburg is the terror of our enemies and electrifies our army and our people, who have boundless faith in him. I view our situation gravely. Our manpower resources are not inexhaustible, and the mood of the people is depressed by food shortages and the way the war drags on. But even should we lose a battle, God forbid, our people would accept such a setback under Hindenburg's leadership, as they would any peace over his name. If this is not done, the duration of the war and its changing fortunes will be chalked up against the Kaiser by the people.[168]

Not only Bethmann argued for Hindenburg on these grounds. Center Deputy Erzberger had warned, "With Hindenburg [at the head of the army] the Kaiser could even lose the war, then he would have done everything possible. Losing the war without Hindenburg means ruin for the Dynasty."[169] This general political sentiment also found expression in a letter of 29 May 1916 by the Württemberger ambassador to his Minister President, Weiszäcker:

> Even if we were to succeed in wearing down the French army at Verdun without too heavy losses on our own side, to defeat the to be expected Russian offensive and so to come to a peace, then its conditions will probably remain far behind the expectations of the nation and will only be accepted with resignation when they were convinced that the Army leadership was not at fault. This belief can only Hindenburg give them. . . . What is at stake is not the "Kommandogewalt" but the Dynasty.[170]

In retrospect the change from Falkenhayn to Hindenburg and Ludendorff cost Bethmann dearly. The duo made short shrift of his hopes to make the peace for which he needed Hindenburg's name and prestige. But what did the situation look like at the time? The crucial question for Bethmann was whether fighting on with Falkenhayn would be better or worse than a chance at peace with Hindenburg and Ludendorff.

Three main reasons explain Bethmann Hollweg's choice. First, Falkenhayn had changed his position from 1915 and now argued strongly

---

[168] Cited from the English translation of Ritter, *The Sword and the Scepter*, vol. 3, pp. 188–89. In this English edition the crucial "jeden Frieden" is mistranslated as "a peace." The correct translation reads "any peace." See for the original German Janssen, *Der Kanzler und der General*, pp. 215–16. In July Bethmann Hollweg again made the connection between Hindenburg's position and the survival of the Hohenzollern Dynasty (Müller, p. 206, diary entry of 26 July 1916).

[169] Müller, pp. 283–84.

[170] Quoted in Janssen, *Der Kanzler und der General*, pp. 291–93.

in favor of unrestricted submarine warfare, which was indeed launched for a short period at the beginning of the year. Bethmann Hollweg saw unrestricted submarine warfare as a desperate gamble, sure to bring the United States into the war and maybe even some of the other neutral nations such as Holland and Denmark, and squashing all hopes for a compromise peace.[171] In contrast, in the spring of 1916 Ludendorff was on record as opposing unrestricted submarine warfare.[172] Craig argues that when Falkenhayn switched his position to throw his support behind submarine warfare, Bethmann decided he had to go.[173]

Second, Bethmann had hoped that Hindenburg and Ludendorff would not be extremist in their war aims. From a conversation with Hindenburg in mid-1915, Bethmann Hollweg had come away strongly impressed with their opposition to the Pan-German extreme annexationist schemes.[174] At the time it looked as if Falkenhayn would demand higher war aims. Falkenhayn had insisted on the Flemish coast, while Hindenburg argued only for possession of Liège.[175] Third, Bethmann considered Falkenhayn a gambler who had cost Germany dearly at Verdun.[176]

Finally, it deserves notice that it was not only the conservative and annexationist forces in German society that wanted to see Hindenburg in command. All forces with their contradictory expectations and hopes could at least agree on the need for Hindenburg.[177]

During previous attempts to remove Falkenhayn Wilhelm II had stood by his chief of staff. Why did he change his mind? The Kaiser was fully conscious of the power Hindenburg and Ludendorff would

[171] Müller, pp. 146–47, diary entry of 11 January 1916.

[172] Craig, p. 369. Ludendorff writes in his memoirs that he and Hindenburg "had both spoken against the proposal for unrestricted [submarine] warfare on the 30th August" (Ludendorff, *My War Memories*, vol. 1, p. 312). On the next page he argues that at least until October Bethmann Hollweg believed that he, Ludendorff, opposed unrestricted submarine warfare. See also Knesebeck, p. 156, where Ludendorff writes in a letter in the beginning of March 1916: "I am so unclear about the U-boat question that I can not make a judgment. In any case it seems good to me that Bethmann stays." See also Birnbaum, pp. 178–79.

[173] Craig, pp. 368–69.

[174] See Bethmann Hollweg's letter to Valentini of 12 March 1915 in Zechlin, "Friedensbestrebungen und Revolutionsversuche," B 22/63, pp. 46–47.

[175] See Gatzke, p. 81; Craig, p. 363; Ritter, *The Sword and the Scepter*, vol. 3, p. 278; and Craig, p. 368. Bethmann Hollweg argued against an annexation of the Flemish coast on 7 April 1915, basing his position on Ludendorff's judgement that the possession of Liège would suffice. See Zechlin, "Friedensbestrebungen und Revolutionsversuche," B 20/63, p. 7.

[176] Ritter, *The Sword and the Scepter*, vol. 3, p. 182.

[177] Deist, *Militär und Innenpolitik*, 1/I, pp. LII, LXI.

command once appointed to the OHL. He compared their appointment to his de facto abdication.[178] He was, however, left no other option; all his advisors, his military Cabinet as well as his government officials, agreed that Falkenhayn had to go.[179] There seemed to be a general consensus that Falkenhayn had miscalculated one too many times. He was held responsible for the failures in Bukinowa and Verdun and had failed to correctly predict Rumania's declaration of war, which Falkenhayn had hoped would not occur for a while. In June the King of Bavaria had visited the Kaiser and apparently discussed the change.[180] The Bavarian Prime Minister had been convinced for a long time that the people would only believe Hindenburg if he were to say, "This and no more can be achieved."[181]

The Kaiser's already weak control over policy eroded even further when Paul von Hindenburg and Erich von Ludendorff took control of the Third High Command. The crucial step in this process took place when they took over from Falkenhayn, because the explicit reason that finally overcame the Kaiser's resistance was the argument that with Hindenburg the people would accept a "meager peace;" without Hindenburg such a peace would lead to revolution and the fall of the Hohenzollern Dynasty. However, the effect of a change from Falkenhayn to Hindenburg and Ludendorff should not be exaggerated. Falkenhayn had also wielded enormous power and had not been shy to use it. As Janssen points out, "the actual power of Falkenhayn was of no lesser magnitude than that of his successors."[182] Moreover, Falkenhayn had been a strong supporter of the conservatives. In February 1915 Dr. Ernst Jäckh, for example, remarked to Gustav Stresemann that "Falkenhayn was the hope of the German parties which are reactionary in matters of domestic politics."[183]

Conclusion

In this chapter I have analyzed how Germany's semirepressive and moderately exclusionary regime reacted to new unfavorable information when in 1916 they learned they would probably lose the war. I found that, as the theory predicts, German war aims rose with the costs

---

[178] Müller, p. 201.

[179] Deist, *Militär und Innenpolitik*, 1/I, p. LII.

[180] Müller, p. 196.

[181] Janssen, *Der Kanzler und der General*, pp. 93–94.

[182] Ibid., p. 166. See also Ritter, *The Sword and the Scepter*, vol. 3, pp. 80–82; Sweet, "Leaders and Policies," p. 249.

[183] Quoted in Sweet, "Leaders and Policies," p. 236.

of the war. Moreover, this increase in war aims was intended to buy off the people. These conclusions are shared by the majority of historians of Germany's war aims in the First World War. In this conclusion I briefly touch upon the fate of Germany's leaders and then turn to a historical argument about postwar Germany that, although not predicted by the theory, seems a natural extension.[184]

Although I focused in this chapter mostly on the elite and the beneficiaries of the old regime rather than on the individual leaders, it deserves notice that both the Kaiser and Ludendorff foresaw an awful personal fate if the war ended in a loss. As Colonel Bauer recalled, Ludendorff told him in the fall of 1918, "What the fatherland was now thinking about was not the war anymore, but his and the Emperor's head."[185] When the war finally ended on 11 November 1918, neither Kaiser William II nor Ludendorff was there to witness the end. Both had fled the country to avoid imprisonment or death at the hands of the Socialist revolutionaries. The Kaiser fled to the Netherlands, Ludendorff, in a false beard and a wig, to Norway.

The wartime dynamic between proponents of high war aims and reformers also played a very important role in postwar Weimar Germany. As Holger Herwig showed, after the war the beneficiaries of the old order went to great lengths to shift the blame of the defeat onto the shoulders of their old opponents, the Socialists. In a systematic campaign, the postwar government "sought to 'organize' materials in order to answer questions concerning the origins of the war."[186] One of the most (in)famous products of this campaign was the "stab-in-the-back" myth, the fundamentally flawed argument that the German army was never defeated but stabbed in the back by a disloyal homefront. Germany's "self-censors," in Herwig's phrase, selectively edited documentary collections, suppressed honest scholarship and subsidized pseudo-scholarship, underwrote massive propaganda, and over-

---

[184] As I argued in the theory chapter, in semirepressive, moderately exclusionary regimes the leadership can only continue the war as long as the people do not learn the true desperate state of affairs and likely unfavorable outcome of the war. Although it is clear that all countries tried to manipulate the flow of information about the war to the people, the Germans surely went the farthest in actually presenting a falsely optimistic picture. The institution of the *Kriegspresseamt* (war press bureau) in November 1915 was very valuable in this respect and went a long way to help control the information from the front back to the homeland. See Bethmann Hollweg, *Betrachtungen* (1989), p. 172; Farrar, *The Short-War Illusion*, pp. 48, 50, 133. Knightley's *The First Casualty* is a compelling book with many insights on the role of the media in war and the struggles and relationships between journalists on the one hand and politicians and soldiers on the other.

[185] Quoted in Bauer, p. 239.

[186] Herwig, p. 263.

saw the export of this propaganda to its former enemies. This campaign, as Herwig notes, was the natural outgrowth of the elite's attempt to avoid punishment by their former enemies:

> Unsurprisingly, some of the self-censors were driven by reasons of personal interest. As Erich Hahn has suggested, the traditional elite of the Wilhelmstrasse fought for its political survival by defending its credibility—be it in 1914 or 1919—both at home and abroad. The war-guilt issue thus served its purpose much in the way that the "stab-in-the-back" legend served the army: as an escape from the political consequences of defeat. In other words, the consequences of the miscalculated risk of July 1914 could be avoided only by keeping the anti-war-guilt campaign alive after the peace. And since the Republic very much depended on the cooperation of former imperial officials, it naturally had an interest in establishing their "innocence." Yet the war-guilt game was dangerous because, as Karl Kautsky had put it in 1919, it was "not only a scholarly question for historians," but "an eminently practical question for politicians." For the authors of the war, the answer to the question of who was responsible amounted to a "death sentence" as they surely would be "cast among the politically dead . . . stripped of all power." It was to be part of the genius of the patriotic self-censors that they managed through their collective efforts at preemptive historiography to escape that "death sentence."[187]

This extension of the wartime dynamic into peacetime is perhaps not surprising, but it offers additional support for my theoretical claims since it integrates a new observation into the analysis. It is also one example where the case study method allows us to tease out implications and new observations that otherwise probably would go unrecognized.

---

[187] Ibid., pp. 298–99.

5

Russia

IN THIS CHAPTER I briefly examine how Russia changed its war aims during the war. Russia's tsarist regime qualifies as a semirepressive, moderately exclusionary regime because it clearly excluded the majority of the population from access to the political decision-making process and lacked—at minimum estimated it lacked—the ability to repress a revolution in case of another defeat in war. This chapter is short because the historical record on Russia's wartime experience is far less complete than for any of the other main belligerents. Therefore, it is much more difficult to assess the leadership's expectations about the outcome of the war and how these changed. This often makes it difficult to infer what would constitute new information and makes changes in Russian war aims more difficult to attribute to its regime type or changed expectations. It is fairly obvious, however, that many if not most of the military leaders were extremely poor learners. In the face of sometimes overwhelming evidence they refused to learn the lessons of the war and stuck to inappropriate strategies and tactics. Notwithstanding the problematic evidence, I conclude that Russia's leaders probably became more pessimistic in 1915 and perhaps also in 1916. Russia's war aims, however, probably increased in 1915 and probably did not change much during 1916.

In 1905, after Russia's defeat in the Russo-Japanese War, the Tsar was forced to make some significant political concessions and give a greater proportion of Russians a greater say to prevent a full-fledged revolution that his advisors told him could not be repressed.[1] However, after the so-called coup of 3 June 1907, the franchise was revised again. Peasant representation dropped from 35 to 19 percent in the Third Duma, worker representation decreased from 33 to 5 delegates, and the landed nobility increased its representation from 28 to 44 percent; non-Russians also lost much of their voice in the Third and Fourth Dumas. As a result of these reforms, most of the Russian population was excluded from access to national policy-making and "only about one 40th of the population voted for the Third Duma," which served until 1912.[2]

With the systematic exclusion of most of the population from access to the policy-making process, imperial Russia employed moderate re-

[1] Verner, pp. 20–23; Pipes, *The Russian Revolution*, p. 43; Hosking, p. 8.

[2] Lieven, *Nicholas II*, p. 187; MacKenzie, p. 71; Pipes, *The Russian Revolution*, pp. 180–81.

pression to keep control of the opposition. However, as Richard Pipes notes, by the beginning of the twentieth century Russia no longer was an effective police state. By the start of the First World War Russia had "a police force that was ubiquitous, meddlesome, and often brutal, but on the whole inefficient. The powers given to the political police were entirely out of proportion to the results achieved."[3]

Two specialized police forces supported the regime. The first, the Okrhana, the security police, specialized in counterintelligence; the second, the Gendarmes, was a paramilitary force to suppress urban disorder and control the railways. The Gendarmes were a relatively small force for a country with Russia's population. Between ten and fifteen thousand strong, this force was, of course, unable to repress massive unrest and disturbances in a general crisis. In those situations the government called in the regular army to help suppress disturbances. However, as William Fuller has shown, after the reforms of 1905 the army fought hard (and successfully) to get out of its internal repression role.[4] The inadequacy of government repression, meanwhile, was clearly shown by the government's inability to prevent new strikes from breaking out in the summer of 1914.[5]

The clearest recognition of the regime's weakness and an uncanny prediction of future developments, both military and political, can be found in a well-known memorandum of February 1914 to the Tsar by the ex-Minister of the Interior, and member of the State Council, Peter Durnovo. Durnovo's memorandum is one big, impassioned plea not to become embroiled in what he saw as the inevitable future war and contained a warning against any attempt to compromise with the middle classes because that would only enable the lower classes to stage

---

[3] Pipes, *Russia under the Old Regime*, p. 315; see esp. pp. 313–15.

[4] William Fuller, pp. 244–58. The civilians and particularly the Police Department agreed, in July 1913, "taking into account the insignificant quantity of troops now detailed to help the civilian powers, and also [taking into account] the fact that, as monthly reports of the Governors received by the Policy Department testify, the general mood of the population is calm, and there are no grounds to expect that a massive revolutionary movement will arise in the near future" (quoted on p. 256).

[5] Unfortunately we lack good statistics to assess the degree of repression before the war. We do know, however that at the height of the revolutionary terror of 1906–7, left-wing terrorists killed or maimed 4,500 officials. When we include private persons, the total death toll climbs to over 9,000. Against this terror the harshest repression of the early Stolypin ministry from August 1906 to April 1907, which introduced field courts for civilians, meted out only a thousand death sentences. In subsequent years, from 1908 to 1909 when political crimes once again were tried before ordinary courts, of those convicted for political crimes and armed assault, almost one-fifth of those convicted, 3,682 persons, were condemned to death. Although substantial, these numbers do not indicate particularly harsh and widespread repression. See Pipes, *The Russian Revolution*, pp. 70, 165; see also Rogger, p. 99.

TABLE 5.1

New Information and Changes in War Aims for Russia

Russia	New Information	Changes in War Aims
1914	*Unfavorable*: 27–30 Aug: Large defeat at Tannenberg. Nov–Dec: Munitions shortages. High casualties? Dec: Limanova; Lodz falls. *Favorable*: 30 Aug–15 Nov: Victories against Austria-Hungary in Galicia? Miracle on the Marne?	14 Sep–21 Nov *Decreases*: Holstein remains part of Germany. Annexation of Silesia only a possibility. No more reparations? Greater concessions to the Allies? *Increases*: Free passage through the Straits; Constantinople neutralized. Northern part of Bukovina. Not just eastern but all of Posen. Further weakening of Germany and Austria-Hungary?
1915	*Unfavorable*: May–Sept: Retreats in Poland? Sept–Oct: Bulgaria enters. Nov–Dec: Serbia defeated. *Favorable*: 23 May: Italy enters. Jan–Feb 1916: Successes in the Caucasus. Munition shortages appear solved.	21 Nov 1914–12 Mar 1916 *Decreases*: Mar: Neutral sphere in Persia a British sphere. 26 Apr: Italian demands—Istria, Dalmatia, and Adriatic—harm Serbia's strategic interests. *Increases*: 4 Mar: Constantinople and surroundings. 12 Mar 1916: Erzerum.
1916	*Unfavorable*: 18 Mar–April: Failure of the offensive at Lake Narotch; Sept–Dec: New Brusilov offensive; Rumanian defeat(?) Oct 1916-Feb 1917: Riots and food shortages in the cities. *Favorable*: Mar–Apr: Caucasus; Trebizond falls; 4 July–Oct: Brusilov offensive (?); Oct: Entente will have a massive superiority in 1917.	6 Mar 1916–15 Feb 1917 *Decreases*: 17 Aug: Treaty of Bucharest; concessions to the Rumanians in the Bukovina and Banat. *Increases*: Sept: Armenia Major to be annexed.

TABLE 5.1 (con't)

New Information and Changes in War Aims for Russia

Russia	New Information	Changes in War Aims
1917	*Unfavorable*: 19 July: Kornilov offensive fails, 19 July–Sept: German counteroffensives successful; Russians pushed back. 3 Sept: Riga falls. Summer–Fall: Drastic increase in desertions and mutinies. Oct–Nov: Increasing fraternization of Russian troops with the Germans. 15 Dec: Armistice signed with Germans, 18–23 Feb 1918: Germans renounce armistice, retake the offensive, advance at record speed.	15 Feb 1917–3 Mar 1918 *Decreases*: 19 Oct: Poland granted unconditional independence. 24 Feb 1918: Any terms as long as they kept the Bolsheviks in power now acceptable.

Notes: Question marks indicate the uncertain status of new information and/or a change in war aims. For Russia's full war aims see chapter 8.

a revolt. Durnovo warned: "If the war ends in victory, the putting down of the Socialist movement will not offer any insurmountable obstacles. . . . But in the event of defeat, the possibility of which in a struggle with a foe like Germany cannot be overlooked, social revolution in its most extreme form is inevitable."[6]

As an ex-Minister of the Interior, Durnovo's estimates about the consequences of defeat were likely shared by many of his former colleagues. Both the strongest personality in the Council of Ministers, the Minister of Agriculture Krivoshein, and the current Minister of the Interior Maklakov explicitly warned their colleagues on the eve of the war of the potential for a repetition of the consequences of the Russo-Japanese War.[7] Especially in Russia, defeat in war would seriously threaten the regime. After all, as Lieven notes,

> The régime had always derived a major part of its legitimacy from its claim that the autocracy alone had been capable of creating a Great Russia and ensuring that the empire was respected and accepted as an equal by the leading European powers. Humiliation in foreign policy thus struck directly at the régime's *raison d'être*. . . . Moreover, . . . any weakness revealed by failures in foreign policy was sure to have unpleasant implications for a régime whose ability to maintain control within Russia depended in part on its reputation for strength and invincibility.[8]

In conclusion, the prewar Russian regime clearly excluded large groups from access to the policy-making process. Based partially on their experience after defeat in the Russo-Japanese War and the revolution of 1905, the regime estimated they could not effectively repress the opposition if the lower and middle classes joined in a revolt. Hence, Russia qualifies as a semirepressive, moderately exclusionary regime.

Overview of the War

To provide a quick overview of the war, table 5.1 summarizes the evidence on the intervening and dependent variables, new information, and changes in war aims for 1914, 1915, 1916, and 1917. I briefly reca-

---

[6] The Durnovo Memorandum is reprinted in Riha, pp. 465–78.

[7] When brought the mobilization order to sign, Maklakov further admitted that "War cannot be popular among the broad masses of the people who are more receptive to ideas of revolution than of victory over Germany" (quoted in Rogger, pp. 109–10). For Krivoshein's statement in the Council of Ministers of 24 July, see Lieven, *Russia and the Origins of the First World War*, p. 143.

[8] Lieven, *Russia and the Origins of the First World War*, pp. 53–54.

pitulate for each year whether the unfavorable new information outweighed the favorable new information and whether war aims overall decreased or increased.

Although Russia's initial expectations about the war are open to dispute, it seems that between late September and late November 1914 the leadership did not change its expectations much but probably became slightly more pessimistic.[9] The demand for free passage through the Straits in particular meant that Russia's war aims increased in this period.[10] Although Russian leaders surely increased their estimates of the expected costs of war during 1915, many generals apparently remained blithely optimistic about Russia's relative strength, largely because they had become much more optimistic about the munitions problem. However, Chief of Staff Alexeiev seems to have been more realistic and lowered his estimate of Russia's relative strength.[11] In all, between November 1914 and March 1915 the leadership must have become more pessimistic. In this period, nevertheless, Russia's war aims increased substantially because of the new demand for Constantinople and its surroundings.[12]

During 1916 the Russian leadership probably became more pessimistic about the costs of the war and about the people's cost tolerance. Although the failure of the offensive at Lake Narotch made the leadership more pessimistic about Russia's relative strength, by early 1917 they were nevertheless relatively optimistic about the prospects for victory in the coming year.[13] Whether this was due to the promises and confidence of their allies or to renewed faith in their own strength is

[9] Much of the secondary literature asserts that Russian leaders expected the war to be short and victorious. Knox, vol. 1, p. xxxii; Lieven, *Russia and the Origins of the First World War*, pp. 108, 133, 186. However, significant secondary and primary sources indicate that the foremost military and political leaders were often much less sanguine about Russia's relative strength and the duration of the war. See Lieven, *Nicholas II*, pp. 199, 205; Daniloff, p. 320; and especially de Basily, pp. 96–97; see also Snyder, *The Ideology of the Offensive*, pp. 157–64. Pokrowski, *Die Internationalen Beziehungen im Zeitalter des Imperialismus* (hereafter *IBZI*), II. Reihe, 6. Band 2, Halbband, no. 476, p. 416, no. 555, pp. 475–76; Linke, p. 40; Stone.

[10] On Russia's war aims in 1914, see Dallin, "The Future of Poland," pp. 7–8; Dallin, *Russian Diplomacy*, p. 131; Smith Jr., "Legacy to Stalin," pp. 5–15, 59–73, 121–31; *IBZI*, II, 6, 1, no. 318, pp. 243–44, no. 256, pp. 193–94, no. 318, p. 244, no. 546, pp. 468–69; *IBZI*, II, 6, 2, no. 484, p. 422, no. 506, p. 441, no. 500, p. 436. Linke, pp. 43–44, 184.

[11] Stone, *The Eastern Front*, pp. 212, 227; Lieven, *Nicholas II*, p. 217; Knox, vol. 1, p. 364, vol. 2, p. 395. For Alexeiev's pessimism, see Knox, vol. 2, p. 387. See also Cherniavsky, pp. 36, 103.

[12] Smith Jr., "Legacy to Stalin," pp. 553–54, 591; Linke, pp. 55–56, 199, 220.

[13] Stone, pp. 227–41, 270–74, 282, 545–49; Knox, vol. 2, p. 495, 544, 551–52; Vulliamy, pp. 157, 216, 263–64; Gourko, pp. 262–69, 298; Linke, p. 119.

unfortunately impossible to discern. War aims, however, probably increased somewhat.[14] During 1917 the Russian leaders became dramatically more pessimistic about the people's cost tolerance and Russia's relative strength. The people, moreover, had lost all faith in the old regime and the army leadership. Popular discontent and lack of faith in victory produced two revolutions; the second revolution brought Lenin and the Bolsheviks to power. Realizing that a continuation of the war would only increase the chances they would lose power at home, the Bolsheviks lowered their war aims and accepted the harsh terms of Brest-Litovsk. Chapter 8 takes up a detailed analysis of 1917.

The Causal Mechanism: The Domestic Consequences of the Terms of Settlement

Although much less evidence is available, it seems that Russia's leaders, like Germany's, formulated war aims to cover the costs of the war and buy off the domestic opposition to forestall a postdefeat revolution. Two of the foremost scholars on the military and diplomatic aspects of Russia's participation in the First World War, Norman Stone and Horst Günther Linke, respectively, both argue that Russian leaders recognized that a peace that failed to reward the Russian people for their sacrifices would surely lead to a revolution. Stone argues:

> There seems to have been very little thought, in circles that mattered, of a separate peace with the Germans, and peace-feelers never went beyond surreptitious and insincere conversations, although the Germans kept trying for more. On the contrary, Russian war aims went up, parallel with the sacrifices being demanded of the people; and ministers feared that the whole system would be overthrown if they did not offer satisfaction to the national aspirations.[15]

Linke similarly has concluded: "it had to appear questionable whether the autocratic regime, which could not and would not politically cooperate with the bourgeoisie nor offer social reforms for the workers and farmers, could survive the internal pressures, which in spite of the people's hankering for peace, would result from a victoryless end to the war."[16]

---

[14] Linke, pp. 55–57, 240, 224; Dallin, "The Future of Poland," pp. 30, 72; Gourko, pp. 399–410, see also pp. 248–49; Smith Jr., "Legacy to Stalin," pp. 12–13; Smith Jr., *The Russian Struggle for Power, 1914–1917*, pp. 363–82, 420–24; Abrash, p. 119.

[15] Stone, p. 218.

[16] Linke, p. 243, see also p. 237. See also Farrar, *The Short-War Illusion*, pp. 122–23.

There exists some credible evidence that the Tsar recognized that a meager peace would lead to revolution. On 27 June 1915 the Tsaritsa sent a letter to the Tsar, in which she recounts a conversation she had with Grand Duke Paul, the Tsar's only living uncle:

> Well to begin with, [French Ambassador to Russia] Paléolog[ue] dined with him [Grand Duke Paul] a few days ago & then they had a long private talk & the latter tried to find out from him, very cleverly, whether he knew if you had any ideas about forming a separate peace with Germany, as he heard such things being spoken about here, & as tho' in France one had got wind of it—& that there they intend fighting to the very end. Paul answered that he was convinced it was not true, all the more, as at the outset of the war we & our allies had settled, that peace could only be concluded together on no account separately. Then I told Paul that you had heard the same rumour about France; & he crossed himself when I said you were not dreaming of peace & knew it would mean revolution here & therefore the Germans are trying to egg it on.[17]

The Tsar replied two days later: "I thank you with all my heart for your sweet, long letter, in which you give me an account of your conversation with Paul. You gave perfectly correct answers on the questions of peace."[18] Zechlin notes that a year later, in mid-June 1916, both the Tsaritsa and the Tsar told Paléologue that Russia did not and could not entertain any thoughts about peace, specifically a separate peace with Germany, because that would bring about a revolution.[19]

The evidence is clear that at least as early as 1915 the leadership calculated they would not be able to maintain the regime and repress an attempted revolution if the war ended in even a moderate defeat.[20] Given their fears about imminent domestic unrest, the Council, reluctantly, explored their options. Many in the Council (always excluding Goremykin) felt that with the worsening military situation, a dramatic domestic political change was needed. The retreat and enormous losses of the spring and the summer brought increasing pressures from the Duma for domestic political reform. The ministers concluded that either the domestic moderate opposition would have to be bought off with political concessions and reform—some form of parliamentary

---

[17] Pares, *Letters of the Tsaritsa to the Tsar 1914–1916*, p. 93.

[18] Vulliamy, *The Letters of the Tsar to the Tsaritsa, 1914–1917*, p. 61.

[19] Zechlin, *Krieg und Kriegsrisiko*, p. 359.

[20] Cherniavsky, pp. 100–101, 128, 179, see also 163–65; Poincaré, vol. 7, pp. 103–4; Knox, vol. 1, p. 334. German and British leaders also recognized the danger of revolution in Russia in case of a defeat. See German Under-Secretary Jagow's draft of a letter from Bethmann-Hollweg to Falkenhayn in Janssen, *Der Kanzler und der General*, pp. 279–81, and French, *British Strategy and War Aims*, p. 167.

government—or there would have to be a dictatorship that would ruthlessly repress the unrest. As the Minister of Internal Affairs put it, "Either dictatorship or a policy of reconciliation is necessary. . . . Our duty is to tell the Emperor that, in order to save the State from the greatest perils, one must move either to the left or to the right. The internal situation of the country does not allow for continued sitting between two chairs."[21] One of the most astute and powerful members of the Council, the Minister of Agriculture A. V. Krivoshein, similarly declared in mid-August 1915: "We must tell His Majesty that the internal situation . . . allow[s] of only two solutions: either a strong military dictatorship, if one can find a suitable person, or reconciliation with the public."[22] But the notes of the Council of Ministers show that a majority of ministers was pessimistic about the regime's ability to institute any effective "strong military dictatorship."[23]

The more liberal ministers Krivoshein and Sazonov (and Grand Duke Nicholas) strongly favored "reconciliation with the public" and domestic political reforms, whereby the government would "open up an upward safety-valve."[24] However, Prime Minister Goremykin, Tsar Nicholas II, and especially Tsaritsa Alexandra strongly opposed any reforms. But the defeats in Poland in the spring and summer of 1915 enabled the reform-minded ministers to win a temporary and rather meager victory when the Council made a very cautious opening to the Progressive bloc in the Duma at the end of August 1915.[25] Such minimal progress was swept away when the majority of the ministers in favor of reform were dismissed in subsequent months after the worst dangers had subsided and the German advance had been brought to a halt in September.[26] There was to be neither reform nor full-blown dictatorship, no decisive movement to either the left or the right; the leadership continued to muddle through and be irrelevant to the great majority of Russians.

[21] Cherniavsky, pp. 157–58. The conservative Supreme Procurator of the Holy Synod, A. D. Samarin, was opposed to any concessions, believing they would inevitably lead to demands for still more concessions (pp. 163–64; see also p. 165).

[22] Cherniavsky, p. 142.

[23] Ibid., esp. p. 179. Lieven, *Nicholas II*, p. 211.

[24] Daniloff, pp. 173–74.

[25] Cherniavsky, pp. 163–65, 183–208.

[26] Pipes, *The Russian Revolution*, p. 227. Pipes notes that "as the days went by the crisis subsided because in September the German offensive ground to a halt, lifting the threat to the Russian homeland. Newspapers favorable to the Progressive Bloc now began to argue that everything possible had been done and there was no point in pressing the government further. At the end of September, the Central Committee of the Constitutional-Democratic Party, the core of the Progressive Bloc, decided to postpone further demands for political reform until the conclusion of the war."

By 1916 the writing on the wall was there for all to see. On 12 January Buchanan begged the Tsar to change his internal policies and grant a government responsible to the Duma "while there was yet time, pointing out the danger of a starving and exasperated capital."[27] More and more people, including several Grand Dukes, warned the Tsar about the dangers to his crown. Grand Duke Nicholas told the Tsar on 6 November: "Do you really not see, that you are on the point of losing the crown! Come to your senses at last, before it is too late! Give the country a responsible government!"[28] In some military and political circles plans were broached for a palace revolution. The Tsar and his wife would be forced to abdicate, the Tsarevitch would be the successor under a regent, and the Autocracy would be reformed into a democratic Monarchy. Rumors about such a coup received a favorable reception among the privileged classes, who saw this as the last opportunity to prevent a revolution from below and reinvigorate the people in favor of the war.[29] But the Tsar would not listen. The Tsaritsa in particular continued to urge him not to give in to the demands for a responsible Cabinet and a constitution.[30]

Without political reform, the regime was left with the only remaining alternative: war aims formulated to buy off the domestic opposition. The most important war aims that would buy off the people were a united Poland and especially Constantinople. For both the nationalists and Orthodox Russians, the gain of Constantinople would fulfill age-old dreams. Russia would finally gain a warm water port, and the Orthodox Cross would finally return to "Tsargrad," as they called Constantinople. The fulfillment of these dreams probably would suffice to buy off the domestic opposition. From very early on in the war, many voices called for the fulfillment of "the old Byzantine dream" whereby Russia would take control over "Tsargrad," the "cradle of the Orthodox faith."[31] As Paléologue recorded the sentiments of the Russian elite in his diary,

> This war will have no meaning for us unless it brings us Constantinople and the Straits. Tsargrad must be ours, and ours alone. Our historic mission and our holy duty is to set the cross of Pravoslaviye Orthodoxy, the cross of the Orthodox Faith, on the dome of Santa Sophia once more. Russia would not be the chosen nation if at long last she did not avenge the age-old wrongs of Christianity.

[27] Knox, vol. 3, p. 515.
[28] Daniloff, p. 250; see also p. 257; Linke, p. 125.
[29] Linke, p. 125. Knox, vol. 2, p. 517.
[30] Pares, *Letters of the Tsaritsa to the Tsar 1914–1916*, p. 453ff.
[31] Sazonov, *Fateful Years*, pp. 239–61.

According to Paléologue, these demands were echoed in political, religious, and university circles, "and even more in the obscure depths of the Russian conscience."[32] Around the demand for Constantinople almost all groups could rally: nationalists, liberals, the press, even the leader of the Kadets, Paul Miliukov, demanded that Russia seize the Straits and "Tsargrad."[33] Foreign Minister Sazonov foresaw that the "glamour of Tsargrad's name" and the fulfillment of the "age-long dream of Russia placing an Orthodox Cross on the cupola of Saint Sophia" would go a long way to buy off the opposition.[34] With the growing unrest in the capital and elsewhere toward the end of 1916, and with the western Allies' consent, the new Chairman of the Council Trepov announced the existence of the Straits Agreement to the Duma on 3 December 1916, in an attempt to pacify the opposition and forestall further unrest.

In another striking parallel with German plans to reward the people, the Russian Supreme Command hoped to reward its most suffering and most deserving soldiers with land grants at demobilization to prevent them from turning their arms against the regime and ruling classes. "The allotment," according to the demands by Stavka as relayed by A. V. Krivoshein, "should be not less than six to nine desiatins [between roughly 15 and 20 acres]. The allotments can be made from government land and the land of the Peasant Bank, but should primarily be from the confiscated estates of German colonists and enemy subjects."[35] Krivosein himself favored annexations in Armenia and the Caucasus for such purposes.[36]

Conclusion

In summary, we find (often indirect) evidence that the Russian leadership considered three options. First, they could continue the war. However, a choice to continue the war may have been the result of two very different, even diametrically opposed, chains of reasoning. On the one

---

[32] Quoted in Smith, "Legacy to Stalin," p. 349.

[33] MacKenzie, p. 108.

[34] See Sazonov, *Fateful Years*, p. 251. Smith Jr., "Legacy to Stalin," pp. 377, 390–91, 524–26.

[35] Cherniavsky, p. 22. According to Pipes, "Russian troops began to show signs of demoralization. To appease them General Ianushkevich unsuccessfully urged the government to issue a pledge that after victory every war veteran would receive twenty-five acres of land" (*The Russian Revolution*, p. 219). I am not sure whether this refers to the same demand, but it seems likely.

[36] Linke, pp. 211, 225.

hand, the leadership may have been relatively *optimistic* as they could, and apparently some did, hope that more shells and more Allied help would get them out of the mess they were in on the Eastern Front. On the other hand, the leadership may have been *pessimistic* about its prospects on the battlefield and may have chosen to continue the war because settlement on losing terms meant revolution. Especially for 1915, the evidence suggests that the leadership had become more pessimistic about the war.

The Russian leadership had two further alternatives. They could end the war on losing terms and try to *repress* the domestic unrest, or end the war on losing terms but beforehand open up the political system and *make concessions* to the domestic political opposition. The notes of the Council of Ministers make clear that during 1915 most leaders estimated they would not be able to repress a revolution and that the Tsar was strongly opposed to any significant reform. While we do know that Russia rejected several attempts at a separate peace and chose to continue the war, the very limited available historical evidence allows only weak conclusions about the reasons underpinning the choice to continue it. At the end of 1915 and again at the end of 1916 Russian leaders may have chosen to continue the war in the hope that the army now finally had the necessary equipment and expectation of Allied support, or out of fear of a revolution if they signed an insufficient peace, or some combination of these motivations.[37] Particularly for 1915 the evidence suggests that the Russian regime chose to continue the war out of fear of domestic punishment. Moreover, the leadership increased its war aims even when they became more pessimistic about the war. The increase in Russian war aims during 1915 also appeared to be intended to buy off the opposition. Thus, with the caveats mentioned above in mind, for 1914 and 1916 the evidence is at minimum consistent with the theory, while the case of 1915 supports the theory.

[37] As Linke concludes, the Russian government's unwillingness to make a separate peace with either Germany or Austria-Hungary could have resulted from "the expectation to finally achieve victory, out of fear to lose her trustworthiness as an ally in the eyes of her current Allies, and in the mistaken hope to prevent revolutionary unrest through further perseverance" (p. 237).

6

France

THIS CHAPTER TRACES how French leaders changed their war aims, with a heavy emphasis on the period of late 1916 to late 1917. Two main conclusions emerge from my analysis. First, as the theory predicts, France's nonrepressive, nonexclusionary regime lowered its war aims as it lowered its estimate of France's relative strength and increased its estimates of the costs of war. Second, for French leaders the anticipated domestic political consequences of the terms of settlement did not influence French war aims, whereas *international* consequences of the terms of settlement did play an important role in the formulations and changes in French war aims. For French policy makers, France's postwar relative power, vis-à-vis Germany *and* their allies, remained a major consideration throughout the war.[1]

The chapter also examines two competing explanations. A first competing explanation derived from the work of Bueno de Mesquita et al. and Downs and Rocke suggests that Democratic leaders gamble for resurrection to avoid losing power.[2] This argument fails because the respective French Prime Ministers were willing to lower their war aims and settle on relatively poor terms when they became more pessimistic. The second competing explanation argues that the continuous French demand for the return of Alsace-Lorraine—although this meant different things at different times—served to buy off the people after the war. Since the return of Alsace-Lorraine would cover the costs of war, this argument goes, the French government could lower its demands elsewhere if necessary. Thus, the finding that French leaders did indeed lower their demands when they became pessimistic about the war is insufficient to show that France's leaders formulated their war aims by a different logic than Germany's regime. Although the argument is plausible, the evidence suggests that the demand for the return of Alsace-Lorraine was less intended to reward the people than

---

[1] Renouvin; "Die Kriegsziele der französischen Regierung 1914 bis 1918," pp. 129–30. The same article was originally published in French under the title "Les Buts de guerre des gouvernement français, 1914–1918." See also Stevenson, *French War Aims against Germany, 1914–1919*, p. 199.

[2] Bueno de Mesquita, Siverson, and Woller; Bueno de Mesquita and Siverson, "War and the Survival of Political Leaders"; Bueno de Mesquita and Siverson, "Political Survival and International Crises"; Downs and Rocke.

to redress the strategic imbalance between Germany and France. Thus, the anticipated international consequences rather than any anticipated domestic consequences drove the demand for Alsace-Lorraine.

To make these points, I divide this chapter into four main sections. As before, these sections measure the independent and dependent variables and detail the historical fit of the proposed causal mechanism. In the first section I code prewar France on the independent variable of regime type. The second section then offers a brief overview of the new information and changes in French war aims in each year of the war and shows that the French leadership became more pessimistic in 1914, 1915, and 1917. I turn to a detailed examination of 1917 in the third section, because in that period French leaders most changed their estimates of the outcome of the war and countenanced the possibility the war might end in a moderate loss (perhaps largely at Russia's expense). In this section I first lay out the leadership's initial expectations for 1917, the new information of the year, and expectations at the end of the year. Then I turn to France's war aims at the end of 1916 and 1917, respectively, and examine the changes. In the fourth section I examine the historical fit of the proposed causal mechanisms, the domestic and international consequences of the terms of settlement.

The Independent Variable: Regime Type

Prewar France was a nonrepressive, nonexclusionary regime and probably the most democratic regime on the continent at the time. To show that France is indeed a nonrepressive, nonexclusionary regime, I sketch the political landscape in prewar France and identify the main decision makers and the sources of their political power. France qualifies as a nonrepressive, nonexclusionary regime for three reasons.[3] First, no group was systematically excluded from the policy-making process. Second, no group had to fear an irreversible loss of power and access if it lost one particular political struggle. Third, the regime would not and could not systematically repress and eradicate the domestic opposition.

The Third Republic was born from the French defeat in the Franco-Prussian War of 1870–71. In one catastrophic debacle France lost the war, Alsace and Lorraine, and its emperor, Napoleon III. Initially the republic was thought to be merely a transitory period until a monarchy

---

[3] The classification used in the data analysis in chapter 3 also codes France as a Democracy. In 1914 France scores an 8 on the Democracy index and a 0 on the Autocracy index of Gurr's *POLITY III*.

could be restored, and therefore the Third Republic had only a sketchy and incomplete constitution.[4] What served as a constitution was a combination of three laws, the Law on the Organization of the Senate, the Law on the Organization of the Public Powers, and the Law on the Relations of the Public Powers, passed in the National Assembly on 24 February, 25 February, and 16 July 1875, respectively.[5] This constitution contained no bill of rights, no provisions for the method of appointing ministers or of electing members of the Chamber of Deputies, and no provisions dealing with the judiciary, the budget, or local government. In Schuman's words, it was "severely practical and limited in scope."[6]

The constitution did *not* provide for a separation of powers between an independent legislature, executive, and judiciary.[7] The result was that parliament became the most powerful domestic institution, where all authority was located. The acting executive, the Cabinet, was responsible to parliament, and all legislation had to be passed by a majority of both the Chamber of Deputies and the Senate. Members could introduce bills on their own initiative in both houses. Articles 8 and 9 of the Constitutional Law of 16 July 1875 also dictated the primacy of parliament in foreign affairs. The President could not declare war without the *preliminary* assent of the two chambers. Furthermore, the chambers had the right to be informed of the terms of treaties, specifically including peace treaties, as soon as the interest and security of the state permitted. These treaties would be final only after the chambers had approved them. All cessions, exchanges, and acquisitions of territory, moreover, had to be approved by parliament. Members of parliament were elected in regular and democratic elections with universal manhood suffrage.[8] However, as Gilbert notes, "the voting system by which French senators were chosen favored rural districts and the well-to-do, so the Senate functioned as a conservative counterweight to the more liberal Chamber of Deputies."[9]

The titular head of state, the President, had no independent power because all his acts had to be countersigned by ministers who, in turn,

[4] This description of the institutional framework of the Third Republic is largely based on Schuman, pp. 7–14, and R. K. Gooch.

[5] These laws are reprinted in appendix A of Schuman, pp. 423–25.

[6] Ibid., p. 10.

[7] For a good description of the basic relation between President, Prime Minister, and Cabinet, the Chamber of Deputies, Senate, and National Assembly, and the voters under the constitution of the Third Republic, see Watson, appendices 2 and 3.

[8] Schuman, p. 11. Of course, universal *manhood* suffrage meant that one particular group *was* systematically excluded from access to power. I cannot venture to guess whether giving women the vote would have materially altered the balance of power between the contending factions in the Third Republic.

[9] Felix Gilbert, p. 57.

were answerable to the parliament. The President did name the ministers and picked a "President of the Council," that is, the Prime Minister. However, since each ministry could hold office only so long as it enjoyed the confidence of the majority of both chambers, the President had little discretionary power.[10] He could advise, admonish, and warn, but any additional influence was purely personal and informal. During the war the presidency was held by Raymond Poincaré (*gauche radical*).

Actual executive power resided in the ministry, which was headed by the Prime Minister, who proposed his Cabinet to the chamber. A ministry theoretically acted as a unit at all times, and the Prime Minister was presumably only primus inter pares. No Cabinet could serve without the approval and support of the deputies. When a ministry was defeated in a vote of confidence, its resignation was obligatory. Although the constitution made the ministry answerable to both houses, in practice responsibility was to the Chamber of Deputies rather than to the Senate. The decree of 28 October 1913 gave supreme political control to the ministry in time of war. The ministry had the sole right to determine the political objectives of war. Moreover,

> as a corollary of its control over policy the government . . . could . . . designate the principal enemy; order an offensive at one point and defensive at another; transport troops to such and such a place. The government would determine the objectives, while leaving to the military technicians the responsibility for using the measures necessary for their achievement.[11]

France was governed by five different Prime Ministers during the war. René Viviani had become Prime Minister in early 1914; Aristide Briand took over on 29 October 1915 and stayed in power until March 1917; Alexandre Ribot remained only a short time in power; Paul Painlevé took office in September 1917. From November 1917 onward, Georges Clemenceau, known as "the Tiger," directed the Third Republic with an iron will. The ousted Prime Ministers remained influential, either inside subsequent ministries or in the Chamber of Deputies.

Parties mattered, of course, but party discipline was not very strong, and neither was party organization in the country. Moreover, politicians did not feel particularly bound to their parties; they moved easily from one party to another and often constructed new, (un)official

---

[10] In his memoirs *Au service de la France*, wartime President Raymond Poincaré provides a good picture of the central role of the chambers and their respective Presidents in the selection of a new Prime Minister.

[11] Professor Barthelemy of the École Libre des Sciences Politiques, quoted in King, p. 2.

groups in the chambers.[12] The Third Republic featured a large assortment of larger and smaller parties, with a bewildering assortment of names.[13] No single party could command an electoral majority, and consequently every government was a coalition.[14] An important factor in the stability of the Third Republic was that a small number of the same personalities served again and again in almost every Cabinet. The elections of 26 April and 10 May 1914 led to the following political alignments in the chambers on the eve of the war.[15] On the extreme left there were 104 Unified Socialists (*socialistes SFIO, unifiés*). At center-left, essentially the majority in power, 262 members gravitated around the Radical Party, of which the core of 172 members came from the recently unified *parti républicaine radical* and *radical socialiste*. Next, there were 122 members of the center-right, even though two of its three constituent groups had the word "left" in their name: the *républicains de gauche*, the *gauche democratique*, and the *féderation républicaine*. Finally, on the right sat 82 members, comprising the small catholic group *Action Liberale*, the *nationalistes*, and the noninscribed who refused to list a party affiliation.

The Socialist Party refused to participate in bourgeois ministries to signal their determination that reforms would not suffice or be valuable in and of themselves. Instead, the party held that it would be necessary to take power and replace the whole bourgeois state with the proletarian state. However, quite a few socialists defected from the party and joined and even led so-called bourgeois ministries. The careers of former socialists such as Alexandre Millerand, Aristide Briand, René Viviani, and Albert Thomas illustrate a central characteristic of the Third Republic: Individual ambition and ability played a more important role than did mere party affiliation or party loyalty. Alexandre

---

[12] Felix Gilbert, p. 57; see also Schuman, p. 15. Leon Bourgeois, for example, is alternatively listed as *républicain radical* in the second Ribot ministry, as *gauche democratique* in the fifth Briand, third Ribot, and Painlevé ministries, and as *radical-socialiste* by Duroselle. See Bonnefous, vol. 2, pp. 446, 449–52; and Duroselle, *La Politique extérieure de la France*, p. 19.

[13] The names of these political parties are more often than not misleading. Party names often did not cover their cargo. Names such as "republican," "democratic," "radical," and even "socialist" often do not really reflect the doctrines or programs of the respective parties: "The Radical Socialist party for example, is neither radical nor socialist as a Marxian understands those terms, while the Republican Left in the Senate is a right group just next to the Royalists" (Schuman, p. 17).

[14] The abundance and "multifariousness of the political groupings was chiefly a reflection of tiny differences in economic interests and of variation stemming from local and regional particularities" (Felix Gilbert, p. 57).

[15] These numbers can be found in Duroselle, *La Politique extérieure de la France*, pp. 12–13.

Millerand's decision to join the Waldeck-Rousseau Cabinet as Minister of Trade illustrates the important point that while the socialists did not want to join the bourgeois power structure, this power structure had no problems in co-opting and integrating such socialists.[16]

Compared to Germany, there was little reason to fear a socialist revolution in France. Not only was the existing nonexclusionary structure willing to co-opt individual socialists and socialist ideas, the basis of socialist support was also much weaker. For example, compared with the German Socialist Party, the SPD, the French Socialist Party had one-tenth the membership and half the proportion of votes. Similarly, whereas in Germany fully one-quarter of wage earners belonged to trade unions, in France only 9 percent did.[17] In general, pressure groups were much weaker and less important players in France than in either Germany or Britain, and as a result, political cleavages did not harden into solid social blocs.[18]

Thus, the pronounced democratic nature of prewar French politics and the democratic slack in the policy-making process prevented a zero-sum view of domestic politics among the great majority of Frenchmen. No group was systematically excluded from power or feared that a loss on one particular issue would spell their irrevocable demise. Each group could hope to win on some (other) important issues in the future. As a result, the Third Republic was relatively stable and in no immediate danger of overthrow from either left or right. Moreover, the regime did not (need to) repress the domestic opposition, and it is noteworthy that the Viviani ministry decided in August 1914 not to arrest suspected left-wing agitators and other assorted socialists who featured on the *Carnet B* blacklist. Hence, France qualifies as a nonrepressive, nonexclusionary regime.

Overview of the War

As in the previous chapter, I first summarize the intervening and dependent variables for France in each year of the war in table 6.1. In 1914, 1915, and 1917 French leaders lowered their estimates of the out-

---

[16] Recouly, p. 217.

[17] This is hardly surprising, given that while more than half of the population was involved in agriculture, only one-quarter was employed in industry. Moreover, industrial relations could be problematic by and large only in the Northeast, where much of the heavy industry was located. Much of this territory was, of course, occupied in the first few months of the war (Felix Gilbert, pp. 57–58, 65).

[18] Stevenson, *French War Aims against Germany*, p. 5.

come of the war. Because I go into detail only for 1917, I summarize 1914 and 1915 in a few brief paragraphs here.

The main unfavorable new information of 1914 surely was the failure of the French war plan, Plan XVII, with its feint into the Upper Alsace and main thrust into Lorraine, and the deep penetration of French territory that resulted from the German advance under the Schlieffen Plan. But the first months of the war brought favorable new information as well, in particular, the British decision to join the war. Nevertheless, between the end of July and the end of December 1914, French leaders raised their estimate of the costs of war and surely also lowered their estimate of the probability of victory, since the hoped for quick victory had escaped them. Unfortunately, I can assess the changes in French war aims only between September and late December because the French government formulated its war aims for the first time on 20 September 1914.[19] Note that since these war aims were formulated well after the "miracle on the Marne" of 5–10 September and therefore *after* the major disillusionment of the first month, we can only assess the impact of *subsequent* new information on French war aims. In the interval between late September and late December, the leadership received the unfavorable new information that Turkey had joined the Central Powers, that the attempt to outflank the Germans in the "race to the sea" had failed, that the Russian "steamroller" had performed poorly, and that the war would last longer and be more costly than previously estimated.

A comparison of French war aims as unanimously accepted in the Council of Ministers on 20 September with Prime Minister Viviani's public statement of French war aims on 22 December 1914 seems to indicate at first French war aims had remained unchanged. However, behind closed doors, Prime Minister Viviani was willing to give up Indo-China to get Japanese support and Japanese troops in Europe. Undoubtedly aghast at such generosity, Foreign Minister Delcassé persuaded the Cabinet to accept a more modest proposal to attract Japanese aid. Initially, France would offer Japan the removal of tariff barriers in Indo-China and "the freedom to trade on the same terms as France herself: in other words the immediate prospects of economic dominance in Indochina and the longer-term prospect of political dom-

---

[19] On 5 August then Foreign Minister Doumergue told the Russians and the British that France would at a minimum demand Alsace-Lorraine, "whose retrocession to France must in any event be assured" (Stevenson, *French War Aims against Germany*, p. 12). However, while this seems to set a lower boundary on French war aims, it was not a full statement of French war aims as considered by the government. On 5 August President Poincaré had also called for "legitimate reparations," which France had, according to him, held dear to its heart for over forty years.

inance too."[20] If that would not suffice, further concessions could be considered. Second, and more importantly, the French government accepted the Russian government's demand for free passage through the Straits, as relayed by Sazonov to British Ambassador Buchanan and French Ambassador Paléologue at the end of September.[21] On 13 October Foreign Minister Delcassé told the Russian Ambassador Izvolski that France would "fully support" Russia's demands for "freedom of the Straits and sufficient guarantees on this point."[22] As for Great Britain, the issue had important strategic implications for France, particularly for its naval preeminence in the Mediterranean. In the previous century France and Great Britain had fought the Crimean War to hold off such Russian gains.[23] Thus, as they lowered their expectations, Viviani and Delcassé became willing to make substantial concessions in the French colonies and regarding the Straits and thereby lowered France's war aims.[24] All in all, however, France's war aims in this period were too vague to draw strong inferences.

During 1915 the unfavorable new information, in particular, the costly failures of the French offensives, Russian defeats, and Bulgaria's decision to enter the war on the side of the Central Powers, more than outweighed the favorable new information of Italy's entry on the side of the Entente. The overall new information of 1915 therefore made the French leadership more pessimistic about France's relative strength and the costs of war. Although Joffre was optimistic about his plans for 1916, France's political leaders did not share his optimism that his plans would now bear the fruits he had previously promised and would continue to promise. (Not just among parliamentarians, but even in the military itself doubts were mounting about Joffre's costly offensives.)[25] In his ministerial declaration upon taking power on 3 November, the new Prime Minister Aristide Briand openly acknowledged that victory was still far way; therefore, the country would have to bear further burdens.[26]

---

[20] Andrew and Kanya-Forstner, p. 78.

[21] Linke, p. 184.

[22] Izvolski to Sazonov, 13 October, in M. N. Pokrowski, *Die Internationalen Beziehungen im Zeitalter des Imperialismus* (hereafter *IBZI*), II. Reihe, 6. Band, 1. Halbband, no. 385, p. 304, see also 2. Halbband, no. 551, pp. 472–73, for a report of a conversation between the Japanese ambassador at St. Petersburg Motono and French Ambassador Paléologue of 23 November.

[23] For Paléologue's bitter comment that the program of Tsar Nicholas I had now finally been realized after sixty-one years, see Linke, p. 189.

[24] For the government's willingness to extend greater rights to the French colonial subjects, see Andrew and Kanya-Forstner, p. 82.

[25] Poincaré, vol. 7, p. 169.

[26] Bonnefous, vol. 2, pp. 97, 99–100. See also Poincaré, vol. 7, p. 376.

TABLE 6.1

New Information and Changes in War Aims for France

France	New Information	Changes in War Aims
1914	*Unfavorable*: Sept: German reserves in front lines: Plan XVII fails. 1–4 Nov: Turkey enters? 17–19 Nov: Race to the sea fails? Dec: Russians unsuccessful against Germany? High casualties? *Favorable*: 4–6 Aug: Britain enters, sends BEF. 14–15 Sept: Schlieffen Plan fails. Dec: Russians successful against Austria-Hungary; colonial subjects flock to the colors.	20 Sep 1914–22 Dec 1914 *Decreases*: Japan gets the freedom to trade in Indo-China on the same terms as France. Free passage through the Straits for Russia.
1915	*Unfavorable*: By Sept: Failures at Artois, Champagne, Loos; shortage of effectives looms; Russia suffers severe defeats. Sept–Oct: Bulgaria enters war. *Favorable*: 23 May: Italy enters war.	22 Dec 1914–22 Dec 1915 *Decreases*: 22 Dec: No more demand for the removal of Prussian militarism; no more demand for reparations (?). 10 Apr: Constantinople and surroundings to Russia. 26 Apr: Italian gains in the Adriatic, the Tyrol, Istria, and Dalmatia. *Increases*: Annexation of Syria (before the war a sphere of influence).
1916	*Unfavorable*: 21 Feb–Aug: Verdun; Sept–Dec: Rumania defeated. Oct–Dec: New Brusilov offensive fails; German counteroffensives succeed. *Favorable*: 19 Oct–Dec: Counteroffensives at Verdun; 25 May: Conscription in Britain. 4 May–11 Aug: Brusilov offensive. 5 June: Arab Revolt. 1 July–Nov: Somme attrition; Austro-Hungarian weakness. Aug: Sixth Battle of the Isonzo. 27 Aug: Rumania enters war. Oct–Nov: Germans feel the manpower pinch.	22 Dec 1915–12 Jan 1917 *Decreases*: May 1915 and Sept 1916: Decreased compensation in Turkey, smaller Syria and Cilicia. (17 Aug: Treaty of Bucharest?) Nov 1916–Feb 1917: Concessions to Italy in Turkey (Adana). *Increases*: 12 Jan 1917: Alsace-Lorraine of 1790 instead of 1870, i.e., including the Saar. Neutralization of the Rhineland, to become buffer states? Further claims to Rhineland left open.

TABLE 6.1 (cont.)

France	New Information	Changes in War Aims
1917	*Unfavorable:* 4 Feb: Germans withdraw to the Hindenburg line. 19–31 July: German counteroffensive against Kerenski. Summer-Fall: Russia army dissolving. 16 Apr–4 May: Nivelle offensive. 20 May–June: Mutinies in the French army. 18 Aug, 15 Nov: American slow in coming. 24 Oct: Caporetto. 13 Nov: Second Russian revolution. 15 Dec: Russia drops out of war; armistice on the Eastern Front. *Favorable:* 15–17 Mar: First Russian revolution? 5 April: America enters war.	*Decreases:* June: Annexations on the left bank of the Rhine ruled out; annexation of Luxembourg ruled out. 18–19 Sept: Alsace-Lorraine of 1870 instead of 1790. 28 Oct: Change in sovereignty over the left bank ruled out. 28 Nov: Demand for Syria retracted. Britain gets a free hand in the Ottoman Empire? 27 Dec: Evacuation of occupied Russian territory no longer demanded.
1918	*Unfavorable:* 21 Mar–29 Apr: Successes of the German Stormtrooper offensives. Summer: Intra-alliance bargaining power shifting to Americans? *Favorable:* Mid-July: German offensives have failed. May–July: American troops finally arrive in large numbers. 18 July–Sept: Allied counterattacks push back German army. 15 Sept: Austrians launch peace appeal. 15–24 Sept: Bulgarian forces defeated at the battles of Monastir-Doiran. 19–20 Sept: Decisive Turkish defeat at Megiddo. 24, 26 Sept: Bulgarians request armistice. 27 Sept: Allies break through and turn the Hindenburg line. 30 Sept: Bulgaria surrenders. 3–5 Oct: Germans and Austrians request armistice. 8 Oct–11 Nov: Allied advantage rapidly growing; Germany weaker than previously estimated. 14, 20 Oct: Turks ask for armistice. 31 Oct: Turks accept armistice. 3 Nov: Austria accepts separate armistice. 2–9 Nov: News of the revolution in Germany slowly starts to reach Allied leaders.	*Increases:* 30 Sept, 8 Nov: French demands in Ottoman Empire partially re-instated; French gain the right to establish civil administration in the Occupied Enemy Territories Administration West. 30 Sept: French impose armistice terms on Bulgaria. 29 Oct–5 Nov: Bridgeheads at Mayence, Coblenz, and Cologne; a neutral zone of 30–40 km width along the remainder of the right bank. Demand for reparations re-instated. Treaties of Brest-Litovsk and Bucharest to be annulled. Acceptance of Wilson's Fourteen Points (with reservations on freedom of the seas and reparations)? Hence, demand for change in regime re-instated. Austro-Hungarian army to be demobilized, troops serving on the Western Front withdrawn, half of all artillery surrendered. Serbs to occupy all territory claimed by the Yugoslavs; large part of Austro-Hungarian navy to be surrendered to Italy.

Note: Question marks indicate the uncertain status of new information and/or war aims. For France's full war aims see chapters 8 and 9.

This change in French estimates led to a drastic decrease in French war aims. Pressed on France's war aims in parliament the day he took office, Briand replied, in much the same terms as used by Viviani on 22 December 1914, that although the question of peace was still far away, French soil would have to be liberated, the provinces taken by conquest would have to be restored, Belgium would have to regain its territory and political and economic power, and "valiant" Serbia would have to be rescued and restored to its full integrity. Finally, he demanded guarantees for a durable peace.[27] Briand's statement entailed a marked lowering of French war aims on two points. First, the demand that Prussian militarism be broken was conspicuously absent.[28] Second, it also makes no mention of reparations.[29]

Behind the scenes, an even further modification of French war aims had taken place. During 1915 France was forced to concede gains to Russia and Italy that were against its national interest. Until March Foreign Minister Delcassé had apparently thought that Russia would settle for making Constantinople an international city and the neutralization of the Straits. But a French note of understanding of 10 April conceded the Russian demand for Constantinople and the surrounding area. Notwithstanding some counterclaims on the Ottoman Empire, this constituted a *major* concession on the part of the French and was recognized as such by the Russians.[30] Both Poincaré and Foreign Minister Delcassé were strongly opposed because possession of Constantinople would make Russia a great Mediterranean naval power.[31] Before going into the specifics, it should be emphasized that

[27] Bonnefous, vol. 2, pp. 98–99.

[28] Renouvin, "Die Kriegsziele der französischen Regierung," p. 134. In a letter to the troops at the end of the year, Poincaré declared that France would fight "until victory, until the destruction of Prussian militarism, and the total reconstitution of France" (Bonnefous, vol. 2, p. 111). But Poincaré was always one of the more hawkish French politicians and as President had little on no influence on war aims. Stevenson claims that by "breaking Prussian militarism" Poincaré meant a peace that would protect France against "any renewed offensive by German ambition" (*French War Aims*, p. 17). By this construction "breaking Prussian militarism" is but another term for "guarantees," which seems an oversimplification.

[29] In early February, prodded by Wilson's emissary Colonel House, Briand limited himself to the declaration that France would not accept a peace that would not bring it the expected result of the return of Alsace-Lorraine (Renouvin, "Die Kriegsziele der französischen Regierung," p. 134).

[30] *IBZI*, II. Reihe, 7. Band, 2. Halbband, no. 568, pp. 568–69.

[31] See especially Poincaré's letter to Paléologue of 9 May 1915: "The attribution of Constantinople, Thrace and the Straits and coast of the Sea of Marmara to Russia implies the partition of the Ottoman Empire. We have no good reason to desire that partition. . . . The possession of Constantinople and its environs not only gives Russia some privileges

French counterclaims were seen as a poor second best to the maintenance and indeed revivification of the whole Ottoman Empire. From late 1912 onward, the emphasis of French policy had shifted to the *preservation* and survival of the Ottoman Empire as one of the conditions of the Mediterranean balance of power.[32]

In return for the concession on Constantinople, Sazonov and the Tsar promised to support British and French ambitions in the Ottoman Empire and elsewhere.[33] French ambitions focused mainly on Syria, an area over which they had gradually been extending their control before the war. In 1912 Grey had already given the French a formal statement of British *désintéressement* and recognized France's rights in Syria and Lebanon.[34] Furthermore, it should be noted that in the Franco-Turkish agreement of April 1914 France had gained control of a sphere of economic influence in Syria up to Aleppo, but not quite all the way up north to the port of Alexandretta. Now in 1915 in return for the concession on Constantinople, "the government of the Republic, having considered the conditions of peace which Turkey must sign, desire[d] to annex, Syria, including the province of the Gulf of Alexandretta, and Cilicia to the Taurus Range."[35] These counterdemands were subject to the conditions as stipulated by the British, "that the war was carried to a victorious conclusion and that France and England achieved their aims in the Near East and elsewhere."[36] The "Syria" France negotiated in the Sykes-Picot agreement of February 1916 was substantially smaller than the Syria ("*la Syrie intégrale*") initially demanded. Pales-

---

in the succession of the Ottoman Empire. It would introduce her, through the Mediterranean, in the concert of the western nations and give her, by the free access to the sea, the possibility of becoming a great naval power. Everything would therefore have changed in the European equilibrium" (quoted as "Pa-ap 043-Cambon J v.79, Poincaré to Paléologue 5bis-10 5/9/15, personal letter, copy of late draft," in Bobroff). See also Poincaré, vol. 7, p. 104; Stevenson, *The First World War and International Politics*, p. 126; Stevenson, *French War Aims*, p. 28; Andrew and Kanya-Forstner, pp. 72–73. The concession may even have cost Delcassé his job; see Smith Jr., "Legacy to Stalin," p. 11.

[32] Andrew and Kanya-Forstner, pp. 50–53, 72.

[33] The Tsar had made explicit to Paléologue on 3 March that "elsewhere" referred to the Rhineland: "Prenez la rive gauche du Rhin, prenez Mayence; prenez Coblence, allez plus loin si vous le jugez utile" (Take the left bank of the Rhine, take Mainz, take Koblenz, go farther still if you judge it useful) (quoted in Prete, p. 891).

[34] Poincaré, vol. 7, pp. 206, 219; Andrew and Kanya-Forstner, p. 51.

[35] *IBZI*, II. Reihe, 7. Band, 1. Halbband, no. 370, p. 339; Smith Jr., "Legacy to Stalin," pp. 578–81. Paléologue presented the Russians with a demand for annexation of Syria, but Andrew and Kanya-Forstner argue that it seems much more likely that Delcassé intended to claim Syria as a sphere of influence; see Andrew and Kanya-Forstner, p. 73; see especially note 71, p. 168.

[36] Quoted in Andrew and Kanya-Forstner, p. 73.

tine would come under international control, and the Syria of the Sykes-Picot agreement became a much shallower area penetrating far less deep into modern Jordan, Syria, and Iraq.[37]

The French demand for Syria must be placed in its proper perspective. First, any French claims in the Ottoman Empire were conditional on an actual Arab revolt and Russian approval. Second, in the claim to Syria the anticipated international consequences of a division of the Ottoman Empire played a much more significant role than any attempt to reward the people for their sacrifices. Given the earlier agreements with the Turks and British, these French counterdemands do not seem an attempt to increase French demands but largely an attempt to maintain France's position vis-à-vis the British in the Ottoman Empire. Delcassé, for one, did not think Syria a great prize, declaring he did not think it wise to "risk a quarrel with the English over something of so little value."[38] Although the demand for Syria was clearly pushed by colonial interest groups in France, popular support was decidedly tepid, and Syria could not be used to buy off any political opposition. Andrew and Kanya-Forstner conclude that, at most, the public was opposed to British control over Syria.[39] All in all, then, the French demand for Syria would not compensate for the Russian and British strategic gains in the Ottoman Empire and moreover decreased in substance during 1915.

France had to make further concessions to entice Italy to join the war. Italy's demands ran counter to French national interests, as they would surely lead to a further weakening of France's relative power in the Mediterranean. Thus, as a result of the unfavorable new information of 1915, French leaders substantially lowered their war aims in two respects. First, they substantially lowered their demands against Germany. Second, because French leaders had been forced to lower their estimates of French power relative to their allies and would have to rely more on those allies' efforts in the future, French leaders made concessions to them that carried significant and unwelcome implications for France's postwar position.

Although 1916 brought some important unfavorable new information, the French leadership became much more optimistic about the war, largely because of the successful counteroffensives around Verdun in the fall under the leadership of General Nivelle and because of new information that Germany was starting to experience manpower shortages. Additional good news was the decision by the British to in-

---

[37] See ibid., Maps Appendix, p. 294.
[38] Quoted in ibid., p. 75.
[39] Ibid., p. 77.

stitute full conscription and the Arab Revolt against the Ottoman Empire. The new optimism led to a significant increase in French war aims against Germany (more on these issues below).

However, 1917 became *l'année horrible* for the French. While the French leadership saw the first Russian revolution temporarily as favorable new information, they soon learned better. Already in the summer of 1917 they estimated there existed a good chance that Russia might drop out of the war. The second Russian revolution and the armistice on the Eastern Front of mid-December meant that the Germans would be able to concentrate most of their forces on the Western Front in 1918. In addition, the main basis for the French optimism at the end of 1916 was swept away when the Nivelle offensive totally failed and instead produced mutinies in the French army. Of course, the entry of the United States was favorable new information, but the French soon worried about the unexpectedly slow arrival of American manpower. Because of their new pessimism about the war French leaders dramatically decreased their war aims.

In 1918 the favorable new information of the failure of the German offensives, the defection of Germany's allies, and the increasingly visible weakening of the German army led to an upsurge in French war aims. However, as we will see in chapter 9, because of a shift in intra-alliance bargaining power, the French leadership had to pay more attention to American demands than they would have liked.

In the next section I examine 1917 in greater detail because by 1917 the costs of the war relative to France's cost tolerance had risen so much that if French politicians worried about their ability to reward the people for their sacrifices, the costs of war surely had to have been a major influence by late 1917. My focus on 1917, therefore, allows me to track the change in French war aims when the costs of war should be *most* likely to influence the direction of the change in French war aims.

Expectations, New Information, and War Aims in 1917

To organize the greater detail of my analysis of 1917, this section is broken up into four subsections. The first lays out the French leadership's expectations for 1917. The second presents the new information received during 1917 and focuses in turn on the Russian revolutions and the armistice on the Eastern Front, the entry of the United States, and the Nivelle offensive and the mutinies in the French army. The third examines the leadership's expectations in two periods, late August to mid-September, and November-December 1917. The final subsection shows how France's war aims changed.

To enable the reader to follow the rapidly changing cast of characters at the top of the French leadership during 1917, I briefly sketch the most important changes. During 1917 France was governed by four Prime Ministers. The sixth Briand Cabinet had taken over from the fifth Briand Cabinet on 12 December 1916 but lasted only until March. Alexandre Ribot became Prime Minister for the third time between 20 March and 7 September. Six days later Paul Painlevé took over for only two months, until 13 November 1917. From 17 November until 1920 Georges Clemenceau ruled with maximum determination and minimum coordination with the other ministers of his Cabinet. In late May Henri-Philippe Pétain replaced Nivelle as Commander of the French army.

Expectations in Late 1916 through Early 1917

The evidence strongly suggests that in late 1916 and early 1917 the French leadership, political but especially military, intended to fight what they intended to be the decisive battle in 1917. This battle would crown the Allies' efforts in 1916, especially the preparatory attrition achieved by the results of the Somme offensive and its planned continuation over the winter months.[40] The change in the military leadership when Joffre was replaced by Nivelle in December 1916 only served to increase the politicians' belief in victory that year in the crucial month of January 1917.

To establish French expectations at the end of 1916 in detail, we first turn to Joffre's plans for 1917. At the inter-Allied conference on 15 November, Joffre requested the assembled Commanders-in-Chief to agree with his plans as outlined in a memorandum distributed before the conference.[41] The "decisive effort," according to Joffre's outline, should take place in the spring of 1917.[42] Joffre specifically asked if they agreed

> (a) That *a decision of the war should be sought by resuming co-ordinated offensives in the spring of 1917*, using for this purpose all the resources which can be collected during the winter. (b) That the best way of creating favorable conditions for this offensive consists in pursuing offensive actions during the whole of the winter along all of the fronts, as far as climatic conditions make this possible. . . . That *a powerful attack, intended to be decisive, should be prepared for the spring of 1917* and carried out on the Anglo-Franco-Belgian frontier.[43]

[40] Joffre, *The Memoirs of Marshall Joffre*, p. 485.
[41] See ibid., p. 496; see also Joffre, *Journal de marche de Joffre, 1916–1919*, p. 199.
[42] Joffre, *Memoirs*, p. 502.
[43] Ibid., pp. 507–8, emphasis added.

The conferees replied affirmatively to Joffre's questions. At the conclusion of the conference the representatives of the Allied armies committed themselves to the plan of action as outlined in the memorandum presented to them,

> the object of the plan being to *give a decisive character to the campaign of 1917*. . . . On the Balkan front . . . [t]he Russo-Rumanian forces will operate against Bulgaria from the north while the Allied Army of Salonica operates from the south, the action of these two groups being closely co-ordinated, *the idea being to obtain a decision* on one or the other of the two fronts, according as the operations develop.[44]

The Commanders-in-Chief agreed that "the Germans were in great difficulties on the western front, and that the situation of the allies was more favorable than it had ever been."[45] It deserves note that Briand was also more optimistic about the Russian army, which was now better supplied and might finally make full use of their enormous numbers.[46]

From 17 December 1916 onward, Nivelle assumed command of the military direction of the war. The change in command and the arrival of General Lyautey as War Minister did not mean a change in the overall strategic aims of the government. As Alexandre Ribot recalls a conference at the War Ministry on 12 January 1917,

> After the replacement of General Joffre (12 December) and the arrival at the Ministry of General Lyautey, we maintained the same conception of the policy to be followed in 1917. "The French government puts it as an axiom of the combined action of the Allies that all the Russian, Rumanian, and Balkan questions, including those of Salonica, shall not be resolved except by a very strong, and as rapid as possible, effort on our front, *the French armies being the only ones capable of obtaining a decisive success*. The role of the coalition on all the other fronts is to aid this action."[47]

While Nivelle's reconceptualization of Joffre's plans shifted the burden from the British (where Joffre had put it) onto the French army and the Chemin des Dames, the goal remained a decisive breakthrough to restore a "battle of movement" over the "battle of position" that had been waged on the Western Front since November 1914. Note

---

[44] Ibid., pp. 512–13, emphasis added.

[45] Liddell Hart, p. 298. A large factor undoubtedly was that, as estimated by Joffre, the Allies would enjoy a 17 to 10 superiority on the Western Front. See Joffre, *Memoirs*, p. 510; see also his *Journal*, p. 144. Liddell Hart estimated that the Allies could marshal 3.9 million men against 2.5 million Germans on the Western Front.

[46] Briand in the secret committee 28 November–7 December 1916 (Bonnefous, vol. 2, p. 190).

[47] Ribot, *Lettres*, p. 175, emphasis added.

also the Cabinet's intention to let the victory fall to French forces, with its implications for French demands both against its allies and against its enemies.

Nivelle aimed to achieve a breakthrough by the combination of creeping artillery barrages and a large maneuvering army held in reserve to exploit a breakthrough, what became known, rather infamously, as the Nivelle offensive. Nivelle promised quick and decisive results, and his promise was all the more credible for his victories at Douaumont and Vaux in the battle of Verdun in the late fall of 1916. Nivelle's confidence in his methods is on record. On 15 December 1916, when he bade farewell to his army at Verdun, he said, "The experience is conclusive. Our method has provided its proofs. Victory is certain, I give you my pledge. The enemy shall learn it to his detriment."[48]

At least during January 1917 the most important political leaders shared Nivelle's optimism. The replacement of Joffre by Nivelle significantly increased the government's confidence in a quick and cheaper victory in 1917 than that promised by Joffre.[49] To Prime Minister Aristide Briand, Nivelle promised more decisive and offensive action and, most importantly, less waste of French blood. Briand had already expressed considerable optimism about the upcoming year during the inter-Allied meeting of political leaders held at the same time as the inter-Allied meeting of military leaders in November 1916.[50] France's political leaders, moreover, reacted very positively to the proposed changes for the campaign of 1917 introduced by Nivelle. Nivelle intended to avoid a bloody Somme-type offensive and wanted the French to reap the rewards of his anticipated victory.

Minister of Finance Alexandre Ribot, for one, thought that Nivelle's audacious plan had serious chances for success and compared it to the Brusilov offensives of 1916.[51] Prime Minister Briand himself was, according to Lloyd George and Maurice Hankey, genuinely convinced of Nivelle's chances for success. At the Rome conference of 5–7 January 1917, Briand pointed out to Lloyd George that "*General Nivelle consid-*

---

[48] Quoted in Painlevé, *Comment j'ai nommé Foch et Pétain*, p. 11.

[49] Painlevé, p. 10; see also Ribot, *Lettres*, pp. 145–46.

[50] Briand had argued that the Allies had 50 percent more effectivess than the combined total that the Germans, Austrians, Bulgars, and Turks could raise. He also emphasized that the morale of the Allied soldiers had not been affected, as had allegedly been shown by the fighting at Verdun and the Somme offensive. Moreover, the Allies' situation concerning materiel and munitions was improving daily. Briand, however, put much more emphasis on the offensive in the Balkans against Bulgaria than the military did. See Suarez, vol. 4, pp. 4–5, 8; see also Painlevé, p. 6.

[51] Ribot, *Lettres*, p. 177.

ered it possible to break through," and he emphasized "the importance of the spring offensive being decisive."[52] When Lloyd George warned that "the Generals were just as confident now as they had ever been, but . . . pointed out that they had always been just as confident before previous offensives," Briand was not discouraged.[53] Instead, he told Lloyd George how,

> when General Nivelle had commanded the armies in the region of Verdun, he had come to M. Briand and proposed an attack. M. Briand had felt some doubt about the question, owing to the *usure*. General Nivelle, however, had described exactly how he could conduct the operation, and had stated that he would send telegrams to him at such and such an hour from such and such points, which he had captured. Eventually, M. Briand sanctioned the attack, and General Nivelle carried it out absolutely as he had forecast. This naturally had created a most favorable impression in regard to General Nivelle on M. Briand's mind, and made him feel some confidence in his plans for the future. At Verdun, M. Briand pointed out, the French actually did break through the German lines, but the country was a *cul de sac* and unfavorable to an advance. Nevertheless, they gained invaluable experience. *They were inclined to think that an attack, prepared in a certain way, had now a very good chance of succeeding.*[54]

Briand further emphasized the inferior quality of the German troops the French expected to confront in 1917.

Although very optimistic, the French Cabinet remained cognizant of two preconditions for success. As Paul Painlevé, Minister and member of the War Ministry in the fifth Briand Cabinet (29 October 1915– 12 December 1916), subsequently Minister of War in the third Ribot Cabinet (20 March 1917–7 September 1917) and Prime Minister from 13 September to 13 November 1917, noted, two conditions would be indispensable for success: first, all the Allied armies, British, French, Italian, Russian, Russo-Rumanian, and Salonican, would have to attack simultaneously; and second, these attacks should encompass vast areas.[55] Furthermore, the nagging question remained, in the mind of the ministers, whether it would be possible to break through the enemy's front within twenty-four to forty-eight hours, as Nivelle thought. Would the French have the artillery to destroy, to a depth of seven to

---

[52] Lloyd George, *War Memoirs,* vol. 3, p. 340, emphasis in original.

[53] Ibid., vol. 3, p. 341, emphasis deleted.

[54] Ibid., vol. 3, pp. 341–42, emphasis in original; see also pp. 378–79; and Hankey, *The Supreme Command 1914–1918,* vol. 2, pp. 613–14, 617.

[55] Painlevé, pp. 4–5; see also Ribot, *Lettres,* pp. 174–75.

eight kilometers, the German defenses? Would the offensive not get stuck in only the first or second lines of defense? If that happened, what did Nivelle propose to do?[56]

With regard to their allies and potential allies, many French leaders predicted troubles for the Romanov regime, but few expected that Russia would collapse and drop out of the war.[57] Politicians hoped that Russia's internal troubles could be solved by a "palace coup."[58] With mistaken notions of the French Revolution in mind, they hoped such a coup would result in an upsurge of "revolutionary patriotism," leading to a revitalized, re-energized, and more efficient Russian war effort.[59] As for the United States, the French leadership was not optimistic at the end of 1916 that the Americans would intervene on their behalf any time soon.[60]

The New Information in 1917

The most significant new information received by French leaders in the course of 1917 was the breadth and depth of the Russian revolution, the American entry into the war, the failure of the Nivelle offensive and subsequent mutinies in the French army.[61] The Russian revolution of March 1917 affected France's expectations and plans in two ways. First, the minimum conditions necessary for success of the planned offensive as agreed on at Chantilly were no longer present. The revolution implied Russian military inaction and immobility, which in turn meant that the Rumanian army and the Salonican army would be doomed to inaction. Thus, the basis of the Allies' plan for a decisive breakthrough in 1917, namely, combined offensives on all fronts, had dropped out from under them. As the new Minister of War in the Ribot Cabinet, Paul Painlevé, noted, if the Anglo-French armies would attack as had been foreseen at the Chantilly conference of No-

---

[56] Ribot, *Lettres*, p. 177.

[57] See Paléologue's telegram of 14 January 1917, in Ribot, *Lettres*, pp. 226–27. But Nivelle was apparently worried that Russia might not be able to hold out much longer because of its serious internal troubles. See his note quoted in Painlevé, Annex 2, pp. 363–67.

[58] Poincaré, vol. 9, entry of 16 January 1917, p. 53. Paléologue attended a party on 26 January 1917 at which influential Russians openly discussed a proposed palace coup (Herman, p. 321).

[59] Apparently German and Austrian leaders initially had similar expectations about such a resurgence. See Herman, p. 342.

[60] Ribot, *Lettres*, p. 272.

[61] Ibid., p. 301.

vember 1916, they would attack alone.[62] Second, the possibility that Russia would drop out of the war altogether rapidly became frighteningly real. With the disappearance of the Eastern Front, the Germans would be able to concentrate all their forces on the Western Front.

Initially French leaders hoped that Russia would take up the struggle again with all its energy, willing to bear even greater sacrifices.[63] However, after a few months French leaders saw their worst fears realized. The Russians did not participate in the Allied spring offensives as planned and launched their Kerenski offensive only on 29 June; it petered out by 15 July. While the first stage of the offensive gained substantial territory, largely because the Germans had changed to a defense-in-depth strategy, the German counteroffensive of 19 July caused the total collapse of morale among Russian troops, who refused to fight and fled. The Russian forces retreated in disorderly fashion for two weeks, and the rate of desertions increased.[64]

This unfavorable new information convinced Allied political and military leaders by early August that a Russian collapse was near. They agreed that such a collapse would rule out an Allied victory over the Central Powers. While Foch argued it would not suffice to give victory to the enemy, Prime Minister Ribot acknowledged, however, that the situation could become perilous for the Allies.[65] The Russian defeats at the Second Battle of Riga, 3–21 September, led the new Prime Minister and Minister of War Painlevé to acknowledge to President Poincaré on 19 September that the Russian army was on the verge of dissolution, which, of course, would present new opportunities to the Central Powers.[66]

In the second week of November Kerenski fled, and Lenin and Trotski triumphed in St. Petersburg. The second Russian revolution destroyed any lingering French hopes the Russians would remain in the

[62] Painlevé, p. 31. See also Renouvin, "Die Kriegsziele der französischen Regierung 1914 bis 1918," p. 144.

[63] Ribot, *Lettres*, p. 240. See also Painlevé, p. 31. In the first couple of months French leaders had great hopes for a *reveil* of Russia, with the experience of the French Revolution uppermost in their minds. See Ribot, *Journal d'Alexandre Ribot*, p. 55; see also Renouvin, "Les tentatives de paix en 1917 et le gouvernement français," p. 494.

[64] Herman, p. 408. The offensive failed because the Central Powers had foreknowledge of the Russian plans, and the Russians experienced continued supply shortages and a loss of morale among their soldiers. Moreover, some units refused to fight, while others rejected orders to report to the front, interpreting these orders as a strategy to draw the revolution's defenders away from St. Petersburg (p. 398).

[65] Ribot, Prime Minister at the time, gives an account in his *Journal*, pp. 174–75.

[66] Painlevé's letter is quoted in Poincaré, vol. 9, pp. 289–90. Poincaré noted that "[t]he Deputies are frightened by the economic situation and the Russian events" (p. 291). See also Painlevé, p. 243.

war. At an inter-Allied conference on 29 November, two days before the new Russian government asked for an armistice to quench the "general thirst for peace which brought the Bolsheviks to power," the new Prime Minister, Clemenceau, acknowledged that Russia could no longer be counted on as an ally.[67] He could hope only that the Allies would be able to hold out until the Americans arrived. Although not unexpected, the armistice on the Eastern Front of 15 December put the final nail in the coffin of any hopes that Russia might continue to fight.

Against this unfavorable new information, we must weigh the favorable new information of the American entry in the war, a few weeks after the first Russian revolution. On 6 April the United States declared it would enter the war, notably as an "Associated" but not "Allied" power. For several weeks thereafter France and Britain were not particularly impressed with the material impact of American intervention. Over time, however, the Allies started looking to the American army as the means of their salvation and reason for continuing the war. The main problem for the Allies was that the American army was slow in coming. With a large American army on the Western Front they surely could win the war. The question was, however, whether they would be able to survive long enough for that American army to make the difference.

It is striking to see how little stock French leaders initially put in American military assistance. They estimated that the main American contributions would be U.S. Treasury loans, American shipping, and wheat and oil.[68] The skepticism of the Allies was not unreasonable. The United States had but a small peacetime army, and the British experience showed it would take between one and two years before the American army would be able to participate in any offensives on a grand scale.[69] However, already by mid-June Minister of War Painlevé asked the American General Pershing upon his arrival in France for one million men one year hence. Pershing promised one million men by July 1918 and an additional million after that if necessary.[70] But few believed Pershing could keep his promise. Already by 26 July Pershing

[67] Painlevé, p. 272.

[68] Ibid., p. 205; Renouvin, "Les Tentatives de paix en 1917 et le gouvernement français," p. 494; Poincaré, vol. 9, pp. 58, 106–7. For French skepticism about American capabilities and effectiveness, see Audoin-Rouzeau, pp. 157–58; and Seymour, vol. 3, p. 7.

[69] Ribot, *Lettres*, pp. 212–13. Many believed that the American army would only have decisive effect in 1919—that is, of course, if they could hold out that long. See Renouvin, "Die Kriegsziele der französischen Regierung 1914 bis 1918," p. 144.

[70] Painlevé, p. 206; on p. 242 Painlevé writes that on 16 June he obtained President Wilson's promise of one million American soldiers present on the French front before the end of June.

had to scale back his promises to only twenty-one divisions, comprising about 420,000 men, with an additional 214,975 support troops by 15 June 1918.[71] By July 1918 there would therefore be only approximately 700,000 Americans in France. The bottleneck was shipping. The War Department warned there was small chance of securing the tonnage necessary to bring one million men to France by July 1918. By mid-August Pershing further lowered his estimate to twelve to fifteen American divisions in France by April-May 1918.[72]

By November, seven months after the United States had entered the war, the American effort "remained frustratingly small. . . . American commodities and manufactures, too, were slow in coming, and in November 1917 France was desperately short of the food and raw materials it needed to keep its economy functioning."[73] At the end of November 1917, there were only four American divisions in France, and only one of these was actually training in the line. Shipping and training remained the two great bottlenecks. There was only sufficient shipping to transport one and one-third divisions per month.[74] John J. Pershing, Commander of the American Expeditionary Force, warned that at the current "slow rate of arrival, we should not have more than half of the twenty-one divisions promised by the War Department ready for service by June [1918]."[75] On the basis of the British experience, it was estimated, moreover, that after their arrival American divisions would require some months in a quiet part of the line before they were ready to take an active part in the fighting.[76] By mid-November a careful estimate of the relative power of the combatants led American and Allied staffs to the conclusion that the Germans could have as many as 217 divisions on the Western Front by early spring 1918. The Allies, it was estimated, would be able to raise only 169 divisions; if the American divisions were counted double because of their size, they could muster 171 divisions. There might be additional American divisions by 1 May, but only if these should arrive according to schedule, which was becoming more and more doubtful.[77]

[71] Pershing, vol. 1, p. 118. At 27,802 men, American divisions were about twice the size of French and British divisions. Pershing lists the composition, organization, and command structure of U.S. infantry units in Pershing, vol. 1, p. 101, note 1. See also Poincaré, vol. 9, p. 153; entry of 3 June 1917; Bonnefous, vol. 2, pp. 249–50.

[72] Joffre, *Journal*, p. 226.

[73] Stevenson, *French War Aims*, p. 94.

[74] At this rate the Americans would barely fulfill Pershing's promise of 18 August 1917 that there would be twelve to fifteen American divisions in France by April–May 1918. See Joffre, *Journal*, p. 226.

[75] Pershing, vol. 1, pp. 233–34.

[76] Hankey, vol. 2, p. 744.

[77] Pershing, vol. 1, p. 233.

Although American manpower arrived far more slowly than they had hoped in the early summer, their impending arrival nevertheless had a significant influence on French and British estimates and plans for the coming year. In a meeting of the War Committee of 30 November Clemenceau described his expectations for the near future: "The Germans want to end the war in 1918. We want to await the complete cooperation of the Americans, which implies that the war will not end before 1919. This should guide our behavior."[78]

The combined effect of the Russian collapse and tardiness of American troops affected French estimates in two ways. First, decision makers were forced to lower their estimate of the probability of victory. In late 1916 and early 1917 they had hoped for a *decisive* victory in 1917; now they hoped they would survive the expected German spring offensives. If they could survive, the influx of American manpower would ensure victory. Second, French leaders were forced to increase their estimates of the costs of war. At the beginning of the year decision makers believed the war could end in 1917; now they hoped the war would end in 1919. French troops would have to bear a large share of the additional costs of war. After the failure of the Nivelle offensive and the following mutinies, French leaders were forced to worry whether the French army would be willing to suffer higher war costs.

Several factors doomed the ambitious Nivelle offensive to failure: the Russian Revolution, the German withdrawal to the Hindenburg line, and an arrogant optimism bordering on stupidity that brought French plans into German hands well before the offensive was launched.[79] Nivelle finally did get his chance for glory, even though French leaders were aware of many of these problems well before the offensive was actually launched.[80]

---

[78] Poincaré, vol. 9, p. 393, entry of 30 November 1917. For Lloyd George's pessimism and Clemenceau's optimism see ibid., p. 394.

[79] For details on the Nivelle offensive see King; Clayton; Commandant de Civrieux; Painlevé; Pedroncini, *Les Mutineries de 1917*; Ribot, *Lettres*; de Pierrefeu, *G.Q.G. Secteur I*; de Pierrefeu, *Plutarch Lied*; and Lloyd George, *War Memoirs*, vol. 3, pp. 340–42. For a good sketch of the changes in Joffre's plans introduced by Nivelle, see King, pp. 143–44; and for more detail see Ribot, *Lettres*, pp. 176–77. King also provides a good summary of the raging debates about the merits of the plan (pp. 144–58). For some of the political and military discussions see Poincaré, vol. 9, pp. 97–100; and Painlevé, pp. 17–74.

[80] King, pp. 152–53; Poincaré, vol. 9, pp. 99–100, 106; Painlevé, pp. 40–41; Ribot, *Lettres*, p. 177. Painlevé was also very worried about the public knowledge about the planned offensive, extending even to the planned date. See King, p. 150; Ribot, *Lettres*, p. 186. General Franchet d'Esperey had told Nivelle several times, notably in a letter of 4 March, of the German withdrawal in the Alberich movement. Nivelle replied on 7 March that he thought the withdrawal unlikely and would not change anything in his plan of operations. See Painlevé, pp. 29–30.

As noted above, the Russian Revolution precluded the planned combined offensives on all fronts.[81] But developments on the French's own front also seriously affected the chances of success for the planned Nivelle offensive. The Alberich movement, for example, the withdrawal of German forces to the Hindenburg (Siegfried) line, starting on 4 February, as summarized by Painlevé, "created a situation in which three-quarters of our projected attack would fall upon a void."[82] In spite of such concerns the French political leadership in the end decided to give the green light for the offensive for three main reasons. First, a cancellation at this late date of the offensive would leave the British, who already had started operations on their front, in the lurch.[83] Second, the military leadership basically agreed that the Nivelle offensive would at least lead to some tactical gains for the French.[84] Moreover, General Nivelle promised he would not repeat a Battle of the Somme under any circumstances and to call off the offensive if his ambitious objectives would not have been reached in forty-eight hours.[85] Nivelle went even so far as to suggest that the first two German lines would be taken with *insignificant losses.*[86] Third, the government and military were afraid of leaving the initiative to the Germans.[87] As Jere Clemens King concludes, "further allied passivity pending American intervention seemed to Nivelle and the harassed government to be as dangerous an alternative as a partially successful offensive."[88]

After several postponements, the Nivelle offensive was finally launched on 16 April. It quickly became apparent that Nivelle's high hopes for his offensive would not be met. Painlevé noted that at the end of the first day, 16 April, the French had advanced five hundred meters, instead of the ten kilometers foreseen in the timetable of the

---

[81] Painlevé, p. 30; Ribot, *Lettres*, p. 185.

[82] Painlevé, quoted in King, p. 151. The Germans executed the Alberich movement in February 1917. By this movement they straightened their defensive line and withdrew to the well-prepared defensive Hindenburg (or Siegfried) line. On 24 February the British troops stationed in the region of L'Ancre found to their surprise that they no longer had the enemy in front of them. Initially the French leadership believed that the German withdrawal was to their advantage. See Ribot, *Lettres*, p. 185; Pétain, p. 138; Painlevé, p. 49.

[83] King, pp. 157–58; Painlevé, p. 46. During the last months of 1916 and in early 1917, French leaders started to doubt the British willingness to incur costs and continue the war according to the plans laid out at Chantilly in November 1916. See Joffre, *Memoirs*, p. 486.

[84] King, pp. 155, 157–58; Painlevé, p. 48; Poincaré, vol. 9, pp. 97–98; see especially Poincaré's notes of the crucial meetings of 5 and 6 April 1917, ibid., pp. 105–8.

[85] King, pp. 154, 159; Painlevé, p. 50; Poincaré, vol. 9, p. 108.

[86] Painlevé, p. 49, emphasis in original; see also p. 43.

[87] See Ribot, *Lettres*, p. 174; Painlevé, p. 45; King, p. 157.

[88] King, p. 169.

attack.[89] Poincaré noted on April 17 that "unfortunately, it is certain that a great part of the hopes conceived at the High Command have miscarried."[90] The next day Painlevé gave an account of the military operations in somber terms. Prime Minister Ribot could not hide his disillusionment.[91] Poincaré noted that the French army "had not even obtained what Pétain, who was the least optimistic of everybody, had hoped for."[92] After their high hopes at the end of 1916, persisting, for many, during the first months of 1917, the complete failure of the offensive came as a rude awakening.

By the second week after the start of the offensive, Painlevé and the members of the powerful Army Commission and even General Nivelle himself had concluded that the offensive had failed.[93] Painlevé notes that after five days the French armies had only in rare cases reached the second German position, and even at the most important points failed to pass the first line of the first position:

> These meager results, *so inferior to the most pessimistic forecasts*, cost very heavy losses to our best army corps. The rupture not having been obtained, the vast projects of intensive exploitation perished in the same stroke; the general plan of operations adopted in January 1917 became void.[94]

Painlevé argued convincingly that the attempt to rupture the front cost France more than 33,000 killed on the battlefield and about 85,000 wounded.[95] The total loss at Chemin des Dames in April and the May offensive cost France 61,000 killed, 95,000 wounded, and 9,000 taken prisoner.[96] (Slightly more than one-third of these losses were incurred as a result of the operation in May.) Thus, in six weeks France lost almost the same number as it did in four months of battle on the Somme.[97] As the result of his costly failures, Nivelle was replaced by Pétain.[98]

[89] Painlevé, p. 59.

[90] Poincaré, vol. 9, pp. 113–14.

[91] Ibid., p. 114. In his *Lettres*, Ribot concedes that after their high hopes, the Nivelle offensive became for all, except those who knew the difficulties the French army would have to encounter, "a deception" (p. 192).

[92] Poincaré, vol. 9, p. 114.

[93] King, pp. 163–64; for Nivelle's admission that the operation had been very costly and "had not yielded everything which she could have led to hope," see Poincaré, vol. 9, p. 122, diary entry of 25 April 1917.

[94] Painlevé, p. 67, emphasis added.

[95] Ibid., p. 66.

[96] King, p. 170; Painlevé, p. 133.

[97] Painlevé, p. 133.

[98] King, p. 168.

On 4 May in a meeting with the British, the two allies acknowledged that their optimistic plans for a *decisive* offensive in 1917 had failed. In their protocol they admitted that "the offensive plan began in April had become inoperative. A rupture was no longer to be considered."[99] In mid-September the new Painlevé Ministry evaluated the overall military situation. In its second meeting the new War Committee concluded that "an offensive in which France engages all its forces *cannot give us the decisive victory*, nor prevent the collapse of the Russian front."[100] Compared to their high belief in a decisive battle in 1917, fought and won largely by the French army, French decision makers scaled back their expectations to a calculated risk to stay on the defensive and await the Americans. This constitutes a drastic lowering of French expectations.

As a result of the failure of the Nivelle offensive, morale in the French army was at a low point.[101] The first mutinies broke out on 3 May, to break out again and far more seriously on 20 May. As these mutinies continued into June, the French leadership had to further adjust their estimates of their army's effectiveness and cost tolerance.[102]

Several factors contributed to the mutinies. First, soldiers had become much more pessimistic about the war and "claimed that as Russia crumbled, leaving the German war-machine free to re-mass on the French front, the Government were simply pulling the wool over peo-

---

[99] Painlevé, p. 106. Ribot renders the note written by the Chief of the British General staff at this meeting as follows: "We are nevertheless unanimously of the opinion that the situation has changed since the time when the two governments found themselves in agreement on the offensive plan started in April and that this plan is no longer operative. There can no longer be a question of aspiring to break the enemy front and aspiring to remote objectives" (*Lettres*, p. 211). It is important to recognize that the change in expectations did not come so much from new surprising German tactics (defense in depth) as from the revealed weakness of the French army and its leadership. Joffre had been aware of such new German tactics in October 1916. See Joffre, *Memoirs*, pp. 484–85.

[100] Painlevé, p. 216, emphasis added.

[101] Pétain, pp. 136–37; Stevenson, *French War Aims*, p. 62. An excellent source for the soldiers' perceptions of the war, its conduct, their leaders, and the homefront can be found in a compilation of the French trench press during the war by Audoin-Rouzeau. For the state of morale after the Nivelle offensive, see Audoin-Rouzeau, p. 56. It is interesting to note that Nivelle apparently had written a letter to the Minister of the Interior, Malvy, and to General Lyautey, then Minister of War, at the end of February 1917 in which he warned about the poor morale of the French troops. He blamed this on worker agitation and indiscipline and pacifist agitation in the rear. However, Nivelle almost immediately retracted this letter and did not communicate any doubts about the troops morale to Painlevé. On the contrary, he apparently communicated the highest confidence about troop morale to Painlevé. See Painlevé, pp. 170–73.

[102] Mutinous troops shouted, "We will defend the trenches, but we won't attack!" and "We are not so stupid as to march against undamaged machine guns!" (quoted in Liddell Hart, pp. 300–301).

ple's eyes, and that in fact everyone knew that the Americans would not be able to come into the war in time to be of any use." Second, soldiers complained about their treatment: They "were not getting proper leave; their rations were inadequate; their wives and children were 'starving to death.'" The most important factor, however, clearly was their estimate they were risking their lives in foolish offensives. "They made this point firmly to the Divisional Commander. 'You have nothing to fear, we are prepared to man the trenches, we will do our duty and the Boche will not get through. But we will not take part in attacks which will result in nothing but useless casualties.'"[103]

Pétain and the political leaders did not hesitate to put part of the blame for the mutinies on poor leadership in the French army, a claim supported by later historical analyses.[104] The substantial agreement between Pétain and Painlevé on the underlying causes of the revolts was expressed in their agreement on the solution. Pétain ordered in his very first directive that field commanders had to base "all of their plans upon adequate artillery action, thereby insuring *minimum losses.*"[105] Well aware of the fragile state of his instrument, Pétain recognized the need "to change the character of operations in order to make them less costly to our own troops."[106] As Stevenson points out,

> "It was not only to restore morale that Pétain wished to keep casualties to a minimum. The Army's losses had been so great that it was suffering from a 'crisis of effectives,' and it seemed essential to conserve manpower if France were to have its say in the eventual terms of peace."[107]

Although a certain "malaise" continued well into July, the mutinies subsided in June after the troops became convinced that their lives would not be thrown away in futile offensives.[108] Some local successes in purely limited offensives in July and August, well prepared by artillery barrages, helped to restore morale somewhat.[109] Stevenson agrees that the worst mutinies subsided after June but maintains that "it was February 1918 before the [French] Army's convalescence was com-

---

[103] Pétain's perspective on the mutinies can be found in his detailed analysis of its causes and remedies in Pétain, pp. 132–51. The quotations are from pp. 140–41, emphasis deleted.

[104] Ibid., pp. 132–51; Liddell Hart, p. 301; King, p. 172; and Stevenson, *French War Aims*, p. 62.

[105] King, p. 175, emphasis in original.

[106] Pétain, p. 146.

[107] Stevenson, *French War Aims*, p. 62.

[108] Painlevé, pp. 161, 163.

[109] Ibid., pp. 163–64, but see also pp. 157–58.

plete."[110] Stevenson's point is supported by Pétain's claims, repeated even in December, that the French army had only one more big offensive left in it. Hence the subsequent emphasis on the defensive, with only limited and well-prepared offensives.[111]

There hardly can be any doubt that the mutinies presented French leaders with some unpleasant new information: French relative strength and cost tolerance were lower than they had previously estimated. The French army was simply not willing to lose so much blood for so few expected gains.[112] The failure of the Nivelle offensive also struck a heavy blow to civilian confidence. Poincaré had already noted the spread of pacifism at the end of 1916.[113] Increasing surveys by the government showed a deep pessimism among the populace. In the period between May-June and November 1917, a deep feeling of depression spread over France. With the repeated promises that victory was near and that the next offensive would be the last now totally discredited, the French populace became unwilling to bear quietly any longer the privations imposed by the war. Strikes broke out, and industrial unrest grew rapidly. All in all, though, "like the mutineers, the strikers used pacifist and revolutionary slogans, but also like them they had goals that were generally limited and concrete, and could be satisfied short of political upheaval and a peace of capitulation."[114]

More unfavorable new information about the overall strategic situation came in October when the Italians were routed at Caporetto. This defeat cost the Italians not only over 600,000 men but also many valuable heavy guns. In November the British finally halted the bloody battles at Passchendaele, which had brought them little if any gains at the cost of over 400,000 casualties. Hence, all France's major allies had suffered unexpected and heavy defeats in 1917. The bright point on the horizon, American manpower, was arriving at a dangerously slow tempo.

---

[110] Stevenson, *French War Aims*, p. 62. On 21 October continued worries about the soldiers' morale led the High Command to recommend that the trench newspapers be censored at the division level, and that a copy of each paper should be sent to the General Headquarters (Audoin-Rouzeau, p. 22). Audoin-Rouzeau's detailed study of the French trench press led him to believe that "the terrible setbacks of 1917 ended by instilling doubt and creating a breach in this fine optimism. Henceforward perception of the length of the war was to be modified" (p. 174).

[111] Joffre, *Journal*, pp. 221, 224.

[112] The clearest expression of the French leadership's worries about the morale and resolve of the French army came when they discussed whether or not to grant the French socialists passports to go to the Stockholm Conference, where Russian, French, and German socialists would discuss peace terms. See Poincaré, vol. 9, pp. 148–49.

[113] Poincaré, vol. 9, pp. 24, 33.

[114] Stevenson, *French War Aims*, pp. 62–63.

Expectations for 1918

This section briefly summarizes the expectations for 1918 of two French Prime Ministers: Paul Painlevé, who became Prime Minister in mid-September, and Georges Clemenceau, who took over in mid-November. In his letter of 19 September to President Poincaré, Painlevé summarized the current situation and his expectations for the near future (keep in mind that Poincaré was notoriously hawkish on the war):

> The events occurring in Russia place the allied powers in a new situation. Whatever may now be Russia's future, her military force is tottering and that of the Central Empires finds itself proportionally strengthened. Our enemies see new perspectives opening before them. On the other hand, considering the weariness of the peoples, the shabbiness of the finances and the sacrifices imposed on the belligerent armies, the indefinite prolongation of the war at a slow pace, such as the course it follows at the moment, becomes more and more difficult. Such a modification in the reciprocal situations, especially if one has an eye on the future, merits all our attention. But she should not distract our spirit from the very real and serious advantages obtained so far. There is no doubt that the military situation on the west front is all to our advantage. The moral and material ascendancy of the French army and allied armies confirms itself every day.... Taking these considerations together,[115] it is allowed to conclude that we are approaching a critical point, a "node" of the present war and that, one way or another, we can find ourselves on short term in the presence of overtures to negotiations for peace.[116]

In spite of seemingly tough words about the strength of the French army and the state of affairs on the Western Front, Painlevé's expectations of imminent peace negotiations were not inspired by confidence in imminent victory but by a perceived inevitability of a negotiated and less than victorious peace. As Stevenson concludes, he expected French military prospects to worsen.[117]

When Clemenceau took over from Painlevé in mid-November, he also reviewed the situation together with his military adviser.[118] (With Clemenceau's ascent to power, the domestic pro-war hard-liners defeated those who favored a negotiated settlement, such as Caillaux, Briand, and Painlevé.) The situation was maybe even worse than it had

---

[115] Note that Painlevé does not speak one word about the American army and its potential contributions.

[116] Painlevé's letter is quoted in Poincaré, vol. 9, pp. 289–90.

[117] Stevenson, *The First World War and International Politics*, p. 167.

[118] Clemenceau's estimates are in King, pp. 193–94.

been for Painlevé. Russia and Rumania were out of the war, and the disastrous defeat of the Italians at Caporetto in October reduced them to a defensive posture for a long time to come. Hence, there would be no chance of using Italian manpower in France. Britain would have to replace the 700,000 to 800,000 men it had lost in 1917, and the French army suffered serious shortages in manpower, tanks, planes, long-range heavy artillery, and machine guns.[119] The Germans, in contrast, would be able to move many, if not nearly all, divisions used on the Eastern Front to the west. As Clemenceau's military adviser, General Jean Mordacq, commander of the 24th Division, warned, "The Allies were reduced to the defensive until the Americans could be transported to France in sufficient numbers. Would they arrive in time, and what would be the quality of their troops?"[120]

On separate occasions between 12 and 14 December, Clemenceau laid out his estimates and expectations for the coming year to the Chamber Army Committee, the External Affairs Committee of the Chamber, the Senate Army Committee, and President Poincaré:

> I believe that the Germans will make their greatest effort since the beginning of the war, greater than at Verdun. There is no doubt of it. . . . But, if we hold them, the Germans might not wait any longer before offering peace terms which might be acceptable to us. . . . The German interest is to make a peace in 1918, while ours is to make peace in 1919 when we will have an indisputable victory. . . . If we speak of peace today it would be disastrous, unless we are offered terms in keeping with our dignity. . . . We cannot afford to make a single further mistake, or to run any more risks. We will still lose men in remaining on the defensive, but fewer than if we took the offensive and we would not risk total defeat. . . . I am not for the offensive, because we do not have the means. We must hold on, we must endure. . . . I do not wish at this time to risk the outcome of the war on an offensive.[121]

In a rare moment of agreement between the two old antagonists, Poincaré agreed that France lacked the manpower for an offensive. It should be noted here that, in contrast to the German public, the French public was well aware of the dangerous situation and the impending German

---

[119] The manpower problem remained an overriding concern. On 26 December 1917 Pétain told Clemenceau that with the present numbers of effectives France could not fight more than one more great battle. Clemenceau was urged again to find more men for Pétain. See Poincaré, vol. 9, p. 433.

[120] Quoted in King, p. 194.

[121] Watson, *Georges Clemenceau*, pp. 294–96; Poincaré, vol. 9, pp. 413–14, quoted in King, p. 201.

offensives.[122] Marshall Foch admonished the President and Prime Minister not to exaggerate the dangers.[123] Clemenceau was less confident and urged the British not to redirect manpower to the Turkish Front.[124]

Compared with the French government's optimism of early 1917, therefore, both Painlevé and Clemenceau had become considerably more pessimistic. French estimates of the *long-term* probability of victory could be pretty high, and not much lower from French estimates in late 1916 to early 1917, but survival in the *short-term* seemed much more problematic.

The Change in French War Aims

To evaluate the change in French war aims during 1917, this section first summarizes French war aims at the end of 1916, next those of the end of 1917, and then compares both. On 12 January 1917, the Council of Ministers approved what constitutes the first full-fledged official statement of France's war aims.[125] Prime Minister Briand sent the memorandum to the French ambassador in London, Paul Cambon, to instigate an "exchange of views" on French war aims with its ally.[126] France demanded the return of Alsace-Lorraine, with the frontier of 1790, explicitly formulating this not as "conquest" or profit but as a "recov-

---

[122] At the end of January Joffre does not seem to have been worried about the impending German offensives. He estimated that the Germans would have between 180 and 190 divisions available on the Western Front, against 170 Allied divisions. See Joffre, *Journal*, p. 258.

[123] Poincaré, vol. 9, pp. 413–14.

[124] For the discussions in the Supreme War Council and its decisions in late January, see Joffre, *Journal*, pp. 258–60, and Watson, p. 298.

[125] These war aims differ and are more ambitious than those proposed in the Entente's *collective* reply to President Wilson's note of 18 December, which had asked the belligerents to state their war aims. For Wilson's note, see Scott, pp. 12–15. As Stevenson notes, the Entente's reply "was sufficiently elastic to be compatible with the French territorial programme which was being elaborated in the same weeks" (*French War Aims*, p. 47).

[126] The outlines of this program were agreed upon at a meeting at the Elysée Palace on 7 October 1916 when Poincaré and Prime Minister Briand conferred with Leon Bourgeois, Charles de Freycinet, and the Presidents of the two chambers, Deschanel and Dubost. On 4 November Briand asked Jules Cambon to prepare instructions to his brother on the basis of the agreement reached on 7 October. Jules conferred with his brother Paul, and together they prepared a memorandum dated 6 November, which contained the great bulk of the actual details of the January 1917 program. Note, however, that these aims were substantially higher than those agreed upon on 12 January 1917. See Stevenson, *French War Aims*, p. 42, as well as pp. 43–44; see also Poincaré, vol. 9, pp. 3–4; Soutou, "La France et les marches de l'est, 1914–1919," pp. 356–60; Soutou, *L'Or et le sang*, p. 280; Bonnefous, vol. 2, pp. 253, 259. The important passages of this letter are reprinted in Suarez, vol. 4, pp. 128–30.

ery."[127] The issue of the left bank of the Rhine was raised in deliberately ambiguous terms. On the one hand, the letter argued that some "good spirits" in France would like to reclaim those lands as the lost heritage of the French Revolution. On the other hand, the letter expressed a fear that a claim to these provinces would be seen in France as a conquest and would create "great difficulties."

Although I will return to the issue in more detail below, in this context it is important to note how much questions of Alsace-Lorraine and the Rhineland were connected to the central issue of the *international consequences* of the terms of settlement. These international consequences were captured by the code word "guarantees." Briand's letter to Paul Cambon continued:

> What is more important than a glorious but precarious advantage, is to create a state of affairs which will be a guarantee for Europe as much as for us and which would be security for our territory. In our eyes, Germany must no longer have a foot beyond the Rhine, the organization of these territories, their neutrality, their temporary occupation are to be considered in the exchange of views between the Allies; but it is important that France, being the most directly interested in the territorial status of this region, will have the preponderant voice in the examination of the solution of this grave question.[128]

The government furthermore approved the principle of the League of Nations but suppressed the earlier reference to a break-up of Austria-Hungary and Polish access to the sea.[129] The Council of Ministers decided to leave open the question of what to do with Luxembourg after the war.[130] In negotiations with the Tsar in March 1917, Gaston Doumergue proposed significantly higher French war aims, but since he apparently exceeded his instructions, I feel confident not to count these as authentic French demands.[131]

France's demands at the end of 1916 also contained substantial claims against the Ottoman Empire, largely intended to contain British influence there. These were contained in the Sykes-Picot Agreement,

[127] In the November memorandum the demand was for "at least" the frontiers of 1790. See Stevenson, *French War Aims*, p. 48.

[128] Suarez, vol. 4, p. 130. The earlier, November, version of the memorandum had suggested the alternative of two neutral and autonomous buffer states under Allied protection and temporary occupation. See Stevenson, *French War Aims*, p. 44.

[129] Stevenson, *French War Aims*, p. 48.

[130] Soutou, *L'Or et le sang*, p. 281; see also p. 178; Soutou, "La France et les marches de l'est," pp. 360–61.

[131] Stevenson, *The First World War and International Politics*, p. 118; Suarez, vol. 4, p. 133. For Doumergue's demands, see Suarez, pp. 134–35; Renouvin, "Die Kriegsziele der

which came into force when the Sharif of Mecca launched the Arab Revolt on 5 June 1916.[132] The Sykes-Picot Agreement gave France "priority of right of enterprise and local loans" and the sole right to "supply advisers or foreign functionaries at the request of the Arab State or Confederation of Arab States" in an area marked as (A) on the map accompanying the agreement.[133] This area roughly corresponds to modern Syria and parts of northern Mesopotamia. Britain would enjoy similar rights in area (B), roughly corresponding to modern Jordan and the southern part of Mesopotamia and the coast of the Persian Gulf. Furthermore, the agreement allowed France "in the blue area . . . to establish such direct or indirect administration or control as they desire and as they may think fit to arrange with the Arab State or Confederation of Arab States." This "blue area" roughly corresponds to Lebanon, the coast of Syria, and a large chunk of southeastern Turkey. Britain would enjoy similar rights in a "red area," corresponding roughly to a broad strip along the Tigris and Euphrates rivers from Baghdad to the Persian Gulf. Russia would get similar rights in Armenia. Britain would also gain the ports of Haifa and Acre, but Haifa would remain a free port for French shipping and goods. Palestine would come under international administration. Under pressure from Italy for compensation, the French were forced to make some concessions to the Italians at the end of 1916.[134] (These demands in Turkey were lower on several points than those proposed in 1915, most visibly with regard to Syria and Cilicia.) The Treaty of Bucharest of 17 August 1916 had brought Rumania into the war and promised it large gains at Austria-Hungary's expense, but the effect on French war aims was at best marginal.[135]

Among scholars of French war aims in the First World War, there is a general consensus that France's war aims went down between January and fall 1917.[136] Renouvin argued that "[f]rom March 1917 until the

---

franzözischen Regierung 1914 bis 1918," pp. 139–41. Bonnefous, vol. 2, pp. 259–60, gives a slightly different text.

[132] For official confirmation of the agreement, see Andrew and Kanya-Forstner, pp. 100–102. The Sykes-Picot Agreement and Grey's notes to Cambon can be found in the World War I Documents Archive at www.lib.byu.edu/~rdh/wwi/1916, June 6, 1998.

[133] For the maps, see Stevenson, *The First World War, 1914–1918*, part 2, series H, WWI, 1914–1918, vol. 3, maps on pp. 322–24; Andrew and Kanya-Forstner, appendix.

[134] Andrew and Kanya-Forstner, p. 113.

[135] Rieber, p. 273.

[136] Soutou somewhat hedges his bets. He admits that the general scholarly opinion about France's war aims is that the fall of the Briand Cabinet, the Russian revolution, and the failure of the Nivelle offensive caused the abandonment of the greater part of the objectives defined in the fall of 1916 (*L'Or et le sang*, p. 498). However, in his opinion "this interpretation is excessive. It seems rather that certain options, such as the annex-

very last weeks of the struggle the government limits its demands."[137]
Johnson explicitly ties the decrease in French war aims to "disappoint-
ments" suffered by the French in early 1917:

> The result of these two disappointments [the fall of the Czar government
> in Russia and seemingly hostile conclusions of the Curzon Committee on
> British war aims in the Ottoman Empire], combined with the failure of the
> Nivelle offensive, the wave of mutinies and strikes and increasing diffi-
> culty in maintaining the socialists and radical socialists within the *union
> sacrée*, was that the French Government modified their war aims and in
> public pronouncements went back to the position where they insisted
> upon the return of Alsace-Lorraine and were deliberately vague about all
> other means whereby they would strengthen France's international posi-
> tion against Germany.[138]

By early June 1917 the Ribot government and the two chambers
committed themselves *against* annexations. The rejection of outright
annexations implies a lowering of expectations because the previous
Briand Cabinet had deliberately left this option open.[139] Another indication of the downward adjustment of France's war aims is the government's position on Luxembourg. Recall that previously the council had
decided to leave the option of Luxembourg's annexation by France
open. On 9 June Ribot told the Belgian Minister de Gaifier that "the
annexation of Luxembourg . . . did not figure in France's war aims."[140]
The government's new position on the annexation of Luxembourg was
formalized in an exchange of notes. Although there was substantial
confusion about France's war aims in the spring of 1917, for example,
the difference between the programs of Cambon and Doumergue, it is
clear that, by ruling out options that were previously left open, the
government lowered its war aims.

The most important decrease in French war aims, from the Alsace-
Lorraine of 1790 to the Alsace-Lorraine of 1870, gradually became explicit during the late summer and fall of 1917. Adjusting to the unfa-

---

ation pure and simple, which they had not wanted to discard totally at the end of 1916,
were certainly abandoned, but that others in return had been firmly maintained, in spite
of a certain semantic caution due to the socialist campaigns in favor of a peace 'without
annexation nor indemnity.' " Soutou, "La France et les marches de l'est," p. 368. See also
L'Or et le sang, p. 498. Even by his words, then, French war aims do go down, if only by
discarding some options previously held open.

[137] Renouvin, "Die Kriegsziele der französischen Regierung 1914 bis 1918," p. 130.
[138] Johnson, p. 51.
[139] Soutou, "La France et les marches de l'est," pp. 370, 372.
[140] Stevenson, *French War Aims*, pp. 82–83; Soutou, "La France et les marches de l'est,"
p. 368.

vorable new information of 1917, the diplomacy of Ribot's government became more modest, and in the summer Ribot "felt obliged to launch a campaign of propaganda and Ambassadorial lobbying in Washington on behalf of the claim even to the Alsace-Lorraine of 1870, let alone anything more."[141] The decrease in French war aims becomes more visible after Painlevé became Prime Minister in mid-September. In his letter of 19 September to Poincaré, quoted in part above, Painlevé hints that he is willing to accept a negotiated peace, which, following Soutou, "would be a profound change compared to the politics of his predecessors."[142] In his ministerial declaration on the inauguration of his ministry, Painlevé specified once more France's war aims:

> Disannexation of Alsace-Lorraine, reparation of damages and destruction caused by the enemy, conclusion of a peace which would not be a peace of coercion and violence containing in itself the seeds of future wars, but a just peace, where no people, powerful or weak, would be oppressed, a peace where effective guarantees protect the Society of Nations against all aggression.[143]

Painlevé's declaration leaves open the question of which Alsace-Lorraine is to be "disannexed," that of 1790, 1814, or 1870? The next day Ribot, now Foreign Minister in the Painlevé Ministry, made clear in the chamber that the territory to be "disannexed" was the Alsace-Lorraine of 1870.[144] Painlevé was apparently even willing to give the Germans "unhoped-for" colonial and economic compensation, perhaps in Indochina or Madagascar, if the Germans would agree to return Alsace-Lorraine.[145] At the end of September 1917 Ribot emphasized again that France was now willing to settle for the Alsace-Lorraine of 1870. He instructed the French ambassador in Washington to tell the American

---

[141] Stevenson, *The First World War and International Politics*, p. 172. Stevenson notes that the Americans remained noncommittal.

[142] Soutou, "La France et les marches de l'est," p. 374. Painlevé told Lloyd George at the end of September that he doubted "whether France would continue fighting if it were offered both nine-tenths of Alsace-Lorraine and the whole of Belgium" (Stevenson, *French War Aims*, p. 90). On 19 September former Prime Minister Briand wrote a draft of French war aims on the urging of Poincaré, Painlevé, and Ribot. See Ribot, *Journal*, pp. 205–6. The letter is reprinted in Suarez, vol. 4, pp. 272–73. This memorandum was the result of peace feelers between Briand and the German Baron von Lancken. French war aims were lowered because France now "exclude[s] all possibility to put into question the left bank of the Rhine" (Suarez, vol. 4, p. 273). Hence, France was now willing to forego any change in sovereignty over the Rhineland.

[143] Bonnefous, vol. 2, p. 309; 18 September 1917, *Journal officiel*, Chambre des Députés, 1917, vol. 3, p. 2322.

[144] 19 September 1917, *Journal officiel*, Chambre des Députés, 1917, vol. 3, p. 2359.

[145] Andrew and Kanya-Forstner, p. 119.

government that "there can be no lasting peace without reparation of the violence done to France in 1871." As Stevenson notes, "of the claim he had earlier upheld to the frontier of 1790 he made no mention."[146] In January 1918, finally, the Clemenceau Cabinet limited its demands to the Alsace-Lorraine of 1870 before the Chamber of Deputies.[147]

The change in French war aims from the Alsace-Lorraine of 1790 to the Alsace-Lorraine of 1870 may seem insignificant to the reader not attuned to the particularities of European geography. By reducing its demands, however, France would give up an important part of the Saar coalfield. The Alsace-Lorraine of 1790 would give France roughly two-thirds of this coalfield; the Alsace-Lorraine of 1870 gave France only about one-third. As Stevenson describes it, "In 1913 the Saar coalfield had an output of 17,472 million tonnes, of which only 3,846 million came from the portion south of the frontier of 1815 [i.e., the Alsace-Lorraine of 1870]." In 1913 the Saar, moreover, produced 1.375 million tons of iron and 2.08 million tons of steel. The rest of France produced only 5.207 million tons of iron and 4.687 million tons of steel.[148] The annexation of the Saar by France would therefore change the balance of (industrial) power between France and Germany. Prominent businessmen feared another war and a French defeat in the next ten years if the underlying economic imbalance between France and Germany was not redressed.[149] As Stevenson has noted, "Transferring German Lorraine to France . . . especially if sovereignty over the Saar were altered as well, would in principle go far to redressing the imbalance between French and German heavy industrial capacity."[150] By giving up the demand for the Alsace-Lorraine of 1790, therefore, France made a big concession. With regard to the left bank of the Rhine, French war aims decreased even further in late October. The Cambon letter had first demanded the separation of the left bank from Germany. Then annexation was ruled out, but the option of buffer states was not. In the late fall a change in sovereignty over the left bank was finally ruled out.[151]

The new Clemenceau government was reluctant to be specific on war aims. As Clemenceau proclaimed, his aim was to win. However, Foreign Minister Pichon specified French war aims on 27 December in the Chamber of Deputies, hence, after the Russian armistice:

---

[146] Stevenson, *French War Aims*, p. 83. For a German estimate of Painlevé's demands in the late summer of 1917, see Scherer and Grunewald, vol. 2, no. 231, pp. 378–80.

[147] Stevenson, *French War Aims*, pp. 101–2; Renouvin, "Die Kriegsziele der französischen Regierung 1914 bis 1918," p. 155.

[148] Stevenson, *French War Aims*, appendix I: Alsace-Lorraine and the Saar, pp. 216–18.

[149] Johnson, p. 46.

[150] Stevenson, *French War Aims*, p. 218.

[151] Ibid., note 155, p. 91; see also p. 249.

Liberation of our territories . . . reestablishment of the right to recover the possessions which have been taken from us by force, and, therefore, reintegration of Alsace-Loraine into France. . . . Just reparation of damages, . . . guarantees of a durable peace by . . . the League of Nations. . . . It is no less certain that we have strict obligations with regard to the oppressed nationalities, not only of Belgium, Serbia, Rumania . . . but also of Poland.[152]

While demanding an independent and indivisible Poland, with all necessary guarantees for its free development, the omission of Russia and, more particularly, the occupied territories of Lithuania and Courland is significant. The demand for an independent Poland indicates that the omission of any demand for the Germans to withdraw from the other occupied Russian territories is not the result of a French acceptance of the status quo on the Eastern Front at the time of the armistice. Hence, the omission of a demand for the withdrawal from the occupied territories in Lithuania and Courland clearly implies that France had lowered its war aims in Eastern Europe.

France was willing to scale back its demands against the Ottoman Empire as well. On 28 November, and thus before the Russian request for an armistice, Clemenceau told Lloyd George,

he would make peace with Turkey on any terms; that he did not want Syria for France; . . . that if Lloyd George could get him a protectorate over Syria for France he would not refuse it "as it would please some reactionaries," but he attached no importance to it; he agreed that Palestine should not be given back to Turkey. He gave Lloyd George a free hand to negotiate with Turkey and make the best terms he could.[153]

In his speech before the Chamber of 27 December, Pichon maintained a claim to the internationalization of Palestine but avoided any direct claims to Syria. Hence, French claims against Turkey, *and against Britain*, had decreased by the end of 1917.

Although on occasion hard to trace and disentangle, it is clear that France's war aims went down between January and December 1917.[154] Moreover, war aims went down as the expected costs of war went up. The change in France's war aims between January and December 1917 was the result of the rational adaptation by a nonrepressive, nonexclusionary regime to changed expectations. This conclusion is strongly supported by the most prominent historians of French war aims in the

[152] 27 December 1917, *Journal officiel*, Chambre des Députés, 1917, vol. 4, pp. 3626–31.
[153] Roskill, pp. 466, 570; Hankey, vol. 2, p. 820.
[154] I should note that the drop in France's war aims would be much more dramatic if I had taken French war aims as propounded by Doumergue in his visit to the Tsar in February as my baseline. For Doumergue's war aims see Bonnefous, vol. 2, pp. 259–60.

First World War, Pierre Renouvin and David Stevenson. Stevenson, for example, argues that French war aims went down over 1917 because "these were months of adjustment to a sharp decline in France's relative, and even absolute, power."[155] Analyzing the changes in French war aims, Stevenson concludes:

> Changes in the military balance and in official perceptions of allied intentions were constantly rebounding on the content and on the manner of presentation of French aims. . . . The military balance had a second, less immediate effect. As the prospects of success receded and advanced, so different items among the French leaders' objectives became more prominent in their diplomacy. They approved the Cambon letter at a moment when it seemed that victory might be near and France's contribution to that victory a leading one. By the autumn of 1917, both contingencies were very much in doubt, and French diplomacy and strategy grew less ambitious.[156]

The Causal Mechanisms

There can be no doubt that French leaders did indeed lower their war aims as they became more pessimistic about the outcome of the war. The evidence from both primary and secondary sources is overwhelming.[157] The question remains, however, whether French leaders felt pressured to keep their war aims high enough to prevent their overthrow and punishment.

A careful analysis of the historical evidence leads me to conclude that France's behavior is *consistent* with my theory. The French case does not offer evidence against the proposed causal mechanism but also offers only weak evidence in favor of it. The problem lies in France's demand for the return of at least part of Alsace-Lorraine. It can be

---

[155] Stevenson, *French War Aims*, p. 207. As do I, Stevenson attributes this decline in France's power to the failure of the Nivelle offensive, the resulting mutinies and collapse of civilian morale, and the collapse of Russia. Stevenson, furthermore, agrees that the American entry into the war was only of limited import. See *French War Aims*, pp. 61–63.

[156] Ibid., pp. 207–8; Renouvin, "Les tentatives de paix en 1917 et le gouvernement français," pp. 494–95. This conclusion is also supported by Johnson, who concludes that the most important factors explaining the decrease in French war aims were the changing relations with its allies, the failure of the Nivelle offensive, and the concomitant mutinies and problems in maintaining the socialists and radical socialists in the *union sacrée*. See Johnson, p. 51.

[157] See Bonnefous, vol. 2, pp. 249–51; Poincaré, vols. 4–9; Ribot, *Lettres*; Ribot, *Journal*; Painlevé; Suarez; Renouvin, "Die Kriegsziele der französischen Regierung," pp. 129–30; Renouvin, "Les Buts de guerre des gouvernement français," pp. 494–95; Stevenson, *French War Aims*, pp. 207–8; Johnson, p. 51; Soutou, *L'Or et le sang*, pp. 281, 498; Soutou, "La France et les marches de l' est," p. 368.

argued that, in the age of nationalism, as long as France regained part of these "lost provinces," the gains of war would outweigh the costs of war. There is one piece of evidence that seems to support this contention. In a discussion on 11 February 1916 with the French Minister of War Millerand, the Belgian King Albert "observed that after the war our Governments would have to face a difficult if not critical situation." Millerand responded that he counted "on the liberation of Alsace and Lorraine to allay the recriminations of the French people."[158] Thus, although this evidence is only circumstantial and weak, it still remains plausible to argue that, as long as French leaders could claim after the war they had regained "Alsace-Lorraine" (never mind its precise borders) for the French nation, they would not need to fear the overthrow of the democratic regime and punishment. Therefore, it becomes impossible to conclusively falsify the argument that French leaders formulated war aims to buy off their people and the domestic political opposition.

Although the possibility remains that French politicians insisted on the return of at least part of Alsace-Lorraine for domestic political reasons, I could not find any evidence of upward pressure on French war aims caused by a fear of the domestic consequences of poor terms of settlement. The causal mechanism so prominent in Germany is nowhere to be found in France: French leaders never continued the war out of the fear that only victory could prevent their overthrow and punishment. To be sure, French leaders feared the consequences of defeat, but faced with only two choices, victory or defeat, everyone prefers victory. When faced with a trade-off between victory, defeat, and negotiated settlement, French politicians, especially Briand and Painlevé, became more attracted to a negotiated settlement as they became more pessimistic.[159] Even where internal lobbying was strongest, with regard to France's colonial aims, Stevenson concludes that "the timing of these aims responded more to diplomatic and military developments than to internal lobbying."[160]

[158] Van Overstraeten, *The War Diaries of Albert I*, p. 92. What the consequences would be if the recriminations of the French people could not be allayed, we are left to wonder. In interpreting his statement, moreover, we must consider Millerand's audience. In the postwar intra-alliance bargaining, support from Belgium could be important.

[159] See Painlevé's letter to Poincaré of 18 September 1917 and reports of the Briand-Lancken negotiations in the fall of 1917. See also Soutou, *L'Or et le sang*, pp. 498–99. In September Painlevé's increased pessimism and his estimate of the possibility of a negotiated peace was echoed by his advisers in the Ministry of War. See Stevenson, *French War Aims*, p. 92.

[160] Stevenson, *French War Aims*, p. 22. In an interesting twist on the relative gains argument, Soutou points out several instances in which French industrialists argued against overly extensive annexations in the Saar because it contained the wrong kind of coal.

Although France had its own "'war-aims movement' of right-wing parties, business spokesmen, patriotic journalists and pressure groups, which favored annexations on the eastern frontier ... [this] was smaller and less well co-ordinated than in Germany, and was balanced by the Socialists and the CGT" trade union.[161] Moreover, it deserves emphasis that the industrialists were not behind demands for the return of Alsace-Lorraine and the Saar, because they realized the coke and iron production there would be an economic and industrial disadvantage rather than a boon.[162] As Stevenson points out,

> the industrialists were well able to distinguish their desires as patriotic Frenchmen from their interests as manufacturers. It was primarily for the first motive that they wanted the frontiers pushed forward. They took for granted the return of Alsace-Lorraine, both for sentimental reasons and because it would gravely weaken Germany's military power by depriving the enemy's heavy industry of most of its domestic iron ore. Given this, the Saar must be annexed as well, in order to prevent France's coal deficit from worsening. But the Saar could not relieve the French industry's special shortage of coking coal, and, if coupled with Alsace-Lorraine, would double the capacity of French metallurgy and plunge it into a crisis of overproduction. Pinot and the Peace Treaty commission therefore desired Alsace-Lorraine and the Saar in spite and not because of their private commercial needs, and it was only further annexation beyond this point that they deemed unambiguously in the industry's interest.[163]

If the French regime, or successive governments, feared they could not settle on terms that did not include the return of Alsace-Lorraine, we would at least expect traces of such arguments to survive in the memoirs and secondary literature. However, as noted above, I could find only one instance where the argument was invoked, and that one may have been strategic to ensure France a better position in *intra*-alliance bargaining. Against the argument that a return of the lost provinces was necessary for the regime's survival, Stevenson has concluded that the most a French government that accepted a compromise on Alsace-Lorraine could expect was a "grievous loss of face."[164] Moreover,

---

The addition of this kind of coal would do little to contribute to French industry but would of course help hurt German industry. See Soutou, *L'Or et le sang*, e.g., pp. 183–86.

[161] Stevenson, *The First World War and International Politics*, p. 113. Renouvin points out an interesting parallel to German plans to reward the people. The royalist party *Action française* apparently hoped to reward elite troops with land after the war. See Renouvin, "Die Kriegsziele der französischen Regierung 1914 bis 1918," p. 160.

[162] Soutou, *L'Or et le sang*, p. 188 and throughout.

[163] Stevenson, *French War Aims*, p. 39.

[164] Ibid., p. 12.

the French government also was faced with socialist pressures *against* the demand for straightforward reannexation. The socialists proposed a plebiscite to let the inhabitants of these two provinces determine their own fate, a solution rejected by the government.[165]

Indeed, as the war continued, the opposition on the left became rather less revolutionary and predominantly pacifist, especially after the Nivelle offensive. Ebba Dahlin emphasizes this point in her excellent comparative study of French and German war aims:

> The attitudes found within French Socialism differed from the German views that the French opposition was more pacifist than revolutionary. The issues on war aims were complicated by the difference in the governments—imperial and monarchical in Germany, republican in France. The actual difference in the measure of popular control was not as great as the forms of government might imply, but the republic in France invoked the allegiance of both liberals and radicals, while in Germany the liberals fought for suffrage reform and the radicals desired the downfall of the monarchy. The longer the war continued the greater was the divergence.[166]

The opposition on the right became further marginalized when it lost the fight over parliamentary control over the army.[167]

Thus, in France neither the opposition from the right, mainly supporters of the army and the Church, nor the socialist opposition from the left posed a real threat to the survival of the French regime.[168] It is not surprising, then, that war aims never became a central issue in the domestic political struggle. Demands for rewards for the sacrifices imposed by the war could be met by relatively minor domestic political concessions. For example, in early 1917 after the terrible suffering of the previous year at Verdun, the government issued a decree that implemented measures to support disabled war veterans and workers injured in industrial accidents.[169] The government reacted with carrot and stick to the strikes of January and quickly established a minimum wage rate for all industries doing business with the government, and it set up permanent arbitration and conciliation commissions to resolve

---

[165] Ibid., p. 114.

[166] Dahlin pp. 90–91.

[167] Ibid., p. 35. A particularly good source on the struggle for parliamentary control is King, *Generals and Politicians*.

[168] There were fears in France about the threat of a military coup inspired by the right and social revolution inspired by the left. However, these fears were about the consequences of a disastrous defeat, not about a settlement on moderately losing terms. See Stevenson, *French War Aims*, pp. 199–200. Pershing dismisses the likelihood of a change in the form of government as unlikely. Pershing, vol. 1, pp. 197–98.

[169] Herman, p. 315.

industrial disputes.[170] Later the government dealt with the mutinies and strikes of the spring and summer of 1917 not by repression but by a conciliatory approach, remedying where appropriate legitimate grievances and settling labor disputes through arbitration. Workers and especially soldiers, as Pétain noted in his diagnosis of the mutinies, demanded justice on the home front, where some were waxing rich and reaping the benefits, while they were paying the costs of the war. The government reacted from late April onward by raising the soldiers' pay, ameliorating working conditions, and clamping down on profits.[171] When Clemenceau came to power he made a special effort to keep a check on spreading pacifism while satisfying legitimate demands of the working classes. In December he met with trade union leaders and promised them he would support them on wages and working conditions in return for their promise not to engage in political strikes. Furthermore, he would not interfere as long as their pacifist expressions were kept private and *in camera*. As a result of Clemenceau's conciliatory policies, the number of strikes and workers involved in strikes fell dramatically in 1918.[172] As Stevenson points out, the demands of the French strikers and mutineers of 1917 were of a much more limited nature than those of their German counterparts and "could be satisfied short of political upheaval."[173]

Successive French governments and even colonialist circles were also willing to reward France's loyal subjects in the colonies. As the secretary of the Comité de l'Afrique Française, Auguste Terrier, wrote in December 1914, "Colonialist circles are unanimously agreed that there must be important changes in native policy because of the élan shown by our Algerian, Tunisian, and Moroccan subjects. . . . A wholesale reform of colonial policy will become unavoidable."[174] When conscription was extended to the major towns of Senegal in 1915 the townspeople gained the formal recognition of their citizenship.[175] Clemenceau was also willing to reward France's colonial subjects, particularly the Algerians, for their sacrifices in the war. The Clemenceau

---

[170] Droz, p. 166; Hardach, *The First World War, 1914–18*, p. 66; Herman, p. 318.

[171] On 22 April the government introduced the *Loi Mistral*, which imposed additional control over profits and working conditions. The balance was further adjusted in favor of the lower classes with the introduction on 31 July of a new income tax that abolished some taxes, for example, on doors and windows after 1 January 1918, and levied new taxes on industrial and commercial profits, turnover and agricultural profits, interest, and other forms of profit. See Herman, pp. 364, 417.

[172] Ibid., p. 485.

[173] Stevenson, *French War Aims*, p. 63.

[174] Andrew and Kanya-Forstner, pp. 81–82.

[175] Ibid., p. 82.

"government committed itself to changing the naturalization laws so that war veterans and their father could become French citizens without having to suffer the loss of their Muslim personal status."[176] On 29 January 1918 the Council of Ministers proposed reforms to reward their loyal subjects in Algeria for their sacrifices by promising indigenous citizenship to Muslims who had been resident for two years. This reform became law on 4 February 1919 and created over a half million new voters.[177]

One additional potential competing explanation can also be ruled out. The theory laid out in chapter 2 argues that leaders and regimes sometimes continue a war because they fear severe domestic punishment in the form of exile, imprisonment, or death. Bueno de Mesquita and his collaborators have argued that the danger of losing political office makes Democratic leaders cautious of entering wars and leads them to select wars they are more likely to win in the first place.[178] Downs and Rocke argue that Democratic leaders should be most likely to gamble for resurrection when they anticipate that the failure of their policies will lead to their removal from power.[179] Extending the arguments of Bueno de Mesquita et al. and Downs and Rocke to the logic of war termination should lead to the prediction that Democratic leaders gamble for resurrection to stay in power when they lower their estimates of the expected outcome of the war. This competing explanation fails because Viviani, Briand, Ribot, Painlevé, or Clemenceau never formulated French war aims to personally stay in power when they became more pessimistic about the outcome of the war. The oversight and debates over war aims in the Chamber of Deputies and Senate would simply not have allowed any such attempts. Through the committee system and especially the secret sessions, French parliamentarians were always well enough informed about the developments on the battlefield to recognize any unrealistically high demands. Painlevé's removal in November also showed that parliament could and would remove a Prime Minister who had lost their support. Clemenceau explicitly acknowledged he could not continue the war against the wishes of parliament. In mid-December 1917 he told President Poincaré, "We shall hold on, we shall hold on. If the Chamber overturns me, she assumes her responsibility. Clearly, I cannot force the country to fight against its will, but between us, we shall hold on."[180]

---

[176] Ibid., p. 139.

[177] Huard, p. 226.

[178] Bueno de Mesquita, Siverson, and Woller; Bueno de Mesquita and Siverson, "War and the Survival of Political Leaders;" Bueno de Mesquita and Siverson, "Political Survival and International Crises."

[179] Downs and Rocke.

[180] Poincaré, vol. 9, p. 414; Watson, pp. 294–96.

From the very beginning of the war, French leaders were always very concerned about the international consequences of the terms of settlement, and it seems much more plausible that demands for Alsace-Lorraine were inspired by security concerns than by domestic political concerns: "With their steel mills, iron ore, and phosphates, and their eastern frontier on the Rhine, the lost provinces could substantially increase French power."[181] Germany's invasion of Belgium and Bethmann Hollweg's referral to Germany's pledge to honor Belgium's neutrality as a mere "scrap of paper" brought out the commitment problem in sharp relief. After the war, how could the French rely on any mere "scrap of paper" to contain German ambitions? Especially after Russia threatened to drop out of the war, France dreaded a future in which it might have to fight a renewed war against Germany, and this time under less favorable circumstances with fewer allies on its side. For France,

> The most likely future was therefore one of indefinite confrontation with a rival of inherently superior strength. It was possible to hope that the artificial alteration of the balance of power caused by . . . Allied victory could be embodied in the Treaty and prolonged by its strict maintenance. Yet few French statesmen felt that this sufficed as an answer to the security problem.[182]

Fearful of a renewed war in the near future on less favorable terms, there existed a lower bound of French war aims below which the leaders would not go. This lower bound was drawn around the restoration of Belgium and some sort of arrangement with regard to the left bank of the Rhine, including Alsace and Lorraine. French leaders felt that lower terms would endanger France's long-term security. German control over Belgium would, of course, further increase Germany's power relative to France. With uncertainty about the future of its alliances and a seriously weakened Russia on Germany's Eastern Front, France was under tremendous pressure to change the balance of power in its favor now while it had the strongest possible coalition on its side.

What French leaders wanted were "guarantees." As President Poincaré put it, "the only peace the Republic can accept is one which will guarantee European security . . . and effectively protect us against any renewed offensive by German ambition."[183] There were two possible

[181] Stevenson, *The First World War and International Politics*, p. 114; see also Stevenson, *French War Aims*, p. 12.

[182] Stevenson, *French War Aims*, p. 208; see also p. 93.

[183] Poincaré's message to the Chamber, 5 August 1915, quoted in Stevenson, *French War Aims*, p. 17. For similar expressions by other French leaders see ibid., pp. 42, 65, 67, 70; Johnson, p. 46; Bonnefous, vol. 2, p. 260; Dahlin, p. 98; Suarez, vol. 4, p. 130. Soutou argues that the accord of 5 September 1914, in which the Allies agreed not to sign a

roads to security guarantees: a deterrent alliance and a change in the relative balance of power by diminishing Germany's strength while increasing France's. The most direct road to a change in France's power relative to Germany led to the left bank of the Rhine.[184] French demands for guarantees were not some code word for annexations on the left bank of the Rhine. German territory there was intended as a buffer in one form or another, such as an autonomous state, a French protectorate, or a demilitarized zone. The demand for the return of Alsace-Lorraine clearly was also motivated by security concerns. While the return of these provinces may have had beneficial domestic consequences, it would surely also improve France's power relative to Germany and give France better borders.[185] France also sought to secure some form of guarantees through its allies. The best-known plan to provide France with adequate "guarantees" and address the commitment problem was, of course, the League of Nations.[186]

The French worried not only how the terms of settlement would affect their relative power vis-à-vis Germany but also their relative power vis-à-vis its allies, specifically Britain. From the beginning of the war French leaders were aware of the implications of their intra-alliance bargaining power for the terms of settlement. One consideration in the decision to go ahead with the Nivelle offensive at the beginning of 1917 was that it seemed to promise a distinctly French victory, which would bring the French maximum leverage at the peace table against allies and enemies alike. In the 12 January letter to Paul Cambon re-

separate peace, has not been appreciated for its self-conscious and systematic character: the decision to pursue the war until total victory or, in any case, until the achievement of serious guarantees against Germany. Indeed, Soutou, argues, a return to the status quo ante would not suffice because the balance of power would have to be modified to contain German ambition (L'Or et le sang, pp. 113, 116–17, 139).

[184] Stevenson, French War Aims, pp. 13, 208; Soutou, L'Or et le sang, pp. 116–17, 139; Johnson, p. 52.

[185] This interpretation was apparently shared at the time by the British, who acknowledged that the French demanded "Alsace-Lorraine, as indemnity and security for the future" (Pershing, vol. 1, p. 220). Junior Minister to Lloyd George's War Cabinet Robert Cecil supported the return of Alsace-Lorraine to France because it would give France better strategic borders. See Rothwell, p. 62.

[186] There was, however, another, almost completely forgotten and subsequently ignored plan to provide guarantees, the so-called Clémentel Plan, which sought guarantees by economic means. French Commerce Minister Etienne Clémentel advocated the control of "four or five of the most important materials," which would give the Allies an "economic card of war" which could become a "powerful diplomatic instrument" (quoted in Soutou, L'Or et le sang, p. 485). Soutou is the best source on the Clémentel plan and its development from the Paris Economic Agreement of 1916 onwards. See also ibid., pp. 487, 489, 496–97; Stevenson, French War Aims, p. 11; and Stevenson, The First World War and International Politics, p. 175.

ferred to above, the French government explicitly recognized the potential problems of the compatibility of French war aims with the demands of its allies: "Each power has its own aspirations, it is important to know them to balance, in some way, the satisfaction which could be granted or the sacrifices which could be demanded from each."[187] French leaders were particularly concerned about France's postwar power relative to Britain in the Balkans and in the Middle East and its relative intra-alliance bargaining power.[188]

In the first instance, the shift in intra-alliance bargaining power expressed itself in Clemenceau's willingness to make concessions to the British in the Ottoman Empire. When the United States entered the war and gradually became more important, French leaders became more worried about President Wilson's pressure on French war aims. As Jusserand, French ambassador to the United States, wrote to Ribot in September, the more France grew dependent on American assistance of all kinds, the more "a Head of State assuredly well disposed to us, but . . . who naturally cannot attach the same importance to our peace terms as we do ourselves, will be free to choose the hour and the circumstances of the ending of the conflict."[189]

In summary, there exists but scant evidence that French leaders worried about the domestic consequences of the terms of a negotiated settlement. In contrast, there exists abundant evidence French leaders worried about the international consequences of the terms of settlement. Thus, while the evidence on the domestic consequences of the terms of settlement is merely consistent with the theory, the evidence on the international consequences supports it.

Conclusion

This chapter has examined how French leaders reacted when they were forced to lower their estimates of the probability of victory and their estimates of French relative strength and cost tolerance and increase their estimate of the expected costs of war. The evidence is unambiguous: As a result of these developments, French leaders lowered their war aims, just as the theory predicted a nonrepressive, nonexclusionary regime would do.

[187] Quoted in Suarez, vol. 4, p. 128.
[188] See Dutton, "The Balkan Campaign and French War Aims in the Great War," pp. 97–113. See also Soutou, *L'Or et le sang*, p. 483.
[189] Quoted in Stevenson, *French War Aims*, p. 82.

While the predictions of the theory were indeed borne out, it proved unfortunately impossible to decisively reject the hypothesis that French leaders formulated war aims that were intended to buy off the people for their sacrifices. The problem lay in the French demand for the return of at least part of Alsace-Lorraine. Was this demand maintained out of a perceived need to buy off the people, or because France needed these provinces and their mineral deposits to redress the (economic) imbalance of power with Germany, or because France remained optimistic it would win the war, if it could survive until the Americans arrived? In this chapter I presented what evidence there is for each of these three interpretations. The overall historical record has led me to conclude that the latter two motivations were much stronger than the first. Although the evidence for it is very weak, it is nevertheless impossible to rule out that French leaders demanded Alsace-Lorraine to reward the people for their sacrifices.

7

Great Britain

T HIS CHAPTER OFFERS a second detailed case study of how a nonrepressive, nonexclusionary regime reacts to unfavorable new information. The main conclusions resemble the conclusions about France with one striking addition. As in France, Britain's leaders lowered their war aims when they became more pessimistic about the outcome of the war, worried little about the domestic consequences of the terms of settlement, but were very concerned about the international consequences of the terms of settlement. The most interesting finding of this chapter is that Britain's leaders were willing to do the one thing that their German counterparts tried to avoid at almost all costs: reward the people for their sacrifices by domestic political reform. The Representation of the People Act of January 1918 more than doubled the franchise and gave the vote not only to most of the men that had been previously excluded but also to women over the age of thirty.

As before, this chapter is divided into four main sections. The first section codes prewar Britain's regime type. The second section then offers a brief overview of the new information and changes in British war aims in each year of the war. The third section analyzes 1917 in detail. The fourth section again examines the historical fit of the proposed causal mechanisms and briefly addresses two potential competing explanations.

The Independent Variable: Regime Type

Hardly anyone will dispute the democratic nature of Great Britain's regime before the war.[1] While I agree that Great Britain was democratic, prewar Britain was by no means a harmonious and peaceful, trouble-free polity. Some historians have even argued that in the summer of 1914 the threat of civil war hung over the country. Any description of the British political organization and its institutions must begin with the observation that Britain had no *written* constitution. However,

[1] The classification used in the data analysis in chapter 3 also codes Great Britain as a Democracy. In 1914 Britain scores an 8 on the Democracy index and a 0 on the Autocracy index of Gurr's *POLITY III*.

policymakers and population were very much cognizant and respectful of an unwritten constitution, derived from precedents whose origins went back to the Magna Carta.

In 1910 a new and relatively unknown King, George V, ascended the throne. He nominally ruled an empire whose constituent parts had varying degrees of political autonomy. Canada and Australia, for example, had autonomous governments and were self-governing while India was ruled by a British viceroy. In sharp contrast with the German Kaiser, the King's powers were very limited and circumscribed. He governed under the doctrine of "ministerial responsibility." In that tradition "the king is bound to act on the advice of his ministers, he must choose his ministers, or rather his first minister, in accordance with the will of the House of Commons."[2] In essence, and especially with regard to foreign policy, the King could take no position that had not been previously agreed upon or that was not in harmony with the policy of his government. Indeed, sovereignty lay not with the King but with Parliament, a tradition that can be traced back as far as 1641.

A Cabinet of ministers, in fact, governed Great Britain, although the title "minister" was unknown until 1916. In the Cabinet the Prime Minister was more than a primus inter pares; his voice and opinions counted disproportionately in the policy-making process. As Daalder puts it, "his voice was weighed, not counted. He could threaten individual ministers with dismissal, and all ministers with his own resignation, which would force their resignation as well. Other ministers were responsible not only to the Law and to Parliament, but also to him personally."[3] After the tenure of Pitt the Younger, it was generally accepted that the Prime Minister could not serve against the wishes of the House of Commons. Great Britain had two Prime Ministers during the war, Herbert Asquith until December 1916, and from then on David Lloyd George.

The House of Commons, then, held a central place in the policy-making process. Every Cabinet and Prime Minister had to spend a considerable amount of time and effort to defend their respective policies before the House. However,

> [t]he Cabinet virtually dominates the legislative process . . . and determines the main lines of policy. . . . Because the Cabinet and the leadership of the majority party are one, for all practical purposes, the House of Commons has become an arena for public debate between the Government and the Opposition, rather than a distinct organ of legislation and control. Parliamentary government has in fact become Cabinet government.[4]

[2] Maitland, p. 397.
[3] Daalder, p. 24.
[4] Ibid., p. 4.

Control in the House of Commons depended on a majority that, especially right before the war, did not necessarily depend on the outright majority of one party. In fact, the wartime Cabinets of Asquith and Lloyd George both depended on majority coalitions, the first a coalition of Liberals and Irish Nationalists and Labour, the second on a highly unusual alliance of some Liberals, Conservatives, Irish Nationalists, and Labour.

In 1911 the powers of the House of Lords had been dramatically curtailed. Already well before that time, defeat in the House of Lords did not entail resignation of the ministry. However, while it retained its right to amend bills, in the Parliament Act of 1911 the House of Lords lost its veto power. Two other major innovations were introduced in 1911. First, the life of Parliament was restricted to five years, which was extended by both houses during the war. Second, Lloyd George's budget of that year for the first time remunerated members of Parliament with a salary of 400 pounds a year.

It may be surprising to learn that before the war, of all the countries with more or less representative governments, Britain and Hungary were the only ones that did not have manhood suffrage.[5] The prewar franchise excluded all women (as was common in most of Europe) and about one-third of the adult male population.[6] It has been argued that the franchise system deliberately was class exclusive and aimed to "disfranchise almost half the industrial working class."[7] In principle, the franchise denied access to paupers, living-in servants, most of the military, and many sons living with their parents. Very rigorous registration requirements further de facto denied the vote to many who might have claimed it. In effect, the right to vote still depended on a successful claim to possession. The system was further biased against the working class by allowing almost a half million plural votes.

Based on this quick sketch of the main political institutions, it becomes apparent that while the industrial working class had less access than the more privileged classes in Britain, it was by no means systematically excluded from access. By means of the franchise, the British political system did to some extent discriminate against one group, as was the case in Germany in general and Prussia in particular. However, in Britain, the representatives elected by this group, that is, Labour, did have real political power and access to the policy-making process. Its votes and initiatives in the House of Commons could be

---

[5] This section on the prewar franchise is largely based on Matthew, McKibbin, and Kay.

[6] "According to the Home Office Return for 1915, the electorate, which, of course, consisted entirely of men, was 8,357,000 out of a population of 43,500,000." These figures included Ireland (Fraser, p. xxi).

[7] Matthew, McKibbin, and Kay, p. 735.

essential to the survival of the government. Moreover, the party was represented in the four standing committees in proportion to its numbers in the House. These committees reviewed the bills that were regularly referred to them, unless the House directed otherwise. In the last election before the war, that of December 1910, the four major contenders were Liberal, Conservative, Irish Nationalist, and Labour. The Independent Labour Party was founded by Keir Hardie in 1893, but the Labour Party as we know it stems from the LRC, the Labour Representative Committee, set up in 1900. Notwithstanding the discrimination in the franchise, Labour increased its seats from 2 in 1900 to 42. At this election the Conservatives and Liberals both gained 272 seats, and the Irish Nationalists gained 84 seats.

Three movements, each with a potential for violence, put considerable stress on these prewar institutions: Irish Home Rule, trade unions, and suffragettes. The political conflict over Irish Home Rule can largely be traced back to the fight between Liberals and Conservatives. U.S. Ambassador Walter Hines Pages put it simply and straightforwardly:

> The Conservatives have used Ulster and its army as a club to drive the Liberals out of power: and they have gone to the very brink of civil war. They don't really care about Ulster. I doubt whether they care very much about Home Rule. They'd slip Ireland out to sea without much worry— except their own financial loss. It's the Lloyd George programme that infuriates them, and Ulster and anti-Home Rule are all mere weapons to stop the general Liberal Revolution.[8]

Because of the Parliament Act of 1911, the House of Lords could no longer function as a constitutional barrier to Irish Home Rule, and by 1914 some form of Irish Home Rule appeared inevitable. Although the dispute between Irish Nationalists and Ulster Volunteers seemed to forebode violence, maybe even civil war,[9] autonomy for Ireland would never entail the same drastic change in structure that would result from a change in the Prussian franchise.

Another movement with the potential for violence was the marked increase in Trade Union activity and the number of work stoppages. From 1908 onwards there was a very sharp increase in the numbers of workers involved in strikes, peaking in 1912 to about one and a half million. Although Dangerfield argues that the war basically prevented

---

[8] Quoted in Shannon, p. 206.

[9] Daalder, p. 29. A few months after the war broke out Sir William Birdwood remarked, "*What* a piece of real luck this war has been as regards Ireland—just averted Civil War and when it is over we may all be tired of fighting" (quoted in Gooch, *The Plans of War*, p. 300). Even Prime Minister Asquith apparently initially welcomed the developing crisis in Europe as possibly having the "good effect of throwing into the background the lurid picture of 'civil war' in Ulster" (quoted in Cassar, p. 12).

a general nationwide strike during the fall and winter of 1914, T. O. Lloyd correctly concludes that the trade unions' "militancy had mainly economic causes, and was not a sign that anarchy and revolution were at hand."[10] Simultaneously, under the zealous leadership of Christabel Pankhurst, the women in the suffragette movement broke windows, staged protest rallies and hunger strikes, and agitated in increasingly violent ways for the right to vote.

Although these three movements made many uneasy about the stability of the British monarchy, the regime and its structure were simply not under the same kind of pressures as the German regime. One important reason was that the governing class did not present a monolithic front. Many of the great political quarrels such as parliamentary reform, Irish Home Rule, divestiture of the Church of England in Wales, even the suffragette movement cut across social lines and boundaries.[11] Historians have debated whether the country was prepared to go to civil war over Ireland or revolution by syndicalists. Some see the years before the war as a period of golden tranquility; others see revolution or civil war lurking just around the corner. Both these views seem extreme. A more balanced view leads to the conclusion that "[w]hile England in 1914 was not on the verge of plunging into disorder and chaos, people were uneasy and uncertain about what was happening."[12]

Most importantly, in sharp contrast to the German leadership, British policymakers saw the rise of the working class as *a change in degree, not in kind*. If necessary, the British Democratic leadership was willing to compromise and give up some of their power, to the smallest possible degree to be sure, to the working classes. One particularly cynical lord of the Whig Party pithily

> compared Parliament to a traveller in a sledge, pursued by a band of famished wolves. From time to time he throws them quarters of venison to distract their attention and keep them back so that, half-satiated, they may be less ferocious when they gain the horse's head. Of course, it is necessary to husband the venison, and make it last as long as possible by cutting it up into little pieces. Part of our nobility . . . meritoriously devote themselves to this ungrateful task.[13]

In summary, the rise of the working class in Britain was not seen in zero-sum terms as it was in Germany. Because no group was systematically excluded from access to the policy-making process, because a

---

[10] Lloyd, p. 38; Dangerfield.

[11] Le May, p. 13.

[12] Lloyd, p. 53.

[13] Quoted in Le May, p. 20.

loser in one round could hope to win in future rounds, and because the polity neither wanted to nor could repress the domestic opposition, Great Britain qualifies as a nonrepressive, nonexclusionary regime.

Overview of the War

Table 7.1 summarizes the intervening and dependent variables for Britain in each year of the war. Like the French, British leaders lowered their estimates of the outcome of the war in 1914, 1915, and 1917. Because I go into detail only on 1917, I summarize 1914, 1915, 1916, and 1918 in a few brief paragraphs here.

In contrast to many of the continental powers, British leaders, largely under the influence of Lord Kitchener, estimated from very early on that the war would not end until 1917.[14] Informed members of the British Cabinet were under no or few illusions about the length of a war with Germany. In 1912 the General Staff had refused to give an estimate of the maximum duration of such a war, instead warning that "it would not be safe to calculate the war lasting less than six months."[15] When war broke out in August 1914, some Cabinet members may have initially been more optimistic about the duration of the war, but Kitchener's dire predictions of a long war apparently carried the day.[16] Kitchener's predictions had very important implications for British strategy in the first two years of the war. Not only did it mean that British economic strength would carry its maximum weight, but it also seemed to hold out the attractive possibility of weakening Germany *and* France *and* Russia at the same time, letting them bleed each other white.

The new information of the first months of the war dispelled any initial or lingering optimism about a quick end to the war against Germany. With the high loss rate of the first months on the Western Front, Britain would probably have to pay a higher blood price than the leadership had hoped and estimated.[17] On the other hand, the success of

[14] Foreign Minister Grey's well-known lament in the first days of the war, "The lamps are going out all over Europe; we shall not see them lit again in our lifetime," surely says as much about his expectations of the duration as about the consequences of the war.

[15] Quoted in French, *British Strategy and War Aims*, p. 15.

[16] Farrar, *The Short-War Illusion*, p. 6; Guinn, pp. 27, 31. Gooch, *The Plans of War*, pp. 301–7; French, *British Strategy and War Aims*, pp. 14–15. Although at the end of August 1914 Asquith may not yet have accepted Kitchener's estimate that the war would last at least three years, he apparently did recognize the war would not be over by Christmas. See Cassar, p. 45.

[17] French, *British Strategy and War Aims*, pp. 58, 65. According to his biographer Cassar, Asquith had anticipated that the war would be very costly, but even his worst fears were exceeded (Cassar, p. 45).

TABLE 7.1

New Information and Changes in War Aims for Britain

Britain	New Information	Changes in War Aims
1914	*Unfavorable:* 1–4 Nov: Turkey enters. Nov: High casualty rate. *Favorable:* 23 Aug: Japan declares war on Germany? Sept: France withstands German attack? 25 Dec: One million volunteers answer Kitchener's call.	2–6 Aug 1914–9 Nov 1914 *Decreases:* 9 Nov: Free passage through the Straits for Russia.
1915	*Unfavorable:* Sept–Oct: Bulgaria enters war. Sept–Nov: Loos, Britain has to share the costs of war earlier; Dardanelles a costly failure; Russia suffers severe defeats. 23 Nov: Defeat at Ctesiphon. 5 Dec: Kut besieged. *Favorable:* 23 May: Italy enters war. 9 July: Southwest Africa occupied? 18 Oct: Sharif Hussein promises an Arab revolt. Feb 1916: Cameroons occupied?	9 Nov 1914–23 Feb 1916 *Decreases:* 10 Mar: Constantinople and surroundings to Russia. Ottoman Empire to be dismembered? 26 Apr: Italian gains in the Adriatic. *Increases:* 10–19 Mar: Formerly neutral zone in Persia a British sphere; direct control over Basra; direct or indirect control over Baghdad vilayet.
1916	*Unfavorable:* 29 Apr: Kut surrenders. 1 July–Nov: Somme (?). Sept–Dec: Rumania defeated; German counteroffensives in Russia succeed. 15 Oct–Dec: German restricted submarine warfare costly. *Favorable:* Feb–April: Russian offensives in Caucasus successful. 5 June: Arab Revolt. 4 July 1916–Nov 1917: Brusilov offensive, Austro-Hungarian weakness. Aug: 6th Battle of the Isonzo. 27 Aug: Rumania enters war. Oct: Central Powers themselves estimate they would henceforth decline. Oct: Greece enters war? 19 Oct–Dec: French counteroffensives at Verdun successful. Dec: American intervention more likely?	23 Feb 1916–10 Jan 1917 *Decreases:* 5 June: Sykes-Picot Agreement, break-up of the Ottoman Empire. Nov 1916–Feb 1917: Concessions to Italy in Turkey. *Increases:* 5 June: Sykes-Picot Agreement, Southern Mesopotamia? 10 Jan 1917: Liberation of the Slav and Czecho-Slovaks?

TABLE 7.1 (cont.)

New Information and Changes in War Aims for Britain

Britain	New Information	Changes in War Aims
1917	*Unfavorable*: Jan/Feb–Dec: Unrestricted submarine warfare (especially April). 19–31 July: German counteroffensive against Kerenski. Summer–Fall: Russian army dissolving. 9 Apr–17 May: Costly failure of Battle of Arras. 16 Apr–4 May: Nivelle offensive. 31 July–10 Nov: Passchendaele? 18 Aug, 30 Nov: Americans slow in coming. 27 Oct: Caporetto. 13 Nov: Second Russian Revolution. 15 Dec: Russia drops out of the war; armistice on the Eastern Front. *Favorable*: 11 Mar: Baghdad falls. 15–17 Mar: First Russian Revolution? 5 Apr: America enters. Summer: Convoys work. 9 Dec: Jerusalem occupied.	10 Jan 1917–5 Jan 1918 *Decreases*: 5 Jan 1918: "Reconsideration" of Alsace-Lorraine? Demand for change in German regime withdrawn. Demand for evacuation of invaded Russian territory withdrawn; hence, Germany might gain control over Courland and Lithuania. Only indirect control over Mesopotamia? *Increases*: 5 Jan: Ottoman Empire not broken up; Russia would not gain Constantinople and the Straits. British control over Palestine?

TABLE 7.1 (cont.)
New Information and Changes in War Aims for Britain

Britain	New Information	Changes in War Aims
1918	*Unfavorable*: 21 Mar–29 Apr: Successes of the German Stormtrooper offensives. Summer-Fall: Intra-alliance bargaining power shifting to the Americans? *Favorable*: Mid-July: German offensives have failed. May–July: American troops finally arrive in large numbers? 18 July–Sept: Allied counterattacks push back German army; Foch's strategy works. 8 Aug: Tanks work? 15 Sept: Austrians launch peace appeal. 15–24 Sept: Bulgarian forces defeated at the battles of Monastir-Doiran. 19–20 Sept: Decisive Turkish defeat at Megiddo. 24, 26 Sept: Bulgarians request an armistice. 27 Sept: Allies break through and turn the Hindenburg line. 30 Sept: Bulgaria surrenders 3–5 Oct: Germans and Austrians request an armistice. 14, 20 Oct: Turks first ask Wilson for armistice, then Britain for an immediate peace treaty, accept on 31 Oct. 3 Nov: Austria accepts a separate armistice. 2–9 Nov: News of the revolution in Germany slowly starts to reach Allied leaders.	5 Jan 1918–9 Nov 1918 *Increases*: 11 June: Treaties of Brest-Litovsk and Bucharest cannot be accepted. Sept: Sykes-Picot Agreement to be revised in Britain's favor at France's expense. 27–31 Oct: Increased demands against Ottoman Empire: Allied occupation of the forts in the Dardanelles, occupation of Batum and Baku, control of Transcaucasian railway. 29 Oct–5 Nov: Germany must surrender 160 U-boats; 10 battleships and 6 battle cruisers to be interned, none to be returned to Germany. Germany to withdraw from the occupied territories in the east. Germany left unable to exploit armistice and resume hostilities under better conditions. Reparations. Acceptance of Wilson's Fourteen Points (with reservations on freedom of the seas and reparations)? Hence, demand for change in regime re-instated. Austro-Hungarian army demobilized, troops serving on the Western Front withdrawn, half of all artillery surrendered. Serbs to occupy all territory claimed by the Yugoslavs; large part of Austro-Hungarian navy to be surrendered to Italy.

Notes: Question marks indicate the uncertain status of new information and/or a change in war aims. For Britain's full war aims see chapters 8 and 9.

Kitchener's recruitment drive probably made the leadership more optimistic about the nation's cost tolerance. Turkey's entry implied a greater drain on Britain's—mainly imperial—resources than had been originally estimated and therefore a downward revision of Britain's relative strength and an upward revision of the costs of war. Given the cabinet's acceptance of Kitchener's early estimates, the new information revealed between August and December most likely led the British leadership to only marginally revise its estimates about Britain's relative strength and the costs of war.

When we consider British war aims in the First World War, one thing stands out. British war aims were formulated to contain not just the Central Powers but also Britain's wartime allies. This dynamic was a crucial factor in the government's reluctance to discuss its war aims in the first place and helped keep those aims vague.[18] For 1914 we unfortunately can only compare the Cabinet consensus on British war aims of early August with the aims as stated by Prime Minister Asquith on 9 November 1914.[19] (Asquith's statement of 1 March 1915 and the Cabinet decisions of the first two weeks of March 1915 were undoubtedly influenced by new expectations about the Dardanelles expedition.) It deserves note that on 9 November the Allies were still "racing to the sea" in France, and the British government had just five days earlier declared war on Turkey. The comparison reveals few if any changes in British war aims against Germany and Austria-Hungary, but as was the case for France, the evidence does not really permit strong inferences either way.

However, British war aims clearly decreased in the Middle East. On 9 November, with approval from Asquith and the Cabinet, Foreign Minister Grey told the Russian ambassador in London, Count Benckendorff, that the final disposition of Constantinople and the Straits would be settled in accordance with Russia's wishes after Germany

[18] Britain's intention to impose its terms on both friend and foe is one of the main themes of French, *British Strategy and War Aims*. For Asquith's and Grey's reluctance to discuss British war aims see Cassar, p. 70; and Gooch, "Soldiers, Strategy and War Aims in Britain 1914–1918," p. 26.

[19] For British aims in early August, see French, *British Strategy and War Aims*, pp. 21–22. As do I, Soutou attaches more importance to restoring the balance of power than French seems to be willing to acknowledge in spite of his own arguments. See Soutou, *L'Or et le sang*, p. 115. See also Ekstein, pp. 23–24, and Asquith's speech on the Vote of Credit for the War on 6 August 1914, quoted in Spender and Asquith, vol. 2, pp. 111–16. For Asquith's statement of 9 November, see the speech by the Rt. Hon. H. H. Asquith at the Guildhall, 9 November 1914, in *War Speeches by British Ministers 1914–1916*, p. 59. See also Rothwell, pp. 19 and 25; and Cassar, p. 71.

had been crushed.[20] This constitutes a decrease in Britain's aims because the issue of the Straits had been a long-standing source of conflict between Great Britain and Russia, and Great Britain had repeatedly refused to make any concessions to Russia. Between 1853 and 1856 Great Britain and France had fought Russia over the issue of the Straits in the Crimean War. In 1908 and again in 1911, the Russian government unsuccessfully attempted to persuade the British government to accept a unilateral revision in Russia's favor of the agreements on the Straits of 1871 and 1878.[21] The concession is all the more remarkable since Grey had told Ambassador to the Ottoman Empire Sir Louis Mallet on 25 June 1914 that in the question of the Straits, Great Britain intended to hold to its point of view of 1908.[22] From a British imperial perspective, a weakened Ottoman Empire would also make it harder to balance against Russia. A weaker Turkey would obviously offer a weaker counterweight to any Russian influence and expansion specifically in Persia, where Russia and Great Britain had a history of competing claims. Greater Russian influence there could threaten British imperial interests in India. Furthermore, free passage through the Straits, no longer compensated for by free passage for all, would seriously affect the naval balance of power in the Mediterranean. Overall, hence, the new information of 1914 led to a lowering of British war aims.

For British leaders the actual and potential intervention by three outside actors constitutes a large part of the new information of 1915. Italy's decision to enter on the side of the Entente, although at a high price, more than compensated for the unfavorable new information of Bulgaria's decision to join the Central Powers. In the Middle East the promise of an Arab revolt held out by Sharif Hussein could only partially compensate for the costly failure of the Dardanelles expedition and the defeat of a largely imperial force at Ctesiphon. The failures of the French spring offensives and Russia's severe defeats convinced the leadership that Britain would have to bear its share of the costs of the war earlier than had been previously estimated. This recognition led to British participation in the set-piece battle of Loos in September, the first of many

---

[20] This promise was intimately connected with Grey's warning that the Russians not become distracted by the prospects of gaining Constantinople and keep their military efforts firmly focused on Germany. See Pokrowski, *Die Internationalen Beziehungen im Zeitalter des Imperialismus*, II. Reihe, 6. Band, 2. Halbband, no. 484, p. 422; French, *British Strategy and War Aims*, pp. 45–46; Cassar, pp. 71, 74. King George V also told the Russian ambassador in London on 13 November that Constantinople "must be yours" (no. 506, p. 441). For the demand of the islands of Imbros and Tenedos, see no. 500, p. 436.

[21] Linke, p. 17.

[22] Ibid., p. 187.

battles whose meager gains in no way justified the high costs. But British leaders did not change their belief in the effectiveness of wearing down the Germans or their estimate of the probability of victory.[23] They also seem to have stuck by their timetable for victory in 1917.

The main effect of the unfavorable new information of 1915 again fell on the expected costs of war and induced the British leadership to make substantial concessions to Britain's allies, thereby lowering British war aims. Questioned about British aims on 23 February 1916 in the House of Commons, Asquith purposively repeated the language he had used on 9 November 1914 at the Guildhall. But behind the scenes, Britain made a major concession to Russia in the form of a promise to let Russia gain control over Constantinople and its surroundings if the war ended in victory. Grey had promised Sazonov in November 1914 that Britain would support Russia's wishes with regard to the Straits and Constantinople, but that Britain "refused to consider any settlement with regard to Turkey until after the war."[24] However, by March 1915 the British Cabinet recognized they could not postpone the settlement of this question until after the war. On 10 March the Cabinet accepted that if the war ended successfully, Russia would get Constantinople, the western shores of the Bosphorus, the Sea of Marmara, southern Thrace up to the Enos-Midia line, part of the Asiatic shore, and the Islands of Imbros and Tenedos at the mouth of the Straits.[25] As a quid pro quo, Russia would support French and British demands, not only in the Ottoman Empire but also elsewhere.

The promise to Russia was a major concession, as possession of Constantinople implied a great deal more than free passage through the Straits. With access to a warm water port, the Russian empire would be considerably strengthened and a bigger threat to British interests.[26]

---

[23] Rothwell, p. 34; Riddell, pp. 84, 144; French, *British Strategy and War Aims*, pp. 107, 141, 168. French shows that Kitchener and Robertson used dramatic arguments about the necessity to win the war in 1916 to convince the War Committee of full British participation in the planned spring offensives of 1916 (*British Strategy and War Aims*, p. 174). Given Robertson's memoranda and Kitchener's previous dissembling about strategic affairs in early 1915, it seems much more likely that these arguments were strategic than that they really believed them at that time. The main contention seems to have been that Britain's allies would make a separate peace if Britain did not participate to the fullest extent in the combined Allied offensive (pp. 158–59, xiv). Guinn notes the absurdity of a French separate peace (p. 93). The main effect of this fear falls clearly on the expected costs of the war.

[24] Cassar, p. 74.

[25] Ibid., pp. 74–75; see also Linke, pp. 197–99.

[26] In his memoirs Grey acknowledges the importance of this concession and adds that this secret treaty "would have been the most important of all if Russia had not subsequently cancelled it by breaking her agreement with her allies of September 1914 and

Russian control over Constantinople would rule out a naval expedition and invasion of Russia through the Black Sea as had happened in the Crimean War. To pass through the Straits, warships would need Russia's consent. Furthermore, the dismemberment of the Ottoman Empire would remove a still formidable enemy on Russia's southern flank. Britain's demands in Mesopotamia were designed to balance the expected increase in Russian power. It was expected that Russia would annex its zone in Persia outright, once the Ottoman Empire would fall under the carving knife. To counter the threat to India, Britain would need control of the Gulf and therefore demanded Basra and the Baghdad vilayet.[27]

To buy Italy's entry into the war British leaders were forced to make further strategic concessions. In the Treaty of London of 26 April, Italy was vouchsafed substantial gains mainly at Austria-Hungary's but also Turkey's expense.[28] Italy would obtain the Trentino, Cisalpine Tyrol, the counties of Gorizia and Gradisca, all of Istria with its islands, the province of Dalmatia and several islands along that coast, Valona and the island of Saseno, and the islands in the Dodecanese. British leaders deemed Italy's aims to be "very sweeping" and agreed only reluctantly.[29]

---

making peace without them" (Viscount Grey of Fallodon, *Twenty-five Years, 1892–1916*, vol. 2, p. 189).

[27] The de Bunsen Committee recommended in 1915 that the Ottoman Empire except for Constantinople and Basra be preserved as an independent federal state. The least preferred solution would be to divide Turkey into spheres of influence. See Cassar, p. 77, note 45, p. 249; Rothwell, pp. 26–27. Both Asquith and Grey also strongly preferred *not* to cut up the Ottoman Empire. See Smith Jr., "Legacy to Stalin," p. 542; Cassar, p. 76; Andrew and Kanya-Forstner, p. 72. However, conditional on the materialization of the Arab Revolt, the British accepted their least preferred outcome in the Sykes-Picot Agreement of January (confirmed in an exchange of letters in May) 1916. Because the Sykes-Picot Agreement would *only* come into effect if the Arab revolt actually occurred, the agreement did not, at any time during 1915, constitute minimum demands for settlement for the British. The negotiations between the French and British leading to the Sykes-Picot Agreement were triggered by the offer of an Arab revolt by the Sharif Hussein in mid-October. Stevenson notes that "Grey supported the agreement . . . in the belief that its realization depended on an Arab Revolt that he still thought unlikely to occur" (Stevenson, *The First World War*, p. 129). For other British counterdemands, see French, *British Strategy and War Aims*, pp. 81–82. Rothwell fails to mention free passage through the Straits but does include that Britain demanded a free hand in Arabia (p. 26). Russia, in turn, asked for other concessions that the British government did not explicitly accept (Linke, pp. 197–99).

[28] See Toscano, pp. 183–89.

[29] Quoted in Stevenson, *The First World War and International Politics*, p. 53. Britain was forced to make two additional minor concessions to its allies. Japan gained concessions in China that "left a nasty taste in British mouths," and France gained concessions in the former German Cameroons. See French, *British Strategy and War Aims*, p. 184; Rothwell, p. 11.

Summing up, the effect of the new information of 1915 was to increase the British leadership's estimate of their share of the expected costs of war. Britain's leaders reacted as the theory predicts. During the year they offered concessions to allies who would help them share these burdens: Russia and Italy. These concessions resulted in lower British aims at the end of 1915.

The overall effect of the new information of 1916 is difficult to assess because some of the new information led British leaders to somewhat raise their estimates of the costs of the war, whereas other information led British leaders to somewhat raise their estimates of the probability of victory. The bloodbath on the Somme and the successes of the German submarines in the fall of 1916 surely increased the leadership's estimates of the costs of the war.[30] However, the success of the Russian Brusilov offensive and the revealed weakness of the Austro-Hungarians, the Arab Revolt, but in particular the successful attrition on the Somme and elsewhere and the knowledge that the Central Powers themselves estimated that their power would henceforth decline all made the leadership more confident about Britain's relative strength.[31] These revisions work in opposite directions: Increased estimates of the costs of war should lead the British to lower their aims; increased estimates of the probability of victory should lead the British to raise their aims. The overall effect on British demands is therefore difficult to predict, but because in both aspects the new information of 1916 was relatively minor, we should expect little if any change in British war aims. The only real change of British war aims was the result of the Arab Revolt, which triggered the Sykes-Picot Agreement, and the subsequent revision of this agreement to win Italy's participation. This change more likely qualifies as a decrease than an increase in British war aims, but this depends on whether the acquisition of southern Mesopotamia balances the strategically disadvantageous breakup of the Ottoman Empire and the increase in French and Italian influence in the Middle East.

The most important favorable new information of 1917 came from the successes against the Ottoman Empire, the entry of the United States, and the success of the convoy system. Although considerable, this favorable new information was simply overwhelmed by the unfa-

---

[30] The Battle of Jutland, 31 May and 1 June, produced no new information. As Liddell Hart concluded, "Its value as a battle was in every sense negligible" (p. 292). It may have made the British slightly more optimistic, as it was becoming clearer that the blockade was working, and the Germans could not do much about it. See Cassar, p. 185.

[31] See French, *The Strategy of the Lloyd George Coalition*, p. 34; French, *British Strategy and War Aims*, pp. 209–11; and Lloyd George, *War Memoirs*, vol. 3, p. 1394.

vorable new information of 1917, specifically the Russian Revolution and the armistice on the Eastern Front and the failures of the French and British offensives in the spring and fall. As shown below, the new pessimism about the war led to a drastic decrease in British war aims by the end of 1917. In 1918, as a result of the German Stormtrooper offensives, the British leadership initially became more pessimistic, estimating even that the war would not end before 1920. It took quite some time before the British became optimistic that the war would end in 1918. This optimism finally was brought about by the defection of Germany's allies and especially the Austrian armistice of 3 November. As shown in chapter 9, this optimism resulted in increased war aims. Nevertheless, both British military leaders and politicians consistently maintained a higher estimate of Germany's relative strength than the French and urged caution in the armistice terms to be demanded from Germany.

In the following section I examine 1917 in greater detail, because by 1917 the costs of the war relative to Britain's cost tolerance had risen so much that if British politicians worried about their ability to reward the people for their sacrifices, the costs of war surely had to have been a major influence by late 1917. My focus on 1917, therefore, allows me to track the change in British war aims when the costs of war should be *most* likely to influence the direction of the change in British war aims.

Expectations, New Information, and War Aims in 1917

To organize the greater detail of my analysis of 1917, this section is broken up into four subsections. The first subsection lays out the expectations of British leadership for 1917. The second presents the new information received during 1917 and focuses briefly on the Russian revolutions and the armistice on the Eastern Front but goes into greater detail on the British offensives at Arras and Passchendaele, the Italian defeat at Caporetto, the resumption of unrestricted submarine warfare, the capture of Baghdad and Jerusalem, and the United States' entry into the war. The third examines the leadership's expectations in November-December 1917. The final subsection compares British war aims at the end of 1916 with those of early 1918. Before we turn to an analysis of 1917, we should note an important change at the head of the British government. On 11 December 1916 David Lloyd George took over the position of Prime Minister from Asquith. In the new Cabinet much of the power shifted away from the Liberals to the Conservatives. A small group of five to seven ministers now focused all energies on the prosecution of the war. This group was the so-called War Cabinet; its most important members were Lloyd George, Curzon, Bonar Law, Milner, and, later on, the South African General and statesman Smuts.

Expectations for 1917

When Lloyd George became Prime Minister in December 1916, he asked the Chief of the Imperial General Staff (CIGS) William "Wully" Robertson for a memorandum "of any points connected with the war which particularly required his attention, together with [Robertson's] candid opinion as to our prospects of winning it."[32] In his memorandum for Lloyd George of 8 December 1916 Robertson expressed his confidence in ultimate and decisive victory and in Russia's war effort:

> I have no hesitation in saying that we can win if we will only do the right thing. If I thought otherwise I would tell you so. . . . I have never yet heard any military officer of standing express any other opinion. But there are many important things to be done, and done quickly. We must organize our man-power at home. . . . We must insist upon the overseas Dominions sending more men. . . . We must get a much larger share in the control of the war. . . . We must considerably enlarge our ideas as to the magnitude of the war. . . . The strain will become greater and greater as time goes on, and we are undoubtedly in for a bad time for the next few months, as we cannot get going until next spring, and the people may become impatient. On the other hand, we may hope to have some little success in Egypt and Mesopotamia during the winter, and the Russians are reinforcing their troops in the Caucasus and seem to mean business. So we may hope to shake up the Turk a little. Still, we must not expect any very great relief before the spring, or expect the war suddenly to come to an end.[33]

Robertson was confident that Germany would be decisively defeated but estimated that "we shall be well advised not to expect the end at any rate before the summer of 1918. How long it may go afterwards I cannot even guess."[34] Robertson's memorandum served to dispel any lingering hopes in Kitchener's early estimate that the war would be won by Britain in 1917. Asquith, Lloyd George, and Robertson all

---

[32] Robertson, *Soldiers and Statesmen*, vol. 1, p. 286.

[33] Memorandum quoted in Robertson, *Soldiers and Statesmen*, vol. 1, pp. 286–87, emphasis deleted.

[34] Estimate presented to the War Committee on 3 November 1916, quoted in Guinn, pp. 159–60.

agreed that the war would not be won before 1918.[35] While Robertson hedged his bets, the politicians seem to have estimated the war would end in 1918.[36] In sharp contrast to German efforts to control information, at the end of 1916 British leaders explicitly warned the people not to expect an end to the war any time soon.[37]

In their specifics the politicians favored a different approach in 1917 than did the military. The military leadership was determined to concentrate all forces on the Western Front, but a majority of the cabinet favored less costly attacks in eastern theaters, such as Salonika, Italy, or Turkey to "knock the props from under Germany." Lloyd George intended to force a change in the British military strategy and was a convinced "easterner," largely because he wanted to keep casualties down.[38] He favored an offensive against Austria-Hungary, through Russia or Italy, to exploit its recently revealed weakness and argued such an attack opened up "the prospect of a triumph which would have a determining effect on the fate of the struggle."[39] However, as Cabinet Secretary Hankey recorded on 26 December 1916, "The new War Cabinet . . . don't believe in Robertson's 'Western Front' policy, but they will never find a soldier to carry out their 'Salonica' policy."[40]

Facing a united front among the generals, the British government had accepted the conclusions reached by the military conference at Chantilly on 15 November 1916, which proposed a combined offensive by the Allies. Although French leaders had hoped this offensive would be decisive, British leaders were not optimistic that more of the same would bring about a quick end to the war. From the British perspective, the plans of the Allied military were basically the same as those of a year earlier.[41] However, Nivelle managed to convince Lloyd George

[35] French, *The Strategy of the Lloyd George Coalition*, p. 16; Riddell, p. 214. In mid-February Lloyd George had still thought that the war would be won in 1917 (Riddell, p. 154).

[36] Hankey, vol. 2, pp. 703–7; see also Fest, "British War Aims and German Peace Feelers during the First World War," p. 289; French, *British Strategy and War Aims*, p. 234; Cassar, pp. 207–8; and Lloyd George's speech of 19 December in *House of Commons*, 5th series, vol. 88, cols. 1338–56.

[37] Cassar, p. 207; *House of Commons Debates*, 5th series, vol. 88, col. 1338; Rothwell, p. 96; Guinn, p. 213.

[38] See Turner, *British Politics and the Great War: Coalition and Conflict 1915–1918*, p. 169.

[39] Hankey, *The Supreme Command 1914–1918*, vol. 2, pp. 598–99, see also pp. 610–11; Lloyd George, *War Memoirs*, vol. 3, pp. 1393–94. See also Lloyd George's memorandum presented to M. Briand, 15 November 1916, at the Paris conference of Allied politicians, which was held at the same time as the Allied military conference at Chantilly. Quoted in Guinn, p. 166.

[40] Diary entry for 26 December in Hankey, p. 596.

[41] Most Allied politicians were not happy about these plans, but their front crumbled when French Prime Minister Aristide Briand endorsed the conclusions of the military conference. See Cassar, p. 205.

that the new offensive planned for 1917 would not follow the old pattern, and after their discussions Lloyd George found Nivelle's plan "more to his liking than he had expected."[42] One reason must have been that Nivelle shifted the main burden of the attack away from the British, as previously intended by Joffre, and onto the French.[43] Eventually, on 16 January, the War Cabinet endorsed Nivelle's plans. While supporting his plans, the British High Command was apparently far less optimistic about the plan than the French were.[44] Lloyd George hoped that if the Nivelle offensive failed or was less than successful, his scheme for a combined offensive in Italy would be revived.[45]

From 15 October 1916 onwards Germany resumed *restricted* submarine warfare in accordance with the rules of cruiser warfare. Without delay both Hankey and Admiral Jellicoe warned about the mounting threat. By late October 1916 the British government started to seriously worry about the mounting shipping losses,[46] which produced "real fears that food supplies would be inadequate."[47] However, while submarine warfare looked threatening in the short run, it also made it more likely that the United States would come in on the Allied side.[48]

To sum up, at the end of 1916 British leaders estimated they would be able to achieve a decisive victory over the Germans, most likely in 1918. Germany was starting to show the strain of fighting on two fronts and would now also have to support Austria-Hungary with its own manpower. Austria-Hungary was crumbling while Russia looked stronger than it had a year before, and Turkey would be hard pressed because of the Arab Revolt. Moreover, the probability of American intervention on the Allied side had increased. Amid such grounds for optimism, the mounting shipping losses introduced a note of caution in the British leadership's expectations for 1917.

---

[42] Hankey, vol. 2, p. 613.

[43] Liddell Hart, p. 299.

[44] Hankey, vol. 2, pp. 613–14; see also French, *The Strategy of the Lloyd George Coalition*, pp. 54–55.

[45] Hankey, vol. 2, p. 621.

[46] French, *British Strategy and War Aims*, pp. 231, 224; Bourne, *Britain and the Great War 1914–1918*, p. 68; and Lloyd George's memorandum to Briand for the Paris conference of 15 November, quoted in Guinn, p. 166.

[47] Turner, introduction in Turner, *Britain and the First World War*, p. 6.

[48] See "Wilson's Note on Sussex Affair and on General Submarine Warfare against Merchant Ships," his address to Congress on the Sussex Affair, and his note to Germany in Shaw, pp. 257–70. See also Stevenson, *French War Aims*, p. 46; Lloyd George, *War Memoirs*, vol. 3, p. 1111. The Allies designed their replies to Wilson very carefully, with the intended result: "They brought [America's] intervention on the side of the Allies appreciably nearer" (Lloyd George, p. 1115).

The New Information of 1917

The events of 1917 would make British statesmen much more pessimistic about the outcome on the battlefield. Historians agree that "by August 1917 the War Cabinet had come to have profound doubts about the Entente's chances of a decisive military victory."[49] The main unexpected shock to British statesmen in 1917 undoubtedly was the rapid collapse of Russia and the subsequent armistice between Russia and Germany on 15 December 1917. But, as Hankey noted, 1917 brought a whole string of defeats and unexpected bad news.[50]

Like the French, British politicians were at first unsure of the effects of the first Russian revolution. For some time they clung to their hopes that the revolution might actually strengthen the Russian war effort.[51] However, the failure of the Kerensky offensive (and the failure of the coup by Kornilov) convinced Allied leaders that Russia could no longer be counted on. In mid-July, at a military conference, the Allies concluded that "Russia might well leave the war entirely before the end of the year. . . . *In that event . . . the Allies should proceed to re-define their war aims.*"[52] At the end of September Robertson warned that if the Russians defected, British prospects of victory would vanish.[53] When the Russians signed an armistice at Brest-Litovsk on 5 December, the British knew they could expect a major assault on the Western Front. Leaders such as Asquith and Milner—the latter a prominent member of the War Cabinet—no longer hoped for victory but now started speaking of avoiding defeat.[54] Clearly, Russia's defection from the war led British leaders to lower their estimate of a decisive victory over the Germans.

The failure of the Allied spring offensive destroyed any remaining hopes for a quick and relatively cheap victory for the foreseeable future.[55] The British effort in the Allied offensive of 1917 has become

[49] Cline, p. 168.

[50] Hankey, vol. 2, pp. 598–99.

[51] Ibid., pp. 623, 690; French, "Allies, Rivals and Enemies," p. 30; French, *The Strategy of the Lloyd George Coalition*, pp. 46–49. Lloyd George told Lord Riddell on 14 January 1917 that "the position [in Russia] is similar to that in France before the French Revolution" (Riddell, p. 237). See also Van Overstraeten (1954), p. 159; Lennox, vol. 2, pp. 105–6; Guinn, p. 223.

[52] Guinn, p. 234, emphasis added.

[53] Foch and Haig disagreed and apparently were less pessimistic. See Hankey, vol. 2, pp. 734–35.

[54] Guinn, pp. 274–75. Asquith saw a chance to regain his former position by arguing for a negotiated peace.

[55] French, *The Strategy of the Lloyd George Coalition*, p. 61.

known as the Battle of Arras. "In conjunction with the other attacks planned for the spring of 1917," as Liddell Hart argues, the goal of the British attack was "to complete the overthrow of German power and manpower which it was believed that only the onset of winter had prevented on the Somme."[56] The first phase of the battle failed to bring strategic success but did yield substantial numbers of captured prisoners and heavy guns. The second phase, however, was a bitter failure. Between 9 April and 17 May the British suffered their highest daily losses of the war up until that time, exceeded only by the losses during the German spring offensives of 1918.[57]

The failure of the Allied spring offensive had two important results. First, the Allies gave up hopes for a decisive breakthrough of the German front and were left with no alternative to a strategy of attrition.[58] The strategy of attrition virtually ensured the Allies would suffer very high casualties before they would come close to victory. Second, British leaders learned that the French army was seriously damaged and demoralized.[59] The upshot was that not only the overall war effort would be more costly, but the British share of those costs would also increase. By this double whammy British leaders were forced to increase their estimate of the costs of war. However, the failure of the French offensive and inconclusive reports about the state of French morale also allowed British leaders to raise their estimate of Britain's strength relative to France.

Lloyd George's last hopes to avoid the costly and futile offensives of the Western Front for a cheaper victory elsewhere were destroyed when his alternative plan for an offensive in Italy was shunted aside for another costly battle of attrition, the infamous Passchendaele offensive. When plans for the offensive in Flanders, known as the Third Battle of Ypres or Passchendaele, re-emerged in the spring of 1917, they provoked stern questioning and probing. The Cabinet was frankly worried, if not downright skeptical, about its potential for success and the losses it would produce.[60] However, the navy came to Haig's support. The Admiralty supported the offensive on the grounds that the plan aimed for the Flanders coast and the ejection of the enemy from the

---

[56] Liddell Hart, p. 321.

[57] Bourne, p. 72.

[58] At a conference on 4–5 May in Paris the Allies agreed that "It is no longer a question of aiming at breaking through the enemy's front and aiming at distant objectives. It is now a question of wearing down and exhausting the enemy's resistance and if and when this is achieved, to exploit it to the fullest possible extent" (quoted in Hankey, vol. 2, p. 678).

[59] Guinn, p. 246, note 3; Hankey, vol. 2, p. 671; Liddell Hart, p. 338.

[60] Hankey, vol. 2, pp. 680–84, 701.

ports of Ostend and Zeebrugge. Jellicoe's intervention proved decisive. He warned that unless Haig's plan was carried out successfully, Britain would not be able to continue the war in 1918 for lack of shipping.[61] Hankey records that "No one believed that a strategical result could be achieved, and all shrank from the terrible losses which they knew it must involve. But the consensus of naval and military opinion was so overwhelming that the War Cabinet could not take the responsibility of rejecting the advice thrust upon them with so much cogency."[62]

The offensive was launched on 31 July. By mid-August it was clear the attack would be another failure not worth the terrible costs. Lloyd George witnessed all his gloomy predictions of a few weeks earlier come horribly true.[63] Nonetheless, the offensive continued and did not come to a halt until 10 November. The results confirmed the Cabinet's worst expectations. The offensive produced exactly the costly and indecisive results the Cabinet had wanted to avoid. Robertson had told the cabinet that, on the basis of estimates furnished by GHQ, during the offensive the British would suffer no more than 130,000 casualties along their whole front.[64] The grisly toll of Passchendaele far exceeded this optimistic estimate. For the price of almost no gains the British suffered 400,000 casualties. Moreover, the British army became seriously demoralized and forced to assume a defensive posture.[65] Although the Cabinet had been pessimistic about the offensive, the overall result surely made them more pessimistic about the costs of war and Britain's relative strength than they had been at the end of 1916. The initial success of the British tank offensive at Cambrai beginning on 20 November increased the belief of British leaders in the potential of the tank. But the successful German counteroffensive of 30 November quickly turned elation into reproach, and by 7 December the British had lost almost as much ground as they had gained.[66]

More bad news was on the way. The Italian collapse and rout at Caporetto must have come as a complete surprise to the British. Although Italian civil and military leaders had been anxious about the possibilities of an attack on their flank from the Trentino, British leaders were under the impression that the morale of Italian soldiers was good.[67] On 27 October the bad news about the collapse of the Italian Front reached

[61] Ibid., pp. 679–80. Hankey judges Jellicoe's strong support to have been decisive (p. 701).

[62] Ibid., p. 684.

[63] Ibid., p. 711.

[64] Lloyd George, *War Memoirs*, vol. 5, p. 6.

[65] Herman, p. 417; Hankey, vol. 2, note 1, pp. 743–44, 756; Turner, introduction, p. 4.

[66] Liddell Hart, pp. 344–56.

[67] Hankey, vol. 2, pp. 672, 675.

Britain. The Italian position was seen as critical in the extreme, until the Italians made a successful stand on the Piave River on 10 November. By then the Italians had lost many valuable heavy guns and over 600,000 men.[68] Not only was the Italian army condemned to a defensive posture, but it had to be reinforced by French and British troops. The French and British eventually sent twelve divisions to the Italian Front to provide the backbone for the Italian armies—so much for Lloyd George's plan to defeat Austria-Hungary through an offensive from Italy. The only good thing to come out of Caporetto was the creation of the Supreme Inter-Allied War Council.[69]

The failure of the Allied spring offensives, the poor state of the French and Italian armies, not to mention the complete collapse of the Russian army all meant that the costs of war would increase and that Britain would have to suffer a larger proportion of those costs. The unexpected increase in the costs of war was further highlighted by the rapidly worsening manpower problem.[70] As we have seen above, the "wastage"—as the War Policy referred to the attrition of British manpower—increased substantially during the remainder of 1917. The slaughter at Passchendaele was all the more galling to British politicians because well before the offensive they had emphasized "the importance of not exhausting our dwindling reserves of manpower before the United States could bring their strength to bear."[71] Further "wastage" lay ahead because, as *The Times* warned in its first leader of 21 December 1917, "The defection of Russia and the demands of the Italian campaign impose a fresh and unforeseen drain upon our Armies."[72] At the end of 1917 the government estimated a shortage of about 880,000 men to replace losses and fill the ranks of the new services.[73] These manpower problems were further exacerbated by the urgent demands of industry and especially shipbuilding.[74]

The War Cabinet's main preoccupation during the first half of 1917 undoubtedly was Germany's unrestricted submarine warfare campaign. While concerned about shipping losses in late 1916, the British

---

[68] Liddell Hart, p. 361. British estimates of Italian losses were even higher, approximating three-quarters of a million men.

[69] Hankey, vol. 2, p. 716.

[70] Ibid., vol. 2, p. 674. In May Lloyd George promised to consider, once again, Irish Home Rule, which had been withdrawn after the Easter Rebellion, so that the British troops stationed there could be withdrawn and Irishmen would be more willing to serve in the armed forces. See Schaeffer, *Warpaths: The Politics of Partition*, p. 97.

[71] Hankey, vol. 2, pp. 681–82.

[72] Quoted in Guinn, p. 281.

[73] Hankey, vol. 2, p. 740.

[74] Hankey, vol. 2, pp. 627, 674, especially pp. 730–41.

government came close to panic in April 1917 before their fears subsided again by the late fall, but these fears never completely disappeared. The Cabinet had been informed on 28 December 1916 that Germany would probably resume unrestricted submarine warfare in the next year from March on and that the Germans were in the process of constructing two hundred long-range submarines.[75] A month earlier than expected, on 1 February, the Germans indeed proclaimed unrestricted submarine warfare. In one month losses more than doubled, from 153,666 to 313,486 gross tons. And the numbers continued to climb. Losses for the first half of 1917 were almost twice as much as for the whole of 1916 and exceeded the shipbuilding output by one and a half million gross tons. Under Lloyd George's pressure the Admiralty finally agreed on 30 April to adopt the convoy system.[76] Even though the convoy system eventually brought losses under control, the shipping situation still played a major role in British decision making, well into late 1917 and early 1918.[77] Thus, while British leaders suffered a period of extreme anxiety in April, American assistance and the convoy system managed to defuse the worst threat to British shipping. As Liddell Hart argues, "by the end of 1917 the menace, if not broken, was at least subdued."[78]

In addition to the success of the convoy system, the American decision in April to join the war as an "associated power" and the successes against the Ottoman Empire were the only important favorable new information of the year. Although American entry into the war took away some of the fears of British statesmen about Britain's financial position and continued ability to pay for the war, British leaders initially put little stock in the material effect of American intervention.[79] British soldiers, and especially Robertson, thought that the American decision to "form an army independent of the British and

[75] Fest, p. 291. This was subsequently confirmed in January by Sidney Reilly, the British master spy. See Herman, p. 312.

[76] On 1 April Lloyd George discussed the naval and shipping situation with his friend and confidant Lord Riddell, who noted in his diary, "Lloyd George regard[ed] the situation as very menacing but says he thinks he can see his way to feed the people until the spring of 1918. He remarked, 'we want to find a genius who can discover some method of destroying submarines. Where we are to look for him it is difficult to say' " (Riddell, p. 247).

[77] Guinn, p. 236. For Jellicoe's warning on 30 June that Britain would not be able to continue the war for lack of shipping after 1917, see Hankey, vol. 2, p. 654. Hankey claims that he himself stopped fearing that the submarine warfare would "prove our undoing" when Lloyd George forced the Admiralty to adopt the convoy system (p. 650).

[78] Liddell Hart, p. 310.

[79] Rothwell, p. 102. Apparently neither British nor French leaders were in favor in early 1917 of the United States' raising a large army. See Seymour, vol. 3, pp. 5–7.

French military commands meant that American troops would be unable to effect any serious operation on the Western Front for 'a very long time,' if at all."[80] While Wilson soon committed all America's resources, from experience British politicians knew that it would take time to build and send the American army to France. The slow pace of the arrival of American troops nevertheless disappointed them.[81]

In early December there were only four American divisions in France, of which only one was actually training in the line. The bottleneck was in the shipping shortage. As late as 30 November Hankey wrote in a memo for Clemenceau of the *"potentiality* of the gradual accumulation of American forces on the Western Front in 1918. That . . . depended on . . . the effect of American co-operation in improving the shipping situation."[82] Currently, the British estimated, "The amount of shipping available was sufficient to transport only one and one-third divisions a month, and it was estimated, on the basis of British experience, that after arrival American divisions would require some months in a quiet part of the line before they were fit for battle."[83]

It is likely that British leaders deliberately exaggerated the severity of the shipping shortage. The whole question of shipping was inextricably linked with the question of amalgamation, the use of American manpower in the British and French armies. The European Allies wanted on the one hand to maximize the American contribution to the war effort to maximize their probability of victory in the upcoming German offensives. On the other hand, they wanted to minimize American bargaining power at the postwar peace table, and American leaders were well aware of this dynamic.[84] British and French leaders hoped to escape their dilemma by amalgamation. But they could press for amalgamation only as long as there were too few American troops in Europe for Pershing to field an independent army. Then Lloyd George and Clemenceau could argue that American troops could be brought into the line much faster if they were integrated and trained with existing French or British units.[85] Hence, to further the cause of amalgamation, the British had the seemingly perverse incentive to

[80] Guinn, p. 236.

[81] French, *The Strategy of the Lloyd George Coalition*, pp. 178–79.

[82] Hankey, vol. 2, pp. 731–32, emphasis added.

[83] Ibid., vol. 2, p. 744.

[84] See the reports of the American Mission, reprinted in *Foreign Relations of the United States, 1917*, pp. 334–445, 355–57. Excerpts from House's report are reprinted in Seymour, vol. 3, pp. 300–302. See also Pershing, vol. 1, p. 295; and Trask, p. 72.

[85] Trask, pp. 70–99. On the general amalgamation issue around this time see Pershing, vol. 1, pp. 246–97; Esposito, p. 118.

slow down the shipping of American troops to Europe. To be sure, British leaders publicly bewailed the slow arrival of American troops. But their behavior regarding the transport of American troops shows a radically different picture. As David Trask succinctly argues, "the British hoped to barter tonnage in return for American acceptance of amalgamation. Pershing was forced to strike periodic bargains with the British in order to obtain ships for the transportation of American soldiers to Europe. [Pershing] found he could not resist amalgamation without encountering a British tendency to withhold shipping."[86] (Note that when the situation became really threatening, the British had little problem finding the necessary shipping to transport 500,000 Americans to Europe in two months.)[87]

Already by mid-October Lloyd George and others had come to the conclusion that the American army would not be able to contribute substantially to the fighting before 1919.[88] While the American troops were disappointingly slow in coming, American intervention was nevertheless a crucial factor in British calculations. Indeed, Lloyd George argued it was the reason for hanging on in September 1917.[89] If true, this shows how much British statesmen had changed their estimate of the probability of victory and the costs of war since late 1916.

The only significant successes recorded by British armed forces came in the war against Turkey. Baghdad fell in March, and Jerusalem was occupied on 9 December 1917. As a result, British leaders became more optimistic about their chances against Turkey in 1918. By September 1917 Milner had come to agree with Lloyd George that in the coming year any offensive effort should be directed against Turkey.[90] In late December 1917 the British government therefore persuaded its allies to launch a "decisive offensive" against Turkey in 1918 and so consolidate its position in the Middle East.[91] The Allies agreed, but they attached the condition that there would be no relaxation of British efforts on the Western Front and no forces would be diverted.[92]

---

[86] Trask, pp. 74–75. Note also that in a resolution on "the Transport Problem," passed by the Supreme War Council on 1 December 1917, the decision was made to prioritize *not* the transport of American troops, but rather "the transportation problems as affecting the Italian and Salonika situations" (resolutions quoted in Seymour, vol. 3, pp. 288–90).

[87] Esposito, pp. 126–27.

[88] This was at least Lloyd George's conclusion at the War Cabinet meeting as a "Council of War," on 11 October 1917. See Guinn, p. 261; see also Hankey, vol. 2, p. 706.

[89] Stevenson, *The First World War*, p. 170.

[90] Hankey, vol. 2, p. 697.

[91] French, "Allies, Rivals and Enemies," p. 33.

[92] Hankey, vol. 2, p. 768.

Expectations at the End of 1917 through Early 1918

In this section I examine the *overall* effects of the new information of 1917 on British estimates. In a nutshell, I share Rothwell's conclusion that "The year's warfare, culminating in the battle of Passchendaele in which apparently very meager results had been purchased at a cost of 300,000–400,000 casualties, had forced a conclusion that the defeat of the German army might be either impossible or prohibitively costly."[93]

By October 1917 Lloyd George had drastically scaled down his expectations for victory. He divulged his expectations about the duration and costs of the war to Hankey in a talk on 15 October 1917.[94] Although he still believed that Britain could win militarily eventually, he drastically redefined what he meant by victory. He now estimated that "an allied victory which drove the Germans back to the Meuse would . . . mark the defeat of Germany."[95] He had come to the conclusion that victory "could not possibly be achieved in 1918 by any method."[96] Estimating that the American army would have not reached sufficient strength in 1918, he concluded that the blow that would defeat the enemy would have to be postponed to 1919. Hankey noted that this was the first time he had heard 1919 mentioned as the year of the decisive attack and suggested the Prime Minister inform his colleagues of his conclusion.

After the Russian-German armistice was signed on 15 December 1917 British statesmen became much more pessimistic about the probability of decisive victory. By the end of the year only very few ministers still believed in a crushing military victory.[97] On 8 December Secretary of State for War Derby, a staunch defender of the military High Command, admitted that "So far from there being any question of our breaking through the Germans, it was a question whether we could prevent the German breaking through us."[98] Milner expressed similar feelings. After warning that the British were now fighting for their lives, he told his audience that "it is not now a question of destroying Prussian militarism. The question is, whether Prussian militarism should destroy us."[99]

---

[93] Rothwell, p. 109.

[94] Hankey, vol. 2, pp. 703–7. The following paragraph on Lloyd George's expectations in October 1917 is based on Hankey's notes of that conversation.

[95] Rothwell, p. 99.

[96] Hankey, vol. 2, p. 705; see also pp. 703–7.

[97] Rothwell, pp. 147–48.

[98] Quoted in ibid., p. 144.

[99] Quoted in Guinn, p. 275.

British leaders became more pessimistic in part because they anticipated a major German offensive for the spring of 1918.[100] While the
Germans could transfer troops from the Russian Front, the Allies
would have to withstand the expected onslaught with manpower
problems in the British army, morale problems in the French army, and
(too?) few American troops in the line.[101] As for the French, the question was whether the Americans would come in time.[102] Moreover,
even if the Allies would withstand the German offensive, the costs
would undoubtedly be horrendous.

On 28 December Lloyd George told his colleagues in the War Cabinet that "it was time to consider whether it was worth while to continue fighting. It would be worth going on if Germany could be defeated in two years, but if this was not possible, one should try to find
out what terms one could obtain."[103] Lloyd George for a while had been
toying with the idea of a new public statement of British war aims. In
preparation for such a restatement of British war aims the War Cabinet
asked the General Staff on the last day of 1917 about their estimates of
the probability of victory and the costs of the war:

> Can the General Staff foresee a victorious ending to the War? If so, when
> and under what circumstances? Do the General Staff foresee such an im-
> provement in the future military situation of the Allies as would induce
> the enemy to assent to peace terms more favourable to the Allies than
> those offered, or likely to be obtained, at the present moment? If the an-
> swer is in the affirmative, will the improvement be on such a scale as to
> justify the sacrifice involved in continuing the struggle? Can the General
> Staff foresee, either in 1918 or in 1919, a reasonable probability of the in-
> fliction on the enemy of a defeat that would not leave the military domina-
> tion of Prussia successful and intact?[104]

The government's query is interesting in itself and reveals that the government explicitly based its terms on estimates of the Allies' relative
strength and the costs of war. As we will see below in the section on
Britain's war aims, from Robertson's answers Lloyd George concluded
that a defeat that would not dismantle Prussia's military domination
now probably lay beyond the Allies' capabilities.

---

[100] Haig as always remained optimistic, but his optimism was by now thoroughly discredited in the eyes of the politicians. See Rothwell, pp. 143–44.

[101] Robertson, vol. 2, pp. 267–68.

[102] Gooch, "Soldiers, Strategy and War Aims in Britain 1914–1918," p. 35, note 61,
"Note by the DMI" of 17 November.

[103] Fest, p. 304.

[104] Memorandum quoted in Robertson, vol. 2, p. 281.

In his answer to the government's request, Robertson referred explicitly to the new information of 1917. Of America, he said that "she may be expected to make her weight felt in the field in the autumn of next year."[105] The bad news of 1917 had also made Robertson more pessimistic: "The Entente side, owing to the final collapse of Russia, the defeat of Italy, heavy shipping losses and consequent shortage of certain supplies, general war-weariness and shrinkage of manpower, especially in England and France, might appear bleak, but the enemy's side was not wholly bright."[106]

With regard to the question whether the military situation would improve enough to get the Allies more favorable terms, Robertson referred back to his memorandum of 27 December 1917 in which he had summed up the prospects for Britain and its allies:

> The conclusion is that we must be prepared for a great battle, or rather series of battles, early in the coming year which we shall have to fight defensively; that, being on the defensive, we shall have difficulty in deciding where the enemy's main attack will fall; that we must be prepared for losses of ground, prisoners and guns; . . . If we defeat the enemy's offensive, as we may reasonably hope to do if we make suitable and adequate preparations and do not send our reserves off in wrong directions, how much nearer shall we be to getting a favourable peace? This depends not only upon ourselves but also upon the extent to which the other members of the Entente keep in the field, and upon when America can enter in force. . . . If we do this, and if we determine to endure, and if our allies do likewise, until America is ready, we may hope to get eventually a favourable peace.[107]

Hedging his bets, pointing to the weakness of Britain's allies, Robertson's *hope* to get a favorable peace *eventually* could hardly inspire confidence. Robertson's confidence seems all the more feeble when compared to his statement of late 1916 when he told the War Cabinet, "I have no hesitation in saying that we can win. . . . I have never yet heard any military officer of standing express any other opinion."[108]

[105] In his answer to the Cabinet's query, Robertson referred back to his earlier memorandum of 27 December. This quote is from that earlier memorandum. Quoted in Robertson, vol. 2, pp. 278–80. The memorandum of 3 January 1918 is in Robertson, vol. 2, pp. 282–84.

[106] Ibid., vol. 2, p. 282.

[107] Memorandum quoted in ibid., vol. 2, pp. 278–80. Note that at an inter-Allied conference at Boulogne on 25 September 1917, "Robertson had expressed the view that [if Russia defected] our prospects of victory would vanish" (Hankey, vol. 2, p. 734).

[108] Robertson, vol. 2, pp. 286–87. On the question whether further sacrifices would be justified and the need for American manpower, see Robertson, vol. 2, pp. 283–84.

Lloyd George's concern about the costs of the war is well known. On more than one occasion he deplored the loss of British lives on the battlefields of Flanders.[109] As the costs of war rose, he feared the British were coming dangerously close to the limits of their cost tolerance.[110] Lloyd George's concern for the costs of war and their implications for British war aims also had an international political dimension. He feared the British army reduced to the state of the French army, with its numbers and morale seriously weakened. Without a first-class British army it would fall to America to deal the fatal blow to the Central Powers and reap the rewards of victory. Therefore, as Lloyd George told Hankey, "it was vital to our national policy that, at the end of the war, our Army should not be exhausted and demoralized."[111]

On the extent of victory, Robertson clearly no longer foresaw a decisive defeat of the German army. He argued, "it is certain that we shall never get a satisfactory peace unless and until we exert such pressure on land against the enemy's armies as will show to Germany it is useless to continue the struggle."[112] Note the parallel with Falkenhayn's plans for the Battle of Verdun: The goal here is explicitly to influence the opponent's estimates, not to achieve some kind of decisive victory.

As a result of their own worries and Robertson's answer to their query, the Cabinet surely became more pessimistic about Britain's relative strength and the expected costs of war than they were at the end of 1916. The war would continue at least until 1919, the British would have to bear a greater part of the costs of war—at least until the Americans arrived in force—and even then, the best that could be hoped for was to "show Germany that it is useless to continue the struggle."[113] It is not surprising, therefore, that in meetings of the War Cabinet between 28 December and 3 January the Cabinet concluded that "the magnitude of . . . victory would probably be limited."[114]

---

[109] See his *War Memoirs*; Bourne, p. 71; Hankey, vol. 2, p. 705; and Gooch, *The Plans of War*, p. 312.

[110] According to French, the War Cabinet "feared that the British people might not tolerate in 1918 a repetition of the heavy losses which Haig's armies had suffered in 1917. By the autumn the National War Aims Committee . . . had discovered that amongst leaders of organized labour commitment to military victory as an end in itself, was waning" (French, *The Strategy of the Lloyd George Coalition*, p. 193).

[111] Hankey, vol. 2, p. 706. See also French, *The Strategy of the Lloyd George Coalition*, pp. 9–10, 157–58.

[112] Robertson, vol. 2, p. 283.

[113] Robertson, vol. 2, p. 283. Haig apparently doubted in January 1918 whether the Americans could even seriously contribute to the Allied war effort in 1919. See Fest, p. 306.

[114] French, *The Strategy of the Lloyd George Coalition*, p. 202.

Prospects for victory against Germany now looked bleak, but the prospects of victory against the Ottoman Empire had improved. By early October Lloyd George had come to the conclusion that "the only way to bring the War to an end was by removing her Allies from Germany one by one, ultimately completing isolating Germany," a policy known as "knocking the props from under Germany."[115] He hoped to start this process by knocking Turkey out of the war.

The Change in British War Aims

A comparison of British war aims of December 1916–January 1917 and January 1918 unambiguously yields the conclusion that British war aims substantially decreased during 1917. At the end of 1916 Lloyd George stated Britain's war aims almost immediately after he became Prime Minister, in response to German Chancellor Bethmann Hollweg's proposal for peace negotiations of 12 December 1916.[116] On 18 December, moreover, President Wilson sent the belligerent powers a note suggesting a statement of peace terms.[117] Addressing the Chancellor's note in his first speech as Prime Minister a day later, on 19 December 1916, Lloyd George formulated his statement of British war aims in similar terms as had Asquith: "The only terms on which it is possible for peace to be obtained and maintained in Europe . . . [are] complete restitution, full reparation, effectual guarantees." The main effectual guarantee remained, as in 1915, the destruction of Prussian militarism and the removal of "the Prussian military caste," whose "arrogant spirit" according to Lloyd George, lay at the root of this war: "The Allies entered this War to defend themselves against the aggression of the Prussian military domination, and having begun it, they must insist that it can only end with the most complete and effective guarantee against the possibility of that caste ever again disturbing the peace of Europe."[118]

In his speech on that same day in the House of Lords as a member of Lloyd George's new War Cabinet, Lord Curzon provided a few more specifics. He argued that Britain was fighting

> to recover for Belgium, France, Russia, Serbia, and Rumania the territories which they have lost, and to secure for them reparation for their cruel wrongs. But you may restore to them all, and more than all, the losses

[115] Quoted in ibid., p. 154.
[116] The German Chancellor's speech and official proposal can be found in Scott, pp. 1–3.
[117] Ibid., pp. 12–15.
[118] House of Commons, *Debates*, 5th series, vol. 88, cols. 1335–38.

they have experienced; you may pile indemnities upon them such as no Treasury in Europe could produce, and yet the War would have been in vain if we had no guarantees and no securities against a repetition of these things in the future.

Moreover, the peace of Europe was to be "reestablished on the basis of the free and independent existence of nations, great and small."[119]

On 10 January 1917 the Entente replied to President Wilson's suggestion in a joint note. Its reply was drafted by Briand's *Chef de Cabinet*, Philippe Berthelot, but the final response was largely drafted by the British.[120] While the French argued for even less detail in the Entente's reply to Wilson, upon British insistence a final paragraph was included that set out the Allies' aims in more detail.[121] These details were to be an elaboration of the earlier reply to the German Chancellor's proposal:[122]

[The Entente's] objects in the war are well known; they have been formulated on many occasions by the chiefs of their divers Governments. Their objects in the war will not be made known in detail with all the equitable compensations and indemnities for damages suffered until the hour of negotiations. But the civilized world knows that they imply in all necessity and in the first instance the restoration of Belgium, of Serbia, and of Montenegro and the indemnities which are due them; the evacuation of the invaded territories of France, of Russia and of Roumania with just reparation; the reorganization of Europe, guaranteed by a stable regime and founded as much upon respect of nationalities and full security and liberty, economic development, which all nations, great or small, possess, as upon territorial conventions and international agreements suitable to guarantee territorial and maritime frontiers against unjustified attacks; the restitution of provinces or territories wrested in the past from the Allies

[119] *War Speeches by British Ministers 1914–1916*, pp. 373, 353. See also Asquith's speech of 9 November 1916 at the Guildhall, in ibid., pp. 134–40. In February and May the Allies had guaranteed the restitution of Belgium and the Belgian Congo. See Stevenson, *The First World War and International Politics*, p. 108; Gatzke, p. 76; Stevenson, *The First World War, 1914–1918*, part 2, series H, WWI 1914–1918, II: June 1915–November 1916, docs. 280 and 283, pp. 318–20.

[120] Hankey, vol. 2, p. 602; Stevenson, *French War Aims*, p. 48.

[121] Stevenson, *French War Aims*, p. 47.

[122] The Entente had replied to the Germans "that no peace is possible as long as the reparation of violated rights and liberties, the acknowledgment of the principle of nationalities and of the free existence of small States shall not be assured; as long as there is no assurance of a settlement to suppress definitely the causes which for so long a time have menaced nations and to give the only efficacious guarantees for the security of the world" ("Entente Reply to German Proposals," 29 December 1916, in Scott, pp. 26–28). The reply was drafted by Jules Cambon, the French bureaucrat from the Quai d'Orsay. See Stevenson, *French War Aims*, p. 46.

by force or against the will of their populations, the liberation of Italians, of Slavs, of Roumanians and of Czecho-Slovaks from foreign domination; the enfranchisement of populations subject to the bloody tyranny of the Turks; the expulsion from Europe of the Ottoman Empire decidedly [*sic*] to western civilization. The intentions of His Majesty the Emperor of Russia regarding Poland have been clearly indicated in the proclamation which he has just addressed to his armies. It goes without saying that if the Allies wish to liberate Europe from the brutal covetousness of Prussian militarism, it never has been their design, as has been alleged, to encompass the extermination of the German peoples and their political disappearance. That which they desire above all is to insure a peace upon the principles of liberty and justice, upon the inviolable fidelity to international obligation.[123]

Compared to British war aims at the end of 1915, most of the new language of this reply can be traced back to the earlier statements of Asquith and Curzon about the "rights of the smaller nationalities of Europe," to Wilson's declaration that "every people has a right to choose the sovereignty under which they live," and to earlier agreements among the Allies, such as the Treaty of London and the Treaty of Bucharest.[124] Thus, the call for the liberation of Italians and Rumanians was largely the public recognition of the earlier negotiations and treaties.[125] The demands against the Ottoman Empire reflected the agreement with Sharif Hussein, the recently published Straits Agreement with Russia, and the amended Sykes-Picot Agreement (more on which below).

Two caveats about these war aims are in order. First, the passage about Poland refers to the Tsar's declaration of 26 December: "The

---

[123] "Entente Reply to President Wilson," 10 January 1917, in Scott, pp. 35–38. A slightly different wording is in *The Case of the Allies*, pp. 6–7.

[124] "Wilson's Address before the League to Enforce Peace," Washington, 27 May 1916, in Shaw, pp. 271–75.

[125] The liberation of Italians and Slavs had been promised in the negotiations among Russians, French, British, Italian, and Serbian leaders for the Treaty of London of 1915 that brought Italy into the war. See Petrovich, pp. 162–93. The call for liberation of the Rumanians reflects the Treaty of Bucharest, signed on 17 August, which brought Rumania into the war. In this treaty the Allies undertook to guarantee the territorial integrity of Rumania, not to make a separate peace, and to secure in the final peace settlement the annexation of the Austro-Hungarian territories of Transylvania, the Banat of Temesvar, and a large slice of the Bukovina. For summaries and dates of British promises and obligations, see *British Documents in Foreign Affairs: Reports and Papers from the Foreign Office Confidential Print*, part 2, vol. 3, pp. 312–18; see also the maps on pp. 322–24. See also French, *British Strategy and War Aims*, p. 209. With Allied consent, Russia had published the Straits agreement in the first days of December.

achievement of the tasks which Russia faces as a result of the war—the attainment of Tsargrad [Constantinople] and the Straits, as well as the creation of a free Poland out of all three of her presently dispersed parts—has not yet been assured."[126] Moreover, the explicit mention of Poland must also be seen in the context of the Central Powers' declaration of 5 November whereby the Austro-Hungarian and German emperors promised to create an "independent" Polish state. Especially Britain and France thought the Entente needed to counter Germany's bid for Polish manpower by an offer of Polish self-government or autonomy of their own. Second, the references to the liberation of the Slavs and of Czecho-Slovaks were included under pressure by the French.[127] However, as Rothwell notes, "the French made it clear to Benes that there was no possibility of the war being continued simply for the benefit of east European nationalism; while in Britain those newspaper and publicists who favoured the break up of the [Dual] Monarchy took the realistic line that the inclusion of the Czechs was a mere rhetorical flourish."[128]

The Sykes-Picot Agreement grew out of Sharif Hussein's promise of mid-October 1915 to launch an Arab revolt if the British would accept him as the ruler of an independent Arabia. In return for this concession, he would agree to rule with the aid of British advisors, give the British control over the Basra vilayet, and offer the French concessions in Syria, specifically the area of Aleppo-Damascus-Hama and Homs. In their encouraging reply, the British demanded further concessions in the Baghdad vilayet. The impending disintegration of the Ottoman Empire required negotiations with the French, which led to the Sykes-Picot Agreement, confirmed in an exchange of notes of 15 and 16 May 1916.[129]

---

[126] Quoted in Dallin, "The Future of Poland," p. 72. Hankey's note that the passage on Poland referred to "the Proclamation issued on behalf of the Czar by the Grand Duke Nicholas on August 14, 1914, promising autonomy" must be mistaken since the Grand Duke never promised "autonomy." It is likely that Hankey was thinking of Goremykin's promise of 1 August 1915, as quoted in Dallin, reiterated on 15 November 1916. See Hankey, vol. 2, p. 602; Dallin, "The Future of Poland," p. 30.

[127] Abrash, p. 118, note 83.

[128] Rothwell, p. 79. Moreover, the situation of the Slavs had been already discussed with regard to the Treaty of London, which brought Italy into the war.

[129] It is striking to note that Grey told Cambon already on 19 May that it would be better if the agreement would never become public and put into force. See Linke, p. 224. The notes of Sir Edward Grey to Paul Cambon of 15 and 16 May 1916 confirming the acceptance of the Sykes-Picot Agreement can be found at the World War I Document Archive site, www.lib.byu.edu/~rdh/wwi/1916/sykespicot.html. Stevenson notes that "Grey supported the agreement . . . in the belief that its realization depended on an Arab Revolt that he still thought unlikely to occur" (*The First World War*, p. 129).

After the Arabs launched their revolt the British were bound to the French in respect to their war aims against Turkey. As long as the war ended in victory, Britain would have the right to establish any form of government it chose in both the Basra and Baghdad vilayets while France would enjoy similar rights along the Syrian coast. In addition Britain would get a naval base at Haifa. Sharif Hussein would get his Arab kingdom, which would be nominally independent but in reality divided into spheres of interest. Britain and France would each have exclusive rights to appoint advisors to the sharif in the south and southeast and north and west, respectively. Palestine would be placed under international administration, which not incidentally would keep France at a safe distance from Egypt. The French sphere of influence would stretch from the Gulf of Alexandretta to Kurdistan and the Persian frontier, which would conveniently keep the Russians away from Mesopotamia. In return for their acceptance of these terms in May 1916, the Russians would get Turkish Armenia.[130] Finally, after Italy got word of the Sykes-Picot Agreement in May, Italian Foreign Minister Sonnino loudly complained that his country had not received adequate compensation in Turkey and therefore demanded a larger slice of southern Turkey.[131] It deserves notice that the Italian demands as presented in January 1917 constituted a significant increase over the southwest corner of Asia Minor they had been promised in principle two years before. Elsewhere on

[130] French, *British Strategy and War Aims*, pp. 147–48. Compared to the government's stance at the end of 1915, this agreement probably does not qualify as an increase in British war aims for two reasons. First, the British now agreed to let the French appoint advisors in Syria and northern Mesopotamia. This entails a decrease in British demands, since in October 1915 McMahon had informed Hussein that "it is understood that the Arabs have decided to seek the advice and guidance of Great Britain only, and that such European advisers and officials as may be required for the formation of a sound form of administration will be British." Excerpts of McMahon's letter can be found at the World War I Document Archive, www.lib.byu.edu/~rdh/wwi/1916/mcmahon. Second, the breakup of the Ottoman Empire was not in Britain's strategic interest and was the least favored option of the de Bunsen Committee. Undoubtedly, given British attempts to draw Russian attention away from Persia and India, allowing Russia to annex Turkish Armenia was against British interests and must be interpreted as a lowering of British war aims. As David French notes, the Sykes-Picot Agreement "marked a clear departure from Britain's prewar policy, reformulated by the Bunsen Committee in June 1915, of upholding the integrity of the Turkish Empire in Asia" (*British Strategy and War Aims*, p. 148). Both Asquith and Grey were very averse to cutting up the Ottoman Empire, but Asquith acknowledged that Britain might be forced to protect its interests against its French or Russian allies. See ibid., p. 83; Smith Jr., "Legacy to Stalin," p. 52; Cassar, p. 76; Andrew and Kanya-Forstner, p. 72.

[131] Rothwell, p. 57; Smith Jr., *The Russian Struggle for Power*, pp. 424–31.

the periphery, the Japanese forced the Allies in the spring of 1916 to grant them concessions in China.[132]

Less than one year later, as noted above, Lloyd George had started toying with the idea of a new public statement of British war aims. Upon their return from talks with representatives of Austria and Turkey on peace feelers, Kerr and Smuts reported that Mensdorff, the Austrian representative, and the Turkish spokesman had both "suggested that it would be very useful if the Allies would restate their war aims."[133] The publication of the Central Powers' account of their preliminary peace negotiations with the Russians convinced the British to follow up on this suggestion. Lloyd George asked Hankey to produce a memorandum, which was circulated to the War Cabinet and was further refined by Smuts, Robert Cecil, a junior minister in Lloyd George's Cabinet, and Lloyd George. Before his speech Lloyd George had gained the assent of the Dominions, Asquith, and the leaders of the Labour Party.[134] Lloyd George delivered this new statement at a strategically chosen occasion, on 5 January at a Trade Unions Congress meeting at Caxton Hall.[135]

British demands for the restoration of Belgium, Serbia, Montenegro, and the occupied parts of France, Italy, and Rumania and the reparation of damages remained unchanged. British war aims with regard to Alsace-Lorraine and Poland apparently did not change much either, although an argument can be made that such British demands were also lowered. Concerning Alsace-Lorraine, in January 1917 British leaders had demanded "the restitution of provinces or territories wrested in the past from the Allies by force or against the will of their populations." This claim was now explicitly limited to the promise "to stand by the French Democracy to the death in the demand they make for reconsideration of the great wrong of 1871, when, without any regard to the wishes of the population, two French provinces were torn from the side of France." Note, by the way, that this formulation, together with the announcement "that we feel that government with the consent

---

[132] The Japanese move upset the British and clearly implied a lowering of their war aims. See French, *British Strategy and War Aims*, p. 184.

[133] Hankey, quoting from his diary, vol. 2, p. 737.

[134] Ibid.

[135] "Statement of British War Aims by Prime Minister Lloyd-George," 5 January 1918, quoted in Scott, pp. 225–33, emphasis added. Rothwell concludes that this speech was a genuine statement of British aims and calls it the most important single statement on war aims (pp. 145, 153). For Balfour's view of the domestic political background that necessitated Lloyd George's speech, specifically the relations between labor and the government, see Seymour, vol. 3, p. 340.

of the governed must be the basis of any territorial settlement in this war," left open the option of a plebiscite in Alsace-Lorraine, an option rejected by the French.[136] Lloyd George, afterwards, "proudly boasted that in his reference to Alsace-Lorraine he had achieved a double coup by replacing 'restore' with the more 'elastic' word 'reconsider.' "[137]

In his speech Lloyd George also proclaimed that "an independent Poland, comprising all those genuinely Polish elements who desire to form part of it is an urgent necessity for the stability of Western Europe." This expression of sympathy for an independent Poland aimed to "avert the danger that the Poles, in their despair, might succumb to the blandishments of the Central Powers."[138] But this profession of support was cynical, because, on the other hand, British policymakers were overwhelmingly of the opinion that any inclusion of German territory was not really possible and, in any case, not something for which the war should be prolonged.[139] Moreover, *everybody*, including the old provisional Russian government, had by now promised Poland some form of independence.[140]

While some British demands thus remained unchanged, British war aims were drastically lowered along two main dimensions. First, Lloyd George now explicitly withdrew the previous demand for a change in the German regime. He told his audience that the British people "have never aimed at the break up of the German peoples or the disintegration of their State or country. . . . Nor did we enter this war merely to alter or destroy the imperial constitution of Germany. . . . [A]fter all, *that is a question for the German people to decide.*"[141] Lloyd George had already come to the conclusion that this demand was unrealistic by early October. As French notes, "By 3 October [Lloyd George] had abandoned his intention of continuing the war to impose democracy upon Germany. He was now, albeit unwillingly, content merely to con-

[136] Rothwell, p. 149. For the French government's rejection of a plebiscite see Stevenson, *The First World War*, p. 114. See also Scott, pp. 244–45; and *The "Manchester Guardian" History of the War*, vol. 8, pp. 165–66.

[137] Rothwell, p. 149.

[138] Hankey, vol. 2, p. 729.

[139] Rothwell, pp. 150–51. A debate on the precise nature of a "war aim" in October 1917 seems to have led to the conclusion that "any British declarations to the Poles would be 'aspirations' rather than aims for which the war should, if necessary be prolonged" (p. 156).

[140] On 17 October 1917 the Russian government unconditionally granted Poland independence. See Smith, *Russian Struggle for Power*, p. 484.

[141] Statement of British War Aims by Prime Minister Lloyd George, 5 January 1918, quoted in Scott, pp. 225–33, emphasis added.

tinue fighting to defeat Germany's current bid for hegemony."[142] Prussian hegemony would remain intact, and this obviously constituted a major decrease in Britain's war aims.[143]

Second, Lloyd George now withdrew the demand for the evacuation of invaded *Russian* territory. Britain now conceded control over these territories in one form or another to Germany. Lloyd George said, "I will not attempt to deal with the question of the Russian territories now in German occupation. . . . Under one name or another—the name hardly matters—these Russian provinces will henceforth be in reality a part of the dominions of Prussia." In essence this meant that Germany would be allowed to gain Courland and Lithuania.[144]

On British war aims elsewhere, Lloyd George declared

[W]e regard as vital the satisfaction of the legitimate claims of the Italians for union with those of their own race and tongue.[145] We also mean to press that justice be done to men of Roumanian blood and speech in their legitimate aspirations.[146] . . . Outside of Europe we believe that the same principles should be applied. While we do not challenge the maintenance of the

[142] French, *The Strategy of the Lloyd George Coalition*, p. 154; see also p. 203.

[143] Beginning in early 1914 the British government had insisted on a change in Germany's regime. In October 1914 Asquith defined "the destruction of Prussian militarism" as one of the fundamental prerequisites of peace (Asquith speech at the Guildhall, 9 October 1914, paraphrased in Rothwell, p. 19). For reiterations of this crucial point, see Guinn, pp. 122–23; for 1916 see Fest, pp. 286–87; French, *British Strategy*, pp. 211–16; Rothwell, pp. 42–53. In late March 1917 Lloyd George once again reaffirmed that the destruction of the German regime, what he called the "reactionary military government," was part of the basis for international peace and therefore one of the true aims of the war (Rothwell, p. 71).

[144] Quoted in Fest, p. 301. Lloyd George expressed these sentiments in September 1917. On 18 December Lloyd George had hoped he could trade Courland and Lithuania for Alsace-Lorraine, the German colonies, and Mesopotamia and Palestine (p. 304). Smuts told C. P. Scott in November 1917 that in the case of a separate peace with Russia "it would be difficult to resist" a German proposal that offered to restore Belgium, give up the colonies, and reach a compromise on Alsace-Lorraine on the condition that the Allies would accept the Russo-German treaty (Rothwell, p. 194).

[145] Compare this statement with the rather extensive Italian war aims to which Britain pledged itself by the Italian agreement of 26 April 1915 and the subsequent agreement with regard to Asia Minor of 8 August 1917. See *British Documents in Foreign Affairs: Reports and Papers from the Foreign Office Confidential Print*, part 2, series H, vol. 3, pp. 313–14. For a map of the proposed Italian gains, see ibid., p. 322. Italy was also proposed substantial spheres of influence in Asia Minor in the August 1917 agreement.

[146] Compare with the agreement with Rumania of 17 August 1916, by which Britain undertook "to secure in the final peace settlement the annexation to Roumania of the Austro-Hungarian territories as marked on Map II" (*British Documents in Foreign Affairs*, part 2, series H, vol. 3, p. 315, map on p. 322). This area includes Transylvania, the Banat, and parts of Bukowina, Moldavia, and Hungary.

Turkish empire in the home lands of the Turkish race with its capital at Constantinople,[147] the passage between the Mediterranean and the Black Sea being internationalized and neutralized—Arabia, Armenia, Mesopotamia, Syria and Palestine are in our judgment entitled to a recognition of their separate national condition. *Much has been said about the arrangements we have entered into with our allies on this and on other subjects. I can only say that as new circumstances, like the Russian collapse, and the separate Russian negotiations, have changed the conditions under which those arrangements were made,* we are, and always have been, perfectly ready to discuss them with our allies. With regard to the German colonies, I have repeatedly declared that they are held at the disposal of a conference whose decisions must have primary regard to the wishes and interests of such colonies. . . . Finally, there must be reparation for injuries done in violation of international law. . . . *Apart from this, whatever settlement is made will be suitable only to the circumstances under which it is made, as those circumstances change, changes in the settlement will be called for.* . . . If, then, if we are asked what we are fighting for, we reply, as we have often replied—we are fighting for a just and a lasting peace—and we believe that before permanent peace can be hoped for, three conditions must be fulfilled: First—the sanctity of treaties must be established; secondly, a territorial settlement must be secured based on the right of self-determination or the consent of the governed; and, lastly, we must seek by the creation of some international organization to limit the burden of armaments and diminish the probability of war.[148]

The demands on the Turks constituted a partial *increase* in British war aims. First, the promise of Constantinople and the Straits to Russia was now explicitly withdrawn; second, Lloyd George had now reverted to the preferred position of the de Bunsen Committee to leave the Ottoman Empire intact as far as possible. The change in these demands would substantially improve Britain's strategic position in Egypt and the Mediterranean. (See the sections on 1914 and 1915.)

British war aims against the Ottoman Empire were in flux, not only because of its recent successes there but also because of the second Russian revolution and the armistice on the Eastern Front.[149] British

---

[147] Earlier in his speech Lloyd George had also explicitly denied demanding "the rich and renowned lands of Asia Minor and Thrace, which are predominantly Turkish in race." This stands in sharp contrast with the official acceptance in March 1915 by the British War Council of Russian demands for "Constantinople, the western shores of the Bosporus, the Sea of Marmara, the Dardanelles, southern Thrace up to the Enos-Midia line and the islands of Imbros and Tenedos" (French, *British Strategy*, pp. 81–82).

[148] "Statement of British War Aims by Prime Minister Lloyd George," 5 January 1918, quoted in Scott, pp. 225–33, emphasis added.

[149] Later that same day at lunch Lord Riddell pressed Lloyd George about his speech: "What about Palestine and Mesopotamia? You are not very clear about them." Lloyd

leaders would subsequently use Russia's defection and the new government's rejection of the previous agreements with the Allies as an argument to declare the Sykes-Picot Agreement invalid, since the agreement had required Russian consent. The future of Palestine became especially contested in two aspects. First, several members of Lloyd George's Cabinet wanted to bring it under British (indirect) control, rather than under an international administration.[150] Second, the Balfour Declaration of 2 November declared that the British government would "use their best endeavours to facilitate . . . the establishment in Palestine of a national home for the Jewish people."[151] Britain's war aims in Mesopotamia had, meanwhile, decreased because its leaders now were content with a protectorate or sphere of influence there, instead of direct control.[152]

In summary, Britain's war aims decreased dramatically from January 1917 to January 1918. As French concludes, "These terms represented a major retreat from the maximum war aims programme the British had agreed with their allies between 1914 and 1916 or even from the more moderate but still ambitious programme they had transmitted to Wilson in January 1917."[153] Two changes stand out: the withdrawal of the demand for a change in Germany's regime, and the withdrawal for the evacuation of the occupied Russian territories. With regard to this last change it is important to note that Britain was willing to concede German demands for Lithuania and Courland not just because Russia itself stopped fighting for these provinces. When the full terms of the Treaty of Brest-Litovsk became known in March 1918, Britain became determined to continue fighting for essentially Russian territory.[154]

The events and "changed circumstances" of 1917 led the British to adjust their war aims as I predicted a nonrepressive, nonexclusionary regime would. But there apparently were limits below which Lloyd George would not lower his war aims. After his speech Lloyd George

---

George replied, "Oh, that will have to be worked out hereafter" (quoted in Riddell, pp. 304–5). In mid-December Balfour had apparently offered to make peace with Turkey on the basis of independence for Armenia, Arabia, and Mesopotamia and real autonomy for Palestine and Syria. See French, *The Strategy of the Lloyd George Coalition*, pp. 197–98. In early October Lloyd George told the War Cabinet that Turkey could get very favorable terms, including a loan for reconstruction and protectorate states under nominal Ottoman suzerainty for Syria, Palestine, and Mesopotamia (p. 154).

[150] French, *The Strategy of the Lloyd George Coalition*, p. 134.

[151] Quoted in Stevenson, *The First World War*, p. 176.

[152] Ibid., p. 181.

[153] French, *The Strategy of the Lloyd George Coalition*, p. 205.

[154] Fest, p. 306. In the treaty the Russians ceded to Germany 34 percent of their population, 32 percent of agricultural land, 54 percent of industry, and 89 percent of coal mines (Knightley, *The First Casualty*, p. 151).

told Lords Reading and Riddell that he *"went as near peace as I could."*[155] The evidence clearly demonstrates that such lower bounds to British war aims were set by the anticipated consequences of the *international consequences of settlement.*

The Causal Mechanisms

In this section I examine whether, and if so, how, domestic and international consequences of the terms of settlement influenced British war aims. While British war aims were only marginally, if at all, influenced by the domestic consequences of the terms of settlement, the international consequences of the terms of settlement played a very important role in British war aims from the very beginning of the war. This does not mean there were no strong domestic pressures to reward the British people for their sacrifices. However, contrary to policy in Germany, these pressures were not translated in high war aims because British leaders were willing to reward the British people in exactly the way German leaders were *not* willing to reward the German people: by franchise reform.

The evidence strongly supports the predictions of my theory; British statesmen formulated their "terms on the basis of their estimate of their strength *vis-à-vis* the enemy."[156] As French concludes, however, British policymakers also recognized that the terms of settlement would depend on the strength of its armed forces with regard to its allies.[157] With one exception, historians agree with my conclusion that British war aims were largely determined by the strength of its armed forces, estimates of the probability of victory, and the costs of war.[158] When British leaders became more optimistic as in July and August 1916 and again in the late summer of 1918, they raised their war

[155] Quoted in Guinn, p. 277, emphasis in original.

[156] Rothwell paraphrasing Foreign Minister Grey, p. 21. For example, lowered expectations in May 1917 about Russia's potential defection in 1917 led to attempts to secure a separate peace with Austria-Hungary. See Fest, pp. 295, 297, 299, 303; Guinn, p. 234. For other examples that British soldiers and statesmen connected British war aims with their expectations of the costs of war and probability of victory, see French, *British Strategy,* pp. 174–75, 182, 230.

[157] This conclusion is a major theme in French, *British Strategy and War Aims;* see also French, "Allies, Rivals and Enemies," pp. 22–35; Hankey, vol. 2, pp. 704–5; and Rothwell, p. 1.

[158] Rothwell, p. 200.

aims.[159] When they became more pessimistic as in 1914, 1915, and 1917, they lowered their war aims.

Paul Guinn, however, argues that domestic politics played an important role in the formulations of British war aims. Although he shows the presence of some domestic pressures to reward the people for their sacrifices, he fails to link these pressures concretely to any formulation of British war aims.[160] To bolster his argument, Guinn provides only a few, albeit very interesting, examples to show that British politicians and men of influence shared concerns strikingly similar to those of the German leaders.[161] The most striking examples are quotations from Esher, a professional nonpolitician, and the protectionist Hewings. Esher wrote the King's private secretary on 24 August 1917:

> If we really defeat the enemy England will recover her balance quickly enough. *If we fail to beat the enemy and have to accept a compromise peace, then we shall be lucky if we escape a revolution in which the Monarchy, the Church and all our "Victorian" institutions will founder.* . . . [T]he institutions under which a war such as this was possible whether monarchical, parliamentary or diplomatic, will go under. I have met no one who, speaking his inmost mind, differs from this conclusion.[162]

In early August 1917 Hewings expressed similar fears in his diary: "This government will certainly lose the war, *make a bad peace and produce a revolution*, and must be ended."[163]

These are strong words, but such fears never seem to have affected British war aims, and Guinn fails to make the case. Guinn claims that after the first Russian revolution leading British politicians saw victory

[159] For July and August 1916 see Fest, pp. 285–308; French, *British Strategy*, pp. 211–16; Rothwell, pp. 42–53. For the late summer of 1918, see Fest, p. 307.

[160] However, French refers to some discussions in the first year and a half in which several leading ministers, Kitchener in particular, expressed "the need for some tangible rewards to please the public" and the need to "satisfy the public's desire for territorial spoils." Prime Minister Asquith disagreed and argued that Britain already possessed as much territory as it was able to hold. See French, *British Strategy*, pp. 82–83.

[161] Other interesting analogies between Britain and Germany can be found. In September 1916 Henry Page Croft's National Party was formed: "This party had as its platform the 'complete victory in the war and after the war' and the 'eradication of German influence' " (quoted in Guinn, p. 241). In its extremist policies and even its name, this party reminds the reader of its German counterpart, the *Vaterlandspartei*, founded by von Tirpitz. In June 1917 the British government created a National War Aims Committee chaired by Joint Parliamentary Secretary to the Treasury Captain F. E. Guest (Herman, p. 389).

[162] Quoted in Guinn, p. 242, emphasis added.

[163] Ibid. For an argument that the British government became seriously worried about domestic unrest and potential revolution in 1917, see Turner, *British Politics and the Great War*.

as "the only way to avoid domestic upheaval."[164] I could find only one occasion on which a member of government linked British war aims to a need to reward the people for their sacrifices. In his speech of 19 December Lord Curzon argued that the British people desired "a sufficient and ample return for all the sacrifices that they have made."[165] Nevertheless, as we have seen above, during 1917 British war aims were lowered drastically, and the terms of January 1918 could hardly be said to constitute victory. Stronger yet, the strongest pressures on the British government seem to have been to *lower* their war aims. To counter left-wing allegations that Britain's war aims were imperialistic, one of the specially constituted "Commissions to Inquire into Industrial Unrest" set up in 1917 recommended that the government "should immediately take steps to dispel certain allegations now current that the aims of the Allies are Imperialistic and illiberal, by a declaration of these aims in the spirit of the various pronouncements of the past and present Prime Ministers, and of the formula that the object of the Allies is 'to make the world safe for democracy.' "[166] The War Cabinet almost immediately followed up on these suggestions. Lloyd George and Smuts had already agreed in early June that "drastic changes in the social fabric would be proposed."[167]

It could be argued, however, that analogous to French demands for Alsace-Lorraine, the remaining British war aims in Turkey and the captured German colonies would suffice to reward the people—or, more elaborately, that Lloyd George wanted to shift troops to attack Turkey to secure the required gains there. Although this possibility cannot be excluded with absolute certainty, it seems *highly* unlikely. Most of the captured colonies would go to the dominions, and it is unclear how the British sphere of influence in Mesopotamia and Arabia would reward the British people.[168] As French points out, "The emphasis which policy-makers like Curzon and Amery placed on the Middle East in 1917–18 was not the result of a crude desire to add more territory to the British Empire."[169] Rather, British leaders became worried that with Russia's collapse a dangerous power vacuum was developing along the northern frontiers of Britain's imperial possessions in Asia. Moreover, the recent successes against Turkey seemed to fully warrant these

---

[164] Guinn, p. 242. Rothwell similarly concludes that after the first Russian revolution there was a fear in ruling circles that they needed a victory to validate their position in society (pp. 97–98).

[165] *War Speeches by British Ministers*, p. 352.

[166] Quoted in Turner, *British Politics and the Great War*, p. 193.

[167] Riddell, p. 254.

[168] Rothwell, p. 53.

[169] French, *The Strategy of the Lloyd George Coalition*, pp. 175–76.

demands. Lloyd George's preferred policy of attacking Turkey seems to fit much better with his strategy of "knocking out the props from under Germany" than with ideas that Britain hoped to further expand its empire and thereby reward the people.

The demand for the recognition of the separate national condition of Palestine brings us to a series of events with dramatic consequences for the Middle East and the entire world. It must suffice here to say that this demand and the Balfour Declaration of 2 November 1917 were not the results of an attempt to buy off the people. David Stevenson has concluded that the Balfour Declaration was inspired by *international* considerations, such as the strategic proximity to the British-held Suez Canal and the propaganda value in the United States and Russia.[170]

As I argued in the previous chapter, work by Bruce Bueno de Mesquita et al. and Downs and Rocke suggests that leaders in Democracies might formulate high war aims to stay in power.[171] Some evidence to that effect exists for the fall of 1917. In a speech in Leeds, on behalf of the National War Aims Committee on 26 September, former Prime Minister and current leader of the opposition Asquith insisted on terms that included the evacuation of Russian territory and the return of Alsace-Lorraine to France.[172] French suggests this was a tactical move to prevent Lloyd George from lowering his war aims and that "If Lloyd George had really wished to abandon his commitment to the 'knockout blow' the price of doing so would have been the end of his tenancy of 10 Downing Street."[173] While this may have temporarily shored up British demands, French concludes that "the extent to which Lloyd George was willing to make peace at Russia's expense in 1917 is debatable." French deems it "more likely" that Lloyd George's statement that "Russia ought to pay the penalty" if it were to make a separate peace "was designed to place pressure on the Provisional Government to stay in the war."[174] However, even if we accept that in September 1917 Lloyd George kept British war aims high to stay in power, we saw above that by January 1918 he had significantly lowered British

---

[170] For more background on the Balfour Declaration and British war aims in Palestine, see Stevenson, *The First World War*, pp. 176–81. Note that on 4 June 1917 Jules Cambon had told another Zionist leader, Sokolow, that the French government looked favorably upon Jewish colonization and "the renaissance of Jewish nationality" in Palestine (p. 178).

[171] Bueno de Mesquita et al.; Bueno de Mesquita and Siverson, "War and the Survival of Political Leaders"; Bueno de Mesquita and Siverson, "Political Survival and International Crises"; Downs and Rocke.

[172] The speech is in Scott, pp. 141–47.

[173] French, *The Strategy of the Lloyd George Coalition*, p. 146.

[174] Ibid., pp. 145–46.

war aims on exactly these two points. It seems unlikely, therefore, that the fear of losing power prompted Lloyd George to insist on high British war aims.

In Germany the regime was not willing to reward the people for their sacrifices by domestic political concessions and was, therefore, left with the option of high war aims. The exact opposite was the case for the British government; British leaders *were* willing to reward the people with domestic political concessions. From the summer of 1915 onward, the Labour Party viewed calls for compulsory national service and conscription with deep suspicion. Not only would conscription imply more casualties, but Labour also thought the Conservatives would use compulsory service as a way to break their unions.[175] Thus, Labour leader Henderson warned the Cabinet on the eve of the TUC conference in September 1915 that *"if [conscription] was introduced it should be accompanied by universal suffrage, heavy taxes on the rich and the promise that it would be abandoned at the end of the war."*[176] Henderson's demand clearly aimed to reward the people for the increased costs imposed by conscription. The reaction of British politicians was to grant these concessions and do exactly what the Prussian Junkers refused to do.

On 5 January 1916 Prime Minister Asquith introduced a bill that called for the conscription of all unexempted single men and childless widowers between the ages of eighteen and forty-one.[177] A second bill was introduced later that year that extended conscription to married men. Almost immediately work began on a far-reaching reform of the franchise agreed to by all parties.[178] The Representation of the People Act was first introduced in early 1917 and enacted on 27 January 1918. The bill more than doubled the franchise; it gave the vote to all men over twenty-one and to women over thirty and limited plural voting to one extra vote.[179] In his book on the act Hugh Fraser acknowledges that "[f]rom a historical point of view the present Act owed its origin

---

[175] French, *British Strategy,* p. 118.

[176] Ibid., p. 129, emphasis added.

[177] For a thorough description of the process that led to conscription, see Cassar, ch. 9.

[178] Turner, "British Politics and the Great War," p. 129. Work on the reform started in the Speaker's Conference of late September 1916. Apparently, Lloyd George had concluded already in early 1916 that a reform of the franchise was called for. He told Lord Riddell on 18 June 1916: "Some time before Kitchener's death, the question arose as to votes for soldiers. I am in favour of soldiers having votes. The P.M. is strongly opposed to it. He thinks that the men who are fighting for their country should have no voice in selecting the rulers who are to send them to risk their lives. I think that a monstrous proposition. I may go out on that question. It would be a proper question on which to resign" (Riddell, p. 193).

[179] *Manchester Guardian,* pp. 265–73.

to the fact that it was universally recognized that the electors of members to serve in the Parliament which would have to deal with questions of reconstruction after the War, must include those who had fought for their country in the War."[180]

In addition to franchise reform, the British leadership was also willing to introduce other social reforms. When Lloyd George came to power, he also put Henderson in the War Cabinet and granted concessions to Labour about postwar reconstruction. During 1917, for example, the government introduced bills providing more generous pensions and war disability payments and "a series of education and housing reconstruction programs . . . to allay war weariness and discontent."[181] The government also acted with alacrity upon signs of worker discontent after the first Russian revolution.[182] It conceded Labour demands to abolish leaving certificates and grant wage increases.[183]

The difference in the reactions of British and German leaders to a similar issue, reform of the franchise, strongly supports my theory. As will be shown in the chapter on Germany during 1918, Ludendorff preferred to fight on in an almost hopeless cause, even to lose the war, rather than to reform the Prussian franchise. In sharp contrast, Britain's leaders were willing to more than double the franchise because they never feared such concessions would mean the irrevocable overthrow of the old system. Although the reform could result in a redistribution of the political power among the major parties, no party or leader would have to fear a *permanent* loss of power.

While worries about the domestic consequences of the terms of settlement did not crucially influence British war aims, in large part because the people could be rewarded by other means, war aims were fundamentally influenced by the anticipated *international* consequences of the terms of settlement. British leaders worried about the international consequences of the terms of settlement on two accounts. First, and as emphasized in chapter 2, British leaders worried about the commitment problem. If Germany were allowed to gain power in the settlement, it would become even more difficult for Britain to defend its own security interests. This problem never was far from the minds of British politicians, who only had to point to the example of Germany's violation of Belgian neutrality to emphasize the frailty of

---

[180] Fraser, p. xxii. See also the speech by the Secretary of State for the Home Department on the occasion of the second reading of the bill on 22 May 1917, *House of Commons*, 5th series, session 1917, vol. 93, pp. 2134–35.

[181] Herman, p. 333.

[182] Turner, "British Politics and the Great War," p. 126.

[183] Herman, p. 449.

promises in international politics.[184] Second, British leaders also worried about gains in power by its wartime allies. British policymakers were concerned not to defeat Germany only to have the Russians (or French) take its place as a potential hegemon on the continent.

British wartime concerns about the international consequences of the terms of settlement were a logical extension of its decision to enter the war to maintain the balance of power on the continent. As David French concludes, the British went to war in 1914 to "preserve their country's independence and status as a great power."[185]

Such concerns about changes in the balance of power on the continent with its implications for British security continued throughout the war.[186] In a speech in January 1918 Lloyd George emphasized the commitment problem while he reminded his audience of the political concessions offered by the government:

> If we are not able to defeat the German forces, if we are not able to resist the military power of Prussia, is there any man here in possession of his wits who believes that one of your terms—the least of them—would be enforced? . . . I am talking of the moderate demands of the most pacifist soul in this assembly. Go to von Hindenburg with them. Try to cash that check at the Hindenburg bank. It will be returned dishonored. Whatever terms are set forward by any pacifist orator in these lands, you will not get them cashed by Ludendorff or the Kaiser, or any of those great magnates—not one of them—unless you have got the power to enforce them. A Delegate [interrupting]: Is not the best way to get at the opinion of the German people to allow representatives of this nation to meet representatives of the other Powers at Stockholm or elsewhere? Mr. Lloyd George: The representatives of the German nation would, of course, be chosen by the German Government. . . . You can only make peace with a Government. If the Government does not represent the people of Germany let them change their Government, and if this Government does not represent the people of this country, they can change it. (A Delegate: Give us an opportunity.) We have given you the best opportunity that has been given for a long time, because this Government had introduced a fran-

---

[184] From early on British statesmen insisted that the Entente were fighting "not just for their own physical security but because Germany's invasion of Belgium demonstrated that even its most solemn promises offered no guarantee of a lasting peace" (French, *British Strategy*, p. 60).

[185] Ibid., p. ix; see also p. 21. See also Stevenson, *The First World War*, p. 37; Grey to C. P. Scott, July 1911, quoted in French, *British Strategy*, p. 3.

[186] French similarly concludes that the British government worried that "If Germany's terms were accepted it would be able to resume the war against Britain a few years later in a vastly stronger position" (*British Strategy*, p. 190).

chise bill which has added eight millions to the electorate. You can have your opportunity any time you like.[187]

Not surprisingly, soldiers also worried about the international consequences of a compromise peace, which would increase German strength. Kitchener, for example, warned the American ambassador in late March 1916 that "a compromise peace would probably last only seven years."[188] Robertson expressed similar sentiments in his memorandum of 27 December 1917. He "opposed a compromise peace as merely a 'truce' in which Germany would 'organize' a fresh attempt for securing world domination which she had failed to obtain in the present war."[189]

Concerns about the commitment problem imposed a lower bound of war aims below which the British would not settle. First, Britain insisted on the unconditional restoration of Belgium.[190] British politicians insisted on this because they knew German occupation of Belgium and, in particular, the Belgian coast would seriously change the balance of power on the continent and endanger Britain's future security.[191] In August 1914 Grey had warned of the consequences if Germany were allowed to occupy and control Belgium. This would imply "the whole of the western Europe opposite to us . . . falling under the domination of a single power."[192]

Second, British statesmen also had a lower bound of war aims with regard to German demands against Russia. In September 1917 Lloyd George probed his colleagues in the War Cabinet on a peace at Russia's expense, offering Germany Lithuania, Courland, and an "arrangement" with regard to Poland. His subsequent observation that after such a settlement the German Empire would be equal in power to the British Empire immediately produced second thoughts and an awareness of

[187] Statement of Prime Minister Lloyd George on the Fourteen Points, 18 January 1918, in Scott, pp. 240–41. For another example where Lloyd George warns of the commitment problem, see Lloyd George, "When the War Will End," p. 10.

[188] French, *British Strategy*, p. 194.

[189] Rothwell, p. 148.

[190] See Fest, especially pp. 285–287, 305; French, *British Strategy*, especially p. 212; French, "Allies, Rivals and Enemies," p. 31; Guinn, especially pp. 238, 275; Rothwell, especially pp. 9, 18, 21, 32. Grey had informed the Belgian government in August 1915 that Britain would insist upon the full restoration of Belgian independence in any peace negotiations. In the declaration of Sainte Adresse of February 1916 Britain, moreover, officially declared it would not cease hostilities "unless Belgium is reinstated in her political and economic independence and largely indemnified for the wrongs suffered" (*British Documents*, part 2, series H, vol. 3, p. 316); see also French, *British Strategy*, pp. 165–66.

[191] French, *British Strategy*, p. 21.

[192] Rothwell, p. 18.

the commitment problem. Balfour made it clear he did not want any peace that would leave Germany stronger than it had been in 1914. Milner also noted that such a settlement would mean that Germany would come out of the war stronger than before and there would be another war in ten years' time.[193] We have seen above that Britain was nevertheless willing to offer such terms by January 1918. Rothwell argues that the reason was that "[t]he British now doubted whether there could be any other outcome to the war except perhaps by extending so many lives that Britain's population and economic and military capacity would be so reduced that she would sink to the status of a second-class power."[194]

However, this was all before the draconian terms of the Brest-Litovsk peace settlement between Russia and Germany became known later in 1918.[195] If Rothwell's assessment is correct, the British refusal to settle on terms that would leave intact the Treaty of Brest-Litovsk is all the more proof of British fears of the concomitant change in the balance of power.[196] Rothwell argues that Brest-Litovsk killed the idea of a negotiated peace with Germany at the expense of Russia because that treaty would lead, at a minimum, to a "vast accretion to the resources of the Central Powers and an insidious but certain weakening of Great Britain's position in India."[197] As Robert Cecil put it, "with the resources of Russia and the possibilities of a wealthy country there is no reason why [the Germans] should not fight the world forever and be unconquerable."[198]

It seems that British leaders basically foresaw three possible approaches to solve the commitment problem: a correction in the balance of power, international institutions such as the League of Nations, and, surprisingly, a change in Germany's regime. The first option was, of course, the preferred one. It is important to note that any correction in the balance of power always aimed to leave Germany strong enough to balance off Russia and France.[199] One example of such a change in the balance of power on the continent is British support for French demands for Alsace-Lorraine. The return of Alsace-Lorraine would

---

[193] Fest, pp. 300–301; Rothwell, p. 108.

[194] Rothwell, p. 163.

[195] Fest, p. 306.

[196] Smuts, a member of the War Cabinet, argued: "We could not accept the Brest-Litovsk and Rumanian treaties. They must be placed on the table of the peace conference for revision" (Rothwell, p. 195).

[197] Quoted in ibid., p. 197.

[198] Quoted in ibid., p. 195; see also p. 286.

[199] French, *British Strategy,* p. 21.

stabilize the balance of power on the continent, according to Robert Cecil, because it would give France better strategic frontiers.[200] Another aspect of the rearrangement of Europe's borders was the belief that war would be less likely if "the boundaries of the various States [could be made to harmonize] with the aspirations of their constituent races."[201]

The institutional option was also considered by British statesmen, but always with much skepticism. The British always had few illusions about the efficacy of grandiose schemes about international institutions. This skepticism about the enforcement capabilities of such international institutions came through loud and clear in the British supplement to the Entente's reply to President Wilson's call for a mediated peace of December 1916: "There are those who think that for this disease [i.e., the enforcement problem] international treaties and international laws may provide a sufficient cure," the note warned. "But such persons have ill learned the lessons so clearly taught by recent history. . . . [T]reaty arrangements for maintaining peace were not likely to find much favor at Berlin; . . . such treaties once made would be utterly ineffectual."[202] The British put more faith in much more limited international institutions such as a tripartite treaty of alliance between Belgium, France, and Britain to protect Belgium in the future.[203]

A third option to secure the terms of peace and prevent future conflict was a change in Germany's regime. Although the idea has interesting implications for International Relations theory, this is not the place to deal with the issue at length. Suffice it to note Lloyd George's announcement in his speech of 5 January 1918: "One point of view is that the adoption of a really democratic constitution by Germany would be the most convincing evidence that in her the old spirit of military domination has indeed died in this war, and would make it much easier for us to conclude a broad democratic peace with her."[204]

---

[200] Rothwell, p. 62; Nelson, *Land and Power*, pp. 5–6, 18, 22. This international consequence outweighed domestic consequences for the return of Alsace-Lorraine to France. Nelson notes that "The cession of Alsace-Lorraine . . . could be disadvantageous to the Lancashire textile trade" (*Land and Power*, p. 5).

[201] Rothwell, p. 11.

[202] British supplement to the Entente Reply, to President Wilson, 12 January 1917, in Scott, p. 47. In their reply to Wilson's call for peace, Allied and British decision makers repeatedly stress the need for enforcement of the peace terms. See *The Case of the Allies*, pp. 3, 11, 15. For Balfour's skepticism, see Rothwell, p. 154.

[203] French, *British Strategy*, p. 212.

[204] "Statement of British War Aims by Prime Minister Lloyd George," 5 January 1918, in Scott, pp. 225–33. In 1914 Grey had made a similar argument; see Rothwell, p. 22.

The international consequences of the terms of settlement had a second dimension: the security of Britain and its empire against its allies.[205] Such concerns found their earliest expression in the first months of the war when Britain, France, and Russia agreed in the Pact of London of 5 September 1914 that none of them would sign a separate peace and that each ally's war aims and terms of settlement would have to be agreed on by the others *in advance*. Initially, British leaders hoped the French, Russians, and Germans would bleed each other white, after which Kitchener's New Armies would allow Britain to impose a British peace.[206] Such considerations survived well into 1916. As Robertson wrote to Lord Esher on 9 August 1916, when British leaders were very optimistic about a quick end to the war on favorable terms to the Entente, "I confess that I have anxiety when I think of the day on which we may be seated round the Council Table discussing terms of peace. I am not thinking so much of the enemy as of the Allies."[207]

This examination of British perceptions of the domestic and international consequences of the terms of settlement strongly supports two major casual mechanisms of my theory. On the one hand, the British government was willing to buy off its domestic political opposition with a far-reaching reform of the franchise. On the other hand, there existed a lower bound to British war aims below which British leaders would not settle out of fears for the long-term security of Britain and its empire.

Conclusion

This chapter has established that during 1917 the British government lowered its estimates of the probability of victory and increased its estimates of the costs of war. As a result and as predicted, the government lowered its war aims. Turning to the causal mechanisms, I showed that concerns about the international consequences of the terms of settlement did lead, as predicted, to a lower bound of war aims. The strongest finding of this chapter may well be the willingness of the British government to reward the people for their sacrifices by domestic political concessions. It is striking to note how the British were willing to offer the very thing the German leaders wanted to avoid at all costs: a

[205] This is a central thesis in French's *British Strategy and War Aims*; see, for example, p. ix.

[206] Ibid., pp. xiii, 25.

[207] Quoted in ibid., p. 211. For more on British concerns about intra-alliance bargaining over the terms of settlement, see Nelson, *Land and Power*, pp. 27–52, 71–72.

far-reaching reform of the franchise. This willingness to offer concessions, seen in combination with Britain's prewar political difficulties, clearly shows that it is indeed regime type and not the presence or absence of prewar crises that caused the different reactions to unfavorable new information of Germany and Britain. While Germany increased its war aims to cover the costs of war, Britain lowered its war aims.

8

The Termination of the First World War, I: 1914–1917

T HE PREVIOUS CHAPTERS focused on how nonrepressive, nonexclusionary (France and Great Britain) and semirepressive, moderately exclusionary regimes (Germany and Russia) changed their war aims in the First World War. In this and the next chapter I examine how these changes affect the creation of a bargaining space and, therefore, war termination. In the introductory chapter I argued that if we want to explain the variation between war and peace, the study of the causes of war termination has a great practical advantage over the study of the causes of war. This chapter will try to make the most of this practical advantage and examine the choice between war and peace in each year of the First World War. In other words, I will examine and explain why the war did not end in 1914, 1915, 1916, or 1917. The next chapter examines why the war finally did end in 1918.

This chapter opens with a section that provides a brief overview of the war aims of the main belligerents, including the United States, from 1914 to 1917. The absence of a bargaining space in 1914, 1915, and 1916 will be readily apparent. The years 1917 and 1918, however, merit detailed analysis. The second section focuses on 1917 and addresses three important questions. First, why did the Russian Bolshevik regime agree to a separate peace and accept the Germans' harsh demands? Second, why did the German leadership not push their advantage and ask even higher war aims when they learned the Russian army had basically ceased to exist? The third question is perhaps the most interesting: Why did the German regime not offer a peace on the basis of the status quo ante in the west, or even offer some concessions in Alsace-Lorraine, and try to buy off the people with high(er?) demands in the east? This question has barely been examined in the historical literature, but an answer is crucial to explain why the First World War lasted until 1918.

Overview of the War

To examine whether a bargaining space existed, I list the war aims of the main belligerents in separate tables at five intervals: August–September 1914, November–December 1914, November 1915–March 1916, November 1916–March 1917, and December 1917–March 1918. I examine the war aims of October–November 1918 in the next chapter. These war aims were compiled from a detailed study of the available literature.[1]

While only the latter two periods saw successful war termination negotiations, it deserves emphasis that the continuation of the war at other times was *not* the result of a lack of information about each side's minimum terms of settlement. Although their minimum demands were far apart, the belligerents seem to have had relatively good estimates of their opponents' minimum terms. This information came from public and private sources, as from late 1914 onwards both sides and neutral third parties engaged in numerous, more or less official, probes of their opponents' terms of settlement.[2]

Moreover, leaders in the different states seem to have been well aware that the semirepressive, moderately exclusionary regimes needed higher war aims to buy off their domestic opposition and stay in power. As we saw in chapter 5, German Minister of Foreign Affairs Jagow argued in 1915 that the Tsar could not sign a separate and losing peace because it would lead to a domestic revolution. To prevent a revolution and reward the people for their sacrifices, Jagow argued, the Tsar would insist on the demand for Constantinople.[3] British leaders similarly estimated in August 1915 that Russian peace overtures would produce a revolution.[4] Both American and British leaders also recognized that Germany's regime needed a profit to buy off the people after the war or face revolution. In his Flag Day Address of 14 June 1917, President Wilson told the American people:

---

[1] Full citations for these aims are available at http://www.duke.edu/~hgoemans.

[2] See, for an example of how well Germany's leaders were informed of the basic aims of France and Britain in 1917, Hanssen, pp. 234–35. For Britain's awareness of German terms in September 1917, see French, *The Strategy of the Lloyd George Coalition*, p. 145; see also Stevenson, *The First World War and International Politics*, pp. 165–69. Admittedly, however, the western Allies were surprised and dismayed by the final terms of the Treaty of Brest-Litovsk between Russia and Germany. For more on the probes for peace, see Lafeber; Stadelmann; Steglich, *Der Friedensappell Papst Benedikts XV. vom 1. August 1917 und die Mittelmächte*; Birnbaum; Farrar, *Divide and Conquer*; Fest; Forster; Horak; the voluminous literature on the Sixte affair, for example, de Manteyer; Pedroncini, *Les Négociations secrètes pendant la Première Guerre mondiale*; Renouvin, "Les Tentatives de paix en 1917 et le gouvernement français"; Schwabe, "Die Amerikanische und die Deutsche Geheimdiplomatie"; Wheeler-Bennett; Zechlin, "Friedensbestrebungen und Revolutionsversuche"; Zeman, pp. 121–61.

[3] Fischer, *Griff nach der Weltmacht*, p. 234. Jagow even went so far as to explain the call for the Duma's session as an attempt to shift the blame for the war onto that body. See the draft by Jagow of a reply from Bethmann Hollweg to Falkenhayn, 24 July 1915, in Janssen, *Der Kanzler und der General*, pp. 279–81. See also the "Promemoria aus dem Auswärtigen Amt," U.S.S. of 8 July 1915 in ibid., Anhang III, no. 11, pp. 276–77.

[4] French, *British Strategy and War Aims*, p. 167.

The military masters under whom Germany is bleeding see very clearly to what point Fate has brought them. If they fall back or are forced back an inch, their power both abroad and at home will fall to pieces like a house of cards. It is their power at home they are thinking about now more than their power abroad. . . . They have but one chance to perpetuate their military power or even their controlling political influence. If they can secure peace now with the immense advantages still in their hands, which they have up to this point apparently gained, they will have justified themselves before the German people; they will have gained by force what they promised to gain by it. . . . Their prestige will be secure, and with their prestige their political power. If they fail, their people will thrust them aside; a government accountable to the people themselves will be set up in Germany.[5]

Lloyd George explained the German decision to continue fighting in similar terms on 30 June 1918: "if you were faced with the alternative of certain death now and problematical death two years hence, which would you prefer? Of course you would take your chance and rely on something turning up."[6] The previous year he had already noted that "it would be far easier to make favourable terms" if the German regime could be transformed into a constitutional government. Under the current regime Germany's leaders could not, even if they wanted

---

[5] Wilson's Flag Day Address, Washington, D.C., 14 June 1917, reprinted in Shaw, pp. 411–18; quotation on pp. 416–17. Note how closely these ideas, and even the language, mirror Colonel House's letter to Wilson of 30 May 1917, which suggested Wilson incorporate these themes in his next speech (Seymour, vol. 3, pp. 132–38). With remarkable prescience House predicted to Lord Bryce that if the German regime would fail to secure a profit on the war, "it is probable that the [German] Government will offer the people a liberal monarchy in order to save the present dynasty" (ibid., p. 129).

[6] Riddell, pp. 335–36. Riddell had asked, "How long do you think the war will last, Prime Minister? Lloyd George (laughing): I will write my answer on a piece of paper to be sealed up and opened after the war. But I don't agree with you. In considering the problem I try to feel myself in the position of a German statesman. How would he be likely to regard it? The Germans have great victories to their credit and they have been led to expect more. They think they are winning. How is their view to be changed? Von Kühlmann made the attempt, and you see what happened to him. I think he honestly believed what he said. The hypothetical statesman would receive the illustrious order of the boot. It is a dangerous game. If you break the morale of the people and the peace move does not come off, you are done. Things are different now from what they were in the old days; now you have to conduct your diplomacy in public. Formerly a little junta could decide on peace; to-day you have to obtain the approval of millions of people. That makes negotiations very difficult. R: I agree. But the German statesman would see the red light ahead and would know that the chances were that he would meet disaster before long. LG: Yes, but if you were faced with the alternative of certain death now and problematical death two years hence, which would you prefer? Of course you would take your chance and rely on something turning up."

to, "vacate France and Belgium; there would be too much criticism by sections of their own people."[7] Hence, the failure to end the war before 1917 was *not* the result of a lack of information about each side's war aims or a lack of understanding of how domestic politics affected the war aims of Germany and Russia.

Turning to the specifics, a comparison of the four main belligerents' war aims in the first two months of the war, as presented in table 8.1, reveals trivially that no bargaining space existed. Germany demanded far-reaching gains both in the east and the west, while France and Russia also demanded far-reaching revisions of the prewar status quo. Furthermore, both France and Britain—and perhaps also Russia—demanded that "Prussian militarism" yield its grip on the German Empire. Such high war aims all around should probably not come as a surprise in the initial stages of a major war.

As we saw in the individual chapters on the main belligerents, the new information produced by the fighting between September and November led the respective leaderships to revise their war aims to different degrees. Table 8.2 lays out the war aims of the main belligerents at the end of 1914. Turning first to the Eastern Front, a comparison of Russian and German war aims shows that although the bargaining gap had narrowed, both sides still made demands that were unacceptable to the other. The Germans still demanded border rectifications in Poland, and the Russians still demanded that Prussian territory be included into a new "Poland." In addition, the Russians insisted on the destruction of German militarism and the dissolution of the Austro-Hungarian Empire. What explains the continuation of this bargaining gap?

As we saw in the chapter on Germany, by mid-November 1914 the German leadership explicitly recognized they could not win the war against the combined Entente. They therefore hoped to secure a separate peace with Russia or France. From late 1914 until the summer of 1915, the German leadership tried repeatedly to open a channel of communication with the Russian court to probe the Russian terms for a separate peace. However, the Tsar peremptorily dismissed all peace feelers. Three factors probably played a role in his rejection. First, on 4 September the Allies promised each other in the London Agreement "not to conclude peace separately during the present war. The three Governments agree that when terms of peace come to be discussed, no one of the Allies will demand terms of peace without the previous

---

[7] Both quotations in Riddell, pp. 247, 262. The first statement is from 1 April 1917, the second from 3 August 1917, when Bethmann Hollweg had been replaced as Chancellor by Michaelis. Foreign Minister Grey made a similar argument on 15 May 1916 (Linke, pp. 50–51).

TABLE 8.1

War Aims in August–September 1914

Germany	France	Great Britain	Russia
9 Sept: *France*: not to emerge as a great power. Briey, debilitating war indemnity, economic domination through commerce treaty, Longwy to Luxembourg? Belfort? Western slopes of the Vosges? Fortresses? Coast from Dunkirk to Boulogne to Belgium? *Belgium*: Liège and Verviers annexed; strip of Luxembourg province to Grand Duchy Luxembourg, economically a German province, militarily a vassal. (Antwerp?) *Luxembourg, (GD): A federal German state, gains strip from*	20 Sept: Evacuation of occupied territories, including Alsace-Lorraine; hegemony of Prussian militarism broken; reparations to all Allied countries; guarantees for future peace.	2–6 Aug: Maintain balance of power on the Continent; Germany not allowed to occupy the English Channel coast; Belgian independence; Prussian militarism removed from German politics. Position of the small states?	7 Aug: Trentino, Trieste, Valona to Italy? 14 Aug: United Poland, i.e. German and Austrian Poland annexed. 14 Sept: German power and pretensions to military and political domination broken. Territorial modifications along principle of nationalities; lower course of Niemen and eastern Galicia annexed; newly constituted Kingdom of Poland gets Eastern Posen, Silesia, and the western part of Galicia. France regains Alsace-Lorraine (and Rhenish Prussia and the Palatinate?); Belgium enlarged, Denmark

TABLE 8.1 (cont.)

War Aims in August–September 1914

Germany	Russia
Belgium, corner of Longwy? *Russia*: pushed back as far as possible from German borders; rule over non-Russian peoples broken, specifics left open. *Holland*: Externally independent, internally dependent on Germany. (Offensive and defensive alliance? Antwerp from Belgium?) *Middle European Economic Association*: German economic predominance over Middle Europe, common custom agreements with France, Belgium, Holland, Denmark, Austria-Hungary, Poland, potentially Italy, Sweden, Norway. *Colonies*: Middle African empire, specifics determined later.	regains Schleswig-Holstein; Kingdom of Hanover restored; Austria-Hungary broken up into three kingdoms: Austria, Hungary, and Bohemia; Serbia gets Bosnia, Herzegovina, Dalmatia and northern Albania; Bulgaria compensated in Macedonia; Greece to annex southern Albania, with the exception of Valona, which would go to Italy; England, France, and Japan to partition the German colonies; reparations. 26–27 Sept: Free passage through the Straits with guarantees. 1–3 Oct: Northern Bukovina, southern part to Rumania.

Note: Question marks indicate the uncertain status of a war aim.

TABLE 8.2

War Aims in November–December 1914

Germany	France	Great Britain	Russia
19 Nov–31 Dec: *Russia*: War indemnity; Polish border strip along Njemen-Bobr-Narew. *France*: Longwy added. Otherwise unchanged? *Belgium*: Unchanged?	22 Dec: Alsace-Lorraine; indemnities for France and Belgium; restoration of Belgian independence; Prussian militarism "broken"; tariff concession to Japan in Indo-China (possible outright cession?); Russia free passage through the Straits.	9 Nov: Restoration of Belgian independence and compensation; security guarantees for France; protection of the rights of the smaller nationalities; destruction of military domination of Prussia. Final disposition of Constantinople and Straits to be settled in accordance with Russia's wishes; internationalization of Constantinople and free passage through the Straits.	21 Nov: Destruction of German militarism; Russia accepts any French and British claims; Poland gains Posen, possibly a portion of Silesia; annexation of Galicia, northwestern part of Bukovina; Armenia? Free passage through the Straits, Constantinople neutralized. European Turkey split with Bulgaria; Serbia gets Bosnia, Herzegovina, Dalmatia, and Northern Albania; Greece gets southern Albania minus Valona, which

TABLE 8.2 (cont.)
War Aims in November–December 1914

Russia

goes to Italy; Bulgaria compensation in Macedonia? Austria-Hungary to cede territoy to Russia, Poland, Serbia; southern Bukovina and Transylvania to Rumania, Italian Tyrol and Istria to Italy. Austria-Hungary broken into four parts: Austria, Hungary, Croatia, and Bohemia. Prussia and Hohenzollerns denied the Kaiser's crown; Alsace-Lorraine (the Rhenish provinces?) to France; Belgium to get territory toward Aachen; Schleswig and the Kiel canal zone to Denmark; Kingdom of Hanover revived; France and Britain to divide the German colonies.

Note: Question marks indicate the uncertain status of a war aim.

agreement of each of the other Allies."[8] As the Tsar undoubtedly knew, a separate peace between Russia and Germany would leave Germany free to concentrate all its forces in the west. In a next war, therefore, Russia not only would face a stronger Germany, but would also be a less credible ally to France and Britain. Second, the Tsar remained relatively optimistic about the probability of victory, given the combined force of the Entente and Russia's relative strength—if only the Russian army could be properly supplied. Third, with the experience of the Russo-Japanese War fresh in his mind, the Tsar also knew that any peace that required the Russians to make territorial concessions to Germany would risk revolution at home. Thus, he had relatively little to lose by continuing the war. The Germans, for their part, would not settle on the status quo ante but insisted on moderate gains in the east for probably two reasons. First, they estimated that after a few more defeats Russia would have learned the best they could hope for was a separate peace on moderate losing terms. Second, German leaders from very early on realized they would need gains in *both* the east and the west to buy off the opposition and maintain the domestic political balance of power. I shall return to this issue below in the section on 1917.

Turning to the Western Front, the bargaining gap created by the minimum demands of France, Britain, and Germany had largely remained unchanged. The new German demand for Longwy had actually further widened the bargaining gap. Germany's insistence on high war aims must largely be attributed to the nature of its regime. The German leadership needed substantial gains in the war to offset the already considerable costs of war and buy off the domestic opposition. In addition, the leadership seems to have hoped that a separate peace with Russia would allow them to throw all their forces westward and so thoroughly defeat the western Allies that they could basically impose any terms they wanted. French and British leaders, meanwhile, remained confident of final victory, although they recognized that the costs of war would be higher than they had previously estimated. (This recognition induced them to make a substantial strategic concession to their Russian ally in the form of free passage through the Straits.)

During 1915 most of the new information came from the Eastern Front, where Russia suffered a series of unexpected defeats. As shown in the previous chapters, this new information made the German leadership more optimistic, while France and Britain and perhaps also Russia became more pessimistic. However, the change in their respective

---

[8] This declaration any many other crucial documents from the First World War can be found at http://www.lib.byu.edu/~rdh/wwi/1914/tripentente.html.

TABLE 8.3

War Aims in November 1915–March 1916

Germany	France	Great Britain	Russia
10–11 Nov 1915: *Russia:* Austro-Polish solution. Deeper and broader military, economic, and political ties between Germany and Austria-Hungary. Polish Statelands; tracts of land in the Suwalki province; territory bordering on the Upper Silesian industrial area. Border rectifications with Poland along Kowno-Grondo-Plozk-Warthe line; Lithuania and Courland autonomous Dukedom. 1 Jan 1916: *Belgium:* A defensive alliance with political, economic, military guarantees. Liège? 29 Oct 1915: Annexation of the port triangle of Ostende-Zeebrugge-Antwerp?	10 Apr 1915: Constantinople and surroundings to Russia. Syria to be annexed. 26 April 1915: Italy gets Trentino, cis-alpine Tyrol, Gorizia Gradisca, Istria, Dalmatia, and islands in the Adriatic, Valona, Saseno, and islands in the Dodecanese. 3 Nov 1915: Liberation of French soil; provinces taken by conquest restored; Belgium to regain its territory, political, and economic power; Serbia restored. Guarantees for a durable peace.	10 Mar 1915: Constantinople and surroundings to Russia; neutral sphere in Persia to become British sphere. 19 Mar 1915: Direct control over Basra, direct or indirect control of the Baghdad vilayet; right to make further demands. 26 Apr 1915: Italy gets Trentino, cis-alpine Tyrol, Gorizia Gradisca, Istria, Dalmatia, and islands in the Adriatic, Valona, Saseno, and islands in the Dodecanese. 23 Feb 1916: Belgium and Serbia recover all they have sacrificed. France adequately secured against the menace of aggression; rights of the smaller nationalities secured; military domination of Prussia wholly and finally destroyed.	4 Mar 1915: Constantinople, western shore of the Bosphorus, Sea of Marmora and the Dardanelles, Southern Thrace up to the Enos-Midia line, part of the Asiatic shore between the Bosphorus, Sakkaria River, Bay of Izmid, islands of the Sea of Marmora, Imbros, and Tenedos. France and Britain get the same benevolence for their projects in the Ottoman Empire and elsewhere. Neutral sphere in Persia becomes British sphere. 26 Apr 1915: Italy gets Trentino, cis-alpine Tyrol, Gorizia, Gradisca, Istria, Dalmatia, and islands in the Adriatic, Valona, Saseno, and islands in the Dodecanese. Mar 1916: Tsar sticks to his demands of 21 Nov 1914.

TABLE 8.4

War Aims in November 1916–February 1917

Germany	France	Great Britain	Russia
8 Nov 1916: *Russia*: Recognition of Kingdom of Poland (OHL: Border adjustments along Prussian-Polish border, "Polish borderstrip," economic union with Germany, Polish army under German control). Annexation of territory from Courland and Lithuania to get a good strategic border with Russia (OHL: from the Gulf of Riga to east past Wilna in the direction of Brest-Litovsk). Trade agreement with Russia. *Belgium*: Guarantees in Belgium; if not obtainable to a sufficient degree, annexation of Liège with suitable environs. Congo or parts of it. Increased monthly contributions to 50 million marks? (OHL: exploitation of the Campine). *France*: Briey and	(16 May 1916) 5 June 1916: Sykes-Picot Agreement; Syrian coast, southern Cicilia; right to appoint advisors to the Arab State in Syria and northern Mesopotamia. 12 Jan 1917: Alsace-Lorraine with the frontier of 1790, i.e., including the Saar; security guarantees, specifically neutralization of the Rhineland, (i.e., buffer states?); possibility for claims to the left bank of the Rhine deliberately left open; approval of the League of Nations.	(16 May 1916) 5 June 1916: Sykes-Picot Agreement; Mesopotamia between Baghdad and the Persian Gulf, Acre, Haifa; right to appoint advisors to the Arab State in Jordan and southern Mesopotamia. 11 Dec 1916: Complete restitution, full reparation, effectual guarantees. Removal of the Prussian military caste. Recover for Belgium, France, Russia, Serbia, and Rumania the territories they lost and secure reparations. Guarantees and securities. Free and independent existence of nations great and small. 10 Jan 1917: *Entente reply*: Restoration of Belgium, Serbia, Montenegro with indemnities; evacuation of the invaded territories of France, Russia, and Rumania	17 Aug 1916: Concessions to Rumania: the Banat, the Tisza frontier, Transylvania, and the Bukovina to the Prut. Sept 1916: Amended Sykes-Picot Agreement; Armenia Major to be annexed. 25 Dec 1916: Tsargrad (i.e., Constantinople and surroundings), the Straits, a free Poland out of all three of its dispersed parts.

TABLE 8.4 (cont.)

War Aims in November 1916–February 1917

Germany	Great Britain
Longwy; strategic border adjustments (to Germany's advantage) in Alsace-Lorraine; war indemnity. *Luxembourg*: Incorporated in the German Empire. *Colonies*: Restitution of the colonies with exception of Kiautschou and the Caroline and Mariana islands; acquisition of the Congo or parts of it. *General*: Indemnity for Germans living abroad and for German property abroad. 15 Nov 1916: Freedom of the seas? Freedom of navigation on the lower Danube? Renunciation of all obstructive economic agreements and regulations.[a]	with reparations. Restitution of provinces or territories wrested in the past from the Allies by force against the will of the populations; respect nationalities and full security for all nations, great or small; liberation of Italians, Slavs?, Rumanians and Czechoslovaks? from foreign domination. Expulsion of Ottoman Empire from Europe, enfranchisement of its subjects. Independent Polish state. Removal of Prussian militarism. End of 1916: Concessions to Japan in China; further concessions to Italy in Turkey, larger slice of southern Turkey.

Note: Question marks indicate the uncertain status of a war aim.

[a] 23–24 Dec 1916: OHL (1) Border corrections in Alsace-Lorraine: the western slopes of the Vosges and at Metz. (2) Further protection of the coal basin of Briey and Longwy. (3) The coal basin northerly of Longwy on Belgian territory. More territory around Luxembourg. (4) The corner of Givet to Belgium. (5) The Meuse crossing near Liège; a staging area to the west of the Meuse. A maritime base on the Flemish coast? (6) Further military protection against Poland? (7) More territory from Russia for a good staging area and agriculture. The border between Poland and Russia the narrowest possible. (8) The Sereth as the border between Austria and Russia? The Walachei must be made productive for Germany. Czernawoda-Constanza under German administration, Constanza a free port for Bulgaria. Admiralty: At home: the Belgian and Courlandian coast with the Oesel, Moon, and Faröer Islands. Abroad: in addition to an African colonial empire, as new gains: the Azores, Valona, Dakar with Senegambia, Tahiti; maintenance of the previous possessions: New Guinea with the Bismarck Archipelago and Yap. Potentially Portuguese Timor instead. Tsingtau as German trading port.

war aims made a general peace *less* likely. Table 8.3 lists the war aims of the main belligerents at the end of 1915.

At the end of 1915 the bargaining gap between Germany and Russia had only widened. Germany's demands against Russia now included cession of not only Poland but also Courland and Lithuania, while Russia's demands against Germany remained unchanged. The increase in Germany's demands was due to both favorable new information and domestic pressures to secure gains both in the east and the west to forestall an overthrow of the old order. Russia's refusal to lower its aims in 1915 could be the result of sheer incompetence or the refusal of many among the military leadership to revise their estimates. However, the Chief of Staff to the Tsar apparently did lower his estimates of Russia's relative strength, and most leaders surely recognized that the costs of war would be higher than they had estimated a year earlier. Thus, the lack of change in Russia's war aims against Germany seems to largely be the result of a fear of revolution if the war failed to yield sufficient benefits to reward the people.

On the Western Front, France's withdrawal of its demand that Prussian militarism be broken surely reduced the bargaining gap. However, Germany may well have increased its demands against Belgium, while France and Britain continued to insist on Belgium's complete restoration. Germany's high demands in the west remained an expression of the regime's need to reward the people. France and Britain had probably become somewhat more pessimistic about the war, but the reduction in their war aims again came in the form of strategic concessions to their allies. (The main concession once again benefited Russia, who would be allowed to gain control over Constantinople and the Straits. The Allies also offered substantial strategic concessions to Italy.)

As shown in the previous chapters, the new information of 1916 made German leaders more pessimistic and French leaders substantially more optimistic. The overall effect of the new information on British and Russian expectations about the outcome of the war is more difficult to assess. While Russian leaders probably became somewhat more pessimistic, British leaders probably changed their overall expectations very little, if at all. Because *both* Germany and France raised their war aims, at the end of 1916 the bargaining gap had clearly widened. Table 8.4 lists the war aims of the main belligerents at the end of 1916.

During 1916 Germany's war aims against Russia increased as the leadership now demanded a larger Polish border strip, the annexation of Courland and Lithuania, and a favorable trade agreement. Unfortunately, it is difficult to assess whether and if so by how much Russia's war aims changed. Although the Tsar seems to have recognized by November that the military situation was worsening, and that Russia might have to satisfy itself with its prewar borders in the west, he nevertheless insisted in December on "a free Poland out of all three of her presently dispersed parts." Hence, the Russians maintained the demand that Germany (Prussia) give up Posen. If the Tsar was willing to forego his rather extravagant demands for the internal reorganization of the German Empire—and we have no definite evidence of such a revision—the bargaining gap between Russia and Germany most likely shrank; otherwise the bargaining gap probably widened.

The increased bargaining gap in the east must largely be attributed to the semirepressive, moderately exclusionary regimes in both Germany and Russia. As I argued above, Germany raised its war aims even when it became more pessimistic because the leadership needed to bring home war aims that more than covered the costs of the war or face revolution. At the same time, the Russian leadership continued to insist on the two war aims they hoped would satisfy the domestic opposition, a united Poland and Tsargrad (i.e., Constantinople) and the Straits. (The new Russian demand for Armenia also might serve to reward the homecoming soldiers with land grants.)

In the west both Germany and France increased their demands against each other, while British demands against Germany remained basically unchanged; as a result, the bargaining gap between Germany and the western Allies widened. While the increase in German war aims resulted from the regime's attempt to cover the (increased) costs of the war, the increase in French war aims must be explained by a newfound optimism of the French leadership. As we saw in the chapter on France, this newfound optimism was in large part due to the successes of Nivelle's counteroffensive around Verdun in the late fall of 1916 and the leadership's belief in Nivelle's new methods. Hence, *once we take domestic politics into account*, the absence of a bargaining space from 1914 to 1916 is easily explained.

The events of 1917 helped shape much of the subsequent history of this century. Two revolutions shook Russia, and at the end of the year the world was faced with the first self-declared communist regime. On the other side of the world, the United States decided to intervene in a major war to help shape the future of Europe for the first time. This new information dramatically reduced the bargaining gap between Germany and the members of the Entente and even led to peace on the Eastern Front. Table 8.5 summarizes the war aims of the five main belligerents at the end of 1917, including the United States.

Although I lack the space for a detailed analysis, I should note that the United States' war aims of January 1918 were lower than those of

TABLE 8.5
War Aims in December 1917–March 1918

Germany	France	Great Britain	Russia	United States
Oct 1917: "Penetration of Austria-Hungary"; military convention: defensive and offensive alliance and customs union. 18 Dec 1917: Protection of the Belgian coast; Liège and its foreland including Tongeren. "Attachment" of Belgium by economic, military and territorial concessions. Belgium split into a Flemish and Walloon Federation. France: Longwy-Briey, but no more concessions in Alsace-Lorraine. Luxembourg a German federal state. War reparations from Italy; Italian	June 1917: Annexation in the Rhineland ruled out. Fall 1917: Change of sovereignty in the Rhineland ruled out. 20 Sept 1917: Alsace-Lorraine with frontier of 1870; reparation of damages and destruction caused by the enemy. 28 Nov 1917: Demand for Syria withdrawn? 27 Dec 1917: Liberation of our territories; reintegration of Alsace-Lorraine into France; just reparation of damages; League of Nations; fulfillment of France's strict obligation with regard to the oppressed	5 Jan 1918: Restoration of Belgium, Serbia, Montenegro; evacuation of the occupied parts of France, Italy, and Rumania; reparation of damages. "Reconsideration of the great wrong of 1871." Government with consent of the governed. Some independent Poland, not necessarily including German territory. "The Russian territories now in German occupation ... under one name or another ... will henceforth be in reality a part of Prussia." Turkish empire in the homeland of Turkish people	17 Oct 1917: Poland granted independence. 7 Nov 1917: No annexations, no indemnities; the right of self-determination of peoples. 23 Feb 1918: Any terms that left the Soviet government in power.	8 Jan 1918: Fourteen Points: open covenants of peace; freedom of the seas; removal of economic barriers; reduction of national armaments; impartial adjustment of all colonial claims; evacuation of all Russian territory; Belgium must be evacuated and restored; French territory should be evacuated, "wrong done to France by Prussia in 1871 should be righted": readjustment of the frontiers of Italy should be along lines of nationality; the peoples of Austria-Hungary should be accorded autonomous

TABLE 8.5 (cont.)
War Aims in December 1917–March 1918

Germany	France	Great Britain	United States
colonies to be divided among Germany, England, and France. 9 Feb 1918: Treaty with the Ukraine; economic concessions. 3 Mar 1918: Treaty of Brest-Litovsk: Russia gives up sovereignty over the Ukraine, and territories to the west of the line between the Gulf of Riga and Brest-Litovsk, including Lithuania, Courland, and Poland. They are to be under German military, political and economic control. Possibly Livonia and Estonia while under Russian sovereignty, also under	nationalities of Belgium, Serbia, Rumania, and Poland; independent and indivisible Poland. Jan 1918: Alsace-Lorraine of 1870.	with a capital at Constantinople; Straits to be internationalized and neutralized; Arabia, Armenia, Mesopotamia, Syria, and Palestine entitled to recognition of their separate national condition.	development; Rumania, Serbia, and Montenegro should be evacuated; occupied territories restored; Serbia accorded access to the sea; other nationalities now under Turkish rule should get unmolested opportunity of autonomous development; Dardanelles should be permanently opened; an independent Polish state should be formed; League of Nations must be formed.

TABLE 8.5 (cont.)
War Aims in December 1917–March 1918

Germany
German control. Russia recognizes Finnish independence; Persia and Afghanistan free and independent states; cloaked reparations. 5 Mar 1918: Treaty of Buftea: Control over Rumanian oil fields, railroads, and Danube harbors on the Black Sea; Constanza, Central Power condominium over the Dobrudscha. 7 Mar 1918: Three treaties with Finland with economic advantages to Germany. Mar 1918: Poland: No more "Austro-Polish solution," instead Candidate solution, i.e., now a German prince would become king. Military preponderance, economic concessions, and a border strip (smaller than on 16 August?).

Note: Question marks indicate the uncertain status of a war aim.

April 1917.[9] The decrease in American war aims was the result of the unfavorable new information of 1917, in particular, the second Russian revolution and the armistice on the Eastern Front, and the difficulties and delays in training, outfitting, and shipping American forces to Europe. As a result of these events and nonevents, American leaders estimated at the end of 1917 that the Allied forces were in for a tough time in the spring of 1918, when Germany would launch a massive offensive on the Western Front. If the forces of the Entente and the United States survived this coming offensive, there could be no doubt of their final victory thanks to their overwhelming material and manpower superiority.[10]

[9] America's war aims in early 1917 were the following: 22 January 1917: Equality of nations, equality of rights; government with consent of the governed; a united independent and autonomous Poland; access to the seas; freedom of the seas; moderation of armaments (Shaw, pp. 348–56). 2 April 1917: "Exactly the same things . . . when I [Wilson] addressed the Senate on the 22nd of January." The rights and liberties of small nations; the privilege of men everywhere to choose their way of life and obedience. "The world must be made safe for democracy. . . . We have no selfish ends to serve. We desire no conquest, no dominion. We seek no indemnities for ourselves, no material compensation for the sacrifices we shall freely make. . . . We shall fight for the things which we have always carried nearest our hearts—for democracy, for the right of those who submit to authority to have a voice in their own governments, for the rights and liberties of small nations, for a universal dominion of right by such a concert of free peoples as shall bring peace and safety to all nations" (http://www.lib.byu.edu/~rdh/wwi/1917/wilswarm.html).

While American war aims did not change in most aspects, in one crucial aspect Wilson did modify American demands. In April 1917 the President explicitly declared that one of America's war aims was "the right of those who submit to authority to have a voice in their own governments." All throughout the year Wilson continued to demand the removal of the "arrogant Prussian military caste." By January 1918, however, the President had substantially revised his demands. Now he declared, "Neither do we presume to suggest to [Germany] any alteration or modification of her institutions." (This modification was already visible in Wilson's Fifth Annual Message to Congress of 4 December 1917; see Shaw, pp. 443–54.) All that is left of the earlier demands for a change in Germany's governmental structure is this: "But it is necessary, we must frankly say, and necessary as a preliminary to any intelligent dealings with her on our part, that we should know whom her spokesmen speak for when they speak to us, whether for the Reichstag majority or for the military party and the men whose creed is imperial domination." Unambiguously, by giving up the demand for institutional reform in the German Empire, America significantly lowered its war aims.

[10] For expectations in early 1917 see Lansing's estimates of early April 1917, in Esposito, p. 99; Chief of Staff Major-General Hugh L. Scott's plan of mid-February to raise an army of four million, in Coffman, "The American Military and Strategic Policy in World War I," p. 72; and Assistant Chief of Staff Major General Tasker Bliss's estimates at the end of March that "the war must last practically two years longer before we can have other than naval and economic participation." By Bliss's calculations it would take a year to train one million men and another to transport them overseas (quoted in Trask, note 13, p. 181). See also Esposito, p. 89; Coffman, pp. 72–73. For expectations at the end

As a result of the new information of the year, the Germans raised their war aims during 1917 while the Entente and the United States lowered their war aims. These changes in war aims dramatically narrowed the bargaining gap between the belligerents. On the Eastern Front the new Soviet regime became willing to settle on any terms that maintained the revolution and their government. Accordingly, Germany and Russia were able to reach an agreement to end the war that left both better off than continuing the war. French and British leaders also dramatically lowered their war aims and seemed willing to settle with Germany at Russia's expense. However, German leaders insisted on high demands in the west and may even have increased their demands against France and England. Overall, nevertheless, the bargaining gap between the western Allies and Germany had also narrowed.

1917: Peace . . . and War

While the absence of a bargaining space in 1914, 1915, and 1916 is easily explained, the creation of a bargaining space on the Eastern Front and the absence of a bargaining space on the Western Front in 1917 deserves a more careful analysis. Three questions deserve particular attention. First, why did the new Soviet government accept a separate peace on extremely harsh terms, which would dramatically alter the balance of power on the continent? Second, why did the German regime choose not to press their military advantage in the east, to most likely secure even better terms? Third, and related, why did the German regime choose to launch one last offensive in the spring of 1918 to try to secure high war aims in the west as well? Why did the regime not offer a peace on the basis of the status quo ante or perhaps even offer some concessions in Alsace-Lorraine to persuade France, and maybe Britain as well, to make peace at Russia's expense? This section endeavors to answer these three main questions in turn.

---

of 1917 see Pershing's memorandum of mid-November in Pershing, vol. 1, pp. 234–38. After a meeting of the Supreme War Council of 2 December, Pershing reiterated these conclusions in his cable to the Secretary of War and the Chief of Staff (ibid., pp. 249–50). See also the memoranda of Bliss, Benson, and House composed on the trip home in mid-December from the Supreme War Council meeting in Paris. Bliss's report is reprinted in *Foreign Relations of the United States, 1917*, Supplement 2, The World War, vol. 1, pp. 386–91. See also Esposito, p. 118. The reports of the American Mission are reprinted in *Foreign Relations of the United States, 1917*, Supplement 2, The World War, vol. 1, 1932, pp. 334–445, pp. 355–57. Excerpts from House's report are reprinted in Seymour, vol. 3, pp. 300–302.

To explain why the new Soviet regime decided to accept Germany's harsh terms in February 1918, I focus on the deliberations of the Bolshevik leadership and will not go into the causes of the Russian revolutions. It must suffice to note that the people's rapidly increasing pessimism about the outcome of the war played a crucial role in both revolutions. To briefly recapitulate the events and new information between March and November, the March revolution, which spelled the end of the Romanov regime, ironically brought to power the one domestic group who wanted to continue the war: the liberal constitutionalists.[11] But their tenure produced only ever-increasing evidence of the desperate state of the country and more and more open declarations from all sides that urged peace. Nonetheless, the provisional government under Kerensky attempted another offensive in the first weeks of July, with disastrous results. After scoring some minor gains, the offensive petered out on 17 July, and the German counterattack two days later rang the death knell for the Russian army. Troops mutinied in many units and murdered their officers. As the army dissolved, the Germans advanced and at the end of July captured Tarnopol; in the first week of September Riga fell. The failure of the Kerensky (or second Brusilov or L'vov) offensive led to the first Bolshevik coup attempt on 17 July, which misfired largely because of poor organization. The fall of Riga produced a second coup attempt, this time by General Kornilov. To quell it, Kerensky put arms in the hands of the populace. As Wheeler-Bennett notes, this probably made another and more successful Bolshevik coup attempt only a matter of time.[12]

The day after the Bolsheviks launched their second and successful attempt on 7 November and after a sleepless night, Lenin addressed the Congress of Soviets and immediately zeroed in on the need for peace. "The first thing," he announced, "is the adoption of practical measures to realize peace. . . . We shall offer peace to the peoples of all the belligerent countries upon the basis of the Soviet terms—no annexations, no indemnities, and the right of self-determination of peoples. At the same time, according to our promise, we shall publish and repudiate the secret treaties."[13] He then read the Declaration of Peace, which called for "a just and democratic peace . . . a peace which the Russian workers and peasants have so loudly and insistently demanded since the overthrow of the Tsar's monarchy." The last paragraph contained

---

[11] Wheeler-Bennett, p. 23. Most of this section is based on Wheeler-Bennett's excellent history.

[12] Ibid., p. 56.

[13] Quoted in ibid., p. 68.

the prophetic warning, ironic if we consider Trotsky's future strategy of "No War—No Peace," that "*[w]ars cannot be ended by a refusal [to fight]; they cannot be ended by one side alone.*" The declaration concluded with a proposal for "an armistice for three months—though we are not rejecting a shorter period."[14]

The delegates accepted Lenin's Declaration of Peace, but it would take another two weeks—until 26 November—before the new government was firmly enough established for Trotsky to formally apply to the German High Command for an immediate armistice. Two days later the Soviet Commissar for War and new Commander-in-Chief (former Ensign) Krylenko ordered "firing to cease immediately and fraternization to begin on all fronts."[15] While Trotsky kept the Allied diplomats informed of the Russian peace move, his announcement that an agreement for a preliminary truce was pending met only with a deafening silence. On 15 December, then, Russia signed an armistice with the Central Powers. It was originally to last until 14 January but would be automatically prolonged unless seven days' notice was given. The conference to negotiate the terms of settlement opened on 22 December. Although the western Allies had been invited to participate in negotiations about a general peace at Brest-Litovsk, their refusal meant that the new Russian regime had no choice but to try to negotiate a separate peace with the Germans, Austro-Hungarians, Bulgarians, and Turks.

On the Russian side the crucial fight over peace terms and Russian war aims at Brest-Litovsk was fought back in Russia between Lenin and Trotsky on the one hand and Bukharin on the other; it was, in essence, a struggle for control over the Revolution. The fundamental disagreement between Lenin and Trotsky and Bukharin stemmed from their conflicting estimates of the consequences of resumed hostilities. While the first two had their differences, they were united in the opinion that the war had to be ended and that what was left of the Russian army was in no position to put up any effective resistance whatsoever to the Central Powers' armies. Trotsky, however, was prepared to gamble that the Germans would not be able to retake the offensive because of their troubled domestic situation if the Russians declared, "We shall stop the war, but we shall not sign the peace treaty." He hoped that a renewed German offensive would provoke a revolution in Germany. If the Germans—in spite of his hopes, so argued Trotsky—did take the offensive again, they would stand revealed as naked aggressors to the

---

[14] The Declaration of Peace of 8 November 1917 is reprinted in ibid., appendix 1, pp. 375–78, emphasis added.

[15] Quoted in ibid., p. 75.

world and to the German homefront, and no blame would befall the Soviet government. Lenin had come to a much grimmer estimate of the situation: Russia could no longer fight and had to make peace. There were no signs of other revolutions in the offing. For Lenin, Trotsky's plan entailed a great risk, one he was loath to take with the fledgling Revolution. In sharp contrast to these two, Bukharin urged a resumption of the war in the form of a revolutionary war, a revolutionary crusade.[16]

At the height of this debate, in the third week of January 1918, Lenin summoned Trotsky and Bukharin for a meeting. On 21 January the three battled it out among a group of party leaders. Exasperated by his opponents' poor grasp of the desperate situation, Lenin expounded his Twenty-one Theses. His central claim was that a separate peace with Germany was absolutely essential for the survival of the Russian Revolution. Against Trotsky's proposal, Lenin argued: "If the Germans advance we will have to conclude peace in any case, but the terms will be worse if we do not sign now." Aware that his main opposition lay among those who wanted to continue the war and turn it into a revolutionary war, Lenin predicted the dire consequences of such a course of action. In the seventeenth of his Twenty-one Theses, he argued:

> The question of revolutionary war, therefore, stands as follows: If a revolution should break out in Germany during the next three or four months, then perhaps the tactics of an immediate revolutionary war would not ruin our Socialist Revolution. If [on the other hand] the German revolution does not take place and we go on with the war, Russia would be so badly defeated that she would be forced to sign an even worse peace; such a peace would be signed not by a Socialist government but by some other, by some kind of coalition between the bourgeois *Rada* and the followers of Chernov or some similar government, for after the first shock of defeat the peasant army, which is so badly worn out by the war, would overthrow the Workers' Socialist Government in a few weeks.[17]

His arguments were to no avail. The majority of the sixty-three party leaders present agreed with Bukharin. Unwilling to accept defeat at home, which he believed would spell the demise of the revolution, and a master tactician, Lenin proposed a temporary alliance with Trotsky. He was now willing to give Trotsky's policy of "No War—No Peace"— a trial. "But in that case you won't support the slogan of revolutionary war, will you?" Lenin asked. "Under no circumstances," Trotsky re-

---

[16] Ibid., pp. 185–93.

[17] Lenin's Twenty-one Theses are reprinted in ibid., appendix 3, pp. 385–91. Lenin's retort to Trotsky is in ibid., p. 191.

plied. "Then the experiment will probably not be so dangerous. We will only risk losing Estonia or Livonia, and for the sake of a good peace with Trotsky Livonia and Estonia are worth losing."[18]

On 10 February Trotsky produced his dove from his sleeve, to the astonishment of the assorted delegates and Major-General Max Hoffmann, virtual commander of the Eastern Front and head of the Central Powers' delegation at Brest-Litovsk in particular. "In the name of the Council of People's Commissars, the Government of the Russian Federal Republic informs the Governments and peoples united in war against us, the Allied and neutral countries, that, in refusing to sign a peace of annexation, Russia declares, on its side, the state of war with Germany, Austria-Hungary, Turkey, and Bulgaria as ended." *Unerhört!* (Unheard of!), declared General Hoffmann.[19]

Eight days later Lenin's predictions came true. Hoffman denounced the armistice and retook the offensive. With the Russian army putting up little resistance, Hoffmann's troops advanced at near record speeds. When Lenin heard of the resumption of hostilities, he only hoped that Russia would not have to pay too dear a price for Trotsky's gamble. "There is nothing left for us now but to sign the old terms at once if the Germans will still agree to them."[20] Lenin and Trotsky immediately telegraphed their acceptance of the old terms to German Headquarters, but the Germans did not reply. The Russians' formal acceptance reached Berlin on 21 February. There was still no reply. It was not until the 23rd that the Germans reply arrived—a reply that consisted of new and harsher terms, this time presented as an ultimatum. Its main clauses read:

(2) The Territories which lie west of the line communicated to the Russian representatives at Brest-Litovsk, and which belonged to the Russian Empire, will no longer be under the territorial sovereignty of Russia.[21] In the vicinity of Dünaburg (Dvinsk) the line is to be shifted to the eastern frontier of Courland. . . . Russia renounces all interference in the internal affairs of these territories. Germany and Austria-Hungary intend to determine the future lot of the territories in agreement with their populations. Germany is ready, as soon as a general peace has been concluded and Russian demobilization has been completely carried out, to evacuate the terri-

---

[18] Quoted in ibid., pp. 192–93. See also Stevenson, *The First World War*, pp. 202–3.

[19] Wheeler-Bennett, p. 227. After a night of research, a German delegate managed to find one precedent, several thousand years old, from a war between the Greeks and the Scythians (p. 228).

[20] Ibid., p. 239.

[21] The Provisional Government had already unconditionally granted independence to Poland on 17 October. See Smith Jr., *Russian Struggle for Power*, p. 484.

tory situated east of the line mentioned above, in so far as nothing else results from Article 3. (3) Livonia and Estonia will without delay be evacuated by Russian troops and Red Guards and occupied by a German policing force until the country's institutions guarantee security and political order is restored. . . . (4) Russia shall immediately conclude peace with the Ukrainian People's Republic. Russian troops and Red Guards shall be withdrawn without delay from the Ukraine and Finland. (5) Russia shall do everything in her power to guarantee a speedy and orderly return of the East Anatolian provinces to Turkey. Russia shall recognize the abolition of the Turkish capitulations. [Article 6 required the complete demobilization of the Russian army. Article 7 dealt with economic and trade regulations; Article 8 with indemnification of civil damages and for the maintenance of prisoners of war. Article 9 obliged Russia to cease all agitation and propaganda.] (10) The foregoing conditions are to be accepted within forty-eight hours. The Russian plenipotentiaries must immediately proceed to Brest-Litovsk and there within three days sign the Peace Treaty, which must be ratified within a further two weeks.[22]

When these terms were read to the Central Committee that morning of 23 February, Lenin put the issue starkly in perspective: "It is time to put an end to revolutionary phrases, and get down to work. If this is not done I resign from the Government. To carry on a revolutionary war, an army, which we do not have, is necessary. It is a question of signing the terms now or of signing the death sentence of the Soviet Government three weeks later."[23] After much discussion a vote was taken. Trotsky's abstention, together with three further abstentions, allowed Lenin to carry the day by a vote of seven to four. Next Lenin had to convince the Petrograd Soviet. Lenin reiterated his arguments: There was no army, and further futile resistance and delay would only result in worse terms. He added, "You must sign this shameful peace in order to save the world Revolution, in order to hold fast to its most important, and at present, its only foothold—the Soviet Republic." In his report on the current military situation, Commissar for War Krylenko supported Lenin's arguments. "We have no army," he was forced to tell the delegates. "Our demoralized soldiers fly panic-stricken before the German bayonets, leaving behind them artillery, transport, and ammunition. The divisions of the Red Guard are swept away like flies. Only the immediate signing of peace can save us from ruin." A sailor from Kronstadt reinforced the delegates' view of Russia's precarious position. Upon cries of "Where is our fleet?" he answered, "We

<hr />

[22] These terms are reprinted in Wheeler-Bennett, pp. 255–57.
[23] Quoted in ibid., p. 257.

haven't a fleet anymore, it's a wreck. The sailors have left, and the ships are there for the enemy to take."[24] One last hurdle had to be cleared, the Central Executive of the Congress. Once again Lenin repeated his arguments and came out victorious. Lenin signaled the Soviet government's acceptance of the draconian terms when he came out of this last meeting, in the early hours of 24 February. Now the terms would have to be sold to the people at large. To that end, *Pravda* published Lenin's Twenty-one Theses later that day.

The Treaty of Brest-Litovsk of 3 March 1918 closely mirrored the terms as presented on 23 February.[25] Article IV contained a new Turkish demand:

> The districts of Erdehan, Kars, and Batum will likewise and without delay be cleared of the Russian troops. Russia will not interfere in the reorganization of the national and international relations of these districts, but leave it to the population of these districts, to carry out this reorganization in agreement with the neighboring States, especially with Turkey.

These concessions gave Turkey back its frontiers before the war of 1877–78.

The treaty further stipulated that Russia was to carry out full demobilization without delay, pull its warships into Russian ports, recognize the independence of Persia and Afghanistan, and accept a special economic agreement with the Central Powers. Article IX formally renounced compensations for war expenses and war losses, but in reality Russia was forced to make substantial reparations, under the guise of a reimbursement for the maintenance of prisoners of war, which would eventually amount to 6 billion marks. All in all, Russia lost about one million square kilometers of territory, 34 percent of its population, 32 percent of its agricultural land, 85 percent of its beet-sugar land, 54 percent of its industrial undertakings, one-third of its railways, 73 percent of its iron-ore output, and 89 percent of its coal mines.[26]

On 16 March the twelve hundred delegates to the Congress of Soviets ratified the Treaty of Brest-Litovsk by 784 to 261 votes. Two speeches carried the day. As Wheeler-Bennett records, the first was by "a burly red-headed peasant who followed a long list of opposition speakers. 'Comrades,' he cried in his harsh, uneducated voice, we fought four years; we're exhausted. We have no army. We have no sup-

---

[24] Both quotes in ibid., pp. 258–59.

[25] Ibid., Appendix 5, pp. 404–8.

[26] Ibid., p. 269; French, *The Strategy of the Lloyd George Coalition*, p. 173; Stevenson, *The First World War*, p. 200.

plies. The Germans have an army. It is only a few miles away from Moscow and Petrograd. It is ready to advance. We are helpless. Do you want war or do you want peace?" The second decisive speech was, not surprisingly, by Lenin. To make Russia great again, he argued, time and peace were necessary. He then repeated the peasant's earlier arguments: "Revolutionary phrases will not do. . . . We have no army; we could not keep the army at the front. We need peace to gain a breathing-space to give the masses a chance to create new forces of life."[27]

It is clear that the Soviets' minimum demands centered on the survival of the regime and the Revolution. With their estimate of the effectiveness of the Russian army, it is small wonder that Lenin and the majority of Russian decision makers came to the conclusion that they had no chance on the battlefield. Given these estimates of Russia's chances against the armies of the Central Powers, a continuation of the war would only *increase* the chance that the regime would fall. Under these circumstances any peace that left the Soviet regime intact was acceptable.

Two mechanisms may explain why the commitment problem and the fear of a future war with Germany under worse conditions did not prevent the leadership from accepting the extreme terms of settlement. First, the regime may have had a relatively low estimate of Germany's chances of winning the war on the Western Front. If the Soviets estimated that France, Britain, and the United States would defeat Germany in the near future, they may have anticipated that Brest-Litovsk would not be allowed to stand. In that case it might make sense to shift the costs of war onto Russia's former allies in the west and consolidate Bolshevism at home. This explanation seems unlikely, since the Bolsheviks worried that Britain and France would not be able to defeat the German army and would make a "peace at the Western Front . . . on the bones of the Russian Revolution."[28] Specifically, they feared the western Allies might offer or accept peace on the basis of the status quo ante in the west and give the Germans a free hand in the east.

Lenin used a distinct but related logic to explain the acceptance of the harsh terms to the political homefront. Drawing a comparison with the Tilsit peace imposed by Napoleon on the defeated Prussians, Lenin argued that this time not the remaining great "imperialistic" powers but "the international Socialist proletariat" would come to the Bolsheviks' rescue and free them from the yoke of Brest-Litovsk. As he put it on 14 March in his speech on the ratification of the peace treaty,

---

[27] Quoted in Wheeler-Bennett, pp. 302–4.
[28] The quote is from Trotsky, quoted in ibid., p. 251; see also p. 144.

Our cause is gaining strength, whilst the forces of the imperialists are becoming weaker, and whatever trials and defeats we may suffer from our "Tilsit" peace, we are starting the tactics of retreat, and I repeat once again: there is no doubt whatever that both the conscious proletariat and the conscious peasants are on our side, and we shall prove ourselves capable not only of heroic attack, but also of heroic retreat. We shall know how to wait till the Socialist proletariat comes to our aid and we shall then start a second Socialist revolution on a world scale.[29]

Lenin's belief in a future reversal of fortune undoubtedly goes a long way to explain why he accepted a peace that on the face of it would drastically alter the balance of power in Germany's favor.

Another mechanism, however, may also have played a role. While a principal-agent problem earlier prevented the Russian regime from terminating the war, perhaps now a principal-agent problem made peace possible. As we saw above, the Bolshevik leadership estimated that the continuation of revolutionary war would only guarantee their removal from power and the defeat of the Revolution. To stay in power the Bolsheviks were willing to take the risky course of settlement now, in the hope that future developments would either lead to Germany's defeat or prevent the German regime from exploiting its new advantages. Whereas a unitary rational actor would continue the war to maximize the probability of long-term survival of the state, the Bolsheviks maximized the probability of staying in power. From this perspective, a principal-agent problem made peace possible where it otherwise would not have been. Because the leadership knew that continuation of the war (resulting in a worse loss in the war) would only increase their chances of punishment, they preferred settlement now even on terms that triggered the commitment problem. Lenin's argument that the government had to choose between terminating the war on Germany's harsh terms now or "signing the death sentence of the Soviet Government three weeks later" fits well with this argument. So does his insistence on the need for a breathing space to protect and consolidate the Russian Revolution, after which, perhaps, the struggle could be renewed or the international Socialist proletariat would come to Russia's aid. Of course, as I argue in the next section, the problem was degenerate, because the Germans were basically in a position to take whatever they wanted.

As I argued in chapter 2, an explanation of the Bolsheviks' willingness to lower their demands constitutes only half of the explanation for why the war ended in the east in 1917. For a full explanation, we

---

[29] Speech by Lenin on the Ratification of the Peace Treaty, 14 March 1918, quoted in ibid., Appendix 6, pp. 409–26; quotation on p. 426.

also need to explain why Germany's leaders did not ask even higher demands, such as the removal of the Bolshevik regime. The main reason why the Germans did not further increase their demands or push their military advantage, I argue, is that they were withdrawing large numbers of troops from the Eastern Front to use in the upcoming spring offensives in France.

Germany's leaders certainly recognized the precarious position of the new Russian regime. General Hoffman fully realized that "the only chance the Bolsheviks had of remaining in power, was by signing a peace. They were obliged to accept the conditions of the Central Powers, however hard they might be. . . . The only one of us who doubted this was Count Czernin."[30] After the Germans renewed their offensive on 18 February and rapidly advanced eastward, Hoffmann noted in his diary, "Whether Trotsky will take the road to Canossa in person, or will send someone else, is not yet certain, but this time the Comrades must simply swallow what we put before them."[31]

However, the German leadership had decided already in early November, before the Russian armistice request, to launch one last major offensive in the west with troops withdrawn from the east. Exactly one year before the armistice, on 11 November 1917, in a conference with the army commanders and the Chiefs of their General Staffs at Mons, Ludendorff started to develop his plans for an offensive to win the war in the west.[32] At the end of this conference Ludendorff summarized its conclusions as follows:

> The situation in Russia and Italy will, as far as can be seen, make it possible to deliver a blow on the Western Front in the New Year. The strength of the two sides will be approximately equal. About thirty-five divisions and one thousand heavy guns can be made available for *one* offensive; a second great simultaneous offensive, say as a diversion, will not be possible. Our general situation requires that we should strike at the earliest moment, if possible at the end of February or beginning of March, before the Americans can throw strong forces into the scale. We must beat the British. The operations must be based on these three conditions.[33]

Ludendorff's early plans for an offensive on the Western Front were subsequently boosted by the armistice on the Eastern Front because it would enable the Germans to shift additional manpower to the Western Front. After Hoffman received Trotsky's formal proposals for an

---

[30] Quoted in ibid., pp. 126–27.
[31] Quoted in ibid., p. 246.
[32] Asprey, p. 349.
[33] Quoted in Pitt, p. 60.

armistice in the afternoon of 26 November, Ludendorff asked him whether it was possible to negotiate with the Bolsheviks. Hoffmann replied. "Yes, it is possible. Your Excellency needs troops and this is the easiest way to get them."[34] The prospect of moving troops to the Western Front led Ludendorff to write to his friend von Wyneken the day after the armistice, on 16 December:

> I have to thank you for your last elaborate letter of 26 November. Since then our strategic situation has improved further [i.e., the Russian armistice]. Now the High Command has been relieved of the pressure on the Western Front. I believe we have won the war for Germany. But we should not deceive ourselves. An enormous task still remains. First I have to set up the Western Front again, build there a balance of forces and then— strike.[35]

As Ludendorff told the negotiators for the Central Powers at Brest-Litovsk in early February 1918, further delay was unacceptable because troops *had* to be transferred to the west.[36] Thus, peace in the east would allow Ludendorff to "build a balance of forces" on the Western Front, which would enable him one last major offensive, one last "gambler's throw."

Weakening the Eastern Front had two implications. First, it would make it more difficult to exploit Germany's military advantage. (Although at the end of March 1918, while the spring offensive in the west was in full swing, troops of the Central Powers were still advancing in the Ukraine.[37] The Germans' advance led to increased war aims against Russia and the Ukraine in August, including the surrender of Russian sovereignty over Estonia and Livonia.) Second, weakening the front would make it harder to enforce the terms of settlement. Germany's "moderation" in its demands at Brest-Litovsk, although the word is hardly applicable here, is therefore explained by the need to shift troops to the west.

But why launch an offensive in the west at all? Why did Germany not offer a peace based on the status quo ante in the west, or if necessary offer some concessions in Alsace-Lorraine, and end the war on all fronts? As Wheeler-Bennett notes, the German leadership recognized at the end of 1917 that Germany had to choose between "concluding

---

[34] Quoted in Wheeler-Bennett, p. 79.

[35] Letter of Ludendorff of 16 December 1917, quoted in Knesebeck, p. 163.

[36] Wheeler-Bennett, p. 214.

[37] McEntee calculates that the Germans left fifty-three divisions and thirteen brigades in the east and southeast; as a result 40,095 officers and 1,004,950 men were left in the east (*Military History of the World War*, p. 463).

a peace of conciliation or . . . an attack in the West."[38] While some leaders such as Foreign Minister von Kühlmann and Prince Max von Baden favored the peace policy, Ludendorff, according to Wheeler-Bennett, "had become convinced . . . that the sole hope of Germany's victory lay in 'a gambler's throw,' a blow in the West, swift and terrible."[39] Ludendorff recalls in his memoirs:

In the late autumn, 1917, G.H.Q. was confronted by the decisive question: Should it utilize the favourable conditions of the spring to strike a great blow in the West, or should it deliberately restrict itself to the defensive and only make subsidiary attacks, say in Macedonia or Italy? The Quadruple Alliance was only held together by the hope of a victory by the Germans. The Austro-Hungarian Army was worn out; it had lost 1,800,000 prisoners; it was short of recruits. Its fighting value was slight, though against Italy it had on the whole sufficed. If Russia actually dropped out we might hope that that Army would continue to be equal to its task. . . . In Germany the national spirit appeared to be better than with our allies; nevertheless, it had sunk very low, and feeling had become worse. . . . The Army had come victoriously through 1917; but it had become apparent that the holding of the Western Front purely by a defensive could no longer be counted on, in view of the enormous quantity of material of all kinds which the Entente had now at their disposal. . . . The enormous material resources of the enemy had given his attack a considerable preponderance over our defence, and this condition would become more and more apparent as our best men became casualties, our infantry approximated more nearly in character to a militia, and discipline declined. . . . The condition of our allies and of our Army all called for an offensive that would bring about an early decision. This was only possible on the Western Front. . . . Delay could only serve the enemy's purposes, since he was expecting certain reinforcement. That the attack in the West would be one of the most difficult operations in history I was perfectly sure, and I did not hide the fact. . . . The American danger rendered it desirable to strike in the West as early as possible; the state of training of the Army for attack enabled us to contemplate doing so about the middle of March. . . . If all went smoothly at Brest-Litovsk, if our people there worked with real energy, we could expect to have our forces ready for a successful attack in the West by the time mentioned.[40]

Three potential explanations for the decision in favor of an offensive in the west suggest themselves. A first explanation could be that Germany's leaders were very optimistic about their chances of victory on

[38] Wheeler-Bennett, p. 82.
[39] Ibid.
[40] Ludendorff, *My War Memories*, vol. 2, pp. 539–44.

the Western Front with their newly reinforced army. Such optimism might then rationally underpin high war aims in the west, in which case the upcoming offensive would be intended to convince the western Allies to change their estimates of the outcome of the war and, as a result, their war aims. A second explanation might argue that the gains of the Treaties of Brest-Litovsk and Bucharest would suffice to buy off the people at home but that Germany's leaders estimated that the western Allies would never accept the terms of Brest-Litovsk because they would make Germany too powerful, indeed the hegemon, on the continent. If this was their intent, it is difficult to see how the planned offensive, short of inflicting total defeat on the French and British, would serve to change French, British, and American estimates sufficiently to make them accept the eastern treaties, especially given the anticipated influx of American manpower. The third explanation argues that the gains of Brest-Litovsk and Bucharest would not suffice to buy off the people and keep the semirepressive, moderately exclusionary regime intact. I propose that Germany needed gains in both the east—to satisfy the Junkers—and the west—to satisfy the industrialists—to maintain the balance of power among the regime's ingroups. In this scenario the spring offensive is another high-variance strategy, the only available option to gain the required western aims.

On the first potential explanation, the leadership had indeed become more optimistic about the planned offensive's chances for success, but it was also very much aware of the impending arrival of large numbers of American troops. The peace on the Eastern Front enabled the Germans to shift troops from the east to the west; between November and the end of February the High Command managed to shift some thirty divisions, which gave them 180 divisions on the Western Front.[41] This gave the Central Powers only a small superiority on the Western Front of probably somewhere between ten and thirty divisions.[42] Nevertheless, the representative of the foreign ministry at OHL reported in mid-December: "The generals are talking now very big and full of the idea of smashing the enemy."[43] Although all generals were optimistic of an

---

[41] However, a half million troops were employed in the Ukraine to protect the Hetman in the hope of getting much needed grain and raw materials. Necessitated at least in part by the harsh terms of Brest-Litovsk, about one million German soldiers remained in the eastern theater until October. See McEntee, *Military History of the World War*, p. 463; Wheeler-Bennett, pp. 311–12, 318; Asprey, p. 361. These troops were needed to protect the salient created by Germany's annexations and "border corrections," to protect oil supplies, to put down a Bolshevik rebellion in Finland, and to keep the peace in Rumania.

[42] Liddell Hart, p. 366.

[43] Quoted in Asprey, p. 363.

enormous *initial* success, many, including Ludendorff, were cautious, and a few were even downright pessimistic about Germany's overall prospects.[44] Notwithstanding his boast to von Wyneken, Ludendorff appreciated the difficulties and dangers that awaited his plans and forces. This was the German army's last bolt; Germany could not afford to shoot and miss. In his memoirs Ludendorff recalls:

> The crown of success would be an operation in which we could bring to bear the whole of our superiority. It was our great object. If we did not succeed at the first attack, we should have to do so at the next; by then, indeed, the situation would have become less favorable—how much less favorable would depend upon the rate of arrival and value of the Americans, and the losses which both sides sustained. Everything was based on the assumption that we should do well in this respect and although, of course, I expected our own Army to be weakened, I hoped it would be less so than that of the enemy. By continuing to attack we should still retain the initiative. More I could not aim at.[45]

More specifically, Ludendorff's strategic goal was to "separate the bulk of the English army from the French and crowd it up with its back to the sea."[46] When asked about the operational goal of his offensive by the commander of the northern army group, Crown Prince Rupprecht of Bavaria, Ludendorff retorted: "We make a hole and the rest will take care of itself." What, however, if his troops failed to punch a hole

[44] Ibid., p. 364. Crown Prince Rupprecht of Bavaria, commander of the northern army group, was one of those who warned the Kaiser that while the situation looked favorable, "we still suffered two evils which are beyond remedy, the gradually increasing shortage of troop replacements and horses which would only become worse. We are indeed in a position to strike a few powerful blows at the enemy in the west but scarcely to bring on a decisive defeat, thus it is to be expected that the battle within a few months will once again become a tedious war of position. Who will finally win depends above all on who is able to make do the longest with his effective manpower, and in this respect I am convinced that the enemy is better off, thanks to the Americans, who of course can become effective only gradually" (quoted in ibid.).

[45] Ludendorff, *My War Memories*, vol. 2, pp. 587–88. Hindenburg apparently acknowledged before the beginning of the great offensives to his inner circle that he could not guarantee the spring offensive would bring about a definitive victory over the western Allies in France (Fischer, *Griff nach der Weltmacht*, pp. 822–23).

[46] Ludendorff, *My War Memories*, p. 590. Major George Wetzell, OHL Chief of Operations, had written a memorandum on 12 December 1917 entitled "The offensives in the West and their prospects of success." In it he declared that "the whole offensive action must not consist of a single great attack in one sector. . . . The whole action must rather be composed of several attacks, having the strongest reciprocal effect, in various sectors, with the object of shaking the whole English front" (quoted in Asprey, p. 365). Asprey and Scherer and Grunewald, vol. 2, no. 58, p. 83, give Wetzell the rank of Major; Pitt, however, ranks him as a Lieutenant-Colonel (p. 59).

through the line? Ludendorff's reply when asked this question by Prince Max of Baden in mid-February speaks volumes: "In that case Germany must go under."[47]

A comparison of German leaders' expectations at the end of 1916 and in early 1918 and the new information of 1917 shows that the leadership had increased its estimates of the probability of victory. However, the evidence suggests the German leadership was by no means convinced that France and Britain could be decisively defeated before the United States' manpower would turn the tide. The main source of their optimism was Russia's collapse and the better chance it seemed to offer to win the war *on land* in the spring and summer of 1918. Russia's collapse therefore more than compensated for the failure of the submarine campaign and the realization that the war could not be won at sea. However, if the war would not be won in 1918, Germany's leaders realized, the arrival of American troops would decisively tilt the balance against them. Thus, the question remains: Why was the leadership willing to take the gamble, why not settle now rather than stake *everything* on this last offensive?

It is possible, but unlikely, that the German leadership estimated they would have to defeat the Allies in the west to keep the gains made at Brest-Litovsk and Bucharest, which were necessary to buy off the people at home. Although I found no evidence to support this second explanation, it is true, of course, that the British, and perhaps also the Americans and the French, concluded they could not let the harsh terms of Brest-Litovsk stand. The third and most plausible explanation is that Ludendorff's Stormtrooper offensive amounted to another high-variance strategy.[48] Such a high-variance strategy was necessary because the regime's competing in-groups, the agriculturists and the in-

---

[47] Both cites are quoted in Asprey, p. 367. Final decisions for the offensive were laid down on 21 January. A first offensive, code-named St. Michael, would be launched in late March between Lens and La Fère. Then, in early April it would be followed by a second scheme more northward at the Ypres salient, code-named St. George. For excellent review of these plans and the ensuing battles, indeed, the whole last year of the war, see Pitt and Travers.

[48] Fritz Fischer compares the decision to launch unrestricted submarine warfare with the decision for the spring offensives in a similar vein (*Griff nach der Weltmacht*, p. 826). It was foreseen by the Allies that Germany would attempt such a high-variance strategy. Haig, for one, told the British War Cabinet as much on 8 January 1918: "In my opinion the crucial period for the Allies is the next few months. During this period the Central Powers may make a determined effort to force a decision on the Western front, i.e., on the Italian, French, or British front. I regard such an effort on the part of the enemy in the light of a gamble with the determination to risk everything in order to secure an early and favorable decision." Quoted in McEntee, pp. 463–64. This judgment is also shared by Wheeler-Bennett, p. 82.

dustrialists, worried how the terms of settlement would affect the post-war domestic political balance of power. The demands in the east would mainly benefit the agriculturists, that is, the Prussian Junkers, which would of course strengthen their domestic position against the other main in-group, the manufacturers and industrialists whose interests were mainly focused in the west. To maintain the domestic balance of power, therefore, large gains in the east would have to be offset by substantial gains in the west. The only way to achieve the requisite gains in the west was to convince the western Allies to accept worse terms of settlement—hence the need for a large and successful offensive in the west.

Allied leaders recognized the possibility and dangers of a German offer to make peace on terms close to the status quo ante in the west in return for a free hand in the east. General Pershing, for example, cabled the American Secretary of War on 15 September:

> There is considerable talk of possibilities of peace this winter and discussion is heard among people of all classes, including those high in military rank. Failure to stop German armies and revolt among Russian troops have had depressing effect upon Allies. Present French Cabinet believed to be strongly in favor of continuation of war, but French people in state of mind to accept any favorable proposition. Believe that withdrawal of Germans from Belgium with concessions as to Alsace and Lorraine and return to antebellum status in Balkans would be hard for French to resist, especially with the prospect of giving Germany satisfaction from Russia.[49]

Painlevé apparently told Lloyd George on 25 September 1917 that he doubted "whether France would continue fighting if it were offered both nine-tenths of Alsace Lorraine and the whole of Belgium."[50] General Smuts, an influential member of the inner circle of Lloyd George's War Cabinet, similarly told C. P. Scott in November 1917 that after a separate Russian peace a German proposal to restore Belgium, to give up the colonies, and to reach a compromise on Alsace-Lorraine on the condition that the Allies would accept the Russo-German treaty "would be difficult to resist."[51]

---

[49] Pershing, vol. 1, p. 173.

[50] Quoted in Stevenson, *French War Aims against Germany 1914–1919*, p. 90. Stevenson footnotes Lloyd George, *War Memoirs*, vol. 4, pp. 2100–2101.

[51] Rothwell, p. 194; Smuts quotation in ibid. Lloyd George was apparently well aware of the danger: "Suppose Germany saying: 'You are weary of war; so are we. We are prepared to surrender Alsace and Lorraine. We will evacuate Belgium. We'll cry quits, without indemnities on either side.' Such a proposition—though improbable—was not impossible, and it is conceivable that our Allies might have been willing to accept some such terms, forcing us to an inconclusive peace unless we could carry on alone" (Reiners,

For a while the German leadership seems to have considered the option. In the Crown Council on 11 September 1917, Wilhelm II authorized Foreign Minister von Kühlmann to make peace *before Christmas* on terms that dropped the demand for coastal naval bases in Belgium and offered minimal concessions to the French in Alsace-Lorraine in return for a free hand in the east. However, these terms still insisted on the return of Germany's colonies, Liège, and military guarantees in inland Belgium.[52] Note, thus, that although these concessions substantially narrowed the bargaining gap, the insistence on gains in the west still precluded peace. In the Crown Council at the end of December 1917, even these concessions were withdrawn under pressure from Hindenburg and Ludendorff.[53]

Von Kühlman's attempt to sacrifice some of Germany's demands in the west to get an early peace was probably doomed from the start because demands for high war aims in both the east and the west surfaced very early in the war. As we saw in the chapter on Germany, the Petition of the Intellectuals of April 1915 warned of "the worst discontent from the lower and middle classes ... [and] much bitterness among leading circles" if Germany did not secure "strong extensions of the frontier in east and west." The Petition of the Six Economic Organizations in the spring of 1915 similarly insisted that "the great addition to our manufacturing resources which we anticipate in the west must be counterbalanced by an equivalent annexation of agricultural territory in the east," specifically "annexation of at least parts of the Baltic Provinces and of those territories which lie to the south of them."[54] Much along these lines, the historian Hans Gatzke argues that the need for gains in both the east and the west was necessary to maintain the domestic balance of power between the

---

p. 251). See also Robertson's similar earlier warning of 14 December 1916, in French, *The Strategy of the Lloyd George Coalition*, p. 34.

[52] Stevenson, *The First World War*, pp. 165–69.

[53] Scherer and Grunewald, Kühlmann note of 20 July 1919, vol. 2, p. 549; vol. 3, no. 99, pp. 138–40, no. 225, pp. 341–48; Gatzke, pp. 241–42; Fischer, *Griff nach der Weltmacht*, pp. 547, 629. Hindenburg wrote to the new Chancellor Hertling on 11 December that a reconsideration of Germany's Belgian demands was in order for two reasons. First, the moderation was supposed to produce peace and a British withdrawal from France, both of which conditions were now recognized as unfeasible. Second, Germany's "military situation [had] developed especially favorably." See Gatzke, p. 241; Lutz, pp. 88–89. It deserves note, however, that at the end of June 1918 Ludendorff was apparently willing to probe the possibilities for peace on the basis of the status quo ante in the west and a free hand in the east. Not surprisingly after his clashes on these issues with Ludendorff, Kühlmann insisted that the Supreme Command should make such a proposal itself (Müller, p. 387, entry for 25 June 1918).

[54] The Petition of the Intellectuals can be found in Gatzke, p. 121, the Petition of the Six Economic Organizations in ibid., p. 45.

aristocracy of blood [i.e., the Prussian Junkers] and the aristocracy of coal and iron (ranged respectively behind the Conservative and National Liberal Parties). . . . Many Conservatives realized that an exclusively westward expansion would neither increase their material basis of power, nor check permanently the advance of "western" ideas in Germany. In the end it would benefit solely their commercial and industrial "allies." . . . To maintain the existing balance between Germany's ruling classes, between industrial (and "liberal") and agricultural (and reactionary) interests, the Conservatives looked for material gains adjacent to their eastern holdings.[55]

Mutatis mutandis, the industrialists insisted on gains in the west because an exclusively eastern expansion would mostly benefit their agrarian "allies."

To justify demands on behalf of the industrialists, Ludendorff argued in September that gains in the west were necessary to protect Germany's industry. Crucial deposits of raw materials and industrial regions lay too close to Germany's borders. Upper Silesia, the ore deposits of Lorraine, the Saar, and the coal and industrial district of Westphalia all needed protection from aerial attacks. He claimed that "protection of the Westphalian district by seizure of Belgium . . . is so self-evident, so simple."[56] A similar argument, holding that the gains in the west were necessary in case of any future war, was made in memoranda by the industrialists and by academics (for example, the rector and senate of the Technical College of Hanover). They held that without Longwy-Briey Germany would have to depend in the not too distant future on the import of foreign ore, while with Longwy-Briey, Germany would remain independent of such foreign ore for the next four decades, which had obvious advantages in the case of war.[57]

A second factor in the insistence on demands both in the east and the west connects Germany's federal structure to its war aims. Each of the separate states hoped to share in the spoils of war not only to reward their own people but also to maintain the domestic constitutional and political balance of power among the separate states. For example, in April 1917 the Central Committee of the Conservative Party, the Central Committee of the Pan-German Association, and the Independent Committee for a German Peace together with twenty-four great economic and political associations all argued that the postwar taxes would endanger the financial survival of the sovereign houses and the

---

[55] Gatzke, pp. 5–6. For Ludendorff's motivations to insist on gains in both the east and the west, see Sweet, p. 251.

[56] Ludendorff's letter of September 1917 in Knesebeck, p. 162.

[57] Fischer, *Griff nach der Weltmacht,* p. 792.

independence of the German states and therefore the federative character of the German Empire.[58] These organizations and the individual states hoped to forestall the need for high postwar taxes through their high war aims. Some of the states worried, moreover, that exclusively eastern gains would lead to even greater Prussian dominance of the empire. L. L. Farrar, for instance, argues that "Some of the Bundesstaaten—particularly Bavaria—feared that Prussia would take an inordinate share of the booty and thus dominate the empire even more than it already did."[59] It may, therefore, have been important that Count Georg Hertling, the former Prime Minister of Bavaria, became Chancellor at the end of October 1917.[60] As Chancellor, Hertling insisted on high war aims against Belgium and on keeping Alsace-Lorraine, areas where Bavaria hoped to make substantial territorial gains.[61] After the Treaty of Brest-Litovsk, Bavaria proposed the partition of Alsace-Lorraine, whereby Prussia would gain Lorraine while Bavaria would annex Alsace. Other states raised their own demands; William of Württemberg demanded the Sigmoringen district, and Saxony claimed Upper Alsace.[62] The pressures from the individual states and the industrialists to maintain the domestic political balance of power were largely responsible for the leadership's continued insistence on high war aims in the west and, therefore, for the decision to launch an offensive in the spring of 1918.

Conclusion

Peace was possible between Russia and Germany at the end of 1917 because Russia's Bolshevik leaders were willing to accept any terms that kept them in power, and Germany's leaders showed a modicum of restraint in their demands against Russia. Germany's restraint resulted from the need to shift troops to the Western Front. At the same time, no possibility for a general peace existed because the German leadership insisted on high war aims in the west. Their insistence must be attributed to two factors. First, to maintain the domestic political balance of power, the regime needed to balance the Junkers' gains in

[58] Dahlin, pp. 101–2.

[59] Farrar, *The Short-War Illusion*, p. 44; see also p. 50.

[60] Hertling had warned Bethmann Hollweg already in a letter of 28 March 1915 that a disappointing peace would endanger the monarchy and especially the position of the Kaiser. See Zechlin, "Friedensbestrebungen und Revolutionsversuche," B 22/63, p. 26, note 16.

[61] French, *The Strategy of the Lloyd George Coalition*, p. 210.

[62] Wheeler-Bennett, p. 326.

the east with gains for the industrialists in the west. Second, the armistice on the Eastern Front made it possible to move additional troops to the Western Front and increased the leadership's estimate of their chances in the upcoming offensive there. Now the outcome of the war and the fate of Germany's leaders would be determined by the spring offensives in 1918.

9

The Termination of the First World War, II: 1918

THIS CHAPTER COMPLETES the analysis begun in the previous chapter and explains why peace broke out in late October 1918. I first give a brief overview of the new information and war aims of the main belligerents in 1918. I then examine in greater detail how the German leadership reacted to the new information of 1918. The second half of this chapter examines the reactions of the three democracies: France, Britain, and the United States.

1918 Overview

During 1918 the failures of the Stormtrooper offensives, the successful counteroffensives of the Entente in July, the "black day of the German army," and the steady defection of Germany's remaining allies made the German leadership much more pessimistic not only about the outcome of the war but also about their own fate. Meanwhile, French and British leaders were relatively slow in revising their estimates. While the most important French leaders recognized by mid-October that German resistance was crumbling, even up until the first week of November some of Britain's military leaders still pessimistically estimated that Germany might be able to hold out for another six to nine months. The Austrian decision to accept a separate peace on 4 November finally convinced Lloyd George and others that Germany was now done for and would have to accept harsh terms. Like the French, the Americans had concluded by mid-October that the Germans could no longer withdraw from the armistice negotiations. Two factors were probably responsible for the Americans' optimism. First, American troops were now arriving in large numbers. Second, at the end of September the AEF demonstrated its ability to operate as an autonomous and independent fighting force at St. Mihiel.

As a result of this new information, the war aims of the main belligerents changed sufficiently to finally create a bargaining space. Table 9.1 lists how, as a result of the new information of 1918, Germany, France, Britain, and the United States revised their war aims between March and November 1918 and how a bargaining space finally emerged.

In contrast to previous years, the German leadership now finally lowered their minimum demands. German war aims went down because the leadership recognized that the German people knew, or would soon know, the war was lost. In desperation, the leadership lowered their war aims and tried to buy off the people with a small "revolution from above" to prevent a larger revolution from below. By early November the new German leadership was willing to capitulate outright, while two factors limited the demands of the western Allies. First, until early November some French and especially British leaders estimated that the German army could still hold defensively for a long time. The costs of continuing the war, they estimated, would not be worth the gains, because most of the gains would fall to the United States. Second, as David Stevenson concludes, American pressures to keep French and British war aims low "won the Germans more favorable terms than they could now secure for themselves."[1]

Germany 1918: Peace . . . and Civil War

Following the structure of the previous chapters, I first lay out the new information of March–November 1918. In the next section I detail the changes in Germany's war aims. The third section then explains why Germany's (new) leaders were now finally willing to lower their war aims and how they attempted to buy off the people and prevent a grand domestic revolution.

As we saw in the previous chapter, Germany's leaders started the spring offensive cautiously optimistic. However, the failures of the first Stormtrooper offensive in March and the subsequent offensives of April and May dimmed their optimism, and by May Ludendorff was forced to recognize that Germany would not be able to impose its will on the enemy by force of arms alone.[2] In his general order of 2 August, Ludendorff drastically limited Germany's strategic goals on the Western Front. After the Allied counterattacks abated, Germany would launch only limited attacks and oblige the Allies to negotiate by wearing them

---

[1] Stevenson, *The First World War and International Politics*, pp. 24–25.

[2] Stephen Bailey, pp. 208–9. This conclusion was reiterated by Major Nieman in a memorandum of 20 July 1918; see Direnberger, pp. 99–100. To Ludendorff's outrage this new information was not kept private within the small leadership circle. On 24 June Secretary of State Kühlman told the surprised deputies of the Reichstag that the army had abandoned hope of gaining a decisive victory on the Western Front (Stephen Bailey, pp. 210–11). Ludendorff demanded and got Kühlman's head for this public statement.

TABLE 9.1
War Aims in March–November 1918

Germany	France	Great Britain	United States
30 Sept: Domestic reform: Government drawn from Reichstag: first introduction of parliamentary government.	3 June: A united and independent Poland with free access to the sea.	Mar: Sykes-Picot Agreement to be revised?	6 Apr: Treaties of Brest-Litovsk and Bucharest cannot be allowed to stand.
4 Oct: Accepts Wilson's Fourteen Points and Five Particulars as the basis for the peace negotiations.	27 July: Revision of Treaty of Brest-Litovsk.	11 June: Treaties of Brest-Litovsk and Bucharest cannot be accepted.	8 Oct: Wilson's Fourteen Points and subsequent speeches basis for peace; evacuation of occupied territories.
5 Oct: Belgium restored as an independent state. Reparations not ruled out; cooperation in creation of League of Nations. New states in the east to manage their own constitutions and foreign relations; peace treaties in the east no "obstacle to future peace agreements."	30 Sept: French to establish civil administration in the Occupied Enemy Territories Administration West, in the Ottoman Empire. 29–30 Sept: French impose armistice terms on Bulgaria; Britain and U.S. excluded. 6–7 Oct: Germany to evacuate occupied territories including Alsace-Lorraine and withdraw behind the Rhine; occupation of Alsace-Lorraine but no territory	3 Oct: Sykes-Picot Agreement must be completely revised. 6–8 Oct: Occupied territories to be evacuated. (Alsace-Lorraine not to be occupied by Allies?) Immediate cessation of submarine warfare. 26 Oct: Armistice terms on land as lenient as France, Italy, and U.S. can be made to accept. 22 Oct: British unilaterally impose peace conditions on Turkey.	14 Oct: Process of evacuation and conditions of armistice to be determined by the military advisors of U.S. and Allied governments. Maintenance of present military superiority of U.S. and Allied armies in the field; cessation of unrestricted submarine warfare and destruction by retreating German armies. Change in German regime.

TABLE 9.1 (cont.)

War Aims in March–November 1918

Germany	France	Great Britain	United States
10–12 Oct: Wilson's Fourteen Points and subsequent speeches basis for peace. Evacuation of occupied territories in the west; left open for eastern territories; evacuation under a mixed commission. Germany now governed in agreement with Reichstag. 20 Oct: Halt to unrestricted U-boat warfare; terms of armistice to be left to U.S. and Allied military advisors; present relative strength at the front forms the foundation of agreements? 21 Oct: Poland independent, gets small territorial concessions in Posen; status of Alsace-Lorraine open to discussion?	beyond. Immediate cessation of submarine warfare. 8 Oct: A staging area for renewed military operations: two or three bridgeheads on the west bank of the Rhine, half-circles with a 30 km radius at Rastadt, Strasbourg, and Neuf-Brisach. Occupation of the left bank of the Rhine to ensure reparations? 23 Oct: Bridgeheads at Mayence, Coblenz, and Cologne; occupation of the left bank. 29 Oct–4 Nov: Bridgeheads at Mayence, Coblenz, and Cologne, plus a neutral zone of 30–40 km along the remainder of the right bank. Acceptance of Wilson's "14 points" and subsequent speeches as	26 Oct: No acceptance of Freedom of the Seas; insistence on the right to blockade. 29 Oct–5 Nov 1918: Acceptance of Wilson's Fourteen Points and subsequent speeches as basis for peace; reservations on reparations and freedom of the seas. Abrogation of Brest-Litovsk; German (gradual) withdrawal from Russian territory to 1914 borders. Allies gain right to occupy strategic points in Austria-Hungary to conduct military operations. German colonies in Africa and Asia to be ceded to South Africa and Australia. British protectorate over Mesopotamia and perhaps Palestine;	18 Oct: Austria-Hungary to satisfy the aspirations of Czecho-Slovaks and Yugo-Slavs. 23 Oct: Germans to accept civilian control of the military; preparation of armistice terms to be done by the Allied generals and admirals; Germany to leave all heavy guns behind? Metz, Strasbourg, etc. in the hands of the Allies until peace declared? 27 Oct: Germans to surrender some of their heavy guns? No Allied occupation of Alsace-Lorraine, the Rhineland, and bridgeheads across the Rhine? No surrender of U-boats?

TABLE 9.1 (cont.)

War Aims in March–November 1918

Germany	France	Great Britain	United States
25 Oct: Civilian control over the military accepted; reform of Prussian franchise. 26 Oct: Domestic reform: parliamentary monarchy: Chancellor and Ministers responsible to Reichstag. 31 Oct: Kaiser has to leave? 6 Nov: Capitulation.	basis for peace, but reservations on reparations and freedom of the seas. Abrogation of Treaties of Brest-Litovsk and Bucharest and supplementary agreements, German (gradual) withdrawal from Russian territory to 1914 borders. Austria-Hungary: Allies gain right to occupy strategic points in Austria-Hungary to conduct military operations; navy to Italy, Italy to occupy Austrian territory almost identical as agreed in the Treaty of London. 8 Nov: France and Great Britain agree to help establish native governments and administration in Syria and Mesopotamia.	France to get a sphere of influence in Syria? Surrender of 160 German U-boats; internment of 6 battle cruisers, 10 cruisers, 8 light cruisers, 50 modern destroyers; none ever to return to Germany.	29 Oct–5 Nov: Allies to accept Fourteen Points with the two reservations by the French and British on Freedom of the seas and reparations. British accept to "discuss the principle of Freedom of the Seas" at the peace conference. U.S. accepts French demand for occupation of the east bank of the Rhine because Clemenceau gives his word of honor that France will withdraw after peace conditions fulfilled.

Note: Question marks indicate the uncertain status of a war aim.

out.[3] However, on August 8, the "black day of the German army," the British attacked near Amiens and forced the Germans into a disorderly retreat. In one day the British took 16,000 prisoners and advanced between six and eight miles. This day of 8 August taught Germany's leaders two unexpected lessons: first, the morale of the German army was crumbling; second, tanks were a formidable new weapon of war.[4] Five days later, on 13 and 14 August, Wilhelm II told the assembled leadership in a Crown Council: "We are at the end of our performance. The war must be ended."[5] Ludendorff admitted he lost his earlier confidence that limited offensives would force France and Britain to make peace and scaled down his plans to a pure and simple defensive. All present now agreed that Germany's only remaining hope was to break the enemy's will by a strategic defense.[6] The continued advance of the Allies throughout August forced the Kaiser to acknowledge the bitter reality on 2 September: "The campaign is lost. Now our troops have been running back without a stop since July 18. The fact is we are exhausted."[7]

---

[3] Stevenson, *The First World War and International Politics*, p. 222. It is striking to note that on 4 August, thus well before the defeat of 8 August, Colonel Max Bauer had already come to the conclusion that the military situation had developed so unfavorably that the conclusion of peace could not be put off much longer. To prevent the dangerous internal situation from worsening and potentially developing into a revolution, he recommended that serious steps finally be taken to reform the Prussian franchise (Philipp, p. 221). This was also the first time that Colonel Bauer at General Headquarters concluded that while Germany could not avoid defeat, it could avoid revolution by liberalizing its government in time (Stephen Bailey, pp. 240–41).

[4] Pitt, p. 223; Stephen Bailey, p. 222; see also Ludendorff, *The General Staff and Its Problems*, vol. 2, p. 630. Ludendorff remarked: "On August 8, it was if everything conspired against us. We have done everything possible to prevent the recurrence of something like this so easily. But who can tell me that what was possible once, can not also happen a second time" (Direnberger, pp. 103–4). It can be argued that this *was* already the second time, and Cambrai in 1917 had been the first time.

[5] Direnberger, p. 101.

[6] At the end of the conference Hindenburg expressed the *hope* that Germany would be able "to hold out on French soil and thereby in the end impose our will on the enemies." Where Germany's leaders had seen chances for victory earlier in the year, they were now reduced to the hope—or "pious fraud" by Ludendorff—that an effective defense might still exhaust the Entente and force them to accept German demands. Ludendorff subsequently altered the wording of the protocol of this conference. Where Hindenburg had only expressed a hope, Ludendorff changed the protocol to read that "Hindenburg concludes that [Germany, or OHL] will succeed" (Direnberger, p. 101). See also Stevenson, *The First World War and International Politics*, p. 222; Gatzke, p. 282.

[7] He continued, "When the offensive was opened on the Marne on July 15, I was assured that the French had only 8 divisions left in reserve, and the British perhaps 13. Instead of this, the enemy assembles a crowd of divisions in the forest of Cotterêts, unnoticed by us, attacks our right flank and forces us to retreat. Since then we have received

More unfavorable new information during September further forced the leadership's expectations downwards. On 12 September the Americans eliminated the St. Mihiel Salient.[8] Three days later Austrian Foreign Minister Baron Burian told the new German Secretary of State von Hintze that Austria could not continue the war, and the Austrians issued an appeal "to all" for peace.[9] On the 19th the entire Bulgarian army began to disintegrate, and on 24 September and again two days later the Bulgarians requested an armistice. On 19–20 September Turkey was decisively beaten in Palestine at the battles of Megiddo.[10] On the Western Front, meanwhile, the progress of the Allied forces threatened the supposedly unbreakable Hindenburg line. To counter the threat, OHL finally transported more troops from the Ukraine and the east to the west.[11] But it was too late. On 27 September the Allies turned the Hindenburg line when they broke through at the Cambrai–St. Quentin section.[12] Bulgaria concluded an armistice on 29 September and surrendered outright the following day.[13] (Bulgarian Tsar Ferdinand abdicated on 4 October and fled, first to Austria-Hungary, and then to his native Coburg.)

The unfavorable new information of the last days of September forced the German leadership to draw two unpleasant conclusions. First, defeat in the war was now inevitable. Second, with Bulgaria's armistice and Austria-Hungary's appeal for peace, the people would realize that defeat was now inevitable and that a continuation of the war served only the ends of the old regime. The leadership faced facts at a dramatic conference at army headquarters at Spa on 29 September when Ludendorff told Chancellor Hertling and Vice Chancellor Payer that the situation in the west was hopeless.[14] Germany was left with

---

blow after blow. Our armies can simply do no more" (Müller, p. 406, quoted and translated in Fischer, *Germany's Aims in the First World War*, p. 625).

[8] Not much emphasis should be placed on this success since the Germans were withdrawing at the time.

[9] Herman, p. 621.

[10] Pitt, p. 263.

[11] On 26 September five Germans divisions were withdrawn from the Ukraine and redeployed on the Western Front. The next day more troops were withdrawn from the Russian Front (Herman, pp. 626–27).

[12] Pitt, p. 263; Gleichen, p. 108.

[13] The armistice required Bulgaria to withdraw from the occupied territories in Greece and Serbia, demobilize, with an exception of three divisions to be employed on its eastern frontiers, and surrender its arms, munitions, vehicles, and horses to the Allies. German and military troops were given four weeks to withdraw. In a secret clause Allied military forces were promised passage through Bulgaria and use of its railways, roads, waterways, and harbors. For the terms of the Bulgarian armistice see Scott, pp. 405–6.

[14] Direnberger, p. 110.

no alternative but to conclude an armistice with the enemy as quickly as possible to avoid a catastrophe. In the next few days both other military leaders and the Reichstag were finally informed about the desperate state of affairs.[15]

On 3 October Prince Max of Baden formed a new government based on a coalition of the center and the moderate left that for the first time included members of the Reichstag. Later that same day the new government learned that the Macedonian Front had totally collapsed and that the situation on the Western Front was further deteriorating. Henceforth, significantly spurred on by President Wilson's increasing demands, the new government constantly questioned the military leadership about its estimates and the prospects of the war.[16]

On 9 October the Cabinet learned that the day before a breakthrough had only barely been prevented and that it was becoming questionable whether the troops would hold.[17] In spite of Ludendorff's attempts on 17 October to convince the civilian leadership that War Minister Scheüch's promise of additional manpower made him substantially more optimistic, the government of Prince Max fully realized the situation was deteriorating rapidly.[18] On the 26th news arrived that Austria was going to ask for a separate peace within twenty-four hours. Not only would Germany lose its last ally in the field, but an Austrian surrender also threatened to expose Germany's southern flank to hostile attacks and free up Italian troops for the Western Front.[19]

On 28 October sailors in Kiel mutinied when they heard of plans by the navy for one last desperate, suicidal sailing. However, it took a few days before the extent and seriousness of the mutiny became known because the navy intentionally kept the government in the dark. On 1 November the First American Army broke through the final German positions northeast and west of Buzancy, while the French Fourth Army moved across the Aisne. The Americans, racing through the now open valley of the Meuse, reached Sedan and cut the crucial German supply

---

[15] See Ludendorff's speech of 1 October to the officers at OHL, quoted in "Aus den Tagebuchblättern des Obersten von Thaer vom 1.10.1918," in Miller, *Die deutsche Revolution von 1918–1919*, p. 23. The next day Baron Major von dem Bussche briefed the Reichstag party leaders in somewhat more detail how tanks, the defection of Bulgaria, and Germany's rapidly deteriorating manpower situation had fundamentally changed the military situation and necessitated an armistice (Rudin, pp. 67–70).

[16] For the new government's probing on 3 October, see Ludendorff, *The General Staff and Its Problems*, vol. 2, pp. 634–37; Huber, pp. 562–63; Matthias and Morsey, pp. 115ff., 128ff., 138, 216, 220–56, 384–407, 526–45.

[17] Huber, pp. 562–63; Matthias and Morsey, pp. 115ff., 128ff., 138.

[18] Matthias and Morsey, pp. 216, 220–56; Ludendorff, *The General Staff and Its Problems*, vol. 2, pp. 660–92; Rudin, p. 154.

[19] Matthias and Morsey, pp. 384–407.

line between Mezières and Montmédy. This was exactly the break-through Ludendorff had warned the Cabinet about on 17 October.

On 2 November the army reported the unstoppable dissolution of the front. At the same time several members of the government worried about the possibility of a separate Bavarian peace. The next day Austria signed a separate armistice at the Villa Giusti, near Padua.[20] On 4 November Berlin finally became aware of the seriousness of the events at Kiel when the news broke that the sailors had mutinied and set up a Soviet and that the soldiers sent to suppress the revolt had chosen instead to fraternize. But the threat of revolution was not limited to northern Germany. By now mass protest demonstrations in Munich and elsewhere showed the degree to which the internal situation had deteriorated.

At a meeting of the entire Cabinet on 5 November, General Groener, the new First Quartermaster General after Ludendorff was allowed to resign on 26 October, gave the ministers his estimate of the military situation and its prospects.[21] He noted the unexpected rapidity and extent of the collapse of Germany's allies and warned that as Austria-Hungary came apart, not only Czechoslovakia but also other parts of Germany's erstwhile ally might actively support its enemies. He also alerted the ministers to the danger of a Rumanian re-entry into the war. He painted a bleak picture for the Cabinet: "Only of a short duration can the resistance be that the army can offer against the assault of the external enemy with its tremendous superiority and in the face of the threat from Austria-Hungary." He could not offer an estimate of how long the army could maintain its resistance, because this would depend on the developments on the home front and in the army. (Both Hindenburg and Groener were especially concerned about the dangers of the rapidly spreading Bolshevism to the morale of the army and at home.) General Groener agreed with Erzberger's summary that an improvement of the military situation was not to be expected and that the army would have to withdraw to the German border. Groener hoped they could hold out in their positions for a while longer if the army remained loyal. He promised the politicians there would be sufficient time to negotiate an armistice, but when pressed by Erzberger he could not give the politicians any indication how much time they had left.

The next day, 6 November, Groener had become even more pessimistic. He admitted: "I had hoped that we [could] wait 8–10 days, until we had fixed our positions; after what I have heard in the meantime from Kiel, from Tirol and about the morale in the fatherland, especially in

[20] For the terms of the armistice, see Scott, pp. 446–55.
[21] Matthias and Morsey, pp. 526–45; quotation on p. 532.

Bavaria, with far-reaching political consequences, I have come to the conclusion that we must take this so painful step and ask Foch [for the armistice terms]."[22] Morale at home was crumbling, as unrest and protest demonstrations rapidly spread in Berlin. On 7–8 November revolution broke out in Bavaria, and in Munich a republic was proclaimed. To avoid the fate of the Romanovs, King Ludwig fled. The next day hundreds of thousands marched on Berlin, and when troops joined the revolutionaries revolution broke out there too. In Berlin the new government deliberated on 10 November whether to accept the armistice terms. They had little choice because the army was already dissolving.[23]

The Change in Germany's War Aims

Although between March and late August Germany's leaders became more pessimistic, Table 9.1 shows that little evidence exists that they were willing to lower Germany's war aims in this period.[24] Only after 29 September did Germany's war aims significantly decrease. As shown above, on that day the leadership was informed that the situation was hopeless and that an armistice had to be concluded as soon as possible. Chancellor Hertling begged to be allowed to resign, and a new government was formed under Prince Max of Baden.

With his hand forced by the military, Prince Max had no alternative but to send President Wilson a note late on 3 October asking the American President to bring about and mediate peace negotiations.[25] The note explicitly accepted "the programme set out by the President . . .

---

[22] Ibid., pp. 547–55; quotation on p. 552. The editor notes that the American advance near Verdun was probably largely responsible for Groener's conclusion and pessimism (see note 28). Groener played a crucial role in maintaining the army's loyalty to the new regime. He foresaw that further fighting would worsen rather than improve Germany's position. See Deist, "The Road to Ideological War: Germany, 1918–1945," pp. 355–56.

[23] Miller, *Die deutsche Revolution von 1918–1919*, pp. 23–30.

[24] In the Bucharest treaty of 7 May Germany gained further economic concessions especially with regard to leases of the Rumanian oilfields and a monopoly on the sale and marketing of the entire oil output. Furthermore, the costs of the German occupation of Rumania would be fully borne by Rumania. After Clemenceau made public Emperor Charles of Austria-Hungary's secret attempt at peace negotiations through Prince Sixte on 11 April, Austria-Hungary was forced to make far-reaching concessions to Germany. Austria-Hungary now agreed to negotiate a long-term political, military, and economic alliance whereby the two empires would be linked in a customs and economic union. In August Russia was forced to cede sovereignty over Estonia and Livonia. See Stevenson, *The First World War and International Politics*, pp. 204, 217; Fischer, *Griff nach der Weltmacht*, pp. 599–619, 629–30; Scherer and Grunewald, vol. 3, nos. 61, 62, pp. 88–97, no. 239, pp. 366–67. On the last day of August Foreign Minister Hintze suggested that Germany might now accept a return to the status quo ante with regard to Belgium, subject to certain conditions (Scherer and Grunewald, vol. 4, no. 224, p. 320).

[25] Ludendorff, *The General Staff and Its Problems*, p. 637.

in his message to Congress of January 8, 1918 and his later speeches, particularly his address of September 27, as basis for the peace negotiations."[26] In the ensuing exchange of notes with President Wilson between 8 and 27 October, German leaders incrementally lowered their minimum demands as Wilson gradually increased his. After each note by Wilson the leadership gathered to evaluate Germany's military position and prospects and each time judged that because their military position had deteriorated they had to bow to Wilson's (new) demands. Major issues on which the Germans gradually gave ground were withdrawal from Alsace-Lorraine, withdrawal from the east, a halt to unrestricted submarine warfare, and domestic political reform.[27]

In his third note of 23 October, President Wilson referred to his earlier notes and announced he had forwarded the German request for an armistice to his allies. Wilson had further increased his demands when he argued that "the only armistice he would feel justified in submitting for consideration would be one which should leave the United States and the Powers associated with her in a position to enforce any arrangements that may be entered into and to make a renewal of hostilities on the part of Germany impossible."[28] These "extraordinary safeguards," the President argued, were needed because he could not trust the changes in Germany's system would fully materialize and be permanent.

The German government recognized that Wilson's note represented a new increase in his terms. However, as Solf argued, "If we can promise both [the 'abdication' of Ludendorff and the subordination of the military to civilian control], then we have a good armistice and a good peace."[29] By now the government was in favor of both these demands for reasons of its own, as I will elaborate below.

While the German government was preparing substantial institutional changes at home, the early draft of a reply to Wilson's note maintained that Germany had turned to Wilson to negotiate an armistice, not a surrender.[30] However, on 26 October news arrived that the Aus-

---

[26] The German notes, the American replies, Wilson's speeches, and much more on the armistice negotiations can be found in Marhefka and in Scott. In the next two days the Austro-Hungarian and Ottoman governments issued similar appeals. On 4 October Prince Max provided the leading plenipotentiaries of the Bundesrat more details about his proposed peace program. See Matthias and Morsey, pp. 83–86; Huber, p. 560; Rudin pp. 97–98, 219.

[27] For discussions on Wilson's notes, see Matthias and Morsey, pp. 126–47, 207–21, 281, 292, 294–99, 332ff.

[28] Scott, p. 435.

[29] Huber, p. 578; see also Matthias and Morsey, pp. 332ff.

[30] Matthias and Morsey, pp. 365ff; Huber, pp. 582–83.

trian government was going to ask for a separate peace within twenty-four hours. The effect of the new information of Austria's imminent request for a separate peace was the almost immediate realization that this draft was too "provocative" and challenging. The next day the Cabinet dropped the distinction between an armistice and surrender in the draft of their reply. The Cabinet further softened their reply and lowered their demands when on Erzberger and Scheidemann's suggestion they added the sentence that "the military authorities are . . . subject to [the new people's government]."[31] When they briefly explored the relationship between the armistice and peace conditions, Haussmann warned the Cabinet members that, of course, a bad armistice would bring a bad peace.[32] Later that day, 27 October, the German government sent its brief fourth note to Wilson:

> The German Government has noted the reply of the President of the United States. The President knows the fundamental changes which have taken and are still taking place in the constitutional life of Germany. The peace negotiations will be carried out by a popular government in whose hands lies, in constitutional theory as in fact, the sovereign power. The military powers also are subject to it. The German Government now awaits the proposals for an armistice which shall herald a peace of justice such as the President has described in his declarations.

As the military and domestic situation steadily worsened while the days dragged on without a reply by Wilson, the German leadership became desperate for an armistice. On 6 November Wilhelm II insisted that a delegation be sent to hear Foch's terms, even in the absence of a reply by Wilson, whose note had not yet arrived.[33] Erzberger also agreed that negotiations would have to start on 8 November at the latest. According to Erzberger, the War Cabinet had with complete consent from the Supreme Command come to the conclusion that "If no answer from Wilson would have arrived by that time, then the German delegation *by hoisting the white flag* should on her own initiative carry out the armistice negotiations, *if necessary the capitulation.*"[34]

On the morning of 8 November the German peace delegation led by Matthias Erzberger arrived at Allied headquarters in the Compiègne

---

[31] Matthias and Morsey, pp. 384–407; quotation on p. 386.
[32] Ibid., p. 374, note 49.
[33] Ibid., p. 555. Lloyd George had announced on 5 November in the House of Commons that the Allied governments had asked Wilson to tell Germany that it should apply in the usual way to Marshal Foch if it wanted to hear the armistice terms (ibid., p. 552, note 30).
[34] Erzberger's notes of the War Cabinet meeting of 6 November, in ibid., pp. 556–58, see notes 8 and 14, emphasis added.

forest near Réthonde. There Marshall Foch gave the Germans the terms of the armistice and three days to accept them.[35] The Allied governments had set the following terms (note that the official release by the German government, published in the *Kreuz-Zeitung*, 11 November 1918, is wrong on several details):[36]

1. Effective six hours after signing.

2. Immediate clearing of Belgium, France, Alsace-Lorraine, to be concluded within 14 days. Any troops remaining in these areas to be interned or taken as prisoners of war.

3. Surrender 5,000 cannon (chiefly heavy), 30,000 machine guns, 3,000 trench mortars, 2,000 planes.[37]

4. Evacuation of the left bank of the Rhine, Mainz, Koblenz, Cologne, occupied by the enemy to a radius of 30 kilometers deep.

5. On the right bank of the Rhine a neutral zone from 30 to 40 kilometers deep, evacuation within 11 days.

6. Nothing to be removed from the territory on the left bank of the Rhine, all factories, railroads, etc. to be left intact.

7. Surrender of 5,000 locomotives, 150,000 railway coaches, 10,000 trucks.

8. Maintenance of enemy occupation troops through Germany.

9. In the East all troops to withdraw behind the boundaries of 1 August 1914, fixed time not given.

10. Renunciation of the Treaties of Brest-Litovsk and Bucharest.

11. Unconditional surrender of East Africa.

12. Return of the property of the Belgian Bank, Russian and Rumanian gold.

[35] According to Lloyd George, "when Foch showed our terms to the German envoys they were nearly dumb with astonishment at their severity" (Riddell, p. 379).

[36] Official release by the German government, published in the *Kreuz-Zeitung*, 11 November 1918. It can be found at http://www.lib.byu.edu/~rdh/wwi/1918/prearmistice.html. These do not seem to be entirely consistent with the demands as agreed upon in the Second Paris Conference as listed in Rudin (pp. 306–18) or with the final armistice terms (pp. 426–32). Excluded from Clause 2 was the demand for evacuation of Luxembourg. Not listed were Clause 3, which demanded immediate repatriation of all the inhabitants of the above named countries; Clause 8, which demanded that the German Command reveal all mines and delayed-action fuses, poisoned wells, etc.; Clause 12, under the reservation of all subsequent claims by the Allies, reparation for damages, and restitution of the cash belonging to the Banque Nationale de Belgique and Russian and Rumanian gold taken by the Germans or handed over to them. In Part B detailing clauses for the Eastern Front, Clause 6: Allies to have free access to evacuated territories on Germany's eastern frontier. With regard to the naval clauses the Allies had agreed to demand 6 battle cruisers, 10 cruisers, 8 light cruisers (including 2 mine layers), and 50 destroyers to be interned in neutral ports; Clause 7: maintenance of blockade.

[37] According to Foch's estimates the 30,000 machine guns constituted about half the machine guns and the 5,000 cannon and 3,000 trench mortars about one-third of the artillery of the Germany army (Seymour, vol. 4, p. 144).

13. Return of prisoners of war without reciprocity.

14. Surrender of 160 submarines, 8 light cruisers, 6 dreadnoughts; the rest of the fleet to be disarmed and controlled by the Allies in neutral or Allied harbors.[38]

15. Assurance of free trade through the Kattegat Sound; clearance of mine fields and occupation of all forts and batteries, through which transit could be hindered.

16. The blockade remains in effect. All German ships to be captured.

17. All limitations by Germany on neutral shipping to be removed.

18. Armistice lasts 30 days.

The German delegation tried to consult both the government and the Supreme Command but formulated counterproposals on its own since it could not count on proper instructions from either source in time. A telephone conversation with the Supreme Command on 10 November brought a list of demands, most of which had already been included in the delegation's counterproposals. The conversation ended with the recommendation "Should accomplishment of these points not succeed, then the agreement should nevertheless be signed."[39]

In Berlin the new government deliberated on 10 November whether to accept the armistice terms. After a short declaration by Ebert, Secretary of State for Foreign Affairs Solf read out the armistice conditions and noted the recommendation of the Supreme Command to sign even if an amelioration of these conditions could not be achieved. The total collapse of the front seemed imminent, as he reported: "The Supreme Command begs haste, because the army is already dissolving." A short discussion ensued. Then Ebert asked whether in these circumstances anyone was opposed to accepting the armistice conditions. The record notes that "an awful silence" ensued.[40]

Around 11:30 that night the German delegation in Compiègne received the telegram that authorized them to sign the armistice conditions. Later that night at 5:10, after some negotiations that introduced some largely cosmetic concessions by the Allies, Germany signed the armistice agreement. The German delegation had objected to the surrender of 30,000 machine guns because that would deprive them of the means of firing on the revolutionaries at home.[41] As a concession, in the final agreement Foch limited his demand to only 25,000 machine guns. Furthermore, Germany would have an extra day to evacuate the occupied territories. The final agreement allowed it to surrender 5,000 fewer

---

[38] This was incorrect; see note 36 above for the Allies' naval terms in Clause 4.

[39] Huber, pp. 760–61.

[40] Miller, *Die deutsche Revolution von 1918–1919*, pp. 23–30.

[41] Calahan, p. 177.

machine guns, 300 fewer airplanes, and 5,000 fewer trucks. Germany was also granted an additional three weeks to withdraw from the right bank of the Rhine, and the bridgeheads were reduced to ten kilometers. However, the naval terms increased: Germany now agreed to surrender all submarines in existence, and, in addition to the original demands, ten battleships and fifty destroyers of the most modern type.[42]

Thus, in October and early November Germany's leaders gradually lowered their war aims as they received more and more unfavorable new information. But if Germany's leaders also became substantially more pessimistic during 1916 and at that time raised their war aims, why was the German leadership willing to lower its aims this time? Germany's leaders were now finally willing to lower their war aims because they recognized the war would inevitably end in defeat and that within a short period the people would find out. The unfavorable new information about the developments on the battlefield made clear that the fighting and the losses of the last year had been in vain. No new high-variance strategies were available, and a continuation of the war with further needless sacrifices would only increase the chance of a domestic revolution. Since the people would find out soon that the war was lost, time was of the essence. The German leadership therefore hoped to end the war as soon as possible, still on the best available terms, of course, so they could focus on domestic developments. Thus, the leadership no longer attempted to cover the costs of the war through their war aims but instead formulated their war aims on the basis of their expectations of the outcome of the war. The only way now to buy off the people for their sacrifices would be through domestic political reform.

Domestic Political Reform in Germany in 1918

After the Supreme Command had told the assembled leaders on 29 September that the war was lost and urged an immediate armistice and Chancellor Hertling had been allowed to resign, the discussion that followed once more highlights the connection between the outcome of the war and the anticipated domestic political reaction. As a "solution" to the problem, Secretary of State von Hintze now suggested that the leadership had to choose between a military dictatorship and a "revolution from above."[43] Ludendorff rejected dictatorship,

---

[42] The final armistice terms are from Rudin, pp. 426–32.

[43] Hintze had already ordered his officials at the Foreign Ministry to prepare memoranda on reform and democratization from above the day before. See Direnberger, pp. 109–10; Stevenson, *The First World War and International Politics*, p. 223.

apparently *because* victory was impossible. With Hindenburg, however, he supported the "revolution from above"[44] because "a revolution from above . . . was the only means by which Germany could create a government strong enough to withstand the swell of agitation that an armistice request was bound to produce."[45] "What the fatherland was now thinking about," Ludendorff told Colonel Bauer, "was not the war anymore, but his [own] and the Emperor's head."[46] Von Hintze pictured the revolution from above as follows: "Staged from above through an initiative of the Monarch, [the revolution from above] should fashion a transition, [and] *make the conversion of victory into defeat bearable through the calling into play of as many as possible of those interested in cooperation with the government*; that should be her palliative effect."[47] To that end von Hintze favored a government of national unity that would include parties from the left.[48]

The next day the Kaiser ordered the formation of a new government, composed of members of the Reichstag. For the first time Germany now had parliamentary government. Under the leadership of Prince Max of Baden this new government took office on 3 October and began preparations for far-reaching constitutional reforms of the empire. To start, Prince Max told the members of the federal Upper House two days later that the new government would strongly promote franchise reform in Prussia and would work to establish equal and general suffrage in all federal states. Furthermore, in accordance with the wishes of the majority in the Reichstag, Alsace-Lorraine would become an autonomous federal state with its own parliament. In the next weeks work proceeded on the constitutional reforms.

In his replies to Germany's peace notes of 5 and 12 October, President Wilson continued to insist on the issue of domestic political reform. In their third note to Wilson of 20 October the German leadership declared:

> As a fundamental basis of peace the President indicates the destruction of every military power anywhere that can separately, secretly and of its single choice disturb the peace of the world. To this the German Government replies that hitherto in the German Empire the representatives of the

---

[44] Direnberger, pp. 109–10.

[45] Stephen Bailey, p. 241.

[46] Quoted in Bauer, p. 239.

[47] Quoted in Direnberger, p. 110, emphasis added.

[48] Ludendorff hoped to burden those parties of the left with the "odium of this peace" (quoted in Mai, p. 151). See also Miller, *Die deutsche Revolution von 1918–1919*, p. 23. Some of the conservative leaders similarly hoped that the storm of protest about the expected bad terms would be directed against this new government and bring it down. Then they would reestablish themselves and rule as before (Mai, p. 151).

people have had no influence upon the formation of the Government. The constitution gave the people's representatives no voice in the question of peace or war. There has now been a fundamental change in this matter. The new Government has been formed with the entire approval of a parliament by equal, universal, secret and direct suffrage. It includes among its members the leaders of the great parties in the Reichstag. In future no government can take or retain office which does not enjoy the confidence of the Reichstag majority. The responsibility of the Imperial Chancellor to Parliament is being fixed and secured by the constitution. The first act of the new Government was to lay a bill before the Reichstag, a bill to change the Imperial Constitution by providing that the assent of Parliament is required to all decisions on war and peace. The guarantee for the permanence of the new system is not only these legal provisions but also the firm determination of the German people, the great majority of whom are behind these reforms and mean to see them carried through. Thus the President's question as to with whom he and the Governments allied against Germany have to deal is answered clearly and unequivocally. The proposals for peace and an armistice come from a government which is free from every arbitrary and irresponsible influence and is supported by the overwhelming majority of the German nation.[49]

But the government's reply failed to satisfy the President. In his third note of 23 October he replied

[I]t does not appear that the principle of a government responsible to the German people has yet been fully worked out, or that any guarantees either exist or are in contemplation that the alterations of principle and of practice now partially agreed upon will be permanent. . . . It is evident that the German people have no means of commanding the acquiescence of the military authorities of the Empire in the popular will; that the power of the King of Prussia to control the policy of the Empire is unimpaired; that the determining initiative still remains with those who have hitherto been the masters of Germany. . . . If [the government of the United States] must deal with the military masters and monarchical autocrats of Germany now, or if it is likely to have to deal with them later in regard to the international obligations of the German Empire, it must demand, not peace negotiations, but surrender.[50]

While the German government recognized that Wilson's note represented an increase of his terms, Solf argued on 24 October that the note did not demand the abdication of the Kaiser, but just the removal of

[49] Ludendorff, *The General Staff and Its Problems*, pp. 694–95.
[50] Scott, pp. 434–36.

the "autocratic element," which implied the "abdication" of Ludendorff and the subordination of the military to the civilian authorities. Now the government came out strongly in favor of civilian control over the military. The next day Prince Max wrote the Kaiser that Ludendorff had to go, not least because the new government had to credibly signal that the civilians were in full control. He warned that unless the civilian government showed that it controlled the military, a "peace of agreement" would be impossible. The empire, the army, the throne, and even the Hohenzollern Dynasty would be threatened to the utmost.[51]

Domestic political reforms could now credibly perform two functions at the same time. First, these reforms would implement the "revolution from above" that would prevent the larger revolution from below. Second, at the same time these reforms could buy off Wilson and ease the terms Germany could get in the international bargaining over an armistice. Early on the morning of 25 October, Wilhelm II signed draft legislation that limited his *Kommandogewalt*, which would now be subject to the Chancellor and parliamentary control in matters that had "political significance." Later that day the Upper House of the Prussian Diet passed three electoral reform acts; the next day the Reichstag approved far-reaching constitutional changes. Germany now became a constitutional monarchy, in which the Chancellor and the ministers were responsible only to the Reichstag, and a declaration of war as well as the conclusion of peace or other treaties required the Reichstag's consent. Furthermore, the military authorities were explicitly subordinated to the civilian authorities, and the Chancellor would have to co-sign all military appointments.[52] Three days later the Kaiser accepted the constitutional reform package recommended by the Federal Council.

On the last day of October the government started to seriously debate the fate of Wilhelm II himself. Looking for a scapegoat, many members of the government seemed to agree that the Kaiser should abdicate. His removal would again kill two birds with one stone. First, Vice Chancellor von Payer warned that Germany would have to accept worse terms if the Kaiser did not go of his own volition. Second, if he stayed, von Payer warned, the people would try to find those responsible for the bad peace and look for someone to blame. Then not just the Kaiser but the whole dynasty and the institution of the monarchy would be at stake.[53] But all these reforms had come too late.

[51] Matthias and Morsey, pp. 359–60.

[52] Ibid., pp. 378–82.

[53] Ibid., pp. 446–47. The old industrial magnates, meanwhile, had seen the writing on the wall and had become willing to grant large concessions to their workers to forestall

As a revolutionary tidal wave swept over Germany, Ebert showed up at the Chancellery with the executive board of the Socialist Party on 9 November. He threatened to resign unless the SPD were allowed to take over the government. In response, Prince Max prematurely declared that the Kaiser had abdicated while the Crown Prince had also renounced the throne. At the same time he announced that the SPD had now taken over the government and would call elections for a new National Assembly, in which all citizens over twenty of both sexes could participate in complete equality.[54] To appease the assembled crowds, Philip Scheidemann told them, "The People have won along the line! Long live the German Republic."[55]

To summarize, almost as soon as the leadership recognized Germany would inevitably lose the war and the people would know, work started on domestic political reform whereby the previously excluded groups would now gain full access. Although Prince Max's government introduced some important constitutional changes, these failed to buy off the domestic political opposition. Like President Wilson, the people were not convinced the reforms would be genuine and permanent, and the government could not credibly commit itself to give the people and especially the previously excluded groups a permanent stake in the policy-making process.[56]

During Hindenburg and Ludendorff's tenure, the military leadership enjoyed close to veto power over Germany's war aims. To explain how they lost that power and how the civilians succeeded in pushing

---

a socialist revolution. During October the coal, steel, iron, electrotechnical, and machine manufacturing industries all reached agreement with the trade unions. The industrialists were now willing to grant recognition to the trade unions and agreed to collective bargaining, the eight-hour day, and the formation of a central working committee (Herman, p. 630).

[54] To prevent a further deterioration of the situation, General Groener and Ebert made a pact. Groener promised to support the government if it would fight against radicalism and Bolshevism and work for the return to a state of order. See Herman, pp. 653–54.

[55] Hermann, pp. 653–54.

[56] A crucial factor may have been that Bethmann Hollweg's attempts in 1917 to introduce some limited reform had been successfully sabotaged by the conservatives. As it had become clearer in the spring of 1917 that unrestricted submarine warfare would not bring Britain to its knees, and fearful of a revitalized Russia, Bethmann had persuaded the Kaiser to promise reform of the Prussian franchise. Bethmann Hollweg's policy had led to a conservative backlash that finally cost him his job. But his legacy and the Kaiser's promise lingered in the Prussian parliament. A bill proposing an equal franchise for Prussia had first been introduced on 5 December 1917, only to be immediately relegated to a committee. It came up for a second reading on 30 April, by now amended beyond recognition to propose a new system of *plural* suffrage. This bill, which of course drove a stake through the heart of political reform, finally passed on 4 June. Russia's defeat and their increased optimism about the offensive on the Western Front probably

through lower war aims, I briefly sketch the civil-military struggle of the last month of the war. Throughout that final month the military and civilians leaders clashed over the terms of settlement. But although the civilian leadership was willing to lower Germany's war aims, the military insisted on what they called "honorable terms" that would not damage their prestige too severely.[57] In their meeting of 3 October, for example, Hindenburg insisted that "if German territory was to be surrendered on any considerable scale Germany must fight on. It was better to go down fighting than to lose one's honor." The political leadership, in contrast, argued "[t]hat might be the attitude of the generals, but the Government's business was to save anything that could be saved."[58]

As it became clear the army was crumbling, the civilians gradually became more willing to challenge Ludendorff's judgment and his estimates of the possibilities of continued war. At the same time the new government started to assert its authority against the military leadership, as in the debate whether unrestricted submarine warfare should be halted. At least three factors made it possible for the political leadership to finally subordinate the military to their control. First, the military had lost much of its prestige and domestic political support. Whereas in 1916 Ludendorff and Hindenburg had been called to power because their prestige would enable the regime to sign and survive a losing peace, they could now no longer rely on that prestige to blackmail the politicians to comply with their wishes. Second, the subordination of the military to civilian control also promised to gain Germany better international terms, as President Wilson had made very clear in his notes. Third, worried about their political and physical survival, the politicians tried to squarely put the blame for the lost war on the military. Whereas in early October Ludendorff had blamed

---

made the conservatives confident that domestic reform was no longer absolutely necessary because they could buy off the people with high war aims. See Dahlin, pp. 142–43; Hanssen, p. 279; Gatzke, p. 273.

[57] Stephen Bailey, pp. 239–40; Direnberger, pp. 209–10.

[58] Quoted in Ludendorff, *The General Staff and Its Problems*, p. 637. In his conference with the parliamentarians von dem Bussche had also insisted on an honorable peace (Rudin, pp. 67–70). In discussions on how to reply to Wilson's second note of 14 October, Ludendorff again insisted on an "honorable peace," while the civilian politicians worried about the potentially disastrous consequences of continued war (Matthias and Morsey, pp. 220–56). Ludendorff, *The General Staff and Its Problems*, p. 686. On 16 and 17 October Colonel Heye also told the cabinet members, "We should accept the decisive battle if the terms put to us are dishonorable" (Direnberger, p. 127; see also Matthias and Morsey, pp. 220–56). Again, on 25 October Ludendorff, Hindenburg, and Admiral Scheer argued together that "national and military honor now imperatively demanded [that we] reject the extravagant terms of Wilson" (Direnberger, p. 137).

the politicians of the left for the failure of German arms, Secretary of State Solf tried to set the record straight on 16 October. Solf—correctly—declared that "public opinion was so depressed . . . [b]ecause our military power had been broken. They [the Supreme Command] were now trying to say that our military power would collapse if our national *morale* did not hold out. This attempt to shift responsibility could not be permitted."[59] Like Solf, Chancellor Prince Max also put the blame squarely on the military leadership and declared, "only two decisions are possible: either the fight unto destruction or the attempt after the military collapse to save economically and politically what can still be saved."[60]

As we saw above, by 24 October the civilians agreed that the military would have to be subordinated to civilian control. But Ludendorff would not go quietly. That same day, and without consulting the politicians, Hindenburg and Ludendorff published a note that rejected Wilson's demands on their own authority. To back up their rejection of Wilson's demands and to protest with the Kaiser, Ludendorff and Hindenburg came to Berlin on 25 October against express orders of the government. However, Wilhelm II had just signed the draft legislation that morning that limited his *Kommandogewalt* and therefore referred them to the Chancellor. Because Prince Max was ill, Ludendorff and Hindenburg were now forced to try and convince Vice Chancellor von Payer to reject Wilson's "outrageous demands." Von Payer simply replied that the political representatives had lost their confidence in OHL and wished to hear other representatives of the army. Hindenburg and Ludendorff offered their resignation; while Hindenburg was asked to stay on, Ludendorff's resignation was accepted. He was replaced as First Quartermaster General by General Groener, who had earlier argued that the cooperation of the German workers was necessary to win an industrialized war.[61] At the railway station later that day, Ludendorff predicted to Colonel von Haeften that "In eight days the Field Marshall [von Hindenburg] will be removed and in fourteen days we will no longer have an Emperor."[62] When his prediction came true and revolution broke out, Ludendorff donned a false beard and a wig and fled to Norway.

[59] Quoted in Ludendorff, *The General Staff and Its Problems*, p. 658.

[60] Matthias and Morsey, pp. 216–17. See also Ludendorff, *The General Staff and Its Problems*, pp. 660ff.

[61] Wilhelm Deist, "The Road to Ideological War: Germany, 1918–1945," p. 355.

[62] Matthias and Morsey, p. 365.

France, Britain, and the United States 1918:
Peace and Intra-alliance Bargaining

To complete the analysis of 1918 and explain why peace became possible in October, this section examines how the French, British, and American leaders reacted to the new information of 1918 and changed their war aims. By the end of the first week of November all had come to the conclusion that Germany would have to accept whatever terms it was offered. French and American leaders had already come to a similar conclusion in mid-October, but for a surprisingly long time British leaders continued to believe that Germany could put up effective resistance until the spring of 1919. That each of the western Allies increased their aims is thus hardly surprising. However, the intra-alliance bargaining and mutual fear and suspicion of each other's war aims show that each was concerned almost as much about how the terms of settlement would affect their power relative to their enemy as how they would affect their power relative to their current allies.

By and large, the same set of events constituted new information for France, Britain, and the United States. However, these events did not always carry the same implications for each of the three belligerents. The first new information was the unexpected success of the Stormtrooper offensives in the spring. As a result, French and British leaders became more pessimistic about a quick end to the war. This unfavorable new information led to two important changes in their policies. First, the Allies agreed to a united Allied command under the French Marshall Foch. Second, both French and British leaders urged the Americans to speed up the transportation of American infantry divisions and now became willing to provide the necessary shipping.[63] The pressure from Ludendorff's offensives finally forced the Americans, British, and French to a compromise on amalgamation in early May. Fresh American units would train and gather experience and instruction from the British in quiet sectors of the French front.[64] (Such training was still sadly lacking in many occasions. American forces sometimes went into battle completely unprepared. Apparently "whole U.S. regiments went into battle in 1918 without even knowing how to load

[63] Esposito, p. 125.
[64] The agreement was confirmed on 2 May at Abbeville. See "May–June, 1918, The Allies Appeal for American Assistance" at the World War I Document Archive 1918, http://www.lib.byu.edu/~rdh/wwi/1918/amicome.html.

and fire their rifles.")[65] In return, the British provided the shipping for an additional 500,000 troops to France during June and July.

The urgent request for American manpower produced dramatic results with far-reaching implications. In April there had been only five combat divisions and 284,000 effectives in the AEF in France. In each of the next two months 250,000 American troops came over, and by June twenty-four complete divisions had arrived. In the seven months between 30 March and 2 November, the number of effectives increased sixfold, to 1,872,000. However, for their equipment the American army was almost completely dependent on its allies; they brought almost no aircraft, tanks, heavy artillery, or tools to the front.[66]

The increasing American contribution, of course, carried implications for the intra-alliance balance of power between France, Britain, and the United States, and already on 17 August Clemenceau warned Lloyd George about the implications for the terms of the settlement: "No one appreciates more than I the value of American assistance. But our old Europe, which engaged in war without counting on that help, cannot consider the possibility of 'passing the hand' to its trans-Atlantic ally for the completion of the military task which will found a new Europe."[67] By late October it had become clear that continued fighting would have exposed the French army's weakness relative to the British and especially the American armies.[68] If the war lasted only a couple of months longer, American troops would outnumber those of France. The evidence and bargaining over armistice and peace terms supports David Stevenson's conclusion that "Clemenceau and Foch may therefore not have been unhappy that the fighting ended when it did, particularly as they expected the Peace Treaty to be determined more by troop movements on the ground than by any adherence to the ambiguities of Wilson's speeches."[69]

The French government realized its military strength would inevitably affect its intra-alliance bargaining strength and the terms of peace France would be able to secure. The best way, they thought, to protect their interests would be to try to preempt much of the bargaining over the terms of peace by establishing a favorable situation on the ground through severe armistice terms. Thus, Foreign Minister Pichon argued on 21 October, "It is incontestable that the [terms of the armistice] must

---

[65] Esposito, p. 141, note 3, citing Coffman, *The War to End All Wars*, p. 66.

[66] Knightley, *The First Casualty*, p. 129.

[67] Quoted in Watson, p. 308.

[68] Ibid., p. 335.

[69] Stevenson, *French War Aims against Germany*, p. 131

to a large extent reverberate on the [terms of the peace] and that the necessary guarantees of the peace must find support in the clauses of the armistice destined to precede it."[70] To extract the maximum leverage, therefore, against both enemy and ally, the French government insisted on extensive armistice terms.

Like the French, the British recognized that the huge inflow of American manpower would decisively shift the outcome of intra-alliance bargaining against Great Britain and in favor of the United States. David French summarizes the choices facing the War Cabinet in mid-October:

> If they wished to impose unconditional surrender on the Germans they would probably have to continue fighting into 1919. After considerable deliberation they decided that the likely costs of continuing the war would outweigh the benefits they might gain by doing so. What they found particularly persuasive was the fact that their partners seemed determined to ensure that the British would bear a disproportionately heavy share of the burden of that cost while they reaped the benefits.[71]

The main beneficiary of continued war, British leaders concluded, would be the United States. Thus, Smuts argued on 24 October, "If peace comes now, it will be a British peace." But if the war lasted another year, because Britain insisted on unacceptable terms, while Germany would be "utterly broken and finished," Britain "would have lost the first position; and the peace which will then be imposed on an utterly exhausted Europe will be an American peace." The reason was simple: by 1919 the United States "will have taken our place as the first military, diplomatic and financial power of the world." Reiterating a by now familiar concern, Smuts told the War Cabinet: "our opponents at the peace table will not only be our enemies; and the weaker we become through the exhaustion of war, the more insistent may be the demands presented to us to forgo what we consider necessary for our future security."[72] On 26 October, finally, the War Cabinet agreed that Britain would get a better peace in 1918 than in 1919. Therefore, the armistice terms on land would have to be as lenient as France, Italy, and the United States could be made to accept.[73] On 10 November, likewise, the War Cabinet concluded that it was in Britain's interest to end

[70] Quoted in Lhopital, p. 37.

[71] French, *The Strategy of the Lloyd George Coalition*, p. 271. On 19 October Haig asked, "Why expend more British lives—and for what?" (quoted in Gooch, "Soldiers, Strategy and War Aims in Britain 1914–1918," p. 37).

[72] Quoted in French, *The Strategy of the Lloyd George Coalition*, pp. 276–77.

[73] Ibid., p. 278; Guinn, p. 318.

the war now and not ask for terms that would be unacceptable to Germany and thereby lead to a continuation of the war, which would only work in America's favor.[74]

Returning to the timeline of new information of 1918, the successful Allied counteroffensive launched on 15 July made French and British leaders only marginally more optimistic. In mid-August Lloyd George told the War Cabinet that "he was confident that we should achieve such progress, both actually and from the point of view of the progressive deterioration of internal conditions among the enemy, that we could hope *in 1920* to inflict upon Germany a defeat which she herself would recognize to be a defeat."[75] Even in September the majority of Allied commanders still estimated the war could not be won until 1919.[76]

The good news from the third week of September onward finally convinced French, British, and American leaders to readjust their expectations. In the Middle East, after the unexpectedly big victory at the battles at Megiddo, British troops with Arab assistance drove the Turks out of Palestine and Syria. Under the French General Louis Frenchet d'Esperey Allied forces finally broke out from the Salonika Front on 15–24 September and defeated the Bulgarian forces at the battles of Monastir-Doiran. On the 24th and the 26th the Bulgarians requested an armistice. On 27 September the Allies broke through the Cambrai–St. Quentin section of the Hindenburg line and, in doing so, turned the line.[77] Bulgaria concluded an armistice on the 29th and surrendered late the following day. The Bulgarian army was demobilized, and Bulgarian territory and equipment made available for Entente use.

The German and Austrian requests for an armistice in the first week of October convinced French and British leaders that Germany was in serious trouble.[78] By mid-October, after Turkish requests for an armistice, the French, British, and American governments received more and more intelligence that the Germans were on their last legs and would have to accept any conditions they were offered. Foch told Clemenceau on 18 October that "German military power was in fact sufficiently disorganized militarily and materially to no longer be able

---

[74] Fest, p. 308.

[75] Quoted in French, *The Strategy of the Lloyd George Coalition*, p. 258, emphasis added. That same month Lord Northcliffe even predicted: "We shall none of us live to see the end of this war" (quoted in Andrew and Kanya-Forstner, p. 164).

[76] French, *The Strategy of the Lloyd George Coalition*, p. 270; Andrew and Kanya-Forstner, p. 164; Seymour, vol. 4, p. 57.

[77] Pitt, p. 263; Gleichen, p. 108.

[78] French, *The Strategy of the Lloyd George Coalition*, p. 265; Watson, p. 326.

to present for any length of time a serious resistance."[79] The clearly visible disintegration of the Austro-Hungarian Empire further contributed to the Allies' optimism. The French government agreed with Foch, and Foreign Minister Pichon told the British ambassador that Germany "would accept practically any terms we liked to impose."[80] By the end of October General Pershing and Colonel House were similarly convinced that the internal political conditions of Germany would force it to accept the Allies' armistice terms.[81] Lloyd George was now hopeful that the steady defection of Germany's allies would make it possible to reach an armistice before Christmas.[82] However, many British politicians and generals still refused to believe that the German army was beaten.[83]

On 31 October the Turkish government accepted an armistice, on November 4 the Austrians accepted the terms of the armistice, and the first week of November provided the first signs of a political revolution in Germany. These events, in particular the Austrian armistice, significantly boosted the Allies' optimism.[84] French and American leaders were fully confident that the Germans would have to accept Foch's harsh terms.[85] But the British remained doubtful, even after the news of the mutiny in Kiel reached Britain late on 5 November, whether Germany would accept Foch's terms for an armistice on land *and* their own high naval terms. Even four days before the armistice, on 7 November, CIGS Henry Wilson told the War Cabinet that "from a purely soldier point of view [*sic*], there did not appear to be any actual need yet for the Germans to accept the terms."[86] Only on 8 November *after* the Supreme War Council had drawn up and agreed to the armistice terms was Lloyd George finally convinced that "the Germans must accept them [the Allies' armistice terms] in view of our menace through Austria, the internal conditions of Germany & the revolt of the German fleet."[87]

---

[79] Lhopital, pp. 32–33. The Allied military command was meanwhile busy with preparations for an attack with considerable superiority in November into Lorraine.

[80] Quotations cited in Stevenson, *French War Aims*, pp. 122–23; see also Watson, p. 335.

[81] Rudin, pp. 184–85.

[82] Riddell, p. 376.

[83] French, *The Strategy of the Lloyd George Coalition*, pp. 260, 268–71, 282; Riddell, pp. 353, 374; Guinn, p. 319; Seymour, vol. 4, p. 107.

[84] Lloyd George had already predicted a revolution in Germany on 12 October (Riddell, p. 370).

[85] Seymour, vol. 4, pp. 105, 124; Bliss, p. 510.

[86] Quoted in French, *The Strategy of the Lloyd George Coalition*, pp. 284–85. German proponents of the stab-in-the-back myth later, of course, eagerly exploited these estimates and conclusions of the British military.

[87] Quoted in French, *The Strategy of the Lloyd George Coalition*, p. 285.

The Change in French War Aims

As the French government became more optimistic about a quick and decisive end to the war, the leaders increased their war aims but found their position constrained by the strength and aims of both Great Britain and the United States. Thus, in the final bargaining over the respective peace terms, intra-alliance bargaining often played a decisive role.

First on the block was a revision of the Sykes-Picot Agreement. With the ready pretext that Russian acceptance of the agreement and its terms had been a precondition for its fulfillment and the new Bolshevik government had rejected all secret treaties, the British government insisted on revisions.[88] The British success in the Ottoman Empire had been extensive and larger than French leaders anticipated, and the French had no choice but to lower their aims in the region.[89] But in the Balkans the French government successfully exploited their military upper hand. On 29 and 30 September France managed to steal a march on both Great Britain and the United States in the negotiations over the Bulgarian armistice. The commanding general Franchet d'Esperey basically imposed terms on the Bulgarians, after having been instructed by Clemenceau to exclude both the British and Americans from the negotiations.[90]

As the French become more optimistic during October, they gradually increased their demands against Germany.[91] On 24 October Clemenceau conferred with Marshall Foch and General Pétain about the armistice conditions. The previous day Foch had written that as a result of the continued Allied successes since October, the Allies should no longer aim for the Rhine of Neuf-Brisach, Strasbourg, Rastadt, but that of Mayence, Coblenz, and Cologne and carry their armies there.[92] Clemenceau apparently supported such terms, because he told Foch that the military clauses had to "give the armies of the western allies a complete security and deliver into the hands of the allied governments important pawns. . . . One looks forwards to," he added, "the left bank of the Rhine." The naval conditions should be seen similarly. The blockade

[88] Herman, p. 626.

[89] France would now get the right to "encourage and help establish native governments" in Syria (Andrew and Kanya-Forstner, pp. 160–61); see also *The New York Times*, 8 November 1918.

[90] For the terms, see Rudin, appendix B, pp. 404–5.

[91] For discussions of the First and Second Paris Conferences of 5–8 October and 29 October–5 November, see Stevenson, *French War Aims against Germany*, pp. 118–32; Watson, pp. 332–35; see also Lhopital, pp. 13–17.

[92] Quoted in Lhopital, p. 50.

would have to be maintained, and the armistice would have to have a sufficiently short duration. At the end of their conference Clemenceau charged Marshall Foch to draw up terms on the bases he indicated.[93]

The second Paris Conference from 29 October to 5 November produced some intense intra-alliance bargaining over the specific armistice terms, and this time Colonel House was present for the Americans.[94] Following his new estimates, Foch now proposed armistice terms with bridgeheads at Mayence, Coblenz, and Cologne. Moreover, Foch's new terms included a neutral zone of 30 to 40 kilometers width along the remainder of the right bank of the Rhine. This demand would leave the crucial industrial Ruhr area and Frankfurt exposed and vulnerable. Lloyd George and Colonel House initially expressed reservations about the need to occupy the left bank and the bridgeheads but finally conceded on 1 November.

While House insisted that the Allies should also accept President Wilson's Fourteen Points, the French and British had serious reservations. The French particularly insisted on the need for reparations. Lloyd George, meanwhile, vehemently opposed the American President's demand for "freedom of the seas" because that might detract from the right to blockade. Colonel House threatened that if the Allies refused to accept Wilson's Fourteen Points, the United States might defect from the coalition and pursue negotiations with Germany on its own, which might lead to a separate peace. Colonel House's acknowledgment that Wilson "had insisted on Germany accepting all his speeches, and from these you could establish almost any point that anyone wished against Germany" took much of the sting from his demand.[95] On 30 October Lloyd George broke what remained of the logjam and forced Clemenceau's hand when he proposed to accept peace on the basis of Wilson's speeches and his Fourteen Points with two reservations. These reservations as proposed by Lloyd George together with the Allies' acceptance of Wilson's speeches as the basis for peace were published on 5 November at the end of the second Paris conference.[96]

Clemenceau also fought for France's aims in Eastern Europe. Most prominent among these was the demand that the Treaty of Brest-Litovsk be annulled and Germany withdraw its troops from Russian

---

[93] Clemenceau, quoted in ibid., p. 53.

[94] This section relies heavily on Stevenson, *French War Aims*, pp. 124–32; Watson, pp. 333–35; see also Rudin, pp. 290–95.

[95] Quoted in Watson, p. 334.

[96] *Foreign Relations of the United States*, Washington, D.C., 1918, supplement 1, pp. 468–69.

soil.[97] The Allies agreed to demand the annulment of the Brest-Litovsk, Bucharest, and supplementary agreements of 27 August between Russian and Germany. Because the British and Americans were worried the Bolsheviks would exploit the power vacuum, they insisted on a gradual withdrawal. France first demanded the restoration of Poland with its borders of 1772 but withdrew this demand under pressure from British Foreign Minister Balfour.

David Stevenson concludes that Clemenceau was willing to give way on minor demands in Eastern Europe and the Clémentel Plan in return for support or at least goodwill for core French demands in the west. These core demands were Alsace-Lorraine, "guarantees" by means of the occupation of the left bank of the Rhine and bridgeheads, and reparations.[98] Thus, compared to late 1917 and early 1918, French aims rose markedly. The main increase lay, not surprisingly, in the claim to a strategic frontier on the Rhine. Note that, as a result of these higher demands, the French government could hope to reward its people with the return of Alsace-Lorraine and substantial reparations.

Although French demands were very high, they were clearly based on the leadership's estimate that within a matter of weeks, if not days, the Germans would be forced to concede such severe terms. With the outcome of the war now certain, continued fighting would only lead to an unnecessary waste of blood. Some, such as President Poincaré and the American Generals Pershing and Tasker Bliss, wanted to impose unconditional surrender on Germany and perhaps fight all the way to Berlin. When asked by Clemenceau what he thought of such ideas, Foch replied, "To continue the struggle would incur great risk. It would mean that perhaps fifty or a hundred thousand more Frenchmen would be killed, not counting the Allies, and for quite problematic results. . . . Enough blood, alas! Has already been shed, and that should suffice." Prime Minister Clemenceau agreed: "Marshall, I am entirely of this same opinion."[99] Thus, for both Clemenceau

---

[97] This demand was raised already in the spring of 1918, clearly indicating that France was worried about the postwar balance of power. Foreign Minister Pichon told Wilson that France could not afford to sacrifice Russia: "We would consider abandoning Russia to the Germans to be to lose the War" (quoted in Stevenson, *French War Aims*, pp. 105, 107, 128).

[98] Ibid., p. 128. The conference also agreed on armistice terms for Austria. Italy was to be the main beneficiary. It not only would gain much of the Habsburg navy but also was allowed to occupy Austrian territory to a line almost identical to that agreed upon in the 1915 Treaty of London.

[99] Quoted in King, pp. 238–39. See for similar sentiments Rudin, pp. 286, 288.

and Foch, the costs of war now helped create a bargaining space and led them to—ever so slightly—moderate their demands short of full unconditional surrender.

The Change in British War Aims

The first major revision in British war aims during 1918 came early on. Whereas Lloyd George had left open the possibility of a peace with Germany at the expense of Russia in early January, the harsh terms of Brest-Litovsk made such a deal impossible. Protection of the empire (India) and the balance of power on the Eurasian continent mandated that Brest-Litovsk not be allowed to stand.[100]

After the successes of September and October, the British government revised its aims, against both Germany and its own allies. In the first major revision, British aims in the Middle East, against both the Ottoman Empire and France, increased. After all, as Lloyd George argued, "Britain had won the war in the Middle East and there was no reason why France should profit from it."[101] In the armistice negotiations with the representatives of the Ottoman government on the island of Mudros between 27 and 31 October and under explicit instructions from the War Cabinet, the British Vice-Admiral Calthorpe excluded representatives from the other Allied governments from the negotiations.[102] He managed to drive a hard bargain and secured far harsher terms than the minimum terms the War Cabinet had proposed.[103]

It should come as no surprise that British leaders considered the naval terms crucial to Britain's long-term security. As the new Commander-in-Chief of the Grand Fleet, Sir David Beatty, told Hankey, "the existence of the Empire depends on our Sea Power [so] we must ensure that no Fleet in being is left which can threaten our supremacy."[104] On 19 October the Board of Admiralty proposed an initial list of the naval armistice terms to be offered to Germany. These included the surrender of all their submarines, ten battleships, six battle cruisers, eight light cruisers, and fifty of their most modern destroyers.[105] But several members of the Cabinet worried that the demands of the

[100] See Rothwell, pp. 195–96.

[101] Quoted in French, *The Strategy of the Lloyd George Coalition*, p. 262.

[102] See Riddell, pp. 379–80.

[103] French, *The Strategy of the Lloyd George Coalition*, pp. 265–66. For the official British paraphrase of the armistice terms, see Scott, pp. 444–46. For the full terms see Rudin, appendix D, pp. 410–11; see also p. 270.

[104] Quoted in French, *The Strategy of the Lloyd George Coalition*, p. 281.

[105] Ibid., p. 281, emphasis added.

Admiralty, in combination with Foch's terms for an armistice on land, would be too severe for the Germans to accept.[106] Therefore, in their deliberations of 26 October the War Cabinet merely agreed that "The naval conditions of the armistice should represent the admission of German defeat by sea in the same degree as the military conditions recognize the corresponding admission of German defeat by Land."[107] Central in the Cabinet's naval demands was their determination not to give up the right to blockade or entrust that to the new League of Nations, or surrender to Wilson's demands about "freedom of the seas."[108]

In the Supreme War Council's Second Paris Conference (29 October–5 November) the Allies had to deal with several thorny issues that would affect their future relative power. The council agreed quickly on terms for Austria-Hungary but found much less agreement on the terms to be offered to Germany. Extensive discussions ensued over the Fourteen Points "as a basis" for the peace negotiations. The British were determined to maintain their freedom of action and not be forced into Wilson's conception of peace in Europe. Colonel House threatened that the United States would conclude a separate peace if the Allies refused to accept the Fourteen Points. In return, both Lloyd George and Clemenceau threatened to continue the fight on their own.[109] Mollified by House's assurance that the positions and speeches of President Wilson were vague and open to a wide variety of interpretations, on 30 October Lloyd George accepted the Fourteen Points with two important reservations. First, the issue of freedom of the seas would be set aside for further discussion at the peace conference. As Lloyd George pointed out to Colonel House,

> I could not accept the principle of the Freedom of the Seas. It has got associated in the public mind with the blockade. It's no good saying I accept the principle. It would only mean that in a week's time a new Prime Minister would be here who would say that he could not accept this principle. The English people will not look at it. On this point the nation is absolutely solid. It's no use for me to say that I can accept when I know that I am not speaking for the British nation.[110]

---

[106] Seymour, vol. 4, p. 118.

[107] Quoted in French, *The Strategy of the Lloyd George Coalition*, p. 278.

[108] For Lloyd George's rejection of Wilson's demand for freedom of the seas, see Riddell, pp. 366, 374; French, *The Strategy of the Lloyd George Coalition*, p. 279.

[109] Seymour, vol. 4, pp. 165–66. For more on the debates on the Fourteen Points, see ibid., pp. 161–88. For a detailed examination of the debates and issues of the Second Paris Conference, see Rudin, pp. 285–319.

[110] Quoted in Seymour, vol. 4, p. 184. It looked like that agreement was not possible until Lloyd George made clear that Britain's reservation was not a peremptory challenge to Wilson's position. A compromise was reached after Lloyd George told House, "This

Second, at the insistence of the French but with active support from Britain, the Entente leaders reserved the right to demand reparations for damages inflicted.[111] Colonel House accepted Lloyd George's letter with these reservations on 3 November.

On 1 November Geddes presented the naval armistice terms as drawn up by the Admiralty.[112] Out of a fear that the combination of harsh terms for an armistice on land and harsh naval terms would force Germany to reject an armistice, Foch agreed only to ask for the surrender of German submarines, confinement of the High Seas Fleet to the Baltic, and occupation of Cuxhaven and Heligoland.[113] The next day the issue of the naval terms came up again. It was at that point that Lloyd George argued:

> The armistice conditions to be imposed upon Germany depend to a great extent on what will happen with Austria. If Austria accepts our conditions, or if the Italian successes continue we shall, perhaps, be in a position to enforce harder conditions. On the other hand, if Austria does not give in and continues to struggle, then we shall find ourselves faced with grave decisions to make. Until we know that, we cannot decide about what we are going to demand of Germany. We must ask ourselves whether we want to make peace right away or whether we wish to continue the war for a year. I would not wish to make a decision before the Austrian reply. It may be very tempting to take a certain number of ships, but that is not the root of the question. . . . The modification that the Austrian reply might bring is in the form which we will give to our conditions. Thus, if we can march on Munich and Dresden, we shall be able to impose stiffer conditions. Clemenceau: I propose the adjournment of all naval questions to Monday [November 4].[114]

On 4 November, the day after the Austrian government signed the armistice at Villa Giusti, Lloyd George managed to reach a compromise with the American Admiral Benson and persuaded the council to insist on the German surrender of 160 submarines and the internment of 6

---

formula does not in the least challenge the position of the United States. All we say is that we reserve the freedom to discuss the point when we go to the Peace Conference. I don't despair of coming to an agreement" (ibid.).

[111] Trask, p. 169; Herman, p. 642; French, *The Strategy of the Lloyd George Coalition*, p. 279.

[112] Geddes justified the high terms by the argument that "The list of ships to be surrendered has been drawn up on the basis that if the [British] Grand Fleet and the [German] High Sea Fleet were to fight a battle, the German fleet would come out of it with the loss of the equivalent of these ships" (quoted in Seymour, vol. 4, p. 127).

[113] Rudin, p. 304.

[114] Quoted in ibid., pp. 298–99.

battle cruisers, 10 cruisers, 8 light cruisers, of which 2 minelayers and 50 destroyers of the latest type in a neutral—or failing that an Allied—port.[115] Lloyd George assured British Admiral Wemyss that none of the interned ships would ever be returned to Germany.[116] Later that day the Allies discussed and adopted Germany's final armistice terms.[117] Two demands not published by the German government (see above) were particularly important. First, the Allies demanded free access to evacuated territories on Germany's eastern frontier and, second and crucially, maintenance of the blockade.

Once the British leadership learned of the revolution in Germany they were confident that Germany would accept the armistice terms, and they knew for certain late on 10 November.[118] By now, some feared the Bolsheviks more than the old German regime. As Sir Henry Wilson put it, "Our real danger now is not the Boches but Bolshevism."[119] This was the reason why the Allies allowed some delay in the withdrawal of German troops from Russian soil, where "the internal situation" warranted it.

Just like France, Britain had a set of core demands its leaders would fight for against enemy and ally alike. In the Middle East British leaders tried to protect their empire and the threat of French encroachments. In September Britain learned it could basically impose its terms on the Ottoman Empire. With the Ottomans' defeat largely at the hands of British forces, British leaders did not hesitate to exploit their success to retract much that had been promised to France in the Sykes-Picot Agreement. As a result, Britain would now be able to strengthen its strategic position in the Middle East.[120] The British Empire would be further strengthened if the dominions would be allowed to gain some selected former German colonies.[121] On the continent their goal was to reestablish some form of a balance of power.

[115] Ibid., p. 314.

[116] French, *The Strategy of the Lloyd George Coalition*, pp. 282–83; Stevenson, *The First World War*, p. 231; Seymour, vol. 4, pp. 131–32. When no suitable neutral port was found, these ships were finally ordered to Scapa Flow. Rudin, p. 316, note 24, offers a brief description of the subsequent fate of the German High Seas Fleet. He notes that "Spain was apparently the only neutral sounded on the question" of internment.

[117] Rudin, pp. 305–18.

[118] French, *The Strategy of the Lloyd George Coalition*, p. 283.

[119] Gooch, "Soldiers, Strategy and War Aims in Britain 1914–1918," p. 38.

[120] After the war ended, "Lloyd George developed an obstinate concern to win tangible benefits to justify his support for military activity in the Middle East. Only with difficulty was he brought to realize . . . that *if Britain extended her empire in the Middle East, it would bring more burdens than benefits*, quite apart from the fact that quarrels over this area were endangering relations with France" (Watson, p. 366, emphasis added).

[121] Although Lloyd George was consistently opposed to demands by the dominions for all German colonies, he nevertheless insisted that South West Africa and the Asiatic

British leaders were slow to appreciate the desperate condition of the German army in October and November. This may explain their reluctance to bargain for harsh terms, but it seems likely that British leaders also hoped to keep French ambitions in check. After all, it had always been Britain's goal to restore a balance of power and not weaken Germany only to see a new and powerful French threat arise. Nevertheless, Lloyd George basically gave Foch a free hand to establish the armistice terms and did not protest too vigorously against French demands for occupation of the left bank of the Rhine. Finally, and crucially, British leaders fought to maintain Britain's naval superiority. Lloyd George would not accept Wilson's demand for "freedom of the seas," insisted on the right of blockade, and ensured that Germany would have to give up its fleet. Once it became clear that further fighting would not lead to an improvement in these core areas, British leaders preferred to settle rather than fight on.

The Change in American War Aims

The new information of 1918 led to an increase in the United States' war aims against the Central Powers. The first change in American war aims came after the Treaties of Bucharest and Brest-Litovsk became known. Convinced that these treaties would tilt the balance of power on the continent overwhelmingly to Germany's favor, Wilson made clear on 6 April that these treaties could not be allowed to stand.[122] On 27 September he recast his war aims as listed in his Fourteen Points speech in a slightly different language and insisted that "there can be no peace obtained by any kind of bargain or compromise with the Governments of the Central Empires," but he held out the promise of a fair and just peace.[123]

In the exchange of notes that followed the German peace request, the President gradually increased his demands. In October Wilson renewed his demands for a change in the German regime and the right for self-determination for the Czecho-Slovaks and Jugo-Slavs in the Austro-Hungarian Empire.[124] However, Wilson was determined to

---

islands belonging to Germany would have to be ceded to the South African Federation and Australia, respectively (Rudin, p. 270; see also Rothwell, p. 6).

[122] However, it was never simply Wilson's intent to take a leaf from Britain's book and restore or reestablish a balance of power on the continent. See Esposito, pp. 134–36.

[123] "Address of President Wilson in Opening the Fourth Loan Campaign," 27 September 1918, in Scott, pp. 399–405. Wilson also warned against "exclusive, selfish economic combinations" within the League of Nations. This was more than a veiled reference and rejection of the French Clémentel Plan.

[124] Scott, pp. 418–18, 428–29, 434–36, 440–41; Lowry, p. 284; Rudin, pp. 182–84; Trask, p. 160; Seymour, vol. 4, pp. 145–47.

make the armistice as moderate as possible; as he wrote House on 28 October, "because it is certain that too much success or security on the part of the Allies will make a genuine peace settlement exceedingly difficult, if not impossible."[125]

On 29 October the Allied political leaders and Colonel House commenced the Second Paris Conference and quickly agreed that Foch's terms would indeed prevent a resumption of hostilities by Germany. But House was worried that the naval terms as presented that day by the Allied Naval Council were far too severe and estimated that the other leaders would agree with him.[126] He informed Wilson the next day of his conclusions. House recommended that Wilson accept the French demand for occupation of the east bank of the Rhine, a demand Wilson had opposed, because Clemenceau gave his word of honor the French would withdraw after the peace conditions had been fulfilled. The leaders quickly agreed on armistice terms for Austria but on 2 November postponed further discussions on naval armistice terms for Germany until it was known whether Austria accepted the terms.

Both Wilson and House seem to have underestimated the political implications of the military terms of the armistice, which Foch had stressed to the French leadership.[127] Rather, House concentrated on getting their European allies to accept the Fourteen Points as the basis for the eventual peace.[128] After some tough debates and even tougher rhetoric, Colonel House won over the Europeans to Wilson's Fourteen Points, partially with the help of the Cobb-Lippmann memorandum, which provided a more detailed interpretation of the President's demands.[129]

---

[125] Quoted in Rudin, p. 184, and in Trask, p. 160. Because of a garbled transmission, House received Wilson's message as reading "too much severity." According to Esposito, "This accident seriously diminished the impact of his words" (p. 128).

[126] Seymour, vol. 4, p. 118.

[127] It is striking to note that the Fourteen Points played no role in the Austrian armistice even though the Austro-Hungarian government had explicitly asked for an armistice on such terms. Upon cabling President Wilson the terms on 31 October, Colonel House remarked, "Fortunately, I was able [to prevent] discussion of political questions. I regard this feature as most favorable" (quoted in Rudin, p. 191). For the opinions of Wilson's military advisors, see Rudin, pp. 96–97, 176, 178; Seymour, vol. 4, p. 136. It deserves note that Wilson explicitly disapproved of Pershing's terms, which were very similar to Foch's final terms (Lowry, p. 284).

[128] Seymour, vol. 4, pp. 150–51.

[129] On 30 October Wilson accepted the Cobb-Lippmann memorandum as a "satisfactory interpretation of the principles involved;" however, the "details of application mentioned should be regarded as merely illustrative suggestions and reserved for [the] peace conference. One noteworthy aspect of the memorandum was its argument in favor of the complete restoration of Alsace-Lorraine to France, but French claims to the Saar were

Wilson and House did not shy away from some strong-arm tactics to win the Allies' approval. Wilson wrote House on 29 October: "Can be no real difficulty about peace terms and interpretation of fourteen points if the Entente statesmen will be perfectly frank with us and have no selfish aims of their own which would in any case alienate us from them altogether. . . . If it is the purpose of the Allied statesmen to nullify my influence force the purpose boldly to the surface and let me speak of it to all the world as I shall."[130] The big sticking point, which became clear very early on, was the British refusal to accept the second point: freedom of the seas. On 30 October Wilson warned that he was willing to escalate the rhetoric:

I cannot consent to take part in the negotiation of a peace which does not include freedom of the seas because we are pledged to fight not only to do away with Prussian militarism but with militarism everywhere. Neither could I participate in a settlement which did not include league of nations because peace would be without any guarantee except universal armament which would be intolerable. I hope I shall not be obliged to make this decision public.[131]

In keeping with Wilson's instructions, House warned Clemenceau, Lloyd George, and Orlando bluntly that the United States might conclude a separate peace.[132]

On 31 October Wilson wrote House to insist that

terms I, II, III and XIV [Open Diplomacy, Freedom of the Seas, Levelling of Trade Barriers, League of Nations] are the essentially American terms in the programme. . . . Freedom of the seas will not have to be discussed with Germany if we agree among ourselves beforehand but will be if we do not. Blockade is one of the many things which will require immediate redefinition in view of the many new circumstances of warfare developed by this war.

Against British fears Wilson offered the reassurance that "there is no danger of its [blockades] being abolished."[133]

By that time House had played his trump card and threatened that if the European Allies insisted on making reservations and exceptions to the Fourteen Points, "it would doubtless be necessary for the Presi-

---

rejected (quoted in Rudin, p. 267). For the Cobb-Lippmann memorandum, see Seymour, vol. 4, pp. 154–58.

[130] Quoted in Rudin, p. 271.
[131] Quoted in ibid.
[132] Trask, p. 168; see also Rudin, pp. 272–73.
[133] Quoted in Rudin, pp. 274–75.

dent to go to Congress and to place before that body exactly what Italy, France and Great Britain were fighting for and to place the responsibility upon Congress for the further continuation of the War by the United States in behalf of the aims of the Allies."[134] He noted "As soon as I said this Lloyd George and Clemenceau looked at each other significantly."[135] While each of the Prime Ministers had come in with prepared commentaries on the Fourteen Points, House's threat had worked: Only Lloyd George's opposition to Freedom of the Seas and the claim to reparations remained on the table. On 31 October House wrote Wilson: "Everything has changed for the better since yesterday. If you will give me a free hand in dealing with these immediate negotiations, I can assure you that nothing will be done to embarrass you or to compromise any of your principles. You will have as free a hand after the Armistice is signed as you now have."[136]

As noted above, however, Lloyd George stubbornly refused to accept the guarantee of freedom of the seas and, together with Clemenceau, also insisted on reparations. House finally recommended Wilson accept Lloyd George's compromise note, which still claimed reservations on these points: "If I do not hear from you to the contrary, I shall assume that you accept the situation as it now is. This I strongly advise." Wilson accepted Lloyd George's compromise on 4 November, but not before he authorized House to warn the Allies that if they did not accept the principle they could "count on the certainty of our using our present equipment to build up the strongest navy that our resources permit and as our people have long desired." That same afternoon House and the European Allies also reached agreement on the demand for compensation for damages done by Germany's aggression. As he wrote Secretary Lansing on 4 November, House considered that the agreement on the two reservations made "the situation quite satisfactory for the moment."[137] In his diary for 4 November House recorded similar satisfaction with the results: "I am glad the exceptions were made, for it emphasizes the acceptance of the Fourteen Points. If they had not dissented in any way, but had let the Armistice be made without protest, they would have been in a better position at

[134] House's cablegram to Secretary Lansing for the president of 30 October, reprinted in Seymour, vol. 4, pp. 170–71.

[135] Quoted in Trask, p. 169.

[136] Quoted in Seymour, vol. 4, p. 174. To put it mildly, it is interesting to note that House argued the President would have a free hand, while at the same time assuming the hands of the European Allies would be tied by their acceptance of the Fourteen Points.

[137] Quoted in Rudin, pp. 281, 282, and 283.

the Peace Conference to object to them."[138] The Allies published their conditional acceptance of the Fourteen Points the next day, and House cabled Wilson:

> I consider that we have won a great diplomatic victory in getting the Allies to accept the principles laid down in your January eighth speech and in your subsequent addresses. . . . I doubt whether any other heads of the governments with whom we have been dealing realize how far they are now committed to the American peace programme.[139]

On 5 November, finally, after the deliberations in Paris had ended and produced agreement on the terms of the armistice, President Wilson sent his final reply to the German government. Wilson announced the European Allies' "willingness to make peace with the Government of Germany on the terms of peace laid down in the President's address to Congress of January, 1918, and the principles of settlement enunciated in his subsequent addresses," subject to the two reservations about freedom of the seas and reparations laid out above. In the final paragraph the President notified the German government "that Marshal Foch has been authorized by the Government of the United States and the Allied Governments to receive properly accredited representatives of the German Government, and to communicate to them the terms of an armistice."[140]

As did the French and British, Wilson increased his demands when military prospects improved in August, September, and October and as the American army grew in strength and experience. In his central demand for changes in the domestic institutions of the Central Powers, Wilson succeeded. But as was the case for the European Allies, the Americans formulated war aims almost as much against their allies as against the Central Powers. Here Wilson was less successful and was forced to accept British reservations on the freedom of the seas and French reservations on the demand for reparations. The whole purpose of the American insistence on the Fourteen Points was to tie the hands of the European Allies in the final peace negotiations and force them to accept a moderate peace.[141] The American army, however, had not

[138] Quoted in Seymour, vol. 4, p. 188.

[139] Quoted in Rudin, p. 283.

[140] "Reply to Germany on the Result of the Paris Conferences," 5 November 1918, in Scott, pp. 456–57.

[141] Recall that Wilson already on 21 July 1917 had written, "When the war is over we can force [Britain and France] to our way of thinking because by that time they will, among other things, be financially in our hands" (quoted in Stevenson, *French War Aims against Germany*, p. 257; see also p. 131).

fully been deployed, and the timing of the German request for an armistice surely robbed Wilson of much greater influence at the intra-alliance bargaining table.

Conclusion

A bargaining space was finally created in October and November because the German regime realized the war was inevitably lost. No more high-variance strategies could conceivably save them. The only way now to avoid severe domestic punishment was to make peace as soon as possible and institute domestic political reforms through a revolution from above in order to "save what could be saved." France, Britain, and the United States meanwhile increased their demands but stopped (just barely) short of asking for unconditional surrender—even though the Germans would have accepted—because of intra-alliance pressures and fears the others would gain most from continued war while they would have to pay most of the costs.[142]

The armistice agreement was finally signed at 5:10 in the morning. Because the agreement specified that the fighting would come to a halt six hours after it was signed, someone moved the big hand of the clock back ten minutes to 5:00.[143] The First World War finally ended at eleven in the morning, on the eleventh day of the eleventh month of the year, one week short of four years after (then) Chancellor Bethmann Hollweg and Chief of the General Staff Falkenhayn had concluded that Germany could not win. Many of the former leaders of the semirepressive and moderately exclusionary regimes in Bulgaria, Germany, and elsewhere had by then fled their countries. On 28 June 1919 the Ger-

---

[142] In the detailed case studies on France and Britain, I concluded that British and French leaders did not formulate their war aims to stay in office. However, in the intra-alliance bargaining in October and November, Clemenceau, Lloyd George, and even Wilson used the democratic nature of their governments to gain bargaining power. Both Clemenceau and Lloyd George argued that they could not give way or would have to insist on certain core issues because otherwise they would be removed from power by their parliaments. In a similar ploy, Wilson warned that Congress might decide to accept a separate peace if the Allied statesmen would not give in to his demands. Each argued, in effect, that his hands were tied by the democratic institutions of his country. Apparently, each also believed the others' threats were credible. The issue at stake between the United States and Britain—freedom of the seas—focused squarely on postwar relations between these two countries. As we saw, after some fierce rhetoric a compromise was reached. Clemenceau insisted on the occupation of the east bank of the Rhine, but his promise that France would withdraw after the peace conditions were fulfilled again made a compromise possible. On Clemenceau's claim, see Rudin, p. 286.

[143] Calahan, p. 178.

mans signed the Treaty of Versailles and formally ended the war between Germany and the Allies. Clemenceau had posed them an ultimatum on 16 June 1919 to either accept the terms of Versailles or take
up arms again.[144] With the homeland in disarray and facing a dramatic
food shortage as a result of the continued blockade, the Germans
clearly were in no position to fight.

[144] Herwig, p. 270.

10

Conclusion

War cannot be divorced from political life; and whenever
this occurs in our thinking about war, the many links that
connect the two elements are destroyed and we are left with
something pointless and devoid of sense.
(*Clausewitz, book 8, chapter 6, B*)

THIS BOOK MAKES a simple point: Leaders decide to continue
or stop fighting at least partly based on how the terms of settlement affect their postwar fate. To make this point I constructed
two main theoretical stepping stones. Chapter 2 first developed a theoretical framework to provide a necessary condition for war termination, the creation of a bargaining space. For a bargaining space to be
created where none existed, at least one of the belligerents must change
his war aims. Unitary rational actors change their war aims according
to new information provided by fighting on the battlefield. Fighting
credibly reveals information about each side's relative strength, cost
tolerance, and the expected costs of war. Hence, I argue that the strategic interaction between belligerents must be located on the battlefield
where both sides try to signal their own strength and update their estimates of the outcome on the battlefield. In other words, the critical new
information that makes a bargaining space possible is mostly about
capabilities, not preferences. Thus, a bargaining space is created when
as a result of the fighting the actors have convergent expectations
about the outcome on the battlefield. Because war is costly, at that
point symmetric unitary rational actors can make a deal that leaves
both sides better off than continued war does.

The second half of chapter 2 adds domestic politics and argues that
even with convergent expectations and estimates leaders can gamble for
resurrection and rationally choose to continue fighting if that does not
increase the likelihood of severe domestic punishment. Specifically, I
argue that semirepressive, moderately exclusionary regimes face the
same likelihood of severe punishment—exile, imprisonment, or even
death—when they settle on moderately losing terms as when they lose
disastrously. Semirepressive, moderately exclusionary regimes, therefore, have nothing to lose by continuing a losing war. Repressive, exclusionary regimes and nonrepressive, nonexclusionary regimes, in

contrast, face a much lower likelihood of severe punishment if they settle on moderately losing terms than if they lose the war disastrously. Therefore, such regimes will prefer to settle on moderately losing terms rather than continue fighting and risk a much worse outcome.

These different incentives affect how the different regimes change their war aims and choose their military strategies. First, semirepressive, moderately exclusionary regimes formulate and change their war aims to minimize the likelihood of severe punishment. To survive, these regimes and their leaders need to reward the people after the war for their sacrifices; that is why the minimum acceptable terms of settlement for semirepressive, moderately exclusionary regimes are always designed to show a profit on the war. Therefore, semirepressive, moderately exclusionary regimes that estimate they will lose the war formulate war aims to cover the costs of the war; as the costs increase, so will their minimum war aims. Hence, the counterintuitive argument: semirepressive, moderately exclusionary regimes can raise their war aims even while they lower their estimates of the outcome of the war. In contrast, repressive, exclusionary regimes and nonrepressive, nonexclusionary regimes formulate and change their war aims to maximize their return on the war rather than "gamble for resurrection." Thus, such regimes will lower their war aims when they lower their estimate of the outcome on the battlefield. Second, semirepressive, moderately exclusionary regimes that estimate they will lose the war design their military strategy *not* to achieve the maximum terms of settlement but to achieve the minimum likelihood of severe punishment. If leaders in such regimes estimate that their current ("best") military strategy will result in losing the war and severe punishment, they will pick a new military strategy that increases the likelihood of achieving the requisite profit on the war even if the new strategy at the same time creates a much higher likelihood of a much worse loss. (While the mechanism somewhat resembles prospect theory, note that I provide a rationalist basis to construct a "reference point.") In contrast, repressive, exclusionary regimes and nonrepressive, nonexclusionary regimes design their military strategies to achieve the best terms of settlement.

The rest of this book was then devoted to test these claims. The statistical analysis in chapter 3 showed that between 1816 and 1975 leaders of semirepressive, moderately exclusionary regimes did face the same likelihood of severe punishment whether they lost moderately or disastrously. In contrast, leaders of repressive, exclusionary regimes and nonrepressive, nonexclusionary regimes were much more likely to be punished severely if they lost disastrously than if they lost moderately. In addition, an analysis of wars between 1816 and 1985 showed that wars that featured semirepressive, moderately exclusionary regimes as losers lasted almost twice as long as other wars. To trace the causal mechanism that connects the fate of leaders to the duration of wars, I then examined how leaders in Germany, Russia, France, and Britain changed their war aims during the First World War.

In chapter 4 I showed how Germany's leaders updated their estimates of the outcome of the war and how this new information affected their war aims. I found that even when Germany's leaders agreed in late 1916 that they were *unexpectedly* in a worse position than in late 1915, they still *increased* Germany's war aims. The substance and source of this increase, moreover, could be clearly traced to a desire to reap enough profit on the war to buy off the domestic opposition. If the war failed to bring the expected profit, a chorus of voices predicted from very early on, socialists and other groups excluded from the old order would launch a revolution. In addition, I found that Germany's leaders deliberately implemented several risky "high-variance" strategies to increase their likelihood of avoiding punishment. In early 1915 they started their attempts to foment revolution in Russia (which could, and almost did, backfire);[1] in 1917 they launched unrestricted submarine warfare in the knowledge it would probably bring the United States into the war; and in 1918 they launched the Stormtrooper offensives, which sacrificed their best manpower in vain. Chapter 5 examined a second semirepressive, moderately exclusionary regime, Russia. I showed that Russia's leaders feared a repetition of the revolution of 1905 on a grander scale and formulated their war aims to reward the people for their sacrifices. I found no clear evidence to suggest that Russia's leaders ever lowered their war aims before March 1917. The evidence thus is consistent with my arguments but does not allow stronger inferences. One major problem is that we have no good evidence on the leadership's changing expectations and in particular little evidence for how the Tsar evaluated the changing prospects. For example, although everybody surely recognized that the costs of war were higher than had been anticipated, it seems that even after the disasters of 1915 many in the Russian military leadership never really lowered their estimates of the outcome of the war. The chapter on Russia thus provides some evidence against my argument that leaders rationally update their estimates of the outcome of the war. Nevertheless, overall the semirepressive, moderately exclusionary regimes changed or refused to change their war aims as predicted. Moreover, the major leaders of semirepressive, moderately ex-

---

[1] See Zechlin, "Friedensbestrebungen und Revolutionsversuche, Deutsche Bestrebungen zur Ausschaltung Russlands im Ersten Weltkrieg."

clusionary regimes all demonstrated their great fear of popular retribution: Kaiser Wilhelm II, King Ludwig of Bavaria, Tsar Ferdinand of Bulgaria, and General Ludendorff all fled their country to avoid the fate of the Romanovs.

Chapters 6 and 7 examined the two nonrepressive, nonexclusionary regimes, France and Britain. These chapters show that France and Britain both lowered their war aims when they received unfavorable new information. Moreover, in both cases there were few if any traces of an attempt to reward the people and the opposition for their sacrifices by high war aims. While at worst the French case is merely consistent with my arguments, the British case offers some surprisingly strong support. After the leadership introduced full conscription in May 1916, they developed legislation to reward the people for their sacrifices by domestic political reforms. British leaders were willing to offer the very reward their German counterparts wanted to avoid at almost all costs: a reform of the franchise. The Representation of the People Act of January 1918 more than doubled the franchise, withdrew property qualifications, reduced the number of plural votes, and gave women over the age of thirty the vote. Whereas the German in-groups perceived a reform of the Prussian franchise as severe punishment because it would knock out a crucial prop of the old order and their ruling position, the British leadership did not perceive franchise reform as entailing major punishment or loss of power by the ruling elite. The third major nonrepressive, nonexclusionary state, the United States, also lowered its war aims after it received unfavorable new information in the course of 1917. Thus, all three major nonrepressive, nonexclusionary regimes changed their war aims as predicted by the theory.

The evidence in chapters 3–7 showed that leaders of semirepressive, moderately exclusionary regimes have good reason to fear severe domestic punishment if they lose a war and therefore change their war aims by a different logic. Chapters 8 and 9 tie these arguments and findings to the question that motivated this book in the first place: What keeps wars going and what finally makes them stop? Chapter 8 examined why the First World War continued in 1914, 1915, and 1916 and ended on the Eastern Front but continued on the Western Front in 1917. No bargaining space existed in 1914–16 because the German regime insisted on high war aims to buy off the people, while French and British leaders insisted on moderately high war aims because they remained confident of final victory. Whereas the western Allies had moderately high war aims because they remained optimistic about the outcome of the war, the German leadership had high war aims *in spite* of their growing pessimism about the outcome of the war. (It was striking to find that the German leadership recognized they could not win against the combined Entente already on 17 November 1914.) The Russian leadership (or what passed for it) insisted on high war aims in this period at least partially because they also needed to reward their people and partially because they seem to have estimated that the combined Entente would be able to defeat the Central Powers eventually. After the two Russian revolutions of 1917 a bargaining space was created on the Eastern Front because the new Bolshevik leadership recognized that a continuation of the war would bring only worse terms of settlement and lower the chances their revolution and leadership would survive. The Germans, meanwhile, demanded harsh terms but preferred to settle on the Eastern Front because they needed troops for the upcoming Stormtrooper offensive on the Western Front. They chose to continue the war in the west because they needed gains there as well as in the east to buy off the people and maintain the domestic balance of power between the in-groups. The German insistence on high war aims in the west is all the more striking because the French and British substantially lowered their war aims during 1917 and at least considered making peace on terms that restored the status quo ante in the west while giving the Germans a free hand in the east.

While chapter 8 examined why the war continued, chapter 9 examined why it stopped and explains why a bargaining space was finally created in October–November 1918. I found that Germany's leaders finally became willing to lower their war aims when they learned in late September that the war would inevitably be lost and the people would soon know it was lost. In recognition that continued hostilities would now only increase the chances of severe punishment, the leadership urgently sought an armistice. At the same time, it tried to buy off the people with a revolution from above to stave off revolution from below. As the situation on the battlefield and the home front rapidly deteriorated, the leadership became willing to hoist the white flag and capitulate on the battlefield, to save what could be saved on the home front. As the French, British, and Americans received more and more new information that the Germans were in dire straits, they incrementally increased their war aims. However, a failure to appreciate how desperate the Germans' situation truly was and some tough intra-alliance bargaining over the terms of the armistice introduced a modicum of restraint in their demands. Now that a bargaining space was created, termination was easy. In the armistice negotiations the Germans asked only to keep five thousand more machine guns than Foch had demanded—to use on their own people and fight off the revolution.

I have put the blame for four years of war and over ten million deaths squarely on the shoulders of Germany's regime. If Germany had not been a semirepressive, moderately exclusionary regime, would the war have ended sooner? Such counterfactual claims are notoriously hard to evaluate.[2] In particular, the co-tenability issue looms large: Would the war even have started if Germany had been a nonrepressive, nonexclusionary or repressive, exclusionary regime? An argument can nevertheless be made that a nonrepressive, nonexclusionary Germany would have ended the war before 1918, with 1917 a likely termination year. In such a Germany, the Reichstag would probably have had a preponderant voice in policymaking. The Reichstag Peace Resolution of 19 July 1917 may therefore serve as an approximation of the policy of a "nonexclusionary" Germany. After it had become clear that unrestricted submarine warfare had failed, and in fearful anticipation of a combined offensive on all fronts by the Entente, a majority of the Reichstag resolved:

> The Reichstag aspires to a peace based on mutual agreement and the permanent reconciliation of all nations. Forcible territorial acquisitions and acts of political, economic or financial violence are incompatible with such a peace.[3]

In essence, the Reichstag renounced conquests and therefore appears to have been willing to substantially lower Germany's war aims. It was the semirepressive, moderately exclusionary structure of Germany that allowed a new Chancellor, Michaelis, to pull the sting from the resolution by announcing he accepted the resolution "As I interpret it."[4] It seems plausible to argue that a nonexclusionary Germany would have lowered its war aims, and a bargaining space would have been more likely especially in 1917 when the western Allies substantially lowered their own aims. Whether peace with a nonexclusionary Germany would have been possible in 1917 probably depends on the question whether the leaders of such a Germany would have been willing to offer the French some concessions in Alsace-Lorraine. I see no way of answering this question.

Note that, in contrast to Fritz Fischer, I do not argue that Germany's high war aims were the result of a particular *German* grab for hegemony.[5] The continuation of the war did not result from a determination

---

[2] For counterfactuals and their role in constructing explanations, see King, Keohane, and Verba, pp. 77–78; Fearon, "Counterfactuals and Hypothesis Testing in Political Science"; Fearon, "Causes and Counterfactuals in Social Science."

[3] Quoted in Lutz, p. 255. The majority consisted of the Center, the Majority Social-Democrats, and the Progressive Party.

[4] Michaelis wrote the Crown Prince: "Through my interpretation of it [the Peace Resolution] I stripped it of its most dangerous intentions. With the resolution as it stands we can make any peace we like" (quoted in Dahlin, p. 108). For the selection of Michaelis, see Bailey, "Erich Ludendorff as Quartermaster General of the German Army 1916–1918," p. 45.

[5] Fischer, *Griff nach der Weltmacht*.

to win Germany "its place under the sun" but rather was the result of the institutional structure of the empire. Like the German regime, the Russian regime formulated high war aims to buy off the people for their sacrifices. Both empires were caught between the rising lower classes and intransigent upper classes, where the latter foresaw that any loss on the war as well as any domestic political concessions would lead to their demise.

This book combines both quantitative and qualitative analysis, which makes much stronger inferences possible than if I had relied on one method alone. The qualitative analysis made it possible to demonstrate the plausibility of the causal mechanisms in a way that is difficult in quantitative analyses.[6] For example, we observe that Germany's leaders did not end the war on moderately losing terms in 1914 or 1916. But we cannot observe if they would have been punished severely if they *had* chosen to settle on moderately losing terms; the data are censored. However, the qualitative analysis allowed me to show that Germany's leaders chose to continue the war because they *anticipated* severe punishment if they settled on losing terms. However, the qualitative analysis explored the plausibility of the suggested causal mechanisms in only one particular war. This is where quantitative analysis comes into its own. The quantitative analysis allowed me to show that the proposed relationship between domestic politics and war termination holds generally across time and space.

Thus, the particular argument about the First World War holds for war termination in general. Whether new information about the war shrinks or widens the bargaining gap depends in part on the regime types involved in the war. Specifically, new information that shows a semirepressive, moderately exclusionary regime will probably lose the war most likely *widens* rather than shrinks the bargaining gap.[7] The logic is straightforward: As long as pessimistic leaders of such regimes see any chance to reap a profit on the war and buy off their domestic opposition, their minimum demands will be for such a profitable settlement. However, because their optimistic opponent expects to settle on winning terms, both sides will ask for more than the other is willing to concede, and no bargaining space exists. Because leaders of semirepressive, moderately exclusionary regimes anticipate severe domestic punishment even if they settle on moderately losing terms, they will

---

[6] Recent statistical research tries to address exactly the problem discussed here. See Alastair Smith and Signorino.

[7] More precisely, no bargaining space will be created as long as the potential variation in the outcome of the war, and therefore in the terms of settlement, includes an outcome that would allow the semirepressive, moderately exclusionary leaders to buy off their opposition and prevent punishment.

prefer to continue a war and reject settlements that other regimes would accept. Thus, wars in which semirepressive, moderately exclusionary regimes estimate they will lose should last longer than other wars. As we saw, the quantitative analysis supports this argument. However, such regimes can continue a war they are losing only if the people do not know they continue fighting for the leaders' sake. Once the people learn the war will be lost, continued war will only increase the likelihood that the leaders will be punished severely. Thus, once the outcome of the war becomes public knowledge, leaders of semirepressive, moderately exclusionary regimes will finally lower their war aims and try to reform the regime to avoid punishment.[8]

The statistics and case studies complemented each other particularly well in an additional aspect. The statistical analysis left me very confident that semirepressive, moderately exclusionary regimes and repressive, exclusionary regimes face a different fate when they lose a war moderately. In addition, the statistics clearly show that leaders of semirepressive, moderately exclusionary regimes face the same fate whether they lose moderately or disastrously, whereas leaders of repressive, exclusionary regimes are much more likely to face severe punishment when they lose disastrously than when they lose moderately. Moreover, these differences are clearly statistically significant. However, because nonrepressive, nonexclusionary regimes rarely lose wars, one should be cautious in drawing inferences about how the outcome of the war affects the fate of leaders of such regimes and whether their fate then differs significantly from the fate of leaders of other regimes. The case studies of regime types in the First World War complement the strengths and weaknesses of the statistical analysis particularly well. These case studies examine only nonrepressive, nonexclusionary and semirepressive, moderately exclusionary regimes but clearly show they formulate their war aims according to a different logic and prefer to continue fighting or end war based on different incentive structures. The absence of a case study on repressive, exclusionary regimes and how they react to new information and change their war aims is unfortunate but unavoidable. Fortunately, the strong statistical support for the posited differences between semirepressive, moderately exclusionary and repressive, exclusionary regimes goes a long way to mitigate this problem. It might also be argued that wars of mass mobilization, such as the First World War, are different because they inevitably involve mass sacrifices and therefore more powerful and greater demands for postwar rewards. However, the statistics show the pattern

---

[8] This, and the occasional quick defeat, may explain why several Mixed Regimes still ended a war on moderately losing terms.

of punishment and the duration of war held generally. Moreover, restricting the analysis to wars before 1914 did not significantly affect the results.

This book has argued that the inclusion of a simple model of domestic politics yields better predictions than the unitary rational actor model still favored by many international systemic theorists. The sacrifice in parsimony seems well justified by the gains in explanatory power. The inclusion of one additional variable, the anticipated fate of political leaders, made possible not only more accurate predictions about war termination and how states change their war aims but also *new* predictions on how states choose their military strategies. In other words, not only does my framework outperform the unitary rational actor model, but it also offers predictions about a class of events whose connection with war termination had previously gone unrecognized.

Implications

In addition to these broad empirical findings, this book suggests several theoretical implications. First, while the existing literature on crisis bargaining implies that war serves to reveal information, only Pillar, Pape, and Gartner have attempted to thoroughly investigate this claim.[9] With Pape, I argue that to understand war we must understand the interaction of military strategies. This argument goes against the conventional assumptions in the game-theoretic literature. Fearon, for example, models "war" as a "war of attrition" where leaders try to discover each other's preferences.[10] Two empirical findings argue against this assumption. First, as shown in the case studies, it is the interaction of military strategies on the battlefield that provides the new information used by leaders to update their estimates of the outcome of the war and determines how they change their war aims. Thus, again, it is new information about capabilities rather than preferences that is central to war termination. Also, as shown in chapter 8, the leaders of the different belligerents were apparently rather well informed of each other's preferences and regime type.

Second, and a related issue, what is new information for one side is not necessarily new information for his opponent; it all depends on their initial expectations. For example, if one side has high expectations of a new, secret "wonder weapon," its success on the battlefield provides little if any favorable new information, while it may lead the

---

[9] Pillar; Pape; Gartner, *Strategic Assessment in War.*
[10] Fearon, "Rationalist Explanations for War."

other side to drastically readjust its estimates of the outcome of the war. Stronger yet, if the new wonder weapon has only limited success, both sides could become more pessimistic. Thus, whether a particular event or set of developments makes war termination more or less likely depends on each side's initial expectations. Hence, much can be gained from a better understanding how states form their priors.

Third, these arguments have important implications for the study of coercion. To test whether military coercion "works," it is necessary to examine first whether the attempt to coerce provided *new* information to the opponent. Any attempt at coercion that fails to provide new information is doomed to failure. However, as this book has shown, even if new information is provided, leaders can rationally choose not to back down, or even increase their own demands. Specifically, therefore, studies of coercion should take into account how the new information affects the leader's domestic political calculus. Failure to take such considerations into account can lead to a systematic bias against the effectiveness of military coercion. Coercion may fail *not* because it did not affect the opponent's estimate of the costs of continued resistance but because the leadership cannot back down for domestic political reasons.

Fourth, and perhaps most importantly, leaders in a crisis do *not* choose between a negotiated settlement now and a "costly lottery," as war is almost always modeled.[11] Instead, leaders in a crisis choose between a negotiated settlement now and a negotiated settlement later.[12] Therefore, to understand the choice between peace and war, it is necessary to explicitly model how leaders evaluate this "later negotiated settlement." This book has made an informal attempt to do just that. But the argument here adds a novel twist. I have argued that leaders of semi-repressive, moderately exclusionary regimes sometimes adopt "high-variance" strategies to increase the likelihood of avoiding punishment. Germany's decision to launch unrestricted submarine warfare in 1917 was a prime example of such a high-variance strategy. This high-variance strategy brought the United States into the First World War.[13]

---

[11] See Wagner, "Bargaining and War."

[12] As Schelling, *Arms and Influence* and *The Strategy of Conflict*, and Kecskemeti, *Strategic Surrender*, argue, even the worst loser always has some bargaining power left.

[13] Perhaps a similar high-variance strategy also brought the United States into the Second World War. When faced with America's demands for a withdrawal from China, Japan's leaders perhaps chose to implement a high-variance strategy that might lead to full-scale war with the United States because they could not accept the domestic political consequences of withdrawal from China. As Russett argues, "the Army High Command simply would not have tolerated any abandonment of its position in China. Its own prestige and influence had been built up step by step during the war there, and its

Fifth, the case study on Russia in 1917 suggested how moral hazard (or adverse selection) can overcome the commitment problem. We would expect unitary rational actors to be unwilling to settle on terms that leave them substantially worse off in a next conflict or open to exploitation.[14] Rather than allow an opponent the opportunity to absorb his gains, we would expect such unitary rational actors to continue fighting. However, leaders may prefer to settle now, even on terms that trigger the commitment problem, if continued fighting only increases the likelihood they will suffer severe domestic punishment.

Sixth, and more broadly, in recent years International Relations theorists have been captivated by the relationship between the nature of a domestic political regime and the propensity of states to initiate and get involved in militarized international disputes and wars. While producing interesting and important findings, much of this literature suffers from a pronounced and potentially misleading bias. With only few exceptions, the literature on the "Democratic Peace" tends to treat non-Democracies as all the same and lumps all such regimes together under the rubric of "Authoritarian" regimes. However, once we extend our analysis to include the consequences of losing power, it becomes apparent there are major differences among "Authoritarian" regimes. This book offers explicit causal mechanisms to explain why these regimes behave differently during war. Extending my arguments to the causes of war initiation, it seems plausible to suggest that the fear of severe punishment should make leaders of semirepressive, moderately exclusionary regimes reluctant to go to war in the first place.[15] Moreover, because leaders of such regimes will often continue war even when they estimate they will lose, leaders of other regimes should expect wars with semirepressive, moderately exclusionary regimes to be more costly than wars with other regimes. Therefore, holding everything else constant, leaders of other regimes should find war with semirepressive, moderately exclusionary regimes less attractive than wars with other regimes. Taken together, these considerations suggest that semirepressive, moderately exclusionary regimes should be less involved in wars than other regimes. Some recent empirical work seems

---

position in China became its power base in Japanese domestic politics" ("Pearl Harbor: Deterrence Theory and Decision Theory," p. 97). Whether this is a correct depiction of the Japanese decision calculus or not, to explain what causes war requires an understanding of the causes of war termination.

[14] For an argument on such terms in the context of civil wars, see Walter, "The Resolution of Civil Wars"; and Walter, "The Critical Barrier to Civil War Settlement."

[15] However, domestic instability may make semirepressive, moderately exclusionary regimes prone to attempt diversionary wars.

to support this prediction, but much more work is needed.[16] It could also be that while threats by leaders of semirepressive, moderately exclusionary regimes are less credible in pre-war crisis bargaining, leaders of other regimes will be tempted to make harsher demands. Thus, how the logic of war termination affects the logic of war initiation all depends on the structure of the strategic interaction between the antagonists before war begins.

Outside of International Relations, this book also offers some implications for Comparative Politics. Skocpol and Tilly have shown that defeat in international war can often spur domestic revolution.[17] The arguments and findings here suggest that semirepressive, moderately exclusionary regimes should be particularly susceptible to revolution because even a moderate loss suffices to coordinate the expectations and actions of the domestic opposition.

Conclusion

In conclusion, this book offers four basic lessons for statesmen, historians, and political scientists. First, as long as war is an enduring phenomenon of international politics, statesmen need to be aware of the requirements of war termination. Statesmen involved in a war, considering intervention in an ongoing war, or trying to end a war between other parties need to be aware of the fundamental logic of war termination. In all these situations statesmen should be aware of how the terms of settlement affect the postwar fate of the belligerents, leaders. In addition, statesmen considering intervention in an ongoing war need to be aware how their intervention can affect the calculus for war termination. Sometimes intervention can bring war termination closer; sometimes, however, intervention can put off war termination. Intervention can make war termination less likely, for example, if it increases one side's minimum terms more than it decreases the other side's terms. To name but one important example, attempts to end the

[16] Mansfield and Snyder, "Democratization and the Danger of War," pp. 5–38; see especially table 2 on p. 18. Because Mansfield and Snyder's table 2 refers to "Anocracies," I tested my findings by adopting their coding scheme. Extending my analysis offered in chapter 3, I recoded my data using their coding scheme, laid out in notes 8 and 9 on page 9 of their article. The results were not substantially different. "Anocracies" were still likely to be punished whether they lost badly or moderately. Specifically, "Anocracies" faced a 40 percent chance of being punished if they lost small and a 56 percent chance of being punished if they lost big. Other small losers had a 13 percent chance of being punished if they lost small and a 77 percent chance of being punished if they lost big.

[17] Tilly, pp. 6, 12, 102–3, 216–21, 231; Skocpol, pp. 60–64, 73–77, 94–99.

wars in the former Yugoslavia (and pundits calling for "exit strategies") could surely have benefited from a better understanding of the issues and strategic interactions involved in war termination.

Second, this book also offers several suggestions for historians. Diplomatic historians provide an invaluable benefit for International Relations scholars. Without their painstaking research and toil in the archives, it would have been impossible for me to even begin this study. In recent years renewed interest in the First World War has produced some outstanding work on the international diplomacy and war aims of the belligerents.[18] However, most historians tend to focus either on military strategy or on international diplomacy rather than both of them together.[19] When the focus is on international diplomacy, military strategy is often relegated to the background while it is assumed leaders base their decisions on the current situation on the ground, rather than on their *expectations* about the possible implications of any particular strategy. This book has pointed to a strong connection between military strategy and international diplomacy: One informs the other. I have tried to present a history of the First World War that integrates both aspects. This approach has allowed me to explain what otherwise surely would have presented a puzzle. For example, it explains why France increased its war aims at the end of 1916, even after the horrible slaughter at Verdun and Rumania's defeat. French leaders thought Nivelle's new tactics would overcome the stalemate. A concurrent examination of both military strategy and international diplomacy also made it possible to explain why leaders sometimes changed their military strategy; in particular, it helps explain the substance and the timing of Germany's high-variance strategies. Second, this book has pointed to a connection between international diplomacy and domestic politics that is sometimes overlooked. For instance, while many historians go into great detail about the connection between attempts to reform the franchise and German war aims, I was surprised to find that *no* historian of British war aims explored the potential connection between Britain's war aims and the Representation of the People Act of 1918.

Third, this book also suggests that closer cooperation between so-called bombs-and-bullets specialists, on the one hand, and International Relations theorists and especially International Security theorists, on the other hand, may be especially fruitful. Far too often Inter-

---

[18] To name but three prominent examples, Stevenson, *The First World War and International Politics*; Stevenson, *French War Aims against Germany*; Soutou, *L'Or et le sang*.

[19] French's excellent books on Britain's policies during the First World War are a notable exception; see French, *British Strategy and War Aims* and *The Strategy of the Lloyd George Coalition*.

national Security theorists have handed off the study of warfare to bombs-and-bullets specialists. As I have tried to show, the actual details of (potential) warfare have very important implications for the study of the causes of war termination and the study of the causes of war initiation. Vice versa, international and domestic strategic considerations can fundamentally affect the choice of strategy and the course of war.[20]

In the end, however important these implications may be for policymakers and academics, war termination is an important topic in its own right. An explanation of why a declaration of war was given, or a first shot was fired, at a particular hour on a particular day surely is important. But to understand why millions died in war, *more than one hundred million* in this century alone, we must understand why their deaths made peace possible.

---

[20] The work more than a decade ago by Mearsheimer, Posen, Kier, and Snyder and the literature on the offense-defense balance are, of course, notable exceptions. Various authors have recently begun to explore the role, effects, and determinants of military strategy in greater depth. See Gartner, *Strategic Assessment in War*; Reiter; Reiter and Meek; Reiter and Stam; Stam; Bennett and Stam; Biddle, "Recasting the Foundations of Offense-Defense Theory."

BIBLIOGRAPHY

1. THEORY

Abt, C. C. "Termination of General War." Ph.D. dissertation, MIT, 1965.

Albert, Stuart, and Luck, Edward C., eds. *On the Ending of Wars*. Port Washington, N.Y.: Kennikat Press, 1988.

Allison, Graham. *The Essence of Decision: Explaining the Cuban Missile Crisis*. Boston: Little Brown, 1971.

Bade, Bruce C. "War Termination: Why Don't We Plan for It?" In John N. Petrie, ed., *Essays on Strategy XII*, pp. 205–31. Washington, D.C.: National Defense University Press.

Bailey, S. D. *How Wars End: The United Nations and the Termination of Armed Conflicts 1946–1964*. New York: Oxford University Press, 1982.

Banks, Jeffrey S. "Equilibrium Behavior in Crisis Bargaining Games." *American Journal of Political Science* 34, no. 3 (August 1990): 599–614.

Bar-Tal, Daniel, Arie W. Kruglanski, and Yechiel Klar. "Conflict Termination: An Epistemological Analysis of International Cases." *Political Psychology* 10, no. 2 (June 1989): 233–55.

Bates, Robert H., Avner Greif, Margaret Levi, Jean-Laurent Rosenthal, and Barry Weingast. *Analytic Narratives*. Princeton, N.J.: Princeton University Press, 1998.

Beer, Francis A., and Thomas F. Mayer. "Why Wars End: Some Hypotheses." *Review of International Studies* 12 (1986): 95–106.

Bennett, D. Scott, and Allan C. Stam III. "The Duration of Interstate Wars, 1816–1985." *American Political Science Review* 90, no. 2 (June 1996): 239–57.

Biddle, Stephen D. "The Determinants of Offensiveness and Defensiveness in Conventional Land Warfare." Ph. D. dissertation, Harvard University, 1992.

Biddle, Stephen D. "Recasting the Foundations of Offense-Defense Theory." Manuscript, University of North Carolina, 1997.

Blainey, Geoffrey. *The Causes of War*. 3d ed. New York: Free Press, 1988.

Brodie, Bernard. *War and Politics*. New York: Macmillan, 1973.

Bueno de Mesquita, Bruce, and David Lalman. "Domestic Opposition and Foreign War." *American Political Science Review* 84, no. 3 (September 1990): 747–66.

Bueno de Mesquita, Bruce, and David Lalman. *War and Reason: Domestic and International Imperatives*. New Haven, Conn.: Yale University Press, 1992.

Bueno de Mesquita, Bruce, and Randolph M. Siverson. "War and the Survival of Political Leaders: A Comparative Analysis of Regime Types and Accountability." *American Political Science Review* 89, no. 4 (December 1995): 841–55.

Bueno de Mesquita, Bruce, and Randolph M. Siverson. "Political Survival and International Crises." Paper prepared for presentation at the Annual Meeting of the Peace Science Society, Urbana, Ill., 3–4 November 1994.

Bueno de Mesquita, Bruce, Randolph M. Siverson, and Gary Woller. "War and the Fate of Regimes: A Comparative Analysis." *American Political Science Review* 86, no. 3 (September 1992): 638–46.

Bundy, Stephen M. "Commentary on 'Understanding Pennzoil v. Texaco': Rational Bargaining and Agency Problems." *Virginia Law Review* 75 (March 1989): 335–65.

Calahan, H. A. *What Makes a War End?* New York: Vanguard Press, 1944.

Carroll, Berenice A. "How Wars End: An Analysis of Some Current Hypotheses." *Journal of Peace Research* 6 (1969): 295–321.

Carroll, Berenice A. "Victory and Defeat: The Mystique of Dominance." In Stuart Albert and Edward Luck, eds., *On the Endings of Wars*, pp. 47–71. Port Washington, N.Y.: Kennikat Press, 1980.

Cimbala, Stephen J. *Conflict Termination in Europe: Games against War*. New York: Praeger, 1990.

Cimbala, Stephen J., ed. *Conflict Termination and Military Strategy: Coercion, Persuasion, and War*. Boulder, Colo.: Westview Press, 1987.

Cimbala, Stephen J., ed. *Strategic War Termination*. New York: Praeger, 1986.

Clausewitz, Carl von. *On War*. Edited and translated by Michael Howard and Peter Paret. Princeton: Princeton University Press, 1989.

Coser, L. "The Termination of Conflict." *Journal of Conflict Resolution* 5: 347–53.

Craig, Gordon A., and George, Alexander L. *Force and Statecraft: Diplomatic Problems of Our Time*. 2d ed. New York: Oxford University Press, 1990; first publ. 1983.

Currer, Paul M. "Superpower Approaches to War Termination." In Thomas C. Gill, ed., *Essays on Strategy VI*, pp. 51–69. Washington, D.C.: National Defense University Press, 1989.

Daugherty, William E., and Janowitz, Morris. *A Psychological Warfare Casebook*. Baltimore: Johns Hopkins University Press, 1958.

Downs, George W., and Rocke, David. "Conflict, Agency, and Gambling for Resurrection: The Principal-Agent Problem Goes to War." *American Journal of Political Science* 38, no. 2 (May 1994): 362–80.

Doyle, Michael. "Kant, Liberal Legacies and Foreign Affairs." Part 1, *Philosophy and Public Affairs* 12, no. 3 (1983): 205–35; part 2, *Philosophy and Public Affairs* 12, no. 4 (1983): 323–53.

Dupuy, Trevor N. *Numbers, Predictions and War*. Indianapolis: University of Indiana Press, 1979.

Dupuy, R. Ernest, and Trevor N. Dupuy. *The Encyclopedia of Military History from 3500 B.C. to the Present*. Revised ed. New York: Harper & Row, 1970.

Dupuy, R. Ernest, and Trevor N. Dupuy. *The Harper Encyclopedia of Military History, from 3500 BC to the Present*. 4th ed. New York: HarperCollins, 1993.

Eisinger, Peter. "The Conditions of Protest Behavior in American Cities." *American Political Science Review* 67, no. 1 (March 1973): 11–28.

Elster, Jon. *Nuts and Bolts for the Social Sciences*. New York: Cambridge University Press, 1989.

Engelbrecht, Joseph A., Jr. "War Termination: Why Does a State Decide to Stop Fighting? (World War II, Anglo Boer War, Japan, Great Britain)." Ph.D. dissertation, Columbia University, 1992.

Fearon, James D. "Bargaining over Objects That Influence Future Bargaining Power." Manuscript, Department of Political Science, University of Chicago, August 1995.

Fearon, James D. "Causes and Counterfactuals in Social Science: Exploring an Analogy between Cellular Automata and Historical Processes." Paper presented at the conference "Counterfactual Thought Experiments in World Politics: Logical, Methodological and Psychological Perspectives," Berkeley, Calif., 13–15 January 1995.

Fearon, James D. "Counterfactuals and Hypothesis Testing in Political Science." World Politics 43, no. 2 (January 1991): 169–95.

Fearon, James D. "Domestic Political Audiences and the Escalation of International Disputes." American Political Science Review 88, no. 3 (September 1994): 577–92.

Fearon, James D. "Rationalist Explanations for War." International Organization 49, no. 3 (Summer 1995): 379–414.

Fearon, James D. "Threats to Use Force: The Role of Costly Signals in International Crisis." Ph.D. dissertation, University of California, Berkeley, 1992.

Fearon, James D. "War, Relative Power and Private Information." Paper presented at the 1992 Annual Meeting of the International Studies Association, Atlanta.

Foster, James L., and Brewer, Gary D. "And the Clocks Were Striking Thirteen: The Termination of War." Policy Sciences 7 (June 1976): 225–43.

Fox, William T. R. "The Causes of Peace and Conditions of War." In "How Wars End," special issue of Annals of the American Academy of Political and Social Science (November 1970): 1–13.

Fox, William T. R., ed. "How Wars End," special issue of Annals of the American Academy of Political and Social Science 392 (November 1970).

Gagnon, V. P. "Serbia's Road to War." Journal of Democracy 5 (1994).

Gartner, Scott Sigmund. "I'm OK, You're OK, Let's Fight: An Organizational and Game Theoretic Model of War Termination." Paper presented at the 1994 APSA Convention, New York.

Gartner, Scott Sigmund. Strategic Assessment in War. New Haven, Conn.: Yale University Press, 1997.

Geyer, Michael. "German Strategy in the Age of Machine Warfare, 1914–1945." In Peter Paret, ed., Makers of Modern Strategy, pp. 527–597. Princeton: Princeton University Press, 1986.

Halperin, Morton H. "War Termination as a Problem in Civil-Military Relations." In "How Wars End," special issue of Annals of the American Academy of Political and Social Science 392 (November 1970): 86–95.

Handel, Michael. "War Termination—A Critical Survey." In Jerusalem Papers on Peace Problems. Jerusalem: Hebrew University, 1978.

Handel, Michael I. "War Termination—A Critical Survey." In Nissan Oren, ed., Termination of War: Processes, Procedures and Aftermaths, pp. 40–71. Jerusalem: Magnes Press, 1982.

Hardin, Russell. Collective Action. Baltimore: Johns Hopkins University Press, for Resources for the Future, 1982.

Hardin, Russell. *One for All: The Logic of Group Conflict*. Princeton: Princeton University Press, 1995.

Hobbs, Richard. *The Myth of Victory: What Is Victory in War?* Boulder, Colo.: Westview Press, 1979.

Holl, Jane Ellen Kyrstyn. "From the Streets of Washington to the Roofs of Saigon: Domestic Politics and the Termination of the Vietnam War." Ph.D. dissertation, Stanford University, 1989.

Holsti, Kalevi J. *Peace and War: Armed Conflicts and International Order 1648–1989*. New York: Cambridge University Press, 1991.

Howard, M. *The Causes of Wars and Other Essays*. 2d ed. Cambridge, Mass.: Harvard University Press, 1984.

Ikle, Fred Charles. *Every War Must End*. New York: Columbia University Press, 1971.

James, D. Clayton. "American and Japanese Strategies in the Pacific War." In Peter Paret, ed., pp. 703–32. *Makers of Modern Strategy*. Princeton: Princeton University Press, 1986.

Jervis, Robert. "Cooperation under the Security Dilemma." *World Politics* 30 (1978): 167–214.

Jervis, Robert. *Perception and Misperception in International Politics*. Princeton: Princeton University Press, 1976.

Jervis, Robert. "War and Misperception." In Robert I. Rotberg and Theodore K. Rabb, eds., *The Origin and Prevention of Major Wars*, pp. 101–26. New York: Cambridge University Press, 1989.

Kaiser, David. *Politics and War: European Conflict from Philip II to Hitler*. Cambridge: Harvard University Press, 1990.

Kecskemeti, Paul. "Political Rationality in Ending War." In "How Wars End," special issue of *Annals of the American Academy of Political and Social Science* (November 1970): pp. 105–15.

Kecskemeti, Paul. *Strategic Surrender: The Politics of Victory and Defeat*. Stanford, Calif.: Stanford University Press, 1958.

Kennan, John, and Robert Wilson. "Bargaining with Private Information." *Journal of Economic Literature* 3 (March 1993): 45–104.

King, Gary, Robert O. Keohane, and Sidney Verba. *Designing Social Inquiry: Scientific Inference in Qualitative Research*. Princeton: Princeton University Press, 1994.

Kitschelt, Herbert. "Political Opportunity Structures and Political Protest Movements." *British Journal of Political Science* 16 (1986): 57–85.

Klingberg, Frank L. "Predicting the Termination of War: Battle Casualties and Population Losses." *Journal of Conflict Resolution* 10, no. 2 (1966): 129–71.

Kriesi, Hanspeter, Ruud Koopmans, Jan Willem Duyvendak, and Marco G. Giugni. *New Social Movements in Western Europe*. Minneapolis: University of Minnesota Press, 1995.

Kuran, Timur. "Now Out of Never: The Element of Surprise in the East European Revolution of 1989." *World Politics* 44, no. 1 (October 1991): 7–48.

Lax, David A. "Commentary on 'Understanding Pennzoil v. Texaco': Market Expectations of Bargaining Inefficiency and Potential Roles for External Parties in Disputes between Publicly Traded Companies." *Virginia Law Review* 75 March (1989): 367–81.

Lax, David. "Optimal Search in Negotiation Analysis." *Journal of Conflict Resolution* 29, no. 3 (September 1985): 456–72.

Levy, Jack S. "Domestic Politics and War." In Robert I. Rotberg and Theodore K. Rabb, eds., *The Origin and Prevention of Major Wars*, pp. 79–99. New York: Cambridge University Press, 1989.

Levy, Jack S. "Learning and Foreign Policy: Sweeping a Conceptual Minefield." Presented at the 1992 Annual Meeting of the American Political Science Association, Chicago, 3–6 September.

Licklider, Roy, ed. *Stopping the Killing.* New York: New York University Press, 1993.

Linz, Juan J., and Alfred Stepan. *Problems of Democratic Transition and Consolidation.* Baltimore: Johns Hopkins University Press, 1996.

Lipsky, Michael. "Protest as a Political Resource." *American Political Science Review* 62, no. 4 (December 1968): 1144–58.

Lohmann, Susanne. "The Dynamics of Informational Cascades: The Monday Demonstrations in Leipzig, East Germany, 1989–91." *World Politics* 47, no. 1 (summer 1994): 42–101.

Mandel, Robert. "Adversaries' Expectations and Desires about War Termination." In Stephen J. Cimbala, ed., *Strategic War Termination*, pp. 174–189. New York: Praeger, 1986.

Mansfield, Edward D., and Jack Snyder. "Democratization and the Danger of War." *International Security* 20, no. 1 (summer 1995): 5–38.

Manwaring, Max G. "Limited War and Conflict Control." In Stephen J. Cimbala and Keith A. Dunn, eds., *Conflict Termination and Military Strategy, Coercion, Persuasion, and War*, pp. 59–76. Boulder, Colo.: Westview Press, 1987.

Maoz, Zeev. "Resolve, Capabilities, and the Outcomes of Interstate Disputes, 1815–1976." *Journal of Conflict Resolution* 27 (June 1983): 195–229.

Mayer, Arno J. "Internal Causes and Purposes of War in Europe, 1870–1956: A Research Assignment." *Journal of Modern History* 41 (1969): 291–303.

Mayer, Arno J. "Internal Crises and War since 1870." In Charles L. Bertrand, ed., *Revolutionary Situations in Europe, 1917–1922: Germany, Italy, Austria-Hungary.* Montreal: Centre Inter-universitaire d'études Européennes, 1977.

Mayer, Arno J. *The Politics and Diplomacy of Peacemaking.* Princeton: Princeton University Press.

Mayer, Frederick W. "Managing Domestic Differences in International Negotiations: The Strategic Use of Internal Side-payments." *International Organization* 46, no. 4 (autumn 1992): 793–818.

McAdam, Doug, John D. McCarthy, and Mayer N. Zald. *Comparative Perspectives on Social Movements, Political Opportunities, Mobilizing Structures, and Cultural Framings.* New York: Cambridge University Press, 1996.

Milgrom, Paul, and John Roberts. "Bargaining, Influence Costs, and Organization." In James E. Alt and Kenneth A. Schepsle, eds., *Perspectives on Positive Political Economy.* Cambridge: Cambridge University Press, 1990.

Mitchell, C. R., and Michael Nicholson. "Rational Models and the Ending of Wars." *Journal of Conflict Resolution* 27 (September 1983): 495–520.

Mitchell, Christopher R. "Ending Conflicts and Wars: Judgment, Rationality, and Entrapment." *International Social Science Journal* 43, no. 1 (February 1991): 5–19.

Mnookin, Robert H., and Robert B. Wilson. "Rational Bargaining and Market Efficiency: Understanding *Pennzoil v. Texaco.*" *Virginia Law Review* 75 (1989): 295–334.

Morgan, T. Clifton. "A Spatial Model of Crisis Bargaining." *International Studies Quarterly* 28 (1984): 407–26.

Morgan, T. Clifton, and Sally Howard Campbell. "Domestic Structure, Decisional Constraints and War: So Why Can't Democracies Fight?" *Journal of Conflict Resolution* 35, no. 2 (June 1991): 187–211.

Morrow, James D. "Capabilities, Uncertainty, and Resolve: A Limited Information Model of Crisis Bargaining." *American Journal of Political Science* 33 (1989): 941–72.

Morrow, James D. "A Continuous-Outcome Expected Utility Theory of War." *Journal of Conflict Resolution* 29 (September 1985): 473–502.

Morrow, James D. "On the Theoretical Basis of a Measure of National Risk Attitudes." *International Studies Quarterly* 31, no. 4 (1987): 423–38.

Morrow, James D. "Social Choice and System Structure in World Politics." *World Politics* 41, no. 1 (October 1988): 75–97.

Mueller, John. *War, Presidents and Public Opinion.* Lanham, Md.: University Press of America, 1985.

Oren, Nissan, ed. *Termination of Wars: Process, Proceedings and Aftermaths.* Jerusalem: Magnes Press, 1982.

Osterud, Oyvind. "War Termination in the Western Sahara." *Bulletin of Peace Proposals* 20, no. 3 (1989): 309–17.

Pape, Robert Anthony. *Bombing to Win: Air Power and Coercion in War.* Ithaca, N.Y.: Cornell University Press, 1996.

Phillipson, C. *Termination of War and Treaties of Peace.* London: T. F. Unwin, 1916.

Pillar, Paul R. *Negotiating Peace: War Termination as a Bargaining Process.* Princeton: Princeton University Press, 1983.

Przeworski, Adam. *Democracy and the Market.* New York: Cambridge University Press, 1991.

Putnam, Robert. "Diplomacy and Domestic Politics: The Logic of Two-Level Games." *International Organization* 42 (1988): 427–60.

Quester, George H. "War Prolonged by Misunderstood Signals." In "How Wars End," special issue of *Annals of the American Academy of Political and Social Science* 392 (November 1970): 30–39.

Randle, Robert F. "The Domestic Origins of Peace." In "How Wars End," special issue of *Annals of the American Academy of Political and Social Science* 392 (November 1970): 76–85.

Randle, Robert F. *The Origins of Peace.* New York: Free Press, 1973.

Reiter, D. "Military Strategy and the Outbreak of International Conflict." *Journal of Conflict Resolution* 43, no. 3 (June 1999): 366–87.

Reiter, D., and Curtis Meek. "Determinants of Military Strategy." *International Studies Quarterly* 43 (1999): 363–87.

Reiter, D., and Allan Stam III. "Democracy and Battlefield Military Effectiveness." *Journal of Conflict Resolution* 42, no. 3 (June 1998): 259–77.

Richardson, Lewis F. *Statistics of Deadly Quarrels.* Pittsburgh: Boxwood Press, 1960.

Richardson, Lewis F. "War Moods." Part 1, *Psychometrika* 13, no. 3 (September 1948): 147–74; part 2, *Psychometrika* 13, no. 4 (December 1948): 197–232.

Rosen, Stephen. "War Power and the Willingness to Suffer." In Bruce Russett, ed., *War, Peace, and Numbers.* Beverly Hills, Calif.: Sage, 1972.

Rotberg, Robert I., and Thoedore K. Rabb, eds. *The Origin and Prevention of Major Wars.* New York: Cambridge University Press, 1989.

Rothstein, Robert. "Domestic Politics and Peacemaking: Reconciling Incompatible Imperatives." In "How Wars End," special issue of *Annals of the American Academy of Political and Social Science* 392 (November 1970): 62–75.

Russett, Bruce. *Grasping the Democratic Peace: Principles for a Post–Cold War.* Princeton: Princeton University Press, 1993.

Russett, Bruce. "Pearl Harbor: Deterrence Theory and Decision Theory." *Journal of Peace Research* 4 (1967).

Russett, Bruce, ed. *War, Peace, and Numbers.* Beverly Hills, Calif.: Sage, 1972.

Sagan, Scott D. "Origins of the Pacific War." In Robert I. Rotberg and Theodore K. Rabb, eds., *The Origin and Prevention of Major Wars,* pp. 323–52. New York: Cambridge University Press, 1989.

Schelling, Thomas C. *Arms and Influence.* New Haven, Conn.: Yale University Press, 1966.

Schelling, Thomas C. *The Strategy of Conflict.* Cambridge, Mass.: Harvard University Press, 1960.

Schultz, Kenneth A. "Do Democratic Institutions Constrain or Inform? Contrasting Two Institutional Perspectives on Democracy and War." *International Organization* 52, no. 2 (spring 1999): 233–66.

Schultz, Kenneth A. "Looking in Black Boxes: Democracy and Bargaining in International Crises." Unpublished manuscript, Princeton University, spring 1999.

Schumpeter, Joseph A. *Capitalism, Socialism, and Democracy.* 2d ed. New York: Harper, 1947.

Seabury, Paul, and Angelo Codevilla. *War: Ends & Means.* New York: Basic Books, 1989; paperback ed. 1990.

Shillony, Ben-Ami. "The Japanese Experience." In Nissan Oren, ed., *Termination of War: Processes, Procedures and Aftermaths,* pp. 91–103. Jerusalem: Magnes Press, 1982.

Shirer, William L. *The Rise and Fall of the Third Reich.* New York: Simon and Schuster, 1960.

Sigal, Leon V. *Fighting to a Finish: The Politics of War Termination in the United States and Japan, 1945.* Ithaca, N.Y.: Cornell University Press, 1988.

Signorino, Curtis S. "Strategic Interaction and the Statistical Analysis of International Conflict." *American Political Science Review* 93, no. 2 (June 1999): 279–97.

Skocpol, Theda. *States and Social Revolutions: A Comparative Analysis of France, Russia and China.* Cambridge: Cambridge University Press, 1979.

Smith, Alastair. "Testing Theories of Strategic Choice: The Example of Crisis Escalation." Manuscript, Washington University, St. Louis, January 1998.

Smith, D. S., ed., with the assistance of Robert F. Randle. *From War to Peace: Essays in Peacemaking and War Termination*. The International Fellows Program Policy Series. New York: Columbia University, 1974.

Snyder, Jack. *Myths of Empire: Domestic Politics and International Ambition*. Ithaca, N.Y.: Cornell University Press, 1991.

Stam, Allan C., III. *Win, Lose, or Draw: Domestic Politics and the Crucible of War*. Ann Arbor: University of Michigan Press, 1996.

Staudenmaier, William O. "Conflict Termination in the Nuclear Era." In Stephen J. Cimbala and Keith A. Dunn, eds., *Conflict Termination and Military Strategy: Coercion, Persuasion and War*, pp. 15–32. Boulder, Colo.: Westview Press, 1987.

Stein, Arthur A. *The Nation at War*. Baltimore: Johns Hopkins University Press, 1980.

Stein Arthur A. *War Settlement, State Structures, and National Security Policy*. Center for Studies of Social Change, New School for Social Research, Working Paper Series, no. 60, October 1986.

Stein, Arthur A., and Bruce M. Russett. "Evaluating War: Outcomes and Consequences." In Ted Robert Gurr, ed., *Handbook of Political Conflict, Theory and Research*, pp. 399–422. New York: Free Press, 1980.

Stein, Janice Gross. "The Termination of the October War: A Reappraisal." In Nissan Oren, ed., *Termination of Wars: Processes, Procedures and Aftermaths*, pp. 226–45. Jerusalem: Magnes Press, 1982.

Stein, Janice Gross. "War Termination and Conflict Resolution." *International Law* 2: *The Law of Armed Conflict*. London, 1968.

Stein, Janice Gross. "War Termination and Conflict Reduction or How Wars Should End." *Jerusalem Journal of International Relations* 1 (fall 1975): 1–27.

Strachan, Hugh. *European Armies and the Conduct of War*. London: Unwin Hyman, 1983.

Taylor, A. J. P. *How Wars End*. London: Hamish Hamilton, 1985.

Thies, Wallace J. "Searching for Peace: Vietnam and the Question of How Wars End." *Polity* 7 (spring 1975): 304–33.

Tilly, Charles. *European Revolutions, 1492–1992*. Oxford: Blackwell, 1993.

Timasheff, Nicolas S. *War and Revolution*. New York: Sheed and Ward, 1965.

Trask, David F. *The United States in the Supreme War Council: American War Aims and Inter-Allied Strategy, 1917–1918*. Middletown, Conn.: Wesleyan University Press, 1961.

Truman, Harry S. *Memoirs of Harry S. Truman. Vol. 1: Years of Decisions*. New York: Da Capo Press, 1955.

Tsebelis, George. *Nested Games*. Berkeley: University of California Press, 1990.

Tullock, Gordon. *Autocracy*. Boston: Kluwer, 1987.

Van Evera, Stephen. "Why States Believe Foolish Ideas: Non-Self-evaluation by Government and Society." Paper presented at the annual meeting of the American Political Science Association, Washington, D.C., September 1988.

Wagner, R. Harrison. "Bargaining and War." Paper presented at the Annual APSA convention, September 1998, Boston.

Wagner, R. Harrison. "The Causes of Peace." In Roy Licklider, ed., *Stopping the Killing*, pp. 235–68. New York: New York University Press, 1993.

Wagner, R. Harrison. "Peace, War, and the Balance of Power." *American Political Science Review* 88, no. 3 (September 1994): 593–607.

Walt, Stephen M. *The Origins of Alliances*. Ithaca, N.Y.: Cornell University Press, 1987.

Walter, Barbara F. "The Critical Barrier to Civil War Settlement." *International Organization* 51, no. 3 (summer 1997): 335–64.

Walter, Barbara. "The Resolution of Civil Wars: Why Negotiations Fail." Ph.D. dissertation, University of Chicago, 1994.

Waltz, Kenneth N. "Electoral Punishment and Foreign Policy Crises." In James N. Rosenau, ed., *Domestic Sources of Foreign Policy*. London: Free Press, 1967.

Weede, E. *Weltpolitik und Kriegsursachen in 20 Jahrhundert*. Munich: Oldenburg Verlag, 1975.

Wittman, Donald. "How War Ends: A Rational Model Approach." *Journal of Conflict Resolution* 23, no. 4 (December 1979): 743–63.

2. QUANTITATIVE ANALYSIS

Country Studies/Area Handbooks. Washington, D.C.: Foreign Area Studies, American University.

Gurr, Ted R., K. Jaggers, and W. H. Moore. *The POLITY II Codebook*. University of Colorado at Boulder, Center for Comparative Politics, 1989.

Gurr, Ted R., K. Jaggers, and W. H. Moore. *POLITY II: Political Structures and Regime Change, 1800–1986*. ICPSR 9263. Ann Arbor, Mich.: Inter-university Consortium for Political and Social Research, 1990.

Gurr, Ted R., K. Jaggers, and W. H. Moore. "The Transformation of the Western State: The Growth of Democracy, Autocracy and State Power Since 1800." *Studies in Comparative International Development* 25, no. 1 (spring 1990): 73–108.

Jaggers, K., and Ted R. Gurr. *POLITY III: Regime Change and Political Authority, 1800–1994*. Ann Arbor, Mich.: Inter-university Consortium for Political and Social Research, 1996.

Jaggers, K., and Ted R. Gurr. "Transitions to Democracy: Tracking Democracy's Third Wave with the POLITY III Data." *Journal of Peace Research* 32 (November 1995): 469–82.

Legg, Keith R. *Politics in Modern Greece*. Stanford: Stanford University Press, 1969.

Mansfield, Edward D., and Jack Snyder. "Democratization and the Danger of War." *International Security* 20, no. 1 (summer 1995): 5–38.

Plessis, Alain. *The Rise and Fall of the Second Empire, 1852–1871*. Translated by Jonathan Mandelbaum. New York: Cambridge University Press, 1985.

Russett, Bruce. *Grasping the Democratic Peace*. Princeton: Princeton University Press, 1993.

Seton-Watson, Hugh. *Eastern Europe between the Wars: 1918–1941*. Boulder, Colo.: Westview Press, 1982.

Small, Melvin, and J. David Singer. *Resort to Arms*. Beverly Hills: Sage, 1982.

Small, Melvin, and J. David Singer. *Wages of War, 1816–1980: Augmented with Disputes and Civil War Data.* ICPSR 9044. Ann Arbor, Mich.: Inter-university Consortium for Political and Social Research.

Spuler, Bertold. *Rulers and Governments of the World.* London: Bowker, 1977 (also listed under authorship of Martha Ross).

Werner, Suzanne. "Absolute and Limited War: The Possibility of Foreign-Imposed Regime Change." *International Interactions* 22, no. 1 (1996): 67–88.

Werner, Suzanne. "Negotiating the Terms of Settlement: War Aims and Bargaining Leverage." *Journal of Conflict Resolution* 42, no. 3 (June 1998): 321–43.

3. THE FIRST WORLD WAR

Abrash, Merrit. "War Aims toward Austria-Hungary." In Alexander Dallin, ed., *Russian Diplomacy and Eastern Europe 1914–1917*, pp. 78–123. New York: King's Crown Press, 1963.

Acton, Edward. *Rethinking the Russian Revolution.* London: Edward Arnold, 1990.

Adams, R. J. *The Great War, 1914–1918: Essays on the Military, Political and Social History of the First World War.* College Station: Texas A&M University Press, 1990.

Alexinsky, Gregor. *Russia and the Great War.* London: T. Fisher Unwin, 1915.

Andrew, C. M., and A. S. Kanya-Forstner. *France Overseas: The Great War and the Climax of French Imperial Expansion.* London: Thames and Hudson, 1981.

Asprey, Robert B. *The German High Command at War: Hindenburg and Ludendorff Conduct World War I.* New York: William Morrow, 1991.

Audoin-Rouzeau, Stephane. *Men at War, 1914–1918: National Sentiment and Trench Journalism in France during the First World War.* Oxford: Berg, 1992.

Bailey, Stephen. "Erich Ludendorff as Quartermaster General of the German Army 1916–1918." Ph.D. dissertation, University of Chicago, 1966.

Basily, Nicholas de. *The Abdication of Emperor Nicholas II of Russia.* Princeton: Kingston Press, 1984.

Basler, Werner. *Deutschlands Annexionspolitik in Polen und im Baltikum 1914–1918.* Berlin: Rütten & Löning, 1962.

Bauer, Oberst Max. *Der grosse Krieg in Feld und Heimat: Erinnerungen und Betrachtungen.* Tübingen: Osiander'sche Buchhandlungen, 1922.

Becker, Jean-Jacques. *1914: Comment les Français sont entrés dans la Guerre.* Paris: Presses de la Fondation nationale des Sciences Politiques, 1977.

Becker, Jean-Jacques. *Les Français dans la Grande Guerre.* Paris: R. Laffont, 1980.

Becker, Jean-Jacques. *La France en guerre, 1914–1918: la grande mutation.* Paris: éditions Complexe, 1988.

Berger, M., and P. Allard. *Les Secrèts de la censure pendant la Guerre.* Paris: éditions des Portigues, 1932.

Bethmann Hollweg, Theobald von. *Betrachtungen zum Weltkriege. Erster Teil: Vor dem Kriege. Zweiter Teil: Während des Krieges.* Edited by Jost Dülffer. Essen: Reimar Hobbing, 1989.

Bethmann Hollweg, Theobald von. *Betrachtungen zum Weltkriege. Zweiter Teil: Während des Krieges.* Berlin: Reimar Hobbing, 1921.

Birnbaum, Karl-E. *Peace Moves and U-boat Warfare: A Study of Imperial Germany's Policy towards the United States April 18, 1916–January 9, 1917.* Stockholm: Almqvist & Wiksell, 1958.

Blackbourn, David. *Populists and Patricians.* London: Allen & Unwin, 1987.

Blake, Robert, ed. *The Private Papers of Douglas Haig 1914–1919.* London: Eyre & Spottiswoode, 1952.

Bliss, Tasker H. "The Armistices." *American Journal of International Law* 16 (1922): 509–22.

Bobroff, Ronald. "Sazonov's Mazurka: Sergei D. Sazonov and the Question of Polish Autonomy, 1910–1916." Unpublished paper, Duke University, Department of History, 1998.

Bonnefous, Georges. *Histoire Politique de la Troisième République.* 8 vols. *Vol. 2: La Grande Guerre 1914–1918.* 2d ed. Paris: Presses Universitaires de France, 1967.

Bourne, J. M. *Britain and the Great War, 1914–1918.* New York: Routledge, Chapman and Hall, 1989.

Braun, Otto. *Von Weimar zu Hitler.* New York: Europa Verlag, 1940.

Bunselmayer, Robert E. *The Cost of the War, 1914–1919: British Economic War Aims and the Origins of Reparation.* Hamden, Conn.: Archon Books, 1975.

Burgwyn, H. James. *The Legend of the Mutilated Victory; Italy, the Great War and the Paris Peace Conference, 1915–1919.* Westport, Conn.: Greenwood Press, 1993.

Burk, Kathleen. *War and the State: The Transformation of British Government 1914–1919.* London: Allen & Unwin, 1982.

Calder, K. J. *Britain and the Origins of the New Europe, 1914–1918.* Cambridge: Cambridge University Press, 1976.

Cambon, Paul. *Correspondance 1870–1924.* 3 vols. *Vol. 3: Les Guerres Balkaniques, La Grande Guerre, l'Organisation de la Paix.* Paris: Grasset, 1946.

Carnegie Endowment for International Peace. *Preliminary History of the Armistice* (official documents published by the German Reichskanzlei). New York: Oxford University Press, 1924.

The Case of the Allies, Being the Replies to President Wilson and Mr. Balfour's Despatch. London: Hayman, Christy & Lilly, 1917.

Cassar, George H. *Asquith as War Leader.* London: Hambledon Press, 1994.

Charteris, J. *Field Marshall Earl Haig.* London: Cassell, 1929.

Cherniavsky, Michael. *Prologue to Revolution: Notes of A. N. Iakhontov on the Secret Meetings of the Council of Ministers, 1915.* Englewood Cliffs, N.J.: Prentice Hall, 1967.

Christian, David. *Imperial and Soviet Russia.* New York: St. Martin's Press, 1997.

Churchill, Winston S. *The World Crisis, 1911–1918.* 2 vols. New York: Barnes & Noble, 1993.

Civrieux, Commandant de. *L'Offensive de 1917 et le commandement de la guerre.* Paris: Payot & Cie., 1919.

Clayton, Anthony. "Robert Nivelle and the French Spring Offensive, 1917." In Brian Bond, ed., *Fallen Stars,* pp. 52–64. New York: Brassey's, 1991.

Cline, Peter. "Winding Down the War Economy: British Plans for Peacetime Recovery, 1916–1919." In Kathleen Burk, ed., *War and the State: The Transformation of British Government, 1914–1919*, pp. 157–81. Boston: Allen & Unwin, 1982

Coffman, Edward M. "The American Military and Strategic Policy in World War I." In Barry Hunt, and Adrian Preston, eds., *War Aims and Strategic Policy in the Great War*, pp. 67–84. London: Croom Helm, 1977.

Coffman, Edward M. *The War to End All Wars*. New York: Oxford University Press, 1968.

Les Conditions de paix et le sentiment national français. Paris, 1919.

Craig, Gordon A. *Germany 1866–1945*. New York: Oxford University Press, 1978.

Crutwell, Charles R. M. F. *History of the Great War, 1914–1918*. Oxford: Oxford University Press, 1936.

Czernin, Count Ottokar. *In the World War*. New York: Cassell, 1919.

Daalder, Hans. *Cabinet Reform in Britain 1914–1963*. Stanford, Calif.: Stanford University Press, 1963.

Dahlin, Ebba. *French and German Public Opinion on Declared War Aims, 1914–1918*. Stanford University Publications, University Series History, Economics, and Political Science, vol. 4, no. 2. pp. 193–356. Stanford, Calif.: Stanford University Press, 1933.

Dallin, Alexander. "The Future of Poland." In Alexander Dallin, ed., *Russian Diplomacy and Eastern Europe 1914–1917*, pp. 1–77. New York: King's Crown Press, 1963.

Dallin, Alexander, ed. *Russian Diplomacy and Eastern Europe 1914–1917*. New York: King's Crown Press, 1963.

Dangerfield, George. *The Strange Death of Liberal England 1910–1914*. New York: G. P. Putnam's Sons, 1935.

Daniels, Robert V. *Red October: The Bolshevik Revolution of 1917*. New York: Charles Scribner's Sons, 1967.

Daniloff, Jurij. *Grossfürst Nikolai Nikolajewitsch: Sein Leben und Wirken*. Berlin: Richard Schröder, 1930.

Degras, J., ed. *Soviet Documents on Foreign Policy*. 3 vols. London: Oxford University Press, 1951–53.

Deist, Wilhelm, ed. *Militär und Innenpolitik im Weltkrieg 1914–1918*. 2 vols. *Quellen zur Geschichte des Parlamentarismus und der Politischen Parteien*, 2d series, *Militär und Politik*, edited by Erich Matthias and Hans Meier-Welcker. Düsseldorf: Droste Verlag, 1970.

Deist, Wilhelm. "The Road to Ideological War: Germany, 1918–1945." In Williamson Murray, Macgregor Knox, Alvin Bernstein, eds., pp. 352–92. *The Making of Strategy: Rulers, States, and War*. New York: Cambridge University Press, 1994.

Deutsche Nationalversammlung. 1919–20. Untersuchungsausschuss über die Weltkriegsverantwortlichkeit [Parliamentary Committee on Responsibility for the World War]. *Stenographische Berichte über die öffentlichen Verhandlungen des 15. Untersuchungssausschusses nebst Beilagen*. Berlin, 1920.

Deutschland im Ersten Weltkrieg. 2 vols. Vol. 1 edited by Fritz Klein et al. Vol. 2 edited by Willibald Gutsche et al. Berlin: Akademie Verlag, 1968.

Direnberger, Erwin. "Die Beziehungen zwischen Oberster Heeresleitung und Reichsleitung von 1914–18." Inaugural-dissertation Julius-Maximilian-Universität zu Würzburg, Berlin: Junker und Dünnhaupt Verlag, 1936.

Documents and Statements Relating to Peace Proposals and War Aims (December 1916–November 1918. London: Allen & Unwin, 1919.

Droz, Jacques. "Die Politischen Kräfte in Frankreich während des Ersten Weltkrieges." *Geschichte in Wissenschaft und Unterricht* 17, no. 3 (March 1966): 159–68 (translated by Kurt Jürgensen).

Duff Cooper, A. *Haig.* 2 vols. London: Faber, 1935.

Dupuy, R. Ernest, and Trevor N. Dupuy. *The Encyclopedia of Military History from 3500 B.C. to the Present.* Rev. ed. New York: Harper & Row, 1977.

Duroselle, J.-B. *La Politique exterieure de la France de 1914 à 1945.* 3 vols. Paris: Centre de Documentation Universitaire, 1965.

Duroselle, Jean-Baptiste. *La Grande Guerre des Français 1914–1918.* Paris: Perrin, 1994.

Dutton, D. J. "The Balkan Campaign and French War Aims in the Great War." *English Historical Review* 94, no. 370 (January 1979): 97–113.

Ekstein, Michael. "Sir Edward Grey and Imperial Germany in 1914." *Journal of Contemporary History* 6, no. 3 (1971): 121–63.

Epstein, Klaus W. "Development of German-Austrian War Aims in the Spring of 1917." *Journal of Central European Affairs* (April 1957): 24–47.

Esposito, David M. *The Legacy of Woodrow Wilson: American War Aims in World War I.* Westport, Conn: Praeger, 1996.

Falkenhayn, Erich von. *General Headquarters and Its Critical Decisions 1914–1916.* London: Hutchinson & Co., 1919.

Falls, Cyril. *History of the Great War: Military Operations, France and Belgium, 1917.* London: Macmillan and Co., 1940.

Farrar, L. L. *Divide and Conquer: German Efforts to Conclude a Separate Peace 1914–1918.* New York: Columbia University Press, 1978.

Farrar, L. L. "Opening to the West: German Efforts to Conclude a Separate Peace with England, July 1917–March 1918." *Canadian Journal of History* 10, no. 1 (1975).

Farrar, L. L. *The Short-War Illusion: German Policy, Strategy, and Domestic Affairs, August–December 1914.* Santa Barbara, Calif.: Clio Press, 1973.

Feldman, Gerald. *Army, Industry and Labor in Germany 1914–1918.* Princeton: Princeton University Press, 1966.

Ferro, Marc. *The Russian Revolution of February 1917.* Englewood Cliffs, N.J.: Prentice Hall, 1972.

Fest, W. B. "British War Aims and German Peace Feelers during the First World War (December 1916–November 1918)." *Historical Journal* 15, no. 2 (1972).

Fischer, Fritz. *Germany's Aims in the First World War.* New York: W. W. Norton, 1967.

Fischer, Fritz. *Griff nach der Weltmacht: Die Kriegszielpolitik des kaiserlichen Deutschland 1914/18.* Düsseldorf: Droste Verlag, 1961.

Foch, Marshal J.-J. *The Memoirs of Marshal Foch.* Translated by Col. T. Bentley Mott. Garden City, N.Y.: Doubleday, Doran and Company, 1931.

Foreign Relations of the United States, 1918. Supplement 1: *The World War.* Vol. 1. Washington: U.S. Government Printing Office, 1932.

Foreign Relations of the United States, 1917. Supplement 2: *The World War.* Vol. 1. Washington: U.S. Government Printing Office, 1932.

Forster, Kent. *The Failures of Peace: The Search for a Negotiated Peace during the First World War.* Washington, D.C.: American Council on Public Affairs, 1941.

Frankel, Edith Rogovin, Jonathan Frankel, and Baruch Knei-Paz, eds. *Revolution in Russia: Reassessments of 1917.* Cambridge: Cambridge University Press, 1991.

Fraser, Hugh. *The Representation of the People Acts, 1918 to 1921.* 2d ed. London: Sweet and Maxwell, 1922.

French, David. "Allies, Rivals and Enemies: British Strategy and War Aims during the First World War." In John Turner, ed., *Britain and the First World War.* Boston: Unwin Hyman, 1988.

French, David. *British Strategy and War Aims, 1914–1916.* London: Allen & Unwin, 1986.

French, David. "The Meaning of Attrition, 1914–1916." *English Historical Review* 103, no. 407 (1988): 385–405.

French, David. *The Strategy of the Lloyd George Coalition, 1916–1918.* Oxford: Clarendon Press, 1995.

The French Socialist Party and War Aims, Replies to the Questionnaire. New York: George H. Doran Co., 1918.

Fridenson, Patrick. *The French Home Front 1914–1918.* Providence: Berg, 1992.

Fuller, J. G. *Troop Morale and Popular Culture in the British and Dominion Armies 1914–1918.* Oxford: Clarendon Press, 1990.

Fuller, William C. *Civil-Military Conflict in Imperial Russia, 1881–1914.* Princeton: Princeton University Press, 1985.

Gatrell, Peter. "The Economy and the War." In Harold Shukman, ed., *The Blackwell Encyclopedia of the Russian Revolution,* pp. 117–22. Oxford: Basil Blackwell, 1988.

Gatzke, Hans Wilhelm. *Germany's Drive to the West: A Study of Germany's Western War Aims during the First World War.* Baltimore: Johns Hopkins University Press, 1966.

Geiss, Imanuel. *Der Polnischen Grenzstreifen, 1914–1918: Ein Beitrag zur deutschen Kriegszielpolitik im Ersten Weltkrieg. Historische Studien,* no. 378. Lübeck: Matthiesen, 1960.

Geiss, Imanuel, ed. *July 1914, the Outbreak of the First World War: Selected Documents.* New York: Charles Scribner's Sons, 1967.

Gelfland, L. E. *The Inquiry: American Preparations for Peace, 1917–1918.* New Haven, Conn.: Yale University Press, 1963.

Germany, Nationalversammlung (1919–20). *Untersuchungsausschuss über die Weltkriegsverantwortlichkeit. Official German Documents Relating to the World War.* Translated under the supervision of the Carnegie Endowment for International Peace, Division of International Law. New York: Oxford University Press, 1923.

Germany, Reichstag. *Untersuchungsausschuss über die Weltkriegsverantwortlichkeit: Die Ursachen des Deutschen Zusammenbruchs im Jahr 1918.* 4th series. 3. vols. Berlin: Deutsche Verlagsgesellschaft für Politik und Geschichte, 1925.

Geyer, Michael. "German Strategy in the Age of Machine Warfare, 1914–1945." In Peter Paret, ed., *Makers of Modern Strategy: From Machiavelli to the Nuclear Age,* pp. 527–97. Princeton: Princeton University Press, 1986.

Gilbert, Felix. *The End of the European Era: 1890 to the Present.* 2d ed. New York: W. W. Norton, 1979.

Gilbert, Martin. *The First World War: A Complete History.* New York: Henry Holt, 1994.

Gleichen, Edward, ed. *Chronology of the Great War.* Novato, Calif.: Presidio Press, 1988.

Goldstein, Erik. *Winning the Peace: British Diplomatic Strategy, Peace Planning, and the Paris Peace Conference, 1916–1920.* Oxford: Clarendon Press, 1991.

Gooch, John. *The Plans of War: The General Staff and British Military Strategy c.1900–1916.* New York: Halsted Press, 1974.

Gooch, John. "Soldiers, Strategy and War Aims in Britain 1914–1918." In Barry Hunt and Adrian Preston, eds., *War Aims and Strategic Policy in the Great War 1914–1918,* pp. 21–40. London: Croom Helm, 1977.

Gooch, R. K. *The French Parliamentary Committee System.* London: Appleton-Century, 1935.

Gourko, Basil. *War and Revolution in Russia 1914–1917.* New York: Macmillan, 1919.

Graf, Daniel. "Military Rule behind the Russian Front, 1914–1917: The Political Ramifications." *Jahrbücher für Geschichte Osteuropas* 22, no. 3 (1974): 881–912.

Gray, Randall, with Christopher Argule. *Chronicle of the First World War: A Chronology of the First World War.* 2 vols. New York: Facts on File, 1990.

Grey of Fallodon, Viscount Edward Grey. *Twenty-five Years, 1892–1916.* 2 vols. New York: Frederick A. Stokes, 1925.

Groener, Wilhelm. *Der Feldherr wider Willen: Operative Studien über den Weltkrieg.* 3d ed. Berlin: L. S. Mittler & Sohn, 1931.

Groener, Wilhelm. *Lebenserinnerungen.* Göttingen: Vandenhoeck & Ruprecht, 1957.

Groener, Wilhelm. *Das Testament des Grafen Schlieffen.* 2d ed. Berlin: L.S. Mittler & Sohn, 1929.

Guinn, Paul. *British Strategy and Politics, 1914 to 1918.* Oxford: Clarendon Press, 1965.

Hahlweg, Werner. "Das hinterlassene Werk des Parlamentarischen Untersuchungsausschusses." In Rudolph Vierhaus and Manfred Botzenhart, eds., *Dauer und Wandel der Geschichte: Aspekte Europäischer Vergangenheit: Festgabe für Kurt von Raumer zum 15. Dezember 1965.* Münster: Asschendorff, 1966.

Haimson, Leopold. "The Problem of Social Stability in Urban Russia, 1905–1917." 2 parts. Part 1, *Slavic Review* 13, no. 4 (December 1964): 619–42; part 2, *Slavic Review* 14, no. 1 (March 1965): 1–22; "Reply," ibid, pp. 47–56.

Hankey, Maurice. *The Supreme Command 1914–1918.* 2 vols. London: Allen & Unwin, 1961.

Hanssen, Hans Peter. *Diary of a Dying Empire*. Edited by Ralph H. Lutz, Mary Schofield, and O. O. Winther. Translated by Oscar Osburn Winther. Bloomington: Indiana University Press, 1955.

Hardach, Gerd. *The First World War, 1914–18*. Berkeley: University of California Press, 1977.

Heinemann, Ulrich. *Die Verdringte Niederlage: Politische öffentlichkeit und Kriegsschuldfrage in der Weimarer Republik*. Göttingen: Vandehoeck & Ruprecht, 1983.

Herman, Gerald. *The Pivotal Conflict: A Comprehensive Chronology of the First World War, 1914–1919*. New York: Greenwood Press, 1992.

Herrmann, David G. *The Arming of Europe and the Making of the First World War*. Princeton: Princeton University Press, 1996.

Herwig, Holger. "Clio Deceived, Patriotic Self-Censorship in Germany after the Great War." In Steven E. Miller, Sean M. Lynn-Jones, and Stephen Van Evera, eds., *Military Strategy and the Origins of the First World War*, pp. 262–301. Princeton: Princeton University Press, 1991.

Horak, Stephan M. *The First Treaty of WW I: Ukraine's Treaty with the Central Powers of February 9, 1918*. Boulder, Colo.: East European Monographs, 1988.

Horne, Alistair. *The Price of Glory: Verdun 1916*. Abridged edition. New York: Penguin Books, 1964.

Horne, Charles F., ed. *Source Records of the Great War*. Indianapolis: American Legion, 1930.

Hosking, Geoffrey A. *The Russian Constitutional Experiment: Government and Duma, 1907–1914*. New York: Cambridge University Press, 1973.

House of Commons: The Parliamentary Debates. 5th series, vols. 80 and 93. London: Wyman and Sons, no date.

Houston, David F. *Eight Years with Wilson's Cabinet*. 2 vols. New York: Doubleday, Page, 1926.

Huard, Raymond. *Le Suffrage universel en France (1848–1946)*. Lonrai: Aubier, 1991.

Huber, Ernst Rudolf. *Deutsche Verfassungsgeschichte seit 1789. Vol. 5: Weltkrieg, Revolution und Reichserneuerung 1914–1919*. Stuttgart: Verlag W. Kohlhammer, 1978.

Hunt, B., and A. Preston, eds. *War Aims and Strategic Policy in the Great War*. London: Croom Helm, 1977.

Jaffe, Lorna Sue. "British Policy towards Postwar German Disarmament, 1914–1919." Ph.D. dissertation, Yale University, 1982.

Jaffe, Lorna Sue. *The Decision to Disarm Germany*. Boston: Allen & Unwin, 1985.

Janssen, Karl-Heinz. *Der Kanzler und der General: Die Führungskrise um Bethmann Hollweg und Falkenhayn 1914–1916*. Göttingen: Musherschmidt, 1967.

Janssen, Karl-Heinz. *Macht und Verblendung: Kriegszielpolitik der deutschen Bundesstaaten 1914/18*. Göttingen: Musterschmidt Verlag, 1963.

Joffre, J.-J. C. *Journal de marche de Joffre, 1916–1919*. Chateau de Vincennes: Service Historique de l'Armée de Terre, 1990.

Joffre, J.-J. C. *Mémoires*. 2 vols. Paris: Librairie Plon, 1932.

Joffre, J.-J. C. *The Memoirs of Marshall Joffre*. Translated by T. Bentley Mott. London: Geoffrey Bles, 1932.

Johnson, Douglas. "French War Aims and the Crisis of the Third Republic." In Barry Hunt and Adrian Preston, eds., *War Aims and Strategic Policy in the Great War, 1914–1918*, pp. 41–54. London: Croom Helm, 1977.

Journal officiel de la République française: Debats parlementaires: Chambre des députés/Sénat. 1914–19.

Journal officiel de la République française. Chambre des députés, 16 May 1925. Comité secrèt of 1 June 1917, pp. 495ff.

Journal officiel de la République française. Chambre des députés, 2 April 1933. Comité secrèt of 16 October 1917, pp. 545ff.

Journal officiel de la République française. Sénat, 29 September 1968. Comité secrèt of 6 June 1917, pp. 764ff.

Kielmansegg, Peter Graf. *Deutschland und der Erste Weltkrieg.* 2d ed. Stuttgart: Klett-Cotta, 1980.

King, Jere Clemens. *Generals and Politicians: Conflict between France's High Command, Parliament and Government, 1914–18.* Berkeley: University of California Press, 1951.

Klein, Fritz, et al. *Deutschland im Ersten Weltkrieg.* 2 vols. Edited by "einem Kollektiv marxistischer Historiker der DDR." Berlin: Akademie Verlag, 1968. (Note: Vol. 2 is by Gutsche et al.).

Knesebeck, Ludolf Gottschalk von dem. *Die Wahrheit über den Propagandafeldzug und Deutschlands Zusammenbruch: Der Kampf der Publizistik im Weltkriege.* Berlin: Dr. von dem Knesebeck, 1927.

Knightley, Phillip. *The First Casualty.* New York: Harcourt Brace Jovanovich, 1976.

Knox, Alfred. *With the Russian Army 1914–1917: Being Chiefly Extracts from the Diary of a Military Attaché.* 2 vols. London: Hutchinson, 1921.

Koenker, Diane P., and William G. Rosenberg. "Strikers in Revolution: Russia, 1917." In Leopold H. Haimson and Charles Tilly, eds., *Strikes, Wars, and Revolutions in International Perspective: Strike Waves in the Late Nineteenth and Early Twentieth Centuries*, pp. 167–96. Cambridge: Cambridge University Press, 1989.

Koenker, Diane P., and William G. Rosenberg. *Strikes and Revolution in Russia, 1917.* Princeton: Princeton University Press, 1989.

Kousser, J. Morgan. *The Shaping of Southern Politics Suffrage Restriction and the Establishment of the One-Party South, 1880–1910.* New Haven, Conn.: Yale University Press, 1974.

Kuhl, Hermann von. *Der Weltkrieg 1914–1918.* 2 vols. Berlin: Verlag Tradition Wilhelm Kolf, 1929.

Lafeber, Cornalis Victor. *Vredes- en bemiddelingspogingen uit het eerste jaar van wereldoorlog: I. August 1914–December 1915.* Leiden: Universitaire Pers Leiden, 1961.

Lasswell, H. D. *Propaganda Technique in the World War.* London: Kegan Paul, 1927.

Laue, Theodore H. von. "The Chances for Liberal Constitutionalism." *Slavic Review* 14, no. 1 (March 1965): 34–46.

Lauren, Paul Gordon. *Diplomats and Bureaucrats: The First Institutionalist Response to Twentieth Century Diplomacy in France and Germany.* Stanford: Hoover Institution Press, 1976.

Le May, G. H. L. *The Victorian Constitution: Conventions, Usages and Contingencies.* New York: St. Martin's Press, 1979.

Lennox, A. G., ed. *The Diary of Lord Bertie of Thame 1914–1918.* 2 vols. New York: George H. Doran, 1924.

Lhopital, Commandant. *Foch, L'armistice et la paix.* Paris: Plon, 1938.

Liddell Hart, B. H. *The Real War 1914–1918.* Boston: Little, Brown, 1930; re-issued 1964.

Lieven, Dominic. *Nicholas II: Twilight of the Empire.* New York: St. Martin's Press, 1993.

Lieven, Dominic. *Russia and the Origins of the First World War.* New York: St. Martin's Press, 1983.

Lieven, Dominic. *Russia's Rulers under the Old Regime.* New Haven, Conn.: Yale University Press, 1989.

Linke, Horst Günther. *Das zarische Russland und der Erste Weltkrieg: Diplomatie und Kriegsziele 1914–1917.* Munich: W. Fink, 1982.

Livesey, Anthony. *The Historical Atlas of World War I.* New York: Henry Holt, 1994.

Lloyd, T. O. *Empire to Welfare State English History 1906–1985.* 3d ed. New York: Oxford University Press, 1986.

Lloyd George, David. *War Memoirs of David Lloyd George.* 6 vols. London: Nicholson & Watson, 1933–36.

Longley, D. A. "Iakovlev's Question, or the Historiography of the Problem of Spontaneity and Leadership in the Russian Revolution of February 1917." In Edith Rogovin Frankel, Jonathan Frankel, and Baruch Knei-Paz, eds., *Revolution in Russia: Reassessments of 1917.* Cambridge: Cambridge University Press, 1991.

Louis, W. R. *Great Britain and Germany's Lost Colonies, 1914–1919.* Oxford: Clarendon Press, 1967.

Lowry, Bullit. "Pershing and the Armistice." *Journal of American History* 55 (1968–69): 281–91.

Ludendorff, Erich. *The General Staff and Its Problems: The History of the Relations between the High Command and the German Imperial Government as Revealed by Official Documents.* Translated by F. A. Holt. 2 vols. London: Hutchinson, 1920.

Ludendorff, Erich. *Kriegsführung und Politik.* Berlin: Mittler und Sohn, 1922.

Ludendorff, Erich. *Meine Kriegserinnerungen 1914–1918.* Berlin: Ernst Siegfried Mittler und Sohn, 1919.

Ludendorff, Erich. *My War Memories.* 2 vols. London: Hutchinson, 1919.

Ludendorff, Erich. *Urkunden der Obersten Heeresleitung über ihre Tätigkeit 1916/18.* 4th ed. Berlin: Mittler & Sohn, 1922.

Lutz, Ralph Haswell, ed. *The Causes of the German Collapse in 1918.* Translated by W. L. Campbell. Hoover War Library Publications no. 4. Stanford, Calif.: Stanford University Press, 1934.

Lytton, Neville. *The Press and the General Staff.* London: Collins, 1921.

MacKenzie, David. *A History of the Soviet Union.* Chicago: Dorsey Press, 1986.

Mai, Gunther. *Das Ende des Kaiserreiches: Politik und Kriegsführung im Ersten Weltkrieg.* Munich: Deutscher Taschenbuch Verlag, 1987.

Maitland, F. W. *Constitutional History of England.* Cambridge: Cambridge University Press, 1908.

The "Manchester Guardian" History of the War. Vol. 8: *1917–19.* London: John Heywood Publishers, 1919.

Manteyer, G. de. *Austria's Peace Offer, 1916–1917.* London: Constable, 1921.

Marhefka, Edmund, ed. *Der Waffenstillstand 1918–1919.* 3 vols. Berlin: Deutsche Verlagsgesellschaft für Politik und Geschichte, 1928.

Massie, Robert K. *Nicholas and Alexandra.* New York: Atheneum, 1967.

Matthew, H. G. C., R. I. McKibbin, and J. A. Kay. "The Franchise Factor in the Rise of the Labour Party." *English Historical Review* 91, no. 361 (1976): 723–52.

Matthias, Erich, and Hans Meier-Welcker, eds. *Quellen zur Geschichte des Parlamentarismus und der politischen Parteien. Zweite Reihe: Militär und Politik. Vol. 1/I (1/II): Militär und Innenpolitik im Weltkrieg 1914–1918.* Ed. Wilhelm Deist. Düsseldorf: Droste Verlag, 1970.

Matthias, Erich, and Rudolf Morsey, eds. *Die Regierung des Prinzen Max von Baden: Quellen zur Geschichte des Parlamentarismus und der politischen Parteien. Erste Reihe: Von der konstitutionellen Monarchie zur parlamentarischen Republik.* Vol. 2. Düsseldorf: Droste Verlag, 1969.

Mayer, Arno J. *Political Origins of the New Diplomacy, 1917–1918.* New Haven, Conn.: Yale University Press, 1959.

McDougall, Walter A. *France's Rhineland Diplomacy, 1914–1924: The Last Bid for a Balance of Power in Europe.* Princeton: Princeton University Press, 1978.

McEntee, Girard Lindsley. *Military History of the World War.* New York: Charles Scribner's Sons, 1937.

Michaelis, Herbert, ed. *Ursachen und Folgen: Vom deutschen Zusammenbruch 1918 und 1945 bis zur staatlichen Neuordnung Deutschlands in der Gegenwart.* Berlin: Wender, 1959.

Miller, Susanne. *Die Regierung der Volksbeauftragten 1918/19: Quellen zur Geschichte des Parlamentarismus und der politischen Parteien. Erste Reihe: Von der konstitutionellen Monarchie zur parlamentarischen Republik.* Vol. 6, no. 1, 1st part. Düsseldorf: Droste Verlag, 1969.

Miller, Susanne, and Ritter, Gerhard, eds. *Die deutsche Revolution 1918–1919: Dokumenten.* Hamburg: Hoffmann und Campe, 1975.

Miquel, Pierre. *La Grande Guerre.* Paris: Fayard, 1983.

Miquel, Pierre. *La Grande Guerre au jour le jour.* Paris: Fayard, 1988.

Miquel, Pierre. *Le Second Empire.* Paris: Plon, 1992.

Miquel, Pierre. *Poincaré.* Paris: Fayard, 1984.

Mueller, John E. *War, Presidents and Public Opinion.* New York: John Wiley & Sons, 1973.

Müller, Georg Alexander von. *Regierte der Kaiser? Kriegstagebücher, Aufzeichnungen und Briefe des Chefs des Marine-Kabinetts Admiral Georg Alexander von Müller 1914–1918.* Göttingen: Musterschmidt Verlag, 1959.

Murray, Williamson, Macgregor Knox, and Alvin Bernstein, eds. *The Making of Strategy: Rulers, States, and War.* New York: Cambridge University Press, 1994.

Neilson, Keith. *Strategy and Supply: The Anglo-Russian Alliance, 1914–17.* London: George Allen & Unwin, 1984.

Nelson, Harold I. *Land and Power: British and Allied Policy on Germany's Frontiers, 1916–19.* London: Routledge & Paul, 1963.

Nicholson, Harold. *Peacemaking 1919.* New York: Grosset & Dunlap, 1965.

Notestein, Wallace, and Elmer E. Stoll, eds. *Conquest and Kultur: Aims of the Germans in Their Own Words.* Washington, D.C.: GPO, 1917.

Oudin, Bernard. *Aristide Briand, La paix: une idée neuve en Europe.* Paris: Robert Laffont, 1987.

Overstraeten, R. van, ed. *The War Diaries of Albert I, King of the Belgians.* London: William Kimber, 1954.

Painlevé, Paul. *Comment j'ai nommé Foch et Pétain: la politique de guerre de 1917, le commandement unique interallié.* Paris: Librarie Felix Alcan, 1924.

Palo, Michael Francis. "The Diplomacy of Belgian War Aims during the First World War." Ph.D. dissertation, University of Illinois at Urbana-Champaign, 1977.

Panichas, G. A., ed. *Promise of Greatness, 1914–18.* London: Cassell, 1968.

Pares, Bernard. *The Fall of the Russian Monarchy.* New York: Vintage Books, 1961.

Pares, Bernard, ed. *Letters of the Tsaritsa to the Tsar 1914–1916.* New York: Academic International, 1970.

Pedroncini, Guy. *La Défense sous la Troisième République: documents.* Paris: Service historique de l'Armée de terre: Institute d'histoire des conflits contemporains, 1984.

Pedroncini, Guy. *Les Mutineries de 1917.* Paris: Presses universitaires de France, 1967.

Pedroncini, Guy. *Les Négociations secrètes pendant la Premiere Guerre mondiale.* Paris, 1960.

Pedroncini, Guy. *Pétain, général en chef (1917–1918).* Paris: Presses Universitaires de France, 1974.

Pedroncini, Guy. *Pétain, le soldat et la gloire.* Paris: Perrin, 1989.

Pedroncini, Guy. "Remarques sur la décision militaire en France pendant la guerre." *Revue d'histoire moderne et contemporaine* 20 (January–March 1973): 139–52.

Pershing, John J. *My Experiences in the World War.* 2 vols. Blue Ridge Summit, Penn.: Tab Books, 1989.

Pétain, Henri-Philippe. "A Crisis of Morale in the French Nation at War." In *History of Western Civilization,* vol. 9, pp. 132–151. Chicago: University of Chicago Press.

Peterson, H. C. *Propaganda for War.* Norman: University of Oklahoma Press, 1939.

Petrovich, Michael Boro. "The Italo-Yugoslav Boundary Question, 1914–1915." In Alexander Dallin, ed., *Russian Diplomacy and Eastern Europe 1914–1917,* pp. 162–93. New York: King's Crown Press, 1963.

Philipp, Albrecht, ed. *Das Werk des Untersuchungsausschusses der Deutschen Verfassunggebenden Nationalversammlung und des Deutschen Reichstages 1919–1926. Vierte Reihe: Die Ursachen des Deutschen Zusammenbruchs im Jahre 1918.* 9 vols. 1925.

Pierrefeu, Jean de. *G.Q.G. Secteur I: trois ans au grand quartier général par le redacteur du "communiqué."* 2 vols. Paris: L Édition françoise illustrée, 1920.

Pierrefeu, Jean de. *Plutarch Lied.* New York: Alfred A. Knopf, 1924.

Pingaud, A. *Histoire diplomatique de la France pendant la Grande Guerre.* 3 vols. Paris: éditions "Alsatia," 1938–40.

Pipes, Richard. "1917 and the Revisionists." *The National Interest,* no. 31 (spring 1993).

Pipes, Richard. *Russia under the Old Regime.* 2d ed. New York: Collier Books, 1992.

Pipes, Richard. *The Russian Revolution.* New York: Alfred A. Knopf, 1990.

Pitt, Barrie. *1918, the Last Act.* London: Cassell, 1962.

Poincaré, R. *Au service de la France: Neuf années de souvenirs.* 10 vols. Paris: Plon, 1926–33; vols. 4–10.

Pokrowski, M. N., ed. *Die Internationalen Beziehungen im Zeitalter des Imperialismus: Dokumente aus den Archiven der Zarischen und der Provisorischen Regierung.* 2d series. 8 vols. Berlin: Reimar Hobbing, 1931–36.

Ponsonby, Arthur. *Falsehood in Wartime.* London: George Allen and Unwin, 1928.

Prete, Roy A. "French Military War Aims, 1914–1916." *Historical Journal* 26, no. 4 (1985): 887–99.

Recouly, Raymond. *The Third Republic.* London: William Heinemann, 1928.

Reiners, Ludwig. *The Lamps Went Out in Europe.* Translated by Richard and Clara Winston. New York: Pantheon Books, 1955.

Renouvin, Pierre. *L'Armistice de Rethondes, 11 Novembre 1918.* Paris: Gallimard, 1968.

Renouvin, Pierre. "Les Buts de guerre des gouvernement français, 1914–1918." *Revue historique* 235 (January–March 1966): 1–38.

Renouvin, Pierre. *The Forms of War Government in France.* New Haven, Conn.: Yale University Press, 1927.

Renouvin, Pierre. "Die Kriegsziele der französischen Regierung 1914 bis 1918." *Geschichte in Wissenschaft und Unterricht* 3 (1966): 129–43.

Renouvin, Pierre. "Les Tentatives de paix en 1917 et le gouvernement français." *Revue des Deux Mondes* 16 (15 October 1964): 492–513.

Ribot, A. *Journal d'Alexandre Ribot et correspondances inédites 1914–1922.* Paris: Plon, 1936.

Ribot, Alexandre. *Lettres à un ami: souvenirs de ma vie politique.* Paris: Editions Bossard, 1924.

Lord Riddell. *Lord Riddell's War Diary 1914–1918.* London: Ivor Nicholson & Watson, 1933.

Rieber, Alfred J. "Russian Diplomacy and Rumania." In Alexander Dallin, ed., *Russian Diplomacy and Eastern Europe 1914–1917.* New York: King's Crown Press, 1963.

Riha, Thomas, ed. *Readings in Russian Civilization. Vol. 2: Imperial Russia, 1700–1917.* 2d ed. Chicago: University of Chicago Press, 1969.

Ritter, Gerhard A. "Die politische Arbeiterbewegung Deutschlands 1863–1914." In *Aus Politik und Zeitgeschichte, Beilage zur Wochenzeitung Das Parlament,* B 21/63, 22 May 1963, pp. 3–26.

Ritter, Gerhard. *Der Schlieffenplan.* Munich: Verlag R. Oldenbourg, 1956.

Ritter, Gerhard. *The Schlieffen Plan: Critique of a Myth.* Westport, Conn.: Greenwood Press, 1979.

Ritter, Gerhard A. *Staatskunst und Kriegshandwerk: Das Problem des "Militarismus" in Deutschland. Vol. 2: Die Hauptmächte Europas und das wilhelminische Reich (1890–1914). Vol. 3: Die Tragödie der Staatskunst. Bethmann Hollweg als Kriegskanzler (1914–1917).* Munich: Oldenbourg, 1960, 1964.

Ritter, Gerhard A. *The Sword and the Scepter: The Problem of Militarism in Germany. Vol. 2: The European Powers and the Wilhelminian Empire, 1890–1914.* Coral Gables, Fla.: University of Miami Press, 1970. *Vol. 3: The Tragedy of Statesmanship — Bethmann Hollweg as War Chancellor (1914–1917).* Coral Gables, Fla.: University of Miami Press, 1972. *Vol. 4: The Reign of German Militarism and the Disaster of 1918.* Coral Gables, Fla.: University of Miami Press, 1973.

Robertson, W. *Soldiers and Statesmen.* 2 vols. London: Cassell, 1926.

Rogger, Hans. "Russia in 1914." In Walter Laqueur and George L. Mosse, eds., *1914: The Coming of the First World War.* New York: Harper & Row, 1966.

Rosenberg, Arthur. *Die Entstehung der Deutschen Republik, 1871–1918.* Berlin: Ernst Rowohlt Verlag, 1928.

Roskill, Stephen. *Hankey: Man of Secrets.* 3 vols. London: Collins, 1970.

Rothwell, V. H. *British War Aims and Peace Diplomacy, 1914–1918.* Oxford: Clarendon Press, 1971.

Rudin, Harry R. *Armistice, 1918.* New Haven, Conn.: Yale University Press, 1944.

Rumpler, H. "Die Kriegsziele Österreich-Ungarns auf dem Balkan 1915/16." In Hugo Hantsch, ed., *Festschrift Hantsch, 1965: Leopold Graf Berchtold, Grandseigneur und Staatsmann.* 2 vols. Graz, 1963.

Saatmann, I. *Parlament, Rüstung, und Armee in Frankreich, 1914–1918.* Düsseldorf: Droste Verlag, 1978.

Sazonov, Sergiei Dmitrïevich. *Fateful Years, 1909–1916: The Reminiscences of Sergeĭ Sazonov.* London: J. Cape, 1928.

Schaeffer, Robert. *Warpaths: The Politics of Partition.* New York: Hill and Wang, 1990.

Schapiro, Leonard. *1917: The Russian Revolutions and the Origins of Present-Day Communism.* Middlesex: Mauric Temple Smith, 1984.

Scherer, André, and Jacques Grunewald. *L'Allemagne et les problèmes de la paix pendant la première guerre mondiale.* 4 vols. Paris: Presses universitaires de France, 1962–78.

Schleier, Hans. *Die bürgerliche deutsche Geschichtsschreibung der Weimarer Republik.* Berlin (Ost): Akademie-Verlag, 1975.

Schlieffen, Alfred von. *Gesammelte Schriften.* Vol. 1. Berlin: Ernst Siegfried Mittler und Sohn, 1913.

Schmidt, Ernst-Heinrich. *Heimatheer und Revolution 1918: Die militärischen Gewalten im Heimatgebiet zwischen Oktoberreform und Novemberrevolution.* Stuttgart: Deutsche Verlags-Anstalt, 1981.

Schuman, Frederick L. *War and Diplomacy in the French Republic: An Inquiry into Political Motivations and the Control of Foreign Policy.* New York: McGraw-Hill, 1931.

Schwabe, Klaus. "Die Amerikanische und die Deutsche Geheimdiplomatie und das Problem eines Verständigungsfriedens im Jahre 1918." *Vierteljahrshefte für Zeitgeschichte* 19, no. 1 (January 1971): 3–32.

Schwabe, Klaus. "U.S. Secret War Diplomacy, Intelligence, and the Coming of the German Revolution in 1918: The Role of Vice Consul James McNally." *Diplomatic History* 16, no. 2 (spring 1992): 175–200.

Scott, J. B., ed. *Official Statements of War Aims and Peace Proposals, December 1916–November 1918.* Washington, D.C.: Carnegie Endowment for International Peace, 1921.

Seymour, Charles, ed. *The Intimate Papers of Colonel House.* 4 vols. New York: Houghton Mifflin, 1976.

Shannon, Catherine B. *Arthur J. Balfour and Ireland, 1874–1922.* Washington, D.C.: Catholic University of America Press, 1981.

Shaw, Albert, ed. *President Wilson's State Papers and Addresses.* New York: George H. Doran, 1918.

Smith, Clarence Jay, Jr. "Legacy to Stalin: Russian War Aims, 1914–1917." Ph.D. dissertation, Harvard University, 1953.

Smith, C. Jay, Jr. *The Russian Struggle for Power, 1914–1917.* New York: Philosophical Library, 1956.

Smith, S. A. *Red Petrograd: Revolution in the Factories 1917–1918.* Cambridge: Cambridge University Press, 1983.

Snyder, Jack. *The Ideology of the Offensive: Military Decision Making and the Disasters of 1914.* Ithaca, N.Y.: Cornell University Press, 1984.

Soutou, Georges-Henri. "La France et les marches de l'est, 1914–1919." *Revue historique* 260, no. 2 (October–December 1978): 341–88.

Soutou, Georges-Henri. *L'Or et le sang: les buts de guerre économique de la première guerre mondiale.* Paris: Fayard, 1989.

Spender, J. A., and Cyril Asquith. *Life of Herbert Henry Asquith, Lord Oxford and Asquith.* 2 vols. London: Hutchinson, 1932.

Squires, James Duane. *British Propaganda at Home and in the United States from 1914 to 1917.* Cambridge, Mass: Harvard University Press, 1935.

Stadelmann, Rudolf. "Friedensversuche im ersten Jahre des Weltkriegs." In *Historische Zeitschrift* (1937): 156.

Steglich, Wolfgang. *Bündnissicherung oder Verständigungsfrieden: Untersuchungen zu dem Friedensangebot der Mittelmächte vom 12. Dezember 1916.* Göttingen: Musterschmidt Verlag, 1958.

Steglich, Wolfgang, ed. *Der Friedensappell Papst Benedikts XV. vom 1. August 1917 und die Mittelmächte.* Wiesbaden: Franz Steiner Verlag, 1970.

Stevenson, David. *The First World War and International Politics.* Oxford: Clarendon Press, 1991.

Stevenson, D. *French War Aims against Germany 1914–1919*. Oxford: Clarendon Press, 1982.

Stevenson, David, ed. *The First World War, 1914–1918*. 4 vols. Frederick, Md.: University Publications of America, 1989. In Kenneth Bourne and D. Cameron Watt, eds., *British Documents in Foreign Affairs: Reports and Papers from the Foreign Office Confidential Print. Part 2: From the First to the Second World War*. Series H, WWI, 1914–1918, 4 vols.

Stone, Norman. *The Eastern Front 1914–1917*. New York: Charles Scribner's Sons, 1975.

Suarez, Georges. *Briand*. 6 vols. *Vol. 4: 1916–1918*. Paris: Plon, 1940.

Sweet, Paul R. "Leaders and Policies: Germany in the Winter of 1914–1915." *Journal of Central European Affairs* 16, no. 3 (October 1956): 229–52.

Sweet, Paul R. "Germany, Austria-Hungary and Mitteleuropa; August 1915–April 1916." *Festschrift für Hr. Benedict* (1957): 180–212. Berlin: Deutsche Zentral Verlag.

Taylor, A. J. P. *The First World War: An Illustrated History*. New York: Penguin Books, 1980.

Taylor, A. J. P. "The War Aims of the Allies in the First World War." In Richard Pares and A. J. P. Taylor, eds., *Essays Presented to Sir Lewis Namier*, pp. 475–505. London: Macmillan, 1956.

Taylor, A. J. P., ed. *Lloyd George: A Diary by Frances Stevenson*. London: Hutchinson & Co., 1971.

Taylor, Brian Dean. "The Russian Military in Politics: Civilian Supremacy in Comparative and Historical Perspective." Ph.D. dissertation, Massachusetts Institute of Technology, 1998.

Terrail, Gabriel [Mermeix, pseud.]. *Le Commandement unique: Foch et les armées d'occident*. Paris: Presses Ollendorff, 1920.

Terrail, Gabriel [Mermeix, pseud.]. *Les Négociations secrètes et les quatre armistices avec pièces justificatives*. Paris: Ollendorff, 1919.

Terrail, Gabriel [Mermeix, pseud.]. *Nivelle et Painlevé: la deuxième crise du commandement*. Paris: Presses Ollendorff, 1919.

Terraine, John. *Impacts of War, 1914 and 1918*. London: Hutchinson, 1970.

Terraine, John. *The Road to Passchendaele: The Flanders Offensive of 1917*. London: Cooper, 1977.

Terraine, John. *To Win a War: 1918, The Year of Victory*. Garden City, N.Y.: Doubleday, 1981.

Thieme, Hartwig. *Nationaler Liberalismus in der Krise: Die nationalliberale Fraktion des preussischen Abgeordnetenhauses 1914/18*. Boppard am Rhein: Harold Bold Verlag, 1963.

The Times. Documentary History of the War. Vol. 3: Military — Part 2. London: Printing House Square, 1919.

Toscano, Mario. *Il Patto di Londra: storia diplomatica dell'intervento Italiano (1914–1915)*. Bologna: Nicola Zanichelli, 1934.

Trachtenberg, Marc. "The Meaning of Mobilization in 1914." In Steven E. Miller, Sean Lynn-Jones, and Stephen van Evera, eds., *Military Strategy and the Origins of the First World War*, pp. 195–225. Princeton: Princeton University Press, 1991.

Trachtenberg, Marc. *Reparation in World Politics: France and European Economic Diplomacy, 1916–1923*. New York: Columbia University Press, 1980.

Travers, Tim. *How the War Was Won: Command and Technology in the British Army on the Western Front, 1917–1918*. London: Routledge, 1992.

Turner, John. "British Politics and the Great War." In John Turner, ed., *Britain and the First World War*, pp. 117–38. Boston: Unwin Hyman, 1988.

Turner, John. *British Politics and the Great War: Coalition and Conflict 1915–1918*. New Haven, Conn.: Yale University Press, 1992.

Turner, John, ed. *Britain and the First World War*. Boston: Unwin Hyman, 1988.

Verner, Andrew M. *The Crisis of Russian Autocracy: Nicholas II and the 1905 Revolution*. Princeton: Princeton University Press, 1990.

Vogel, Bernhard, Dieter Nohlen, and Rainer-Olaf Schultze. *Wahlen in Deutschland*. New York: Walter de Gruyter, 1971.

Vulliamy, C. E., ed. *The Letters of the Tsar to the Tsaritsa, 1914–1917*. New York: Dodd, Mead and Company, 1929.

Wade, Rex A. *The Russian Search for Peace, February–October 1917*. Stanford, Calif.: Stanford University Press, 1969.

Walworth, Arthur. *America's Moment, 1918: American Diplomacy at the End of World War I*. New York: W. W. Norton, 1977.

War Speeches by British Ministers 1914–1916. London: Fisher Unwin, 1917.

Watson, David Robin. *Georges Clemenceau*. Plymouth: Eyre Methuen, 1974.

Wehler, Hans-Ulrich. *The German Empire, 1871–1918*. New York: Berg, 1985.

Weintraub, Stanley. *A Stillness Heard Round the World: The End of the Great War, November 1918*. New York: Truman Talley Books/ E. P. Dutton, 1985.

Westarp, K. *Konservative Politik im letzten Jahrzehnt des Kaiserreiches*. 2 vols. Berlin: Deutsche Verlagsgesellschaft, 1935.

Wheeler-Bennett, John W. *The Forgotten Peace, Brest-Litovsk, March, 1918*. New York: William Morrow, 1939.

Wickware, Francis G., ed. *The American Year Book, A Record of Events and Progress, 1913–1916*. New York: D. Appleton, 1914–17.

Wieczynski, Joseph L., ed. *The Modern Encyclopedia of Russia and Soviet History*. Gulf Breeze, Fla.: Academic International Press, various years; vol. 10, 1979, vol. 28, 1982.

Wilson, Trevor. *The Myriad Faces of War*. Cambridge: Polity Press, 1986.

Woodward, David. *Lloyd George and the Generals*. London: Associated University Press, 1983.

Zechlin, Egmont. "Deutschland zwischen Kabinettskrieg und Wirtschaftskrieg: Politik und Kriegsführung in den ersten Monaten des Weltkrieges 1914." In *Historische Zeitschrift*. Munich, vol. 199.

Zechlin, Egmont. "Friedensbestrebungen und Revolutionsversuche: Deutsche Bestrebungen zur Ausschaltung Russlands im Ersten Weltkrieg." In *Aus Politik und Zeitgeschichte*, Beilage zur Wochenzeitung *Das Parlament*, Jg.1961, Beilagen 20, 24, 25 Jg.1963, Beilagen 20 und 22. B 20/61 vom 17.5.1961, pp. 269–288 B 24/61 vom 14.6.1961, pp. 325–337 B 25/61 vom 21.6.1961, pp. 341–367 B 20/63 vom 15.5.1963, pp. 3–54 B 22/63 vom 29.5.1963, pp. 3–47.

Zechlin, Egmont. *Krieg und Kriegsrisiko: Zur deutschen Politik im Ersten Weltkrieg*. Düsseldorf: Droste Verlag, 1979.

Zechlin, Egmont. "Probleme des Kriegskalküls und der Kriegsbeendigung im Ersten Weltkrieg." *Geschrifte in Wissenschaft und Unterricht* 16, no. 3 (February 1965): 69–83.

Zeman, Z. A. B. *The Gentlemen Negotiators: A Diplomatic History of the First World War.* New York: Macmillan, 1971.

Zotiades, G. B. "Russia and the Question of Constantinople and the Turkish Straits during the Balkan Wars." *Balkan Studies* (Thessaloniki) 2 (1970): 281–98.

15th Committee of the German Constitutional Assembly (21 August 1919). The Reichstag investigation into both the origins and conduct of the Great War. Twenty-eight members of the *Untersuchungsausschuss* constituted on 21 August 1919 as the 15th Committee of the German Constitutional Assembly. *Das Werk des Untersuchungsausschusses der Deutschen Verfassunggebeden Nationalversammlung und des Deutschen Reichstages 1919–1930.* Berlin: Deutsche Verlagsgesellschaft für Politik und Geschichte, 1927ff.

INDEX